ABOUT THINGS THAT MATTER

ADVANCED INTEGRATION

The Connection Code

Procrastination

Self-Esteem That Matters

Thoughts That Matter

A SELF-IMPROVEMENT SERIES FOR SUCCESS

From Bestselling Author

JC Ryan

Copyright

Your Gift

As a way of saying thanks for your purchase, I'm offering you the first book in the series **About Things That Matter** as a gift.

This book is exclusive to my readers. You will not find this book anywhere else.

You're invited to pause, reflect, and reconsider what truly defines a meaningful life. In a world conditioned to chase money, status, and material achievements, this book challenges the conventional yardsticks of success. Through incisive insight and refreshing authenticity, it guides readers to shift their focus from external validation to the internal foundations that cultivate real fulfillment, purpose, and enduring happiness. It's a call to eliminate distractions, clarify values, and build a life anchored in what matters most.

Visit this link to download your free copy of About Things That Matter or type this address into your browser https://BookHip.com/HLAJBFP

Visit the series page https://mybook.to/Aboutthingsthatmatter

Foreword

I first met JC Ryan some years ago when, as publisher, I interviewed him for Books & Pieces Magazine. We hit it off and became friends. Through his health issues at the time, and the changes he made to his life for the better, we came to discuss this extensive body of work he created, which detailed his journey and served as a blueprint for anyone wanting to improve their lives, both personally and professionally.

Thus came "About Things That Matter," a comprehensive 12-book series that can completely transform your thinking and your successes.

JC wanted my help in putting it all together, and we decided the best way was to offer a series of email courses to complement the books. And to really get it kick-started, JC decided to offer the first course, "Change That Matters," totally free to participants.

Having seen the entirety of this series, I can attest to its robust nature and that it truly is a solid plan for anyone wishing to better their lives, whether personally or in business.

The books and the course(s) have been designed to be followed easily at your own pace and include many additional resources that can be downloaded.

If you've found yourself asking the question: "Is there nothing more I can do with my life?" then this series is definitely for you. It is "About Things That Matter."

Yours in health,

William Gensburger
Publisher & Author
Books & Pieces Magazine (bnpmag.com)
B&P Books (bnpbooks.com)

About Things That Matter

The Complete Transformation System
Your Science-Based Roadmap to a Life of Meaning, Momentum, and Purposeful Living

Most people drift through life reacting to circumstances instead of creating them. They work hard but not strategically. They set goals but struggle to achieve them. They want deeper relationships but don't know how to build them. They feel busy but not fulfilled.

What if there was a better way?

The **About Things That Matter** series is your research-backed, implementation-focused system for transforming intention into achievement and dreams into reality. Based on decades of psychological research and tested by thousands of high achievers, this series provides the specific tools, strategies, and mindsets that separate those who merely wish for better lives from those who actually create them:

The complete "About Things That Matter" series provides a comprehensive, science-based system for transforming every area of your life while reclaiming the fundamental human capacities that have become luxuries in our modern world.

Each book builds on the previous ones, creating a compound effect of growth and transformation. You don't need to read them in order, but starting with your biggest challenge area will create the most immediate impact.

The Research Foundation:
- Harvard's 80-year Grant Study on human flourishing
- Stanford's research on the growth mindset and achievement
- MIT's findings on habit formation and behavioral change
- Decades of organizational psychology research on high performance

Foundation Building

Book 1: Change That Matters
Stop Drifting. Start Directing.

Master the psychology of lasting personal transformation through 8 proven principles that turn intention into achievement.

What You'll Gain:

- The neuroscience-based principles that make change stick
- A systematic approach to breaking limiting patterns
- Proven strategies for overcoming resistance and fear
- The mindset shifts that accelerate personal growth

Readers report feeling more in control of their lives within the first week of implementation.

Book 2: Goals That Matter
Turn Dreams into Done.

Create and achieve meaningful goals through purpose-driven planning that delivers real fulfillment, not just external success.

What You'll Gain:

- The SMART goals framework increases achievement rates by 42%
- How to align goals with your deepest values for sustained motivation
- Systems for maintaining momentum through obstacles and setbacks
- The art of celebrating progress to fuel continued success

Goal completion rates increase by 65% when shared with others using these methods.

Book 3: Time That Matters
Make Every Moment Count.

Transform your relationship with time through proven systems that create freedom, focus, and alignment with what matters most.

What You'll Gain:

- The 80/20 principle applied to daily and weekly planning
- Energy management strategies that multiply your effective working hours

- Digital tools and analog systems that enhance rather than distract
- The art of saying "no" to create space for what matters most

Users gain an average of 8-12 productive hours per week within 30 days.

Book 4: Relationships That Matter
Build Your Social Wealth.

Create deep, meaningful connections through authentic communication and relationship skills that enrich every area of your life.

What You'll Gain:
- The five essential relationship roles that every successful person needs
- Communication skills that transform surface connections into deep bonds
- Digital relationship strategies for authentic connection in a virtual world
- Community-building skills that create belonging and mutual support

Noticeable improvements in relationship quality and communication effectiveness within the first conversations.

Skill Development

Book 5: Emotional Intelligence That Matters
Feel Deeply, Respond Wisely.

Master the art of understanding and managing emotions to enhance relationships, decision-making, and personal effectiveness.

What You'll Gain:
- Advanced emotional awareness and regulation techniques
- Skills to read and respond to others' emotions effectively
- Tools for transforming emotional triggers into growth opportunities
- Leadership abilities rooted in emotional wisdom

Improved emotional responses and relationship dynamics within days of applying core techniques.

Book 6: Happiness That Matters
Choose Joy, Create Fulfillment.

Discover the science of sustainable happiness and build daily practices that create lasting contentment independent of circumstances.

What You'll Gain:
- Evidence-based strategies for cultivating genuine happiness
- Tools to break free from comparison and external validation
- Gratitude and mindfulness practices that rewire your brain for joy
- How to find meaning and purpose in everyday moments

Measurable improvements in mood and life satisfaction within two weeks of consistent practice.

Book 7: The 24-Hour Miracle That Matters
Transform Your Day, Transform Your Life.

Design perfect days that compound into an extraordinary life through intentional morning, work, and evening routines.

What You'll Gain:
- Hour-by-hour blueprints for days that energize rather than drain
- Morning routines that set you up for success and clarity
- Evening practices that restore and prepare you for tomorrow
- Weekend rhythms that rejuvenate and reconnect you to purpose

Dramatic improvements in energy, focus, and life satisfaction within one week of implementation.

Book 8: From Stressful to Successful
Stress Less, Achieve More.

Transform stress from a life-draining force into a success-driving advantage through proven resilience and performance strategies.

What You'll Gain:
- Stress reframing techniques that turn pressure into performance fuel
- Resilience-building practices for bouncing back from any setback

- Peak performance strategies used by top athletes and executives
- Recovery and restoration methods that prevent burnout

Significant reduction in stress levels and improved performance under pressure within days.

Advanced Integration

Book 9: The Connection Code
Crack the Code to Meaningful Relationships.

One-line Summary: Master advanced relationship dynamics, conflict resolution, and influence techniques that create lasting bonds and positive impact.

What You'll Gain:
- Advanced empathy and emotional attunement skills
- Conflict transformation strategies that strengthen rather than damage relationships
- Influence and persuasion techniques rooted in genuine care
- Leadership approaches that inspire and unite rather than divide

Enhanced ability to navigate difficult conversations and deepen existing relationships immediately.

Book 10: Procrastination
Stop Putting Off Your Potential.

Overcome procrastination forever through understanding its root causes and implementing systems that make action inevitable.

What You'll Gain:
- The psychology behind procrastination and how to interrupt the cycle
- Environmental design strategies that make good choices automatic
- Motivation techniques that work even when you don't feel like it
- Completion systems that turn started projects into finished successes

Immediate breakthrough on stuck projects and tasks that have been delayed for weeks or months.

Book 11: Self-Esteem That Matters
Build Unshakable Confidence from the Inside Out.

Develop authentic self-worth through proven strategies that transform self-doubt into genuine confidence and self-respect.

What You'll Gain:
- Tools to overcome negative self-talk and limiting beliefs
- Habits that reinforce your sense of worth daily
- Assertiveness skills to express needs and set boundaries
- The ripple effect of healthy self-esteem on relationships

Noticeable shifts in self-talk and confidence levels within the first week of practice.

Book 12: Thoughts That Matter
Your Brain Is Not Your Boss.

Harness the neuroscience of conscious living to master your mind, emotions, and purpose through proven mental training protocols.

What You'll Gain:
- How to rewire your brain for resilience, clarity, and growth
- Digital detox strategies to reclaim your attention
- Emotional intelligence tools for wise decision-making
- Daily practices to align thoughts with purpose

Mental clarity and emotional regulation improve within days of implementing the core exercises.

Visit the series page https://mybook.to/Aboutthingsthatmatter

Table Of Contents

PART 1 – THE CONNECTION CODE

We live in the most connected age in human history, yet loneliness has become an epidemic. The solution isn't more technology; it's more humanity through technology.

To everyone striving to build genuine connections, across screens, cultures, and time zones, may you always see the human behind the technology.

"People will forget what you said, people will forget what you did, but people will never forget how you made them feel." — Maya Angelou

To everyone who lives in the age of virtual relationships,
who needs bridges over walls,
and authentic connections in a digital world:
may you master the technology without losing your humanity,
scale your influence without sacrificing your integrity,
and remember that behind every screen
is a human heart longing to be understood

The Connection Code

BUILDING RELATIONSHIPS THAT MATTER IN THE DIGITAL AGE

About Things That Matter

A SELF-IMPROVEMENT SERIES FOR SUCCESS

Book 9

JC Ryan

About This Book

The Connection Code: Building Relationships That Matter In The Digital Age is a practical, empowering roadmap for anyone seeking authentic relationships and influence in today's digital age. Rooted in timeless human connection principles and updated for a world of distributed teams, online communities, and cross-cultural communication, this book helps you thrive as a human, without sacrificing effectiveness or wellbeing.

You'll learn:

- The 16 Core Principles that unlock real trust, engagement, and influence through every digital interaction.
- How to build meaningful relationships in remote workplaces, crowded online markets, and global networks.
- Actionable frameworks to communicate authentically, overcome "always on" anxiety, and create an innovation culture on zero budget.

If you've ever felt drained by surface-level networking or struggled to be truly understood across a screen, *The Connection Code* offers solutions to create relationships—and impact—that last.

Who Will Benefit From This Book

The Connection Code: Building Relationships That Matter In The Digital Age is the essential modern companion to the timeless wisdom departed by Dale Carnegie in his 1936 classic, How To Win Friends and Influnce People. The Connnection Code is for those who wants to build authentic relationships across digital channels, inspire teams through screens, and create lasting impact in our hyperconnected world.

If you struggle to build trust through screens, trying to network authentically in digital spaces, or wants to influence others without losing your integrity, this book is for you. Whether you're navigating difficult conversations over email, building community in virtual environments, or simply trying to maintain your humanity while scaling your impact, these principles will transform how you connect.

The frameworks in this book are powerful for distributed teams across cultures and time zones, entrepreneurs building authentic brands in crowded digital markets, and those who want to succeed without sacrificing their values. If you've ever felt frustrated by miscommunication in chat programs, exhausted by performative networking on social media, or overwhelmed by the pressure to be "always on," you'll find practical solutions that honor both effectiveness and wellbeing. This isn't just another communication book; it's a roadmap for thriving as a human in our increasingly digital world, creating the kind of relationships and influence that matter.

Introduction

In 1936, Dale Carnegie published a book that would become one of the most influential works on human relationships ever written. "How to Win Friends and Influence People" IT taught millions of readers the fundamental principles of connecting with others, building trust, and inspiring action. Nearly a century later, Carnegie's insights about human nature remain remarkably relevant—people still want to feel valued, heard, and understood.

But the world Carnegie wrote for no longer exists.

In 1936, most business happened face-to-face. Relationships were built over handshakes and business lunches. Influence flowed through personal presence and carefully crafted speeches. Communication was largely synchronous—when you talked, people listened, and when they responded, you were there to hear it.

Today, we live in a radically different reality. We build relationships through screens, influence through pixels, and connect across continents and time zones. We communicate asynchronously through emails, instantly through messages, visually through videos, and collaboratively through shared digital spaces. We navigate cultural differences in every interaction, manage our presence across multiple platforms, and try to maintain authenticity in an age of performative personal branding.

Carnegie's principles still matter, but they need translation for our digital, global, always-connected world.

This book is that translation, a modern interpretation of timeless relationship wisdom for leaders navigating the complexities of 21st-century connection. Where Carnegie taught readers to remember names and show genuine interest in person, we'll explore how to build authentic relationships across digital channels. Where he emphasized the power of appreciation and acknowledgment in face-to-face interactions, we'll discover how to create belonging in virtual communities. Where he focused on winning people to your way of thinking through persuasion, we'll learn to create collaborative solutions through empathy and shared purpose.

"**The Connection Code**" honors Carnegie's foundational insights while addressing the unique challenges of our hyperconnected yet often lonely digital age. You'll learn not just how to network, but how to build genuine community. Not just how to influence, but how to inspire. Not just how to communicate effectively, but how to connect authentically across any medium, culture, or context.

The principles in this book have been tested in remote teams and global organizations, virtual conferences and digital communities, social media crises and cross-cultural collaborations. They work because they're built on the same fundamental truth Carnegie discovered: people's deepest need is to feel understood, valued, and connected to something larger than themselves.

That need hasn't changed. But how we meet it has evolved dramatically.

Whether you're leading a distributed team, building an online community, navigating workplace conflicts over Slack, or trying to maintain authentic relationships in an age of digital overwhelm, this book provides the frameworks, strategies, and mindsets you need to thrive.

The future belongs to leaders who can create genuine human connection through any medium, inspire trust across any distance, and build communities that transcend geographical and cultural boundaries. In other words, the future belongs to those who master the timeless art of human relationships in the context of modern realities.

Carnegie showed us how to win friends and influence people in his world. This book shows you how to connect, communicate, and lead in yours.

Let's begin.

The 16 Core Principles

Part One: The Connection Code

1. **Be Real** - Authenticity is your superpower in a world of filters
2. **Feel First** - Empathy isn't optional in digital communication
3. **Ask Better** - Curiosity transforms superficial exchanges into meaningful connections
4. **Honor Differences** - Cultural intelligence is essential for global leadership

Part Two: The Communication Compass

5. **Lift While You Shift** - Feedback should empower while correcting
6. **Find the Gold** - Conflict contains information that can transform relationships
7. **Own It All** - Accountability is a competitive advantage in a deflection-filled world
8. **Make It Stick** - Stories move hearts, minds, and mountains

Part Three: The Leadership Legacy

9. **Fuel the Fire** - Create conditions where people motivate themselves
10. **Lead Through Questions** - The best solutions come from empowering others to find them
11. **Make the Impossible Feel Inevitable** - Growth happens when challenges feel conquerable
12. **Connect Work to Why** - Purpose transforms jobs into missions

Part Four: The Future of Connection

13. **Protect Your Humanity** - Boundaries preserve authenticity in hyperconnected world
14. **Create Belonging** - Community is intentionally designed, not accidentally discovered
15. **Evolve With the World** - Adaptability is the meta-skill for changing communication landscape
16. **Leave the World More Connected** - Legacy is measured by the ripple effects you create

Chapter 1: The Authenticity Advantage

PRINCIPLE: BE REAL

We live in strange times. We have more ways to connect than ever before—LinkedIn, Instagram, Slack, Zoom, WhatsApp, and whatever new platform launched while you were reading this sentence. Yet somehow, we're lonelier than ever. We have thousands of "connections" but few real friends. We get hundreds of "likes" but still feel unseen. We're all performing for an invisible audience, carefully curating our digital selves while our real selves quietly starve for genuine human connection.

Here's the truth that no algorithm wants you to know: authenticity is your superpower in a world of filters and facades.

The Great Authenticity Shortage

Let me tell you about Sarah, a marketing director I met at a virtual conference. During the official sessions, she was polished, professional, perfect. Her background was immaculate (fake, but immaculate), her talking points rehearsed, her smile camera-ready. Then her cat jumped on her keyboard, deleted her presentation, and knocked over her coffee—all while she was screen-sharing to 200 people.

She froze. Then laughed. Really laughed. "Well," she said, "meet Mr. Whiskers, my chief chaos officer." She spent the next two minutes telling us about her cat's vendetta against video calls while she cleaned up the mess. When she finally got back to her presentation, something had shifted. People were engaged. The chat came alive. Connections were made. She got more follow-up meetings from that conference than any other.

Why? Because for two minutes, she was real. And in a world of digital facades, real is rare.

Why Genuine Connection Matters More Than Ever

Theodore Roosevelt had a remarkable gift. Before meeting anyone, he would research their interests—whether it was cattle breeding, Dutch art, or local politics. But here's what most people miss about this story: Roosevelt didn't fake interest. He found something genuinely fascinating about each person and let his natural curiosity guide the conversation. He didn't perform interest; he discovered it.

Today, we have LinkedIn profiles, Twitter feeds, and digital footprints that tell us everything about someone before we meet them. Yet most of us use this information to craft the perfect pitch, the ideal approach, the optimal strategy for getting what we want. We've become so good at performing connection that we've forgotten how to create it.

Research in social psychology confirms what our hearts already know: people have finely tuned authenticity detectors. We can sense when someone is genuinely interested in us versus when they're working an angle. Brain imaging studies show that authentic interactions activate reward centers in our brains, releasing oxytocin and building trust. Fake interactions? They trigger the same threat-detection systems as hearing footsteps in a dark alley.

Moving Beyond Transactional Networking

Let's be honest about modern "networking." It's become a sophisticated form of mutual exploitation. I'll endorse your skills if you'll introduce me to your boss. I'll like your post if you'll share mine. We're all so busy climbing that we've forgotten why we wanted to reach the top in the first place.

Consider Marcus, a small business owner who made what seemed like a fatal social media error. He posted a well-intentioned but poorly worded message about diversity that sparked immediate backlash. His first instinct was to defend, to explain, to fight back. Instead, he did something radical: he got real.

"I messed up," he wrote. "I'm still learning, and I clearly have more work to do. Thank you to everyone who took the time to educate me, even when you were frustrated. I'm listening."

Then he did listen. He hosted community conversations. He brought in experts. He shared his learning journey publicly, including his mistakes and misconceptions. Six months later, his business was thriving—not despite his error, but because of how he handled it. His authenticity in the face of criticism built more trust than years of polished marketing ever could.

The Psychology of Digital-Age Relationships

We're wired for connection, but we're living in a world designed for collection. We collect followers like baseball cards, connections like trophies, likes like lottery tickets. But here's what the platforms don't want you to know: the human brain can only maintain about 150 meaningful relationships. That's Dunbar's number, and it hasn't changed just because Mark Zuckerberg invented Facebook.

So what happens when we try to maintain 500 LinkedIn connections, 1,000 Instagram followers, and 2,000 Facebook friends? We default to performance. We create a public persona—Professional You, Version 2.0—and parade it around the digital town square. Meanwhile, the real you, the one with doubts and dreams and a weird obsession with 90s sitcoms, stays hidden.

But authenticity isn't just about being real—it's about creating space for others to be real too. When you drop the mask, you give others permission to drop theirs. When you admit struggle, you invite support. When you share joy without filter, you multiply it.

The Practical Art of Being Real

So how do we cultivate authenticity in a world that rewards performance? Here are some practical strategies:

Start with "I don't know." The three most powerful words in any language. Use them liberally. "I don't know much about that—can you teach me?" instantly transforms you from know-it-all to learner, from presenter to participant.

Share your struggles (appropriately). You don't need to trauma-dump on LinkedIn, but sharing real challenges makes you relatable. "This project is kicking my butt, but here's what I'm learning" is infinitely more engaging than "Thrilled to announce another flawless victory!"

Ask real questions. Not "How are you?" (automatic answer: "Fine"). But "What's actually going on with you?" or "What's got your attention these days?" or "What are you figuring out right now?"

Admit your mistakes quickly and with humor. Everyone screws up. The question is whether you'll try to hide it or mine it for connection. "Well, I just replied-all with my grocery list. Anyone need to know I'm out of milk?" beats panicked deletion every time.

Find genuine points of connection. Before a meeting, don't just scan someone's LinkedIn for ammunition. Look for something that genuinely intrigues you. Maybe you both worked at startups that failed. Maybe you share a hometown. Maybe they have a certification in something you've always wanted to learn. Start there.

The Vulnerability Paradox

Here's the thing about authenticity: it requires vulnerability, and vulnerability feels like weakness. But research by Brené Brown and others shows the opposite is true. Vulnerability is the birthplace of connection, creativity, and change. It's saying "I don't have all the answers" in a world that worships certainty. It's asking for help when everyone else is posturing strength.

During a remote team meeting, a project manager named Maya noticed energy dropping week after week. Instead of pushing harder, she got vulnerable: "I'm struggling here. I miss seeing your faces in person. I miss the bad coffee and the good conversations. I'm finding it hard to lead when I can't read the room. What would help you? What would help us?"

The floodgates opened. Team members shared their own struggles—with isolation, with technology, with work-life boundaries bleeding into work-life chaos. Together, they redesigned their meetings, created virtual coffee breaks, started a weekly "wins and whines" session. Productivity soared, but more importantly, the team reconnected. Maya's vulnerability gave everyone permission to be human.

Building Your Authenticity Practice

Authenticity isn't a destination; it's a practice. Here's how to start:

Morning intention: Before you open your laptop, ask yourself: "How do I want to show up today? What mask am I tempted to wear? What would happen if I left it off?"

The pause practice: Before responding to a message, comment, or email, pause. Ask: "Is this what I really think, or what I think I should say?" Choose real over right.

Connection inventory: Once a week, review your interactions. Which felt genuine? Which felt performed? What patterns do you notice?

The appreciation experiment: Send one genuinely appreciative message daily. Not "Great job!" but "The way you handled that difficult client with patience and humor made my day. Thank you."

The Compound Effect of Authenticity

Here's what happens when you choose real over rehearsed: people remember you. In a sea of digital sameness, authenticity is differentiation. But more than that, it's freedom. Freedom from maintaining multiple personas. Freedom from the exhaustion of constant performance. Freedom to connect with people who like you for you, not your polished avatar.

Authenticity compounds. One real conversation leads to another. One genuine connection introduces you to two more. Before you know it, you've built a network—no, a community—of people who know and value the real you. And in a world where everyone else is performing, that's not just an advantage. It's a revolution.

Chapter Summary

In our hyperconnected yet oddly disconnected world, authenticity has become the rarest and most valuable currency. While we're busy curating perfect digital personas, we're starving for real human connection. The solution isn't more strategies or better performance—it's the courage to be real. When we drop our masks, share our struggles appropriately, ask genuine questions, and create space for others to be human, we transform shallow networking into deep connection. Authenticity isn't just about being yourself; it's about creating permission for others to be themselves too.

Reflection

- When was the last time you felt truly seen and appreciated for who you really are?
- What masks do you wear in professional settings? What would happen if you loosened them a bit?
- Think of someone whose authenticity you admire. What specifically do they do that feels genuine?
- Where in your life are you performing connection rather than creating it?

Action

This week, try the "Three Real Things" challenge:

1. Share one appropriate struggle or learning moment in a professional setting
2. Ask one person a genuinely curious question and listen to their full answer
3. Send one specific, heartfelt appreciation to someone who wouldn't expect it

Track how these authentic moments feel different from your usual interactions.

PRINCIPLE: BE REAL

What's Next?

Now that we've explored why authenticity matters, we need to tackle a harder question: How do we maintain that authenticity when we're communicating through screens? How do we read emotions, create presence, and build safety in digital spaces? In the next chapter, we'll dive into the art of Digital Empathy, because being real is just the beginning. We also need to help others feel real, especially when we can't see their faces or read their body language. Get ready to become fluent in the language of digital emotion.

Chapter 2: Digital Empathy

Last week, I watched a train wreck in slow motion. During a virtual all-hands meeting, a senior executive delivered news about layoffs while checking his phone, glancing at another screen, and occasionally typing. His words said "I understand this is difficult," but his actions screamed "I have more important things to do." The chat exploded. Cameras turned off. The meeting ended in disaster.

He'd forgotten the first rule of digital communication: in a world of screens, empathy isn't optional—it's oxygen.

Reading Emotions Through Screens

Here's the challenge we all face: humans evolved to read micro-expressions, body language, and those tiny facial twitches that signal "I'm upset but trying to hide it." We're built for campfires, not computer screens. Yet here we are, trying to decode emotions through pixelated video feeds and text messages that strip away 93% of communication cues.

But it's not impossible. It just requires a different kind of attention.

Take Lisa, a customer service manager who noticed something odd. Her best-performing agent, Sam, had maintained perfect metrics for months—response time, resolution rate, customer satisfaction scores. All green lights. But in their weekly video check-ins, Lisa noticed Sam's smile never quite reached his eyes. His usual animated gestures had become subdued. He'd started using his virtual background more often, hiding his real environment.

Instead of celebrating the metrics, Lisa sent a simple message: "Hey Sam, you seem a bit off lately. Everything okay? No agenda here—just checking in as a human."

The floodgates opened. Sam's father was in the hospital. He'd been working through grief while maintaining his "professional face." Lisa's digital empathy—reading between the pixels—potentially saved both an employee and a life. They worked out flexible hours, connected Sam with the company's support resources, and his colleagues rallied around him.

The Art of Presence in Virtual Spaces

Being present used to be simple: you showed up, made eye contact, leaned in. Now? Presence is a practiced art form that requires intention, technology management, and a willingness to be deliberately inefficient.

I learned this the hard way during a "digital coffee chat" with a potential collaborator. I thought I was being efficient; responding to "quick" Slack messages, organizing my desktop, half-listening while multitasking. When she said, "I can see you're busy, let's reschedule," I realized I'd blown it. My divided attention had sent a clear message: you're not worth my full focus.

Now, I practice what I call "aggressive presence":

- **Camera at eye level**: Looking down at someone triggers primitive submission/dominance patterns. Eye level says, "We're equals."
- **Close the tabs**: Yes, all of them. That article about productivity hacks can wait. Ironic, isn't it?
- **Phone in another room**: Not flipped over. Not on silent. In. Another. Room. Your brain knows it's there and divides your attention even when it's quiet.
- **Look at the camera, not yourself**: This is harder than quitting sugar. We're all narcissists on Zoom. But when you look at the camera while speaking, the other person feels seen.
- **Use names intentionally**: "That's a great point, Marcus," hits different than "That's a great point." In digital spaces, names are anchors that create connection.

Creating Psychological Safety Online and Offline

Amy Edmondson's research on psychological safety shows that teams perform best when members feel safe to take risks, make mistakes, and be vulnerable. But here's the kicker: psychological safety is harder to build and easier to destroy in digital spaces.

Why? Because digital communication amplifies power dynamics. When the boss sends a Slack message at 10 PM, it feels like a command even if it wasn't intended as one. When someone's critique appears in a shared document, it feels more permanent, more public, more harsh than spoken feedback.

Maya, a team lead at a global tech company, discovered this when her remote team's innovation metrics tanked. People had stopped sharing wild ideas, stopped building on each other's suggestions, stopped taking creative risks. The reason? A single incident where someone's "stupid idea" (meant as self-deprecating humor) was screenshot and shared in another channel with laughing emojis.

Maya rebuilt safety brick by digital brick:

- **The Vegas Rule**: "What's shared in brainstorm, stays in brainstorm." No screenshots, no sharing without permission.
- **Failure Parties**: Monthly celebrations of spectacular failures and what they learned. Maya went first, sharing her most embarrassing coding error.
- **Round Robins**: In video calls, everyone shares ideas in order. No interruptions, no immediate critiques. This prevents the loudest voices from dominating.
- **Anonymous Options**: Using tools like Mentimeter for sensitive feedback or wild ideas. Sometimes safety means invisibility.
- **Vulnerable Leadership**: Maya started each meeting with "Here's where I'm struggling..." It gave everyone permission to be human.

The Empathy Skills That Matter Most

Digital empathy isn't about being "nice" or using more emoji (though a well-placed 😊 can work wonders). It's about developing specific skills:

- **Emotional Granularity**: In person, you might sense someone is "off." Digitally, you need more precision. Are they frustrated? Overwhelmed? Disappointed? The better you can name it, the better you can address it.
- **Pause Fluency**: In digital communication, silence feels heavier. We rush to fill it. But pauses are where empathy lives. "I need a moment to think about what you just shared" shows you're taking someone seriously.
- **Context Imagination**: When someone seems short or distracted, imagine three generous explanations before assuming the worst. Maybe their kid is homeschooling in the next room. Maybe they just got difficult news. Maybe their internet is glitchy and they're struggling to follow.
- **Micro-Affirmations**: Small signals that say "I see you." A thumbs up reaction. A "thanks for sharing that" in chat. A nod on video. These seem tiny but they're the digital equivalent of the supportive murmurs that keep face-to-face conversations flowing.

The Hidden Cost of Digital Coldness

We've all felt it—that sting when someone reads your message and doesn't respond. The anxiety when your video comment is met with silence and blank stares. The creeping feeling that you're shouting into the void.

Digital coldness compounds. One ignored message becomes "they don't value me." One curt response becomes "they don't like me." One meeting where nobody turns on cameras becomes "we're not really a team."

But here's what I've learned: digital warmth compounds too. Exponentially.

When David, a project manager, started sending brief video messages instead of text emails—"Hey team, just wanted to say fantastic work on that client presentation. Sarah, your slide design was chef's kiss. Marcus, the way you handled those tough questions? Masterclass."—something shifted. Team members started sending video replies. Then video check-ins. Then spontaneous video celebrations of small wins.

Six months later, employee satisfaction scores on his team were the highest in the company. The secret? Thirty-second videos that said "I see you" in a way text never could.

Practical Digital Empathy Techniques

- **The Two-Minute Investment**: Before any digital interaction, spend two minutes reviewing the person's recent communications. What's their emotional weather pattern? Stressed? Excited? Overwhelmed? Adjust accordingly.
- **The Emotional Mirror**: Match energy intentionally. If someone shares excitement, bring excitement. If they're processing difficulty, slow down and create space. Don't be a golden retriever when they need a wise owl.
- **The Clarifying Question**: "Help me understand..." is magic. "You sound frustrated—help me understand what's behind that" beats "Don't be frustrated" every time.
- **The Appreciation Specific**: Generic praise is digital noise. Specific appreciation cuts through: "The way you restructured that proposal made complex ideas accessible. I learned from watching you work."
- **The Check-In Ritual**: Regular, brief, no-agenda check-ins. "How are you really?" with time to listen to the answer.

Reading the Unspoken

In digital spaces, what's not said speaks volumes:

- Cameras that stay off might signal disengagement—or might mean someone's in pajama bottoms

- Delayed responses might mean disagreement—or might mean deep thinking
- Brief messages might indicate anger—or might reflect a packed schedule

The key is to get curious, not conclusive. "I noticed you've been keeping your camera off lately—everything okay?" beats assuming they're job hunting.

Building Your Digital Empathy Practice

Start here:

- **Morning Scan**: Before diving into tasks, scan your team's communication from the last 24 hours. What's the emotional temperature?
- **Response Pause**: Before hitting send, read your message as if you're having a bad day. How would it land?
- **Weekly Video Thanks**: Send one video message of appreciation weekly. Make it specific, make it warm, make it under a minute.
- **Empathy Office Hours**: Block time weekly where you're available just to listen. No agenda, no problem-solving required unless requested.

Chapter Summary

Digital empathy isn't about becoming a feelings detective or an emoji enthusiast. It's about recognizing that behind every screen is a human having a human experience. When we learn to read emotions through pixels, create genuine presence despite physical distance, and build psychological safety across digital channels, we transform cold technology into warm connection. The tools may be digital, but the need is ancient: to be seen, heard, and valued. Master digital empathy, and you master the art of making humans feel human, no matter the medium.

Reflection

- When was the last time someone showed you genuine empathy in a digital interaction? What did they do specifically?
- Where do you tend to lose presence in virtual spaces? What pulls your attention away?
- Think of a recent digital miscommunication. How might digital empathy have

changed the outcome?

- What emotions are you best at reading through screens? Which ones do you miss?

Action

This week, practice the "Digital Empathy Triple":

1. Send one video message of appreciation (under 60 seconds, specific praise)
2. Have one virtual conversation with aggressive presence (all tabs closed, phone away)
3. Ask one clarifying emotional question ("You seem stressed—what's on your plate?")

Notice how these small acts of digital empathy shift your relationships.

PRINCIPLE: FEEL FIRST

What's Next?

We've learned to be real, and we've learned to feel what others feel through screens. But empathy without action is just emotional tourism. In our next chapter, we'll explore The Curiosity Principle—how to channel that empathy into questions that build bridges, listening that transforms relationships, and the almost-lost art of following up in ways that make people feel truly valued. Get ready to become the person everyone wants to talk to—not because you have the answers, but because you ask the questions that matter.

Chapter 3: The Curiosity Principle

PRINCIPLE: ASK BETTER

I once killed a conversation with a single question. It was at a networking event (remember those?), and I'd just met a fascinating entrepreneur. Instead of asking about her journey, her challenges, or what excited her about her work, I asked, "So, what's your revenue model?"

Her face fell. The energy drained from our conversation like water from a punctured balloon. She gave a mechanical answer, excused herself to refill her drink, and never came back. I'd committed the cardinal sin of modern conversation: I'd asked a transaction question when what was needed was a transformation question.

Active Listening in a Distracted World

We live in an age of continuous partial attention. While someone's talking, we're composing our reply, checking notifications, planning dinner, and wondering if we remembered to lock the car—all while maintaining eye contact and nodding appropriately. We've become masters of performative listening while actually hearing nothing.

Real listening—the kind that transforms relationships—is becoming as rare as a phone call that isn't trying to sell you an extended warranty.

Consider this scene, repeated millions of times daily: A Zoom meeting where everyone's on mute, cameras optional, while the presenter asks, "Any questions?" Silence. Not because there are no questions, but because no one was really listening. They were on mute in more ways than one—answering emails, browsing news, pretending to take notes while online shopping.

But then there's Priya, a product manager who changed her entire team's dynamic with one simple practice. At the start of each virtual meeting, she'd say, "I'm going to share something for three minutes. Then I want to hear what stood out to each of you—not your opinion, just what you heard."

Suddenly, people listened. They had to. And something magical happened: when people knew they'd need to reflect back what they heard, they actually heard it. Engagement skyrocketed. Ideas built on ideas. The team went from going through the motions to genuine collaboration.

Asking Questions That Build Bridges

Most of us ask questions like we're filling out forms:

- "What do you do?"
- "Where are you from?"
- "How's business?"

These aren't bridge-building questions. They're demographic data collection. They tell you about someone without telling you about someone.

Bridge-building questions sound different:

- "What's got your attention these days?"
- "What are you learning right now?"
- "What's surprising you about your work lately?"
- "If you could change one thing about your industry, what would it be?"

See the difference? The first set asks for facts. The second set invites stories.

During a virtual coffee chat, Alex found himself in a conversation with a potential mentor. Instead of asking, "How did you become successful?"—a question that invites a rehearsed highlight reel—he asked, "What's a belief you held early in your career that you've completely changed your mind about?"

The mentor paused, smiled, and said, "No one's ever asked me that." What followed was a forty-minute conversation about failure, growth, and the danger of being right. They still meet monthly, and that question sparked a relationship that has transformed Alex's career.

The Power of Remembering and Following Up

Here's a truth that will set you apart in our goldfish-attention-span world: People are shocked when you remember things about them. Genuinely shocked. In an era where most people can't remember what they had for breakfast, remembering details about others has become a superpower.

Theodore Roosevelt was famous for this. He'd meet someone once and, months later, ask about their sick mother, their son's baseball game, or their research on butterflies. But Roosevelt had a secret weapon: he took notes. After every encounter, he'd jot down key details about the person.

"But that's manipulative!" you might say. Only if you're remembering in order to get something. If you're remembering because you actually care, it's called being a good human.

Modern tools make this easier than ever:

- CRM systems aren't just for sales—use them for relationships
- Voice memos after conversations to capture key points
- Calendar reminders to follow up on important events
- Simple spreadsheets with columns for name, last conversation, and what matters to them

Sophie, a community manager, keeps what she calls a "connection map." It's a simple spreadsheet where she notes:

- What each community member is working on
- Their current challenges
- Personal milestones coming up
- The last time she reached out

Every Monday, she spends 30 minutes sending personal check-ins based on her notes. "How did the product launch go?" "Did your daughter decide on a college?" "Still struggling with that database migration?"

The result? Her online community has the highest engagement and lowest churn in the industry. Why? Because people feel seen. Remembered. Valued.

The Art of the Follow-Up

Following up is where most relationships die. We have great conversations, exchange contact information with promises to "stay in touch," and then... nothing. The road to forgotten connections is paved with good intentions and no follow-through.

But follow-up doesn't have to be complicated. In fact, the simpler, the better:

The 24-Hour Rule: Within 24 hours of meeting someone, send a brief note. "Really enjoyed our conversation about sustainable packaging. Here's that article I mentioned: [link]. Would love to continue the discussion."

The Unexpected Check-In: No agenda, no ask. Just "Saw this and thought of our conversation about remote team building. Hope the new system is working well."

The Milestone Message: "Remembered you said your book launches this month. Exciting! How are you feeling about it?"

The Learning Share: "Just tried that productivity technique you mentioned. Game-changer. Thank you!"

During the pandemic, Marcus noticed his network was withering. Everyone was "too busy" or "Zoomed out." So he started a simple practice: every Friday, he'd send three voice messages to people he hadn't talked to in a while. Not emails—voice messages. Under 60 seconds. No agenda except "Thinking of you, hope you're well, here's something that made me smile this week."

The response was overwhelming. People sent voice messages back. Real conversations restarted. Some led to collaborations, others to friendships, all to a sense of connection in disconnected times.

Listening Techniques for the Digital Age

The Mirror Method: Reflect back what you've heard before adding your thoughts. "So what I'm hearing is that you're frustrated with the lack of clear communication from leadership. Is that right?" This does two things: confirms you actually listened and gives them a chance to clarify.

The Pause Power: Count to three before responding. In video calls, this feels like eternity. Do it anyway. It signals thoughtfulness and gives introverts space to add their voice.

The Question Behind the Question: When someone asks, "How do I get promoted?" they might really be asking, "Am I valued here?" Listen for the emotion behind the words.

The Summary Send: After important conversations, send a brief summary. "Here's what I captured from our chat. Did I miss anything?" This shows you valued the conversation enough to process it.

Building Your Curiosity Practice

Question Journaling: Keep a collection of questions that spark real conversation. Test them. Refine them. Build your repertoire.

The Daily Curious: Each day, ask one person one genuinely curious question. Not small talk. Real talk.

Listening Sprints: Set a timer for 5 minutes. Ask someone to share something they're working through. Your only job: listen and ask clarifying questions. No advice, no similar stories, just presence.

The Follow-Up Calendar: Schedule follow-ups when you schedule meetings. "Great chat on Tuesday. Follow up in 2 weeks" goes right into the calendar.

The Compound Effect of Curiosity

Here's what happens when you genuinely get curious about people: they become curious about you. But more importantly, they become curious about themselves. Your questions help them think, reflect, discover. You become the person they seek out not because you have answers, but because you help them find their own.

A study by Harvard researchers found that people who ask more questions, particularly follow-up questions, are better liked and perceived as more responsive. But here's the kicker: they also learn more, connect more, and create more opportunities—not because they're networking, but because they're genuinely interested in other humans.

Chapter Summary

The Curiosity Principle isn't about being nosy or manipulative. It's about approaching every interaction with genuine wonder about the human in front of you. When we ask better questions, listen with our full presence, and follow up with care, we transform superficial exchanges into meaningful connections. In a world of distraction and transaction, curiosity is revolutionary. It says, "You matter. Your story matters. And I'm here to witness it." Master this, and you'll never lack for deep connections—because everyone wants to be around someone who makes them feel fascinating.

Reflection

- What questions do you default to in conversation? Are they fact-gathering or story-inviting?
- When was the last time someone's follow-up surprised and delighted you? What made it special?
- Think of your best conversationalist friend. What do they do that makes talking with them so engaging?
- Where does your attention typically go when others are speaking? What pulls you away from presence?

Action

This week, practice the "Curiosity Triple Play":

1. Ask three "What's it like..." questions (What's it like leading a team through this change? What's it like balancing parenthood and your startup?)
2. Take notes after one meaningful conversation and follow up within 24 hours
3. Have one five-minute conversation where you only listen and ask clarifying questions—no advice, no personal stories

Track how these curiosity practices change the depth of your connections.

PRINCIPLE: ASK BETTER

What's Next?

Being real, showing empathy, and getting curious are powerful—but only if we can navigate the beautiful complexity of human diversity. In our next chapter, we'll explore Cultural Intelligence—how to connect across cultures, respect diverse perspectives, and communicate inclusively in our wonderfully global world. Because curiosity without cultural awareness is like trying to drive in a foreign country without learning the traffic rules—dangerous for everyone involved.

Chapter 4: Cultural Intelligence

Last year, I watched a million-dollar deal die in seventeen minutes. An American CEO flew to Tokyo, walked into the boardroom, handed out business cards with one hand while checking his phone, launched straight into his PowerPoint, and wrapped up with, "So, what do you think? Ready to sign?"

The Japanese executives exchanged glances. Twenty minutes of polite non-answers followed. The American left confident. "Nailed it!" he told me. Three weeks later: radio silence. When he finally got feedback through a intermediary, he learned his fate had been sealed before he even opened his laptop. Every gesture had screamed disrespect.

Welcome to the minefield of cross-cultural communication, where your normal is someone else's nightmare.

Navigating Global Relationships

We live in a world where your morning standup includes teammates from Mumbai, São Paulo, and Stockholm. Where your customer in Seoul expects different things than your customer in San Francisco. Where a thumbs-up emoji can either mean "great job" or something anatomically inappropriate, depending on the recipient's location.

Cultural intelligence—CQ, as researchers call it—isn't about memorizing which countries bow and which ones shake hands. It's about developing the awareness, curiosity, and adaptability to connect across any cultural divide.

Maria learned this leading a global product team. Her first few months were a disaster. Her American directness ("Let's cut to the chase") clashed with her Indian team members' preference for relationship-building. Her German colleagues' brutal honesty ("This design is terrible") devastated her Brazilian designers. Her Chinese developers never pushed back on unrealistic deadlines, then missed them entirely.

She was leading by her cultural playbook, and it was failing spectacularly.

Then Maria did something revolutionary: she asked. Not "How do we do things in your culture?" (which invites stereotypes) but "How do you prefer to work? What helps you do your best? What should I know about your communication style?"

The answers transformed her leadership:

- Raj preferred written follow-ups after verbal discussions
- Klaus wanted permission to be direct without offense
- Chen needed explicit invitations to disagree
- Isabella thrived with warm personal check-ins before business

Same team, same goals, wildly different needs. Maria's willingness to adapt didn't dilute her leadership, it amplified it.

Inclusive Communication Practices

Here's an uncomfortable truth: most of us communicate in ways that accidentally exclude. We use idioms that don't translate ("let's touch base," "move the needle"). We assume everyone shares our context. We mistake silence for agreement and loudness for leadership.

Inclusive communication isn't about walking on eggshells. It's about building bridges wide enough for everyone to cross.

Take the case of Zoom fatigue, but not the kind you're thinking of. Amit, a software engineer in Bangalore, was exhausted not from too many meetings but from the cognitive load of translating, cultural code-switching, and speaking his third language while his American colleagues rapid-fired through agendas in their first language, dropping pop culture references and assuming everyone was "on the same page" (there's another idiom that doesn't translate).

His manager, once aware, made simple changes:

- Agendas sent 24 hours in advance
- Key terms defined in shared documents
- Regular pauses for questions
- Round-robin format ensuring all voices heard
- Follow-up summaries in simple, clear language

Small adaptations, massive impact. Amit went from struggling to contributing his best ideas. The whole team benefited from the clarity.

Respecting Diverse Perspectives and Values

Different doesn't mean difficult. It means different.

In some cultures, saying "no" directly is impossibly rude. In others, anything but a direct "no" is dishonestly wasting time. In some cultures, hierarchy is sacred—you don't contradict the boss. In others, hierarchy is evil—everyone's ideas matter equally.

Neither is right. Neither is wrong. Both are real.

James, an Australian manager, learned this the hard way when he proudly introduced "casual Fridays" and first-name basis to his Singapore office. He expected enthusiasm. He got discomfort. His team felt untethered without the structure they valued. Calling the senior director "Bob" felt disrespectful, not friendly.

Instead of forcing his "progressive" approach, James got curious:

- What structures help you feel secure?
- How can we balance innovation with stability?
- What changes would actually improve your experience?

They co-created a hybrid approach: formal titles in client meetings, first names in team huddles. Clear hierarchies for decision-making, open forums for idea-sharing. Not Australian culture or Singaporean culture—their culture.

The Hidden Dimensions of Culture

Edward T. Hall identified "high-context" and "low-context" cultures, and understanding this can save your sanity:

High-Context (Japan, Korea, Arab countries, Latin America):

- Communication is layered, indirect
- Meaning lives in what's not said
- Relationships before tasks
- Silence speaks volumes

Low-Context (Germany, Scandinavia, US, Australia):

- Communication is direct, explicit
- Say what you mean, mean what you say
- Tasks before relationships
- Silence is just... silence

Watch this play out: An American asks her Japanese colleague, "Can you finish this by Friday?" He responds, "It will be difficult." She hears, "Yes, but it'll be challenging." He meant, "No, it's impossible." Friday comes, task isn't done, trust is broken.

The fix? When working across contexts:
- Low-context folks: Listen for the "no" hiding in the "maybe"
- High-context folks: Remember that directness isn't rudeness
- Everyone: Check for understanding beyond the words

Building Cultural Bridges, Not Walls

Priya leads a customer success team spanning twelve countries. Her secret weapon? What she calls "cultural ambassadors"—team members who volunteer to help others navigate their local context.

Before launching in a new market, the ambassador shares:

- How customers prefer to communicate
- What signals respect or disrespect
- Local holidays and observances
- Communication styles that work
- Common misunderstandings to avoid

But here's the key: they share their individual preferences too, preventing stereotypes. "In Mexico, we often start with personal connection, but I personally prefer getting to business quickly" is infinitely more useful than "Mexicans always want small talk."

The Technology Layer

Digital communication adds another complex layer to cultural differences:

- **Email styles**: Americans favor brief and bullet-pointed. Japanese colleagues might write longer, more contextual messages
- **Response times**: Germans expect prompt replies. Spanish colleagues might find immediate responses pushy
- **Video calls**: Some cultures find constant cameras invasive. Others see cameras-

off as disengaged

- **Emojis**: Generational and cultural minefield. That smiley face might read as passive-aggressive

The solution isn't to avoid digital communication. It's to explicitly discuss digital norms:

- How quickly do we expect responses?
- When are cameras required vs. optional?
- What's our emoji policy? (Yes, you need one)
- How do we signal urgency vs. FYI?

Practical Strategies for Cultural Intelligence

The Assumption Audit: Before any cross-cultural interaction, list your assumptions. What are you expecting? What's "normal" to you? Now assume half of those are wrong.

The Phrase Check: Review your communication for idioms, cultural references, and jargon. "Let's hit a home run" means nothing to your cricket-playing colleagues.

The Pace Adjustment: Match the cultural tempo. Pushing for quick decisions in consensus cultures backfires. Building slow relationships in task-focused cultures frustrates.

The Humble Position: "I'm still learning about your culture and communication style. Please tell me if I misstep." This opens doors and prevents misunderstandings.

The Both/And Practice: Instead of "We do it this way OR that way," try "How might we do it this way AND honor that approach?"

When Cultural Intelligence Goes Wrong

Common mistakes that well-intentioned people make:

Over-Stereotyping: "You're from Brazil, so you must love parties!" No. Just no.

Culture Blaming: "This project failed because of cultural differences." Usually it failed because of poor communication about those differences.

Freezing Up: Being so worried about cultural mistakes that you avoid connection entirely.

One-Size-Fits-All: Using the same approach for everyone from a country. India has 22 official languages and countless subcultures. "Indian culture" isn't one thing.

The Competitive Advantage of CQ

Companies with culturally intelligent teams outperform monocultural ones by 35%. Why? Because diverse perspectives lead to better solutions. Because global customers trust companies that "get" them. Because the best talent wants to work where they're understood, not just tolerated.

But the real advantage is personal. When you develop cultural intelligence, every interaction becomes an adventure, not an anxiety. Every difference becomes a learning opportunity, not an obstacle. Every connection becomes richer because you're not trying to make others fit your mold—you're expanding your mold to fit the world.

Chapter Summary

Cultural Intelligence isn't about becoming a cultural chameleon or walking on eggshells. It's about developing the awareness to recognize differences, the curiosity to understand them, and the flexibility to bridge them. In our globally connected world, honoring differences isn't just nice—it's necessary. When we move from "my way is the right way" to "let's find our way," we create connections that transcend borders and build teams that leverage the full spectrum of human brilliance. Master this, and you don't just work in the world—you work with the world.

Reflection

- Think of a time when cultural differences caused misunderstanding. What assumptions were you making?
- Which of your communication habits might exclude or confuse people from different backgrounds?
- Who in your network could teach you about their cultural communication style?
- Where do you feel most comfortable vs. stretched in cross-cultural interactions?

Action

This week, practice the "Cultural Intelligence Trio":

1. Have one conversation where you explicitly ask about communication preferences ("How do you prefer to receive feedback?")
2. Audit one piece of your communication for idioms and cultural references, then simplify it
3. Learn about one cultural dimension you encounter regularly (research or, better yet,

ask someone)

Notice how these practices deepen your connections across differences.

PRINCIPLE: HONOR DIFFERENCES

What's Next?

We've learned to be real, to feel first, to ask better, and to honor differences. Now comes the hard part: what happens when things go wrong? In our next chapter, The Feedback Framework, we'll tackle the delicate art of delivering criticism with care, making mistakes productive, and managing public fumbles with grace. Because in our connected world, how we handle the tough conversations defines our relationships more than the easy ones.

Chapter 5: The Feedback Framework

Three years ago, I destroyed a brilliant employee with a compliment sandwich. You know the technique: say something nice, deliver the criticism, end with something nice. "Sarah, your creativity is outstanding, but your reports are always late and full of errors, though your enthusiasm really brightens the office!"

Sarah heard: "Blah blah blah YOU'RE FAILING blah blah blah."

She quit two weeks later. In her exit interview, she said something that haunts me: "I never knew if you were about to praise me or punch me. Every conversation felt like a trap."

I'd weaponized feedback, turning what should be a gift into a grenade.

Delivering Criticism With Care

Here's the truth no leadership book wants to admit: giving feedback is terrifying. We're afraid of hurting feelings, damaging relationships, or being seen as the bad guy. So we either avoid it entirely (the coward's path) or deliver it badly (the accidental assassin's path).

But feedback isn't the enemy. Bad feedback is the enemy.

Good feedback is like physical therapy—it might be uncomfortable, but it helps you get stronger. Bad feedback is like a random assault—it just leaves bruises.

Marcus, a design director, revolutionized his team's culture with what he calls "Feedback as Love." His rules:

Privacy First: Never critique in public. Ever. Not in Slack channels, not in group emails, not in team meetings. Public praise, private coaching.

Specificity is Respect: "Your designs need work" is lazy and harmful. "The color contrast on mobile makes the text hard to read for users with visual impairments" is actionable and shows you care enough to pay attention.

Future Focus: Instead of "You didn't meet the deadline," try "What would help you hit the next deadline? What got in the way this time?"

Own Your Part: "I realize I wasn't clear about the priorities" or "I should have checked in sooner" shows this is a dialogue, not a decree.

His team went from feedback-phobic to feedback-seeking. They started requesting critiques because they knew it came from care, not control.

The Praise-Progress-Partnership Model

Forget the compliment sandwich. It's manipulative, predictable, and everyone sees through it. Instead, try the Praise-Progress-Partnership model:

Praise (Specific and Genuine): "Your presentation skills have grown tremendously. The way you handled the client's technical questions showed real expertise."

Progress (The Growth Opportunity): "The next level for you is bringing that same clarity to your written reports. Right now, the key insights get buried in details."

Partnership (Co-Creating Solutions): "What would help you structure your reports better? Would templates help? Peer review? Let's figure this out together."

See the difference? It's not a shit sandwich with praise bread. It's a roadmap where appreciation is the starting point, growth is the destination, and you're the GPS, not the driver.

Lisa used this approach with her remote team member who dominated video calls. Instead of "You talk too much," she said:

"Your insights are valuable and you always come prepared—I appreciate that. I've noticed some team members struggle to share their ideas in our current format. How can we structure discussions so your expertise shines AND everyone gets heard? What would work for you?"

They designed a new meeting format together. Problem solved, relationship strengthened.

Managing Mistakes in Public Forums

The internet never forgets, and mistakes that once stayed in the conference room now live forever in screenshots. Managing public mistakes requires a new playbook.

When Alex, a social media manager, accidentally posted a client's confidential campaign data on the company's public Twitter, panic set in. The old playbook said: delete, deny, discipline. The new playbook?

Acknowledge Immediately: "We made an error and shared information we shouldn't have. We're addressing it now."

Take Responsibility: No passive voice. Not "Mistakes were made" but "We made a mistake."

Show the Fix: "Here's what we're doing: 1) Removed the post 2) Notified affected parties 3) Implementing new review process"

Learn Publicly: "We'll share what we learned and how we're preventing this in the future."

Instead of a career-ending catastrophe, it became a masterclass in accountability. Clients appreciated the transparency. The team rallied around Alex instead of throwing him under the bus.

The Digital Feedback Dilemma

Digital feedback hits different. Without tone, body language, or immediate clarification, written feedback often lands harder than intended.

I learned this when my "Quick question: why is this late?" Slack message sent an employee into a spiral. She read frustration and disappointment. I meant genuine curiosity about blockers I could remove.

Now I follow the Digital Feedback Protocol:
Assume Positive Intent Will Be Questioned: Your neutral is their negative. Overcommunicate warmth and support.

Use Video for Sensitive Topics: Nuance needs faces. If it's complex or emotional, switch to video.

The Preview Principle: "Hey, I have some feedback on the proposal. Nothing major, just some thoughts to make it stronger. Good time to chat?"

The Emoji Assist: Strategic 😊 placement softens messages. "Let's revisit this approach 😊" beats "Let's revisit this approach."

The Follow-Up: After written feedback, check in verbally. "Just wanted to make sure my message came across as intended—I'm here to support, not stress."

Creating Psychological Safety for feedback

Amy, a product manager, noticed her team had stopped sharing ideas after one brutal feedback session where an executive demolished a junior developer's proposal. She rebuilt safety systematically:

Feedback Norms: The team created explicit agreements:

- Critique ideas, not people
- Start with questions, not judgments
- "Yes, and..." before "No, but..."
- Everyone gives and receives feedback

The Two-Minute Rule: When receiving feedback, you have two minutes to just listen and ask clarifying questions. No defending, no explaining. This prevents reactive responses.

Feedback Fridays: Optional sessions where people could request feedback on works-in-progress. Low stakes, high learning.

The Vulnerability Lead: Amy went first, sharing a failed project and asking for feedback on what she could have done differently. This opened the floodgates.

The Art of Receiving Feedback

We spend so much time learning to give feedback that we forget receiving it is a skill too. The best feedback receivers:

Say Thank You First: Even if it stings. "Thank you for taking the time to share this" keeps doors open.

Get Curious, Not Defensive: "Can you give me an example?" beats "That's not true!"

Take Notes: Shows you value their input and helps you process later when emotions settle.

Close the Loop: "I've thought about your feedback and here's what I'm doing differently..."

When Tom's 360 review came back brutal—"micromanager," "doesn't trust the team," "control freak"—his first instinct was to argue. Instead, he sent a team message:

"Thank you for your honest feedback. It's hard to hear but important. I'm reflecting on how I can better support your autonomy. In two weeks, let's discuss specific changes I can make. Your success is my success."

His vulnerability transformed him from manager to leader.

Feedback Across Cultures

Remember: feedback that motivates in New York might mortify in Tokyo.

- **Direct cultures** (Netherlands, Israel, Germany): Appreciate blunt, straightforward feedback
- **Indirect cultures** (Japan, Korea, Thailand): Require subtle, face-saving approaches
- **Individual cultures** (US, UK, Australia): Can handle public recognition
- **Collective cultures** (China, Mexico, India): Prefer team recognition

Samantha leads a global team and learned to adapt:

- For her Dutch developer: "This code is inefficient. Here's why and how to fix it."
- For her Japanese designer: "Your work is always so thoughtful. I wonder if we might explore some alternatives for this particular element?"
- Same feedback, different delivery, equal respect.

The Feedback That Changes Everything

The most powerful feedback I ever received came from a mentor who said: "You're so focused on being right that you're forgetting to be helpful."

It shifted my entire approach. Now, before giving feedback, I ask myself:

- Is this about being right or being helpful?
- Am I sharing this to improve or to prove?
- Will this feedback open possibilities or close doors?

Chapter Summary

The Feedback Framework isn't about softening truth or avoiding difficult conversations. It's about delivering truth in a way that lifts while it shifts. When we give feedback with care, create genuine partnerships for growth, and manage mistakes with grace, we transform criticism from a weapon into a tool for connection. Master this, and you become someone people seek out for feedback—because they know that even when it's tough, it comes from love, not judgment. In a world quick to criticize and slow to care, that makes you revolutionary.

Reflection

- Think of the best feedback you ever received. What made it so effective?
- Where do you struggle most with feedback—giving it, receiving it, or both? Why?
- How might your feedback style need to adapt for different team members?
- What stops you from asking for the feedback you need to grow?

Action

This week, practice the "Feedback Triple":

1. Give one piece of feedback using the Praise-Progress-Partnership model
2. Ask for specific feedback on something you're working to improve
3. Send a thank-you message to someone whose past feedback helped you grow

Notice how intentional feedback practices strengthen your relationships.

PRINCIPLE: LIFT WHILE YOU SHIFT

What's Next?

Feedback is just the beginning of difficult conversations. In our next chapter, Conflict Alchemy, we'll dive into the art of transforming disagreement into dialogue, de-escalating digital disputes, and finding common ground when everyone's convinced they're on different planets. Because in our polarized world, the ability to turn conflict into connection isn't just a nice skill—it's a superpower.

Chapter 6: Conflict Alchemy

Last month, I watched a LinkedIn comment thread turn into digital Armageddon. It started with a post about remote work productivity. Three hundred comments later, people were questioning each other's intelligence, work ethic, and moral character. Former colleagues blocked each other. A partnership dissolved. All because two people disagreed about whether working from home was "real work."

Meanwhile, in a Slack channel across the internet, two developers had a heated disagreement about code architecture. By the end of the day, they'd designed a better solution than either original idea. Same species, same platform capabilities, completely different outcomes.

The difference? One group tried to win. The other tried to understand.

Transforming Disagreement Into Dialogue

Conflict is information dressed in emotion. Strip away the heat, and you find data: unmet needs, different perspectives, clashing values, misaligned expectations. The question isn't how to avoid conflict—it's how to mine it for gold.

Rachel, a startup CEO, discovered this when her co-founders nearly imploded over product direction. The CFO wanted to focus on enterprise clients (reliable revenue). The CTO wanted to perfect the consumer product (technical elegance). The CMO wanted to expand internationally (growth metrics). Board meetings became battle zones.

Instead of picking a winner, Rachel introduced "Conflict Mining Sessions":

Step 1: Map the Values: What does each person care about most? Security? Innovation? Impact? Get beneath positions to principles.

Step 2: Find the Fear: What's the nightmare scenario each person is trying to avoid? The CFO feared bankruptcy. The CTO feared building garbage. The CMO feared irrelevance.

Step 3: Discover the Dream: What does success look like for each person? Not just business success—personal success.

Step 4: Create the Alchemy: How can we honor all these values, address these fears, pursue these dreams? Not either/or. Both/and.

They emerged with a phased strategy: secure enterprise revenue first (CFO happy), use that stability to perfect the consumer product (CTO happy), then expand internationally with a proven model (CMO happy). The conflict revealed the solution.

De-escalation Techniques for Digital Disputes

Digital conflicts escalate faster than a Tesla in Ludicrous Mode. No cooling-off period while you walk to someone's office. No body language saying "I'm upset but still respect you." Just words on screens, often read in the worst possible tone.

The Digital De-escalation Toolkit:

The Pattern Interrupt: When a thread gets heated, change the medium. "This seems important. Could we hop on a quick call?" Voices humanize. Video even more so.

The Perspective Pause: Before responding to that inflammatory comment, write three possible interpretations of what they meant. Respond to the most generous one.

The Curiosity Pivot: Replace "You're wrong because..." with "Help me understand your thinking..." It's impossible to stay angry at someone genuinely trying to understand you.

The Common Ground Callout: "I think we both care about [shared value]. We just have different ideas about how to achieve it." Reminder: you're on the same team.

Watch this in action: Two product managers, David and Lin, got into a Slack fight about feature priorities. Messages got shorter, snippier, meaner. Then David typed:

"Lin, I think we're both frustrated because we care so much about user experience. You're worried about overwhelming new users. I'm worried about boring power users. Both valid. Want to grab virtual coffee and figure out how we can do both?"

The temperature dropped instantly. They designed a progressive disclosure system that satisfied both concerns. Conflict became collaboration.

Finding Common Ground in Polarized Times

We're living through the Great Polarization. Every topic—from pineapple on pizza to political policies—becomes a tribal identity marker. You're either with us or against us. Nuance is dead. Middle ground is no-man's land.

But here's what I've learned: common ground isn't in the middle. It's underneath.

During a diversity training that was going off the rails—half the participants felt it was "woke nonsense," the other half felt it wasn't going far enough—the facilitator did something brilliant. She asked everyone to share a story about a time they felt excluded or misunderstood.

The stories poured out:

- The conservative manager excluded from conversations because of assumptions about his views
- The young woman whose ideas were ignored until repeated by male colleagues
- The immigrant engineer who felt he had to hide his accent
- The veteran who felt his service was either tokenized or dismissed

Suddenly, the room wasn't divided into camps. It was filled with humans who all knew the sting of exclusion. They built the program together from that shared understanding.

The Alchemy Process: A Step-by-Step Guide

1. Acknowledge the Heat: "This is clearly important to both of us, and emotions are running high. That's okay."

2. Separate Positions from Interests:

- Position: "We need to return to the office full-time"
- Interest: "I want to build team cohesion and culture"

3. Look for Hidden Agreements: List everything you agree on. It's always more than you think.

4. Explore the 'Why' Behind the 'What': "What would success look like for you?" "What are you worried might happen?"

5. Generate Options Together: Not "my solution vs. your solution" but "what new solutions could we create?"

6. Test Solutions Against Shared Values: Does this honor what we both care about?

When Conflict Goes Nuclear

Sometimes, despite best efforts, conflicts explode. The key is containing the blast radius.

When Marcus, a community manager, faced a full-scale forum meltdown over content moderation policies, he:

Acknowledged the Pain: "I see many of you are upset, and I understand why. This community matters to you, and you feel unheard."

Created Contained Spaces: "We're creating a dedicated channel for this discussion with clear ground rules. The main channels stay focused on their purpose."

Brought in Neutral Voices: Community members who weren't in either camp helped facilitate discussions.

Made the Process Transparent: Daily updates on what was being discussed, what decisions were being made, and why.

Committed to Experimentation: "Let's try this for 30 days and reassess based on data, not debate."

The community not only survived but emerged stronger, with members feeling more invested in its success.

The Unexpected Benefits of Healthy Conflict

Teams without conflict aren't healthy—they're dying. When everyone agrees all the time, it means:

- People don't feel safe to disagree
- You're missing crucial perspectives
- Groupthink is setting in
- Innovation is impossible

The healthiest teams have what researchers call "task conflict"—disagreement about ideas, approaches, strategies—without "relationship conflict"—personal attacks, character judgments, tribal warfare.

Create the former by:
- Assigning devil's advocates
- Rewarding dissenting views
- Celebrating changed minds
- Making "I was wrong" a badge of honor

Prevent the latter by:
- Attacking problems, not people
- Assuming positive intent
- Taking breaks when heated

- Remembering you'll need to work together tomorrow

Digital Tools for Conflict Resolution

Anonymous Input Platforms: Sometimes people need to share concerns without their name attached. Tools like Mentimeter or anonymous Google Forms let real issues surface.

Structured Discussion Templates: Shared docs with sections for "What we agree on," "Where we differ," "Questions we need to answer," and "Possible solutions."

Breakout Rooms: In large conflicts, small group discussions allow more voices and less grandstanding.

Time-Delayed Responses: Tools that require a pause before posting (like Slack's scheduled send) prevent reactive responses.

The Cultural Layer of Conflict

Remember: conflict styles are cultural.

- **Direct conflict cultures** (Israel, France, Russia): Heated debate is engagement, not aggression
- **Harmony cultures** (Japan, Thailand, Indonesia): Open conflict is failure, resolution happens privately
- **Procedural cultures** (Germany, Switzerland): Conflict follows rules and structures

Maria leads a global team and adapts her conflict approach:

- With her Israeli engineers: Direct debate in meetings
- With her Japanese designers: Private one-on-ones to surface concerns
- With her German analysts: Structured feedback processes

Same conflicts, different containers, equal respect.

The Personal Practice of Conflict Alchemy

Before you can transform conflict with others, practice on yourself:

Daily Conflict Inventory: What internal conflicts are you carrying? Between your ambition and your values? Your needs and others' expectations?

The Both/And Practice: When you catch yourself thinking either/or, ask "How might both be true?"

The Perspective Playlist: Before bed, replay the day's conflicts from the other person's view. What were they protecting? What did they need?

Chapter Summary

Conflict Alchemy isn't about avoiding disagreement or finding mushy middle ground. It's about transforming the energy of conflict into the power of breakthrough. When we stop trying to win and start trying to understand, when we mine conflict for information instead of ammunition, when we create containers strong enough to hold heat without explosion—that's when magic happens. In a world tearing itself apart over differences, those who can transform conflict into connection don't just survive—they lead.

Reflection

- What's your default conflict style? Do you attack, avoid, or something else?
- Think of a current conflict in your life. What might the other person be protecting or needing?
- When has conflict led to a breakthrough in your life? What made that possible?
- Where do you need more courage in conflict? Where do you need more restraint?

Action

This week, practice the "Conflict Alchemy Trio":

1. In one disagreement, ask "What are you worried might happen?" and really listen to the answer
2. Find three things you agree on with someone you usually disagree with
3. Transform one either/or debate into a both/and exploration

Track how these practices shift the energy of conflict in your life.

PRINCIPLE: FIND THE GOLD

What's Next?

We've learned to transform conflict, but what happens when we're the ones who screwed up? In our next chapter, The Accountability Advantage, we'll explore the counterintuitive power of owning mistakes, the art of public apologies, and why admitting fault might be the fastest way to build unshakeable trust. Because in a world of spin and deflection, radical accountability is radical leadership.

Chapter 7: The Accountability Advantage

PRINCIPLE: OWN IT ALL

In 2018, the CEO of a major airline watched in horror as security footage of a passenger being dragged off an overbooked flight went viral. His first response was a masterclass in how not to handle a crisis: "I apologize for having to re-accommodate these customers." Re-accommodate. A man with a bloody face being dragged down an aisle, and the CEO called it "re-accommodation."

The internet exploded. Stock price plummeted. Trust evaporated.

Three days later, he tried again: "I deeply apologize to the customer forcibly removed and to all the customers aboard. No one should ever be mistreated this way." Better, but the damage was done. The half-hearted, corporate-speak first response had already told the world everything they needed to know about the company's values.

Contrast this with another CEO who, when his company's data breach exposed millions of users' information, immediately posted: "We screwed up. Badly. Here's exactly what happened, what we're doing about it, and what we're doing to make sure it never happens again. This is on me, and I'm going to make it right."

Stock price barely wobbled. Customer loyalty actually increased. Why? Because in a world of deflection and spin, taking real responsibility is so rare it's revolutionary.

The Power of Owning Your Mistakes

We live in the Age of the Screenshot. Every email, every tweet, every offhand comment can be preserved, shared, and weaponized. The old playbook—deny, deflect, wait for the news cycle to move on—doesn't work when the internet never forgets.

But here's the paradox: the more permanent our mistakes become, the more powerful owning them becomes.

When Sarah, a marketing director, accidentally sent a private email mocking a client's "stupid questions" to the entire client team (yes, the entire team, including the CEO), her career flashed before her eyes. The old playbook said to claim her email was hacked, or taken out of context, or somehow deflect.

Instead, she immediately called the client CEO: "I sent something awful and I'm mortified. You have every right to be angry. I let frustration get the better of me and I expressed it in the worst possible way. There's no excuse. I understand if you want to work with someone else, but I'd like the chance to rebuild your trust."

The CEO was silent for a long moment. Then: "Thank you for calling. I'm angry, yes. But I also know you're human. Let's talk about how to move forward."

They not only kept the account but deepened the relationship. Two years later, when that CEO moved companies, guess who he brought in for marketing?

Building Trust Through Transparency

Trust is built in drops and lost in buckets. But radical transparency—real, uncomfortable, hold-nothing-back honesty—can refill that bucket faster than years of perfect performance.

Marcus runs a software company that promised a major update by Q4. In October, it became clear they wouldn't make it. The old playbook: say nothing, hope for a miracle, announce the delay at the last possible moment with maximum spin.

Marcus's approach: He recorded a video for customers. Not a polished, scripted video. A real one, from his home office, with his kid's toys visible in the background.

"Hey everyone. Marcus here. I need to share some tough news. We're not going to hit our Q4 deadline for the update. We underestimated the complexity, and frankly, I pushed the team to promise more than we could deliver. That's on me. Here's where we actually are, here's what's taking longer than expected, and here's our realistic timeline. I know this impacts your planning, and I'm sorry. For anyone who needs to switch solutions, we'll help with the transition and refund your last quarter. For those who stick with us, I promise we'll make it worth the wait."

The response shocked him. Sure, some customers left. But the majority stayed, and many reached out with support. "Thanks for being straight with us." "We've all been there." "The honesty means more than the timeline."

Six months later, when they delivered the update (ahead of the revised schedule), customer satisfaction was the highest in company history.

Crisis Communication in the Social Media Age

Every company needs a crisis communication plan. But most plans are built for the old world—craft a perfect statement, run it through legal, release it through official channels, control the narrative.

That world is dead. In the social media age, you have minutes, not days. The narrative is never yours to control. And perfect statements smell like corporate BS from a mile away.

The New Crisis Playbook:

Speed Beats Perfect: A genuine response in one hour beats a polished response in one day. "We're aware and investigating. More soon." buys you time while showing you're not hiding.

Human Beats Corporate: People forgive humans, not corporations. Put a real person's name and face on the response.

Specifics Beat Vagueness: "We take this seriously" means nothing. "Here's what we're doing: 1) 2) 3)" means everything.

Updates Beat Silence: Even "We're still working on it, here's what we've learned so far" maintains trust.

Actions Beat Words: Show what you're changing, not just what you're saying.

When Amy's restaurant got review-bombed after a video showed staff refusing service to someone who appeared homeless, she could have claimed it was policy, or the person was disruptive, or any number of deflections. Instead:

"I watched the video and I'm appalled. That's not who we are, and there's no excuse. I've already met with the gentleman in the video to apologize personally. The staff member no longer works here—not because of the video, but because their actions violated everything we stand for. We're also partnering with the local shelter to provide weekly meals and job training. This never should have happened, and I'm going to make sure it never happens again."

The review-bombing stopped. The story shifted from outrage to redemption. The restaurant became known for its community service.

The Anatomy of a Genuine Apology

Bad apologies are everywhere:

- "I'm sorry if anyone was offended" (not sorry, blaming the offended)
- "I apologize for any misunderstanding" (not my fault, you misunderstood)
- "Mistakes were made" (by whom? Magical mistake fairies?)

A real apology has five parts:

1. Own It Completely: "I did this specific thing and it was wrong."

2. Acknowledge Impact: "I understand this caused specific harm to specific people."

3. Express Genuine Remorse: "I'm genuinely sorry" (not "I apologize" which sounds like a legal statement).

4. Explain Without Excusing: "Here's what happened" not "Here's why it's not really my fault."

5. Commit to Change: "Here's what I'm doing differently" with specifics and timeline.

Watch this in action. When David, a team lead, realized he'd been taking credit for his team's ideas in executive presentations:

"I need to address something I've been doing wrong. In our exec presentations, I've been presenting the team's ideas as if they were mine. I see now how that minimized your contributions and probably affected your career growth. I'm genuinely sorry. I got caught up in looking good upward and forgot to lift up the people doing the actual work. Going forward, I'll always attribute ideas to their source, and I've already emailed the exec team to clarify who drove our recent wins. I know this damaged trust and I'm committed to rebuilding it."

His team didn't just forgive him—they rallied around him. Vulnerability creates connection.

The Competitive Advantage of Radical Accountability

Here's what most people don't understand: accountability is a superpower. In a world where everyone deflects, the person who owns their mistakes becomes:

Trustworthy: If you own your failures, people believe your successes.

Learnable: Mistakes you own become lessons. Mistakes you hide become patterns.

Promotable: Leaders want people who surface problems, not hide them.

Magnetic: People are drawn to those who make it safe to be imperfect.

Lisa discovered this after a $2M mistake. She'd signed a contract without catching a clause that cost her company big. The old playbook: bury it in the numbers, blame the fine print, hope nobody notices.

Lisa's move: She walked into the CEO's office. "I made a expensive mistake. Here's what happened, here's what it cost us, here's how I'm fixing it, and here's how I'll prevent it in the future."

The CEO's response surprised her: "Thank you for telling me. The mistake is expensive, yes. But knowing I have leaders who own their errors immediately? That's priceless."

She was promoted six months later. The CEO's reasoning? "I need leaders I can trust when I'm not in the room."

Building a Culture of Accountability

Individual accountability is powerful. Cultural accountability is unstoppable.

Netflix famously shares their "sunshine" principle: uncomfortably transparent communication. Mistakes aren't just admitted; they're dissected in company-wide emails so everyone can learn.

But you don't need to be Netflix. Start small:
Mistake Mondays: Weekly team shares of "Here's what I messed up and what I learned."

Failure Résumés: Document your failures like achievements. What did you try? Why did it fail? What did you learn?

Accountability Partners: Pair people to check each other's blind spots and surface issues early.

Blameless Post-Mortems: When things go wrong, focus on systems, not scapegoats.

Public Learning: Share lessons from failures as widely as you shared the original goals.

The Personal Practice of Ownership

Before leading others in accountability, master it yourself:

The Daily Ownership Audit: Each night, ask "What did I own today? What did I deflect?"

The Preemptive Strike: When you sense you might have made a mistake, investigate and own it before others find it.

The Apology Practice: Apologize for small things well. It builds the muscle for when big apologies are needed.

The Feedback Request: Regularly ask "What mistakes am I making that I don't see?"

Chapter Summary

The Accountability Advantage isn't about self-flagellation or career suicide. It's about recognizing that in a transparent world, owning your mistakes is the fastest way to move past them. When we build trust through transparency, master the genuine apology, and create cultures where accountability is rewarded, not punished, we transform mistakes from career-enders into career-makers. In a world of spin, deflection, and corporate speak, radical accountability isn't just refreshing—it's revolutionary. Own your mistakes, and you own your power.

Reflection

- What mistake are you still trying to hide or minimize? What would happen if you owned it completely?
- Think of the best apology you ever received. What made it so effective?
- Where in your life do you deflect rather than own? What are you protecting?
- How does your organization handle mistakes? Does it encourage ownership or hiding?

Action

This week, practice the "Accountability Triple":

1. Own one mistake completely—to yourself and someone else affected by it
2. Give one genuine five-part apology for something, however small
3. Ask someone you trust: "What's a mistake I make repeatedly that I might not see?"

Notice how ownership changes your relationships and your own peace of mind.

PRINCIPLE: OWN IT ALL

What's Next?

Accountability builds trust, but stories build movements. In our next chapter, Story Power, we'll explore how to use narrative to inspire, data storytelling that actually sticks, and why the person who tells the best story—not who has the best facts—usually wins. Because in our information-overloaded world, facts tell but stories sell, and the leaders who master narrative master influence.

Chapter 8: Story Power

PRINCIPLE: MAKE IT STICK

In 2007, a Washington Post journalist named Rob Walker bought 200 objects from thrift stores and garage sales. Total cost: $128.74. Average price per item: 64 cents. These weren't antiques or hidden treasures—just random junk. A wooden mallet. A plastic banana. A ceramic horse.

Then he did something interesting. He asked writers to create fictional stories about each object. A simple wooden mallet became "the one my grandfather used to build the desk where he wrote love letters to grandma during the war." The plastic banana had "survived three divorces and somehow always ended up in the fruit bowl of hope."

He put the objects on eBay with their stories. Total sales: $3,612.51. That's a 2,700% increase. The wooden mallet that cost 50 cents sold for $71. The plastic banana went for $41.

The objects hadn't changed. Only the stories had.

Using Narrative to Inspire and Influence

We are wired for story. Before PowerPoint, before writing, before agriculture, we had stories. They're how we make sense of chaos, transmit values, and imagine futures. Yet somehow, in our data-obsessed business world, we've forgotten this fundamental truth: facts inform, but stories transform.

Watch what happens in two different all-hands meetings:

Company A: "Our Q3 revenue was $47.2M, up 12% YoY. EBITDA margins improved to 23%. Customer acquisition cost decreased by 18%. We need to maintain this trajectory through Q4."

Company B: "Let me tell you about Maria, a small business owner in Detroit. Six months ago, she was ready to close her family bakery—third generation, her grandmother's recipes. Then she started using our platform. Last week, she hired her fifth employee and is opening a second location. We helped 10,000 Marias this quarter. That's why our revenue is up—because we're changing lives, not just processing transactions."

Which company's employees leave feeling inspired? Which message gets shared at dinner tables? Which vision attracts top talent?

Data Storytelling That Actually Sticks

Here's the problem with most data presentations: they're autopsies, not narratives. They tell you what happened but not why it matters or what happens next. They're screenshots when what we need is a movie.

The Three-Act Data Story:

Act 1: The Setup (Context): Where we were, what we expected, why this matters. Create tension—what's at stake?

Act 2: The Conflict (Data): What actually happened. But don't just show numbers—show the struggle, the surprise, the gap between expectation and reality.

Act 3: The Resolution (Insight): What this means, what we learned, what we do next. Leave them with a clear next step, not just information.

Example: Instead of "Customer churn increased 23% in Q3," try:

"We started Q3 confident in our customer loyalty. Our NPS was strong, feature adoption was up. Then something shifted. By August, we were losing 100 customers a day—people who'd been with us for years. Sarah from the data team discovered the pattern: every churned customer had contacted support 3+ times about our new interface. They weren't leaving because they found something better. They were leaving because we made their daily workflow harder. Here's how we're fixing it..."

See the difference? Same data, completely different impact.

Creating Memorable Messages

The curse of knowledge is real. Once you know something, you can't imagine not knowing it. So you speak in jargon, acronyms, and abstractions that make perfect sense to you and sound like gibberish to everyone else.

The Memorable Message Formula:

Simple: One core idea. If you can't explain it to a smart 12-year-old, it's too complex.

Unexpected: Break a pattern. Start with what surprises. "We're a tech company that hopes you use our product less."

Concrete: Use sensory language. Not "improve efficiency" but "cut your Monday morning email time in half."

Credible: Back it up, but pick one killer proof point, not seventeen mediocre ones.

Emotional: Make them feel something. Pride, urgency, possibility, even productive discomfort.

Story: Wrap it in narrative. Our brains literally can't resist following a story to its conclusion.

When Melinda needed buy-in for an expensive security upgrade, she could have talked about encryption protocols and compliance requirements. Instead:
"Imagine you wake up tomorrow and every customer's credit card is for sale on the dark web. The calls start at 6 AM. Angry. Scared. Some crying because their kids' college funds were drained. The news vans arrive by 7. By 8, our stock is down 40%. By noon, the lawsuits begin. This isn't fiction—it happened to Company X last year. Their security system was exactly like ours is today. The upgrade costs $2M. The alternative costs everything."

Approved in one meeting.

Visual Storytelling in the Digital Age

A picture is worth a thousand words, but the wrong picture is worth negative ten thousand. We've all suffered through presentations with terrible stock photos of people in suits shaking hands or climbing mountains.

Visual storytelling isn't decoration—it's communication.

The Before/After: Nothing tells a story like transformation. Show the messy desk becoming organized, the frown becoming a smile, the empty store becoming packed.

The Journey Map: Don't just show destinations—show the path. Where did we start? What obstacles did we face? Where are we now? Where are we going?

The Human Face: Data about homelessness is statistics. A photo of James, who used to be an engineer and now lives in his car, is a story.

The Unexpected Visual: Instead of a bar chart showing sales growth, show a map with lights turning on in each new market. Instead of percentages, show faces.

Lisa revolutionized her team's weekly reports with one simple change: every metric was accompanied by a customer photo and quote. Revenue wasn't just up 15%—it was "helping Ana expand her flower shop." Bug fixes weren't just down 30%—they were "giving David two hours back each week."

The engagement with her reports went from "I'll review later" to "Can't wait to see this week's stories."

The Science of Story

When we hear facts, two areas of our brain activate—the language processing parts. When we hear stories, our entire brain lights up. The sensory cortex activates during action sequences. The olfactory cortex engages when someone describes a smell. We're not just understanding the story—we're experiencing it.

This is why story is the ultimate influence tool. You're not just reaching the logical brain that says "yes" or "no." You're engaging the whole brain that says "I feel this" and "I see myself in this."

Stanford's Graduate School of Business found that stories are remembered up to 22 times more than facts alone. When students were asked to recall presentations, 63% remembered the stories. Only 5% remembered individual statistics.

Building Your Story Arsenal

Every leader needs a collection of go-to stories:

The Origin Story: Why you do what you do. Your moment of conviction.

The Failure Story: When you spectacularly screwed up and what you learned.

The Customer Hero Story: When someone used your work to achieve something amazing.

The Team Victory Story: When collective effort achieved the impossible.

The Values Story: A moment when principles mattered more than profit.

The Future Story: Paint a picture of what's possible.

Practice these. Refine them. Know them so well you can tell them in an elevator or expand them for a keynote.

Digital Age Story Techniques

The Serialized Story: Don't dump the whole narrative at once. Release it in chapters. Keep them coming back.

The Interactive Story: Let your audience shape the narrative. Polls, choices, branching paths.

The Multi-Modal Story: Same core narrative told through video, text, audio, graphics. Meet people where they are.

The Micro-Story: Twitter threads, Instagram stories, TikTok narratives. Big impact in small packages.

The Data Story Dashboard: Real-time narratives that update as numbers change. The story evolves with the data.

Common Story Pitfalls

The Humblebrag Disguised as Story: "Let me tell you about the time I saved the company $10M through my brilliant innovation..." 😳

The Rambling River: No clear beginning, middle, or end. Just... words.

The Unrelatable Hero: Stories about people so perfect no one can identify with them.

The Missing Point: Great story, but... what was I supposed to learn?

The Data Decoration: Sprinkling anecdotes on bad data doesn't make it good storytelling.

Chapter Summary

Story Power isn't about manipulation or making things up. It's about recognizing that humans are narrative creatures living in a narrative world. When we use stories to make data meaningful, create messages that stick, and paint pictures of possible futures, we don't just inform—we transform. In a world drowning in information, the person who tells the best story doesn't just get heard—they get followed. Master story, and you master the ability to move hearts, minds, and mountains.

Reflection

- What's a story from your life that illustrates your core values? How could you use it in leadership?
- Think of the last presentation that really stuck with you. What made it memorable?
- Where do you default to facts when a story would serve better?
- What story does your team or organization tell about itself? What story should it tell?

Action

This week, practice the "Story Power Triple":

1. Transform one piece of data into a three-act story (setup, conflict, resolution)
2. Craft one "signature story" about a challenge you overcame—practice telling it in 2 minutes
3. In your next presentation or meeting, open with a story instead of an agenda

Notice how storytelling changes engagement and retention.

PRINCIPLE: MAKE IT STICK

What's Next?

We've learned to transform conflict, own our mistakes, and tell powerful stories. Now it's time to master what makes all of this sustainable: motivation. In our next chapter, Motivation Mastery, we'll dive deep into understanding what really drives people, how to tap into intrinsic motivation, and why the old carrots and sticks are killing engagement. Because when you understand what makes people tick, you don't have to push them—they'll race ahead on their own.

Chapter 9: Motivation Mastery

Daniel Pink ruined everything. Well, not everything—just everything companies thought they knew about motivation. In his research, he discovered something shocking: the traditional carrot-and-stick approach doesn't just fail to motivate modern workers—it actively demotivates them.

He ran an experiment where people solved puzzles. One group got paid for each puzzle solved. The other group did it for fun. The paid group performed worse. Not just a little worse—significantly worse. The money had turned play into work, creativity into compliance.

I learned this the hard way when I tried to "motivate" my team with a sales contest. Grand prize: $5,000 bonus. The result? My top performers sandbagged deals to hit them in contest month. My collaborative team turned cutthroat. My creative problem-solvers became rule-followers, finding loopholes instead of solutions. I'd spent money to make my team worse at their jobs.

That's when I discovered the truth: you can't motivate people. You can only create conditions where they motivate themselves.

Understanding What Drives People

Forget everything you learned in Management 101 about Maslow's hierarchy. Not because it's wrong, but because it's incomplete. People aren't vending machines where you insert money and get productivity. They're complex systems driven by internal fires that burn differently for each person.

The Three Universal Drivers (thanks, Pink):

Autonomy: The desire to direct our own lives. Not anarchy—autonomy. People want to choose their path, not have it chosen for them.

Mastery: The urge to get better at something that matters. Not perfection—progress. The satisfaction of looking back and seeing growth.

Purpose: The yearning to do what we do in service of something larger than ourselves. Not just profit.

But here's what Pink missed: these show up differently for everyone.

Take Sarah and Marcus, both software engineers on the same team:
Sarah's autonomy looks like flexible hours and choosing her tech stack. Her mastery is becoming the best systems architect in the industry. Her purpose is building technology that helps people with disabilities.

Marcus's autonomy looks like picking his projects and working location. His mastery is becoming a full-stack developer who can build anything. His purpose is providing for his family and being a role model for his kids.

Same drives, completely different expressions. Motivate them the same way, and you'll lose one of them.

Autonomy, Mastery, and Purpose in Practice

Autonomy in Action
When Lisa took over a struggling customer service team, the first thing she noticed was the scripts. Scripts for everything. "Thank you for calling, my name is X, how may I provide excellent service today?" Soul-crushing, robot-making scripts.

She burned them. Well, metaphorically. In a team meeting, she said: "You know our customers better than I do. You know what works. Instead of scripts, here are our values and goals. You figure out how to achieve them."

Chaos? For about a week. Then something magical happened. The team started sharing what worked. They created their own best practices—not because they were told to, but because they wanted to help each other succeed. Customer satisfaction went up 32%. Employee satisfaction went up 47%.

But here's the key: Lisa didn't abandon them to figure it out alone. She provided:

- Clear goals (what success looks like)
- Guard rails (what we never compromise on)
- Support (training, coaching, resources)
- Trust (no micromanaging, no surveillance)

Mastery in Motion
Google's "20% time" gets all the press, but the real mastery innovation is their "TGIF" meetings where engineers present their projects to the entire company. It's not the time to work on passion projects that matters—it's the stage to show mastery that motivates.

72

Watch what happens when people can showcase growth:

- The junior developer who presents their first feature
- The designer who shows their evolved style over five projects
- The manager who shares how their team's velocity improved

Public progress is motivating. Private progress is satisfying. But progress made visible? That's rocket fuel.

David, a sales manager, created "Mastery Maps" for his team—visual representations of skills from "exploring" to "teaching others." Each person chose their development path. The magic wasn't in the maps—it was in the ownership. People started seeking out challenges that would move them along their chosen path.

Purpose Beyond Profit

Every company has a mission statement. Most are garbage. "To maximize shareholder value while delighting customers through innovative solutions." Kill me now.

Purpose that motivates sounds like:

- "We help small businesses survive and thrive"
- "We make healthcare accessible to everyone"
- "We protect kids online"
- "We turn waste into resources"

But even the best purpose statement is worthless if people can't see their fingerprints on it.

Maria ran a data entry team—not exactly purpose-rich work. But she connected every project to its outcome: "This insurance data you're processing? It helps families get claims paid faster after disasters." She brought in customers to share stories. She showed the before and after. Suddenly, data entry wasn't just keystrokes—it was helping humans in their worst moments.

Recognition and Encouragement Strategies

Recognition is not a one-size-fits-all solution. What motivates one person mortifies another.

The Recognition Matrix:

- **Private Praise**: For introverts, people from hierarchical cultures, those who value humility
- **Public Recognition**: For those who value status, social contributors, achievement-

oriented personalities
- **Peer Recognition**: Often more powerful than top-down praise
- **Self-Recognition**: Creating systems where people can see their own progress

Amy discovered this when her public "Employee of the Month" program backfired. Her best engineer threatened to quit if nominated again—the public attention was agony for him. Meanwhile, her sales team fought for the spotlight.

Her solution? A recognition menu:

- Public shout-out in all-hands
- Private note from leadership
- Donation to charity of choice
- Extra PTO day
- Lunch with CEO
- Feature in company newsletter
- Choose your own reward

People selected what actually motivated them. Revolutionary concept: asking people what they want.

Digital-Age Motivation Tools

Progress Tracking Apps: People love seeing progress. Habitica, Todoist, even simple spreadsheets that show movement toward mastery.

Peer Recognition Platforms: Bonusly, Kudos, or even a simple Slack channel where people can appreciate each other.

Learning Platforms: LinkedIn Learning, Coursera, internal wikis. Make mastery accessible.

Purpose Dashboards: Show how individual work connects to company impact. Real-time updates on customers helped, lives changed, problems solved.

Autonomy Tools: Let people choose when they work (calendar blocking), how they work (tech stack choices), where they work (remote options).

The Danger Zone: When Motivation Becomes Manipulation

Here's where leaders go wrong: they learn these principles and use them as manipulation tools. "I'll give them the illusion of autonomy while steering them exactly where I want."

People can smell fake autonomy like week-old fish. They know when purpose is propaganda. They feel when mastery is just more work disguised as development.

Real motivation requires real trust:

- Autonomy means they might choose differently than you would
- Mastery means they might outgrow their role
- Purpose means they might question decisions that don't align

If you're not ready for those consequences, you're not ready to truly motivate.

Creating Motivational Environments

Motivation isn't an event—it's an environment. You can't inject it like a vaccine. You have to create conditions where it grows naturally.

Physical Environment (even for remote teams):

- Spaces for both collaboration and deep work
- Visual progress indicators
- Celebration walls (virtual or physical)
- Choice in workspace setup

Cultural Environment:

- Psychological safety to try and fail
- Clear connection between work and impact
- Regular reflection and adjustment
- Celebration of learning, not just achieving

Systemic Environment:

- Hiring for intrinsic motivation
- Promotion based on mastery and impact
- Compensation that doesn't demotivate
- Policies that trust adults to be adults

The Personal Practice of Motivation

Before you can master motivating others, understand your own drives:

The Motivation Journal: Weekly reflection on:

- When did I feel most energized?
- What killed my motivation?
- Where did I feel autonomous/masterful/purposeful?

The Energy Audit: Track what gives energy vs. drains it. Redesign your role to maximize the former.

The Purpose Check: Monthly reminder of why you do what you do. Lost touch with purpose? Time to reconnect or redirect.

Chapter Summary

Motivation Mastery isn't about finding better carrots or bigger sticks. It's about understanding that humans are intrinsically motivated beings who shut down when controlled and light up when empowered. When we fuel the fires of autonomy, mastery, and purpose—in ways that honor individual differences—we don't just get better performance. We get innovation, loyalty, and the kind of engagement that transforms organizations. Stop trying to motivate people. Start creating environments where motivation is inevitable.

Reflection

- What truly motivates you? Not what should motivate you—what actually does?
- Think of a time you felt deeply unmotivated. What was missing—autonomy, mastery, or purpose?
- How does your current environment support or suppress intrinsic motivation?
- Where are you trying to motivate others in ways that would demotivate you?

Action

This week, practice the "Motivation Triple":

1. Give someone more autonomy in one area—let them choose the how, when, or where
2. Create a visible way to track progress toward mastery (for yourself or others)
3. Connect one mundane task to its larger purpose—make the impact visible

Notice how these shifts change energy and engagement.

PRINCIPLE: FUEL THE FIRE

What's Next?

Understanding what motivates people is powerful, but it's only half the equation. In our next chapter, The Empowerment Equation, we'll explore how to lead through questions instead of commands, build ownership instead of compliance, and create cultures where innovation isn't just allowed—it's inevitable. Because the future belongs to leaders who don't just motivate their teams—they unleash them.

Chapter 10: The Empowerment Equation

PRINCIPLE: LEAD THROUGH QUESTIONS

The most powerful question I ever asked cost me nothing and changed everything. I was leading a struggling product team, and my instinct was to swoop in with solutions. The app was buggy, deadlines were missed, morale was tanking. Every fiber of my management training screamed: "Take control! Make decisions! Show leadership!"

Instead, I walked into our Monday standup and asked: "If you could redesign how we work together, what would you change?"

Silence. Then Sarah, our junior developer, raised her hand tentatively. "Could we maybe... not have our deepest technical discussions in Slack threads that go on for hours? I get lost and feel stupid asking questions."

Marcus nodded. "And maybe we could pair program more? I feel like I'm always stuck alone with problems that someone else could solve in five minutes."

Lin jumped in: "What if we had protected focus time? I never get deep work done because of all the meetings."

Twenty minutes later, they'd redesigned their entire workflow. Not my workflow imposed on them—their workflow, created by them, owned by them. Six months later, that team had the highest satisfaction scores and fastest delivery times in the company.

I'd learned the hardest lesson in leadership: the best solutions come from the people closest to the problems, not from the person furthest from them.

Leading Through Questions, Not Commands

We live in the age of the know-it-all leader. The CEO who has an opinion on everything. The manager who swoops in with instant solutions. The team lead who thinks leadership means having all the answers. But here's what I've discovered: in our complex, fast-changing world, the leaders with all the answers are usually asking the wrong questions.

The traditional command-and-control model assumes:

- Leaders have the best information
- Faster decisions are always better decisions
- People need to be told what to do
- Compliance equals engagement

All of these assumptions are not just wrong—they're dangerous.

In our interconnected, information-rich world:

- The best information lives at the edges, not the center
- Better decisions beat faster decisions every time
- People need to understand why, not just what
- Ownership beats compliance every single time

The Question Leader's Toolkit:

"What do you think?" - The simplest way to shift from telling to asking. Use it liberally.

"What would success look like to you?" - Helps align on outcomes while preserving autonomy about process.

"What's your instinct telling you?" - Honors their expertise and intuition.

"What would happen if we tried X?" - Invites scenario planning without prescribing solutions.

"What are we not seeing?" - Opens space for dissenting views and blind spots.

"How would you approach this?" - Transfers ownership from you to them.

Watch this in action: When Jennifer's marketing team was struggling with campaign performance, her first instinct was to audit their process and prescribe fixes. Instead, she asked: "If you were running a marketing agency and we were your client, what would you recommend?"

The shift was immediate. Instead of defensive explanations, she got strategic thinking. Instead of waiting for direction, they started experimenting. Instead of "Jennifer's campaigns," they became "our campaigns." Performance improved 40% in three months.

Building Ownership and Initiative

Ownership isn't assigned—it's earned through involvement in creation. When people help build something, they feel responsible for its success. When they're simply told to execute someone else's vision, they feel responsible for following instructions.

The Ownership Ladder:

Level 1: Compliance - "Do this because I said so"

Level 2: Understanding - "Do this and here's why"

Level 3: Input - "Here's what I'm thinking—what do you think?"

Level 4: Collaboration - "Let's figure this out together"

Level 5: Ownership - "This is your area—what's your recommendation?"

Most managers never get past Level 2. They explain their decisions thoroughly, pat themselves on the back for "transparency," and wonder why their team lacks initiative.

The magic happens at Levels 4 and 5.

David, a sales director, discovered this when his team's close rates plateaued. Traditional approach: analyze the data, identify the problems, prescribe solutions, monitor compliance.

David's approach: "Our close rates have flatlined at 23%. Industry benchmark is 35%. As the people actually talking to customers, what do you think is happening?"

What emerged was gold:

- Prospects were getting confused by the pricing structure
- The demo flow didn't match real customer workflows
- Competitors were offering faster implementation
- The sales materials felt too corporate for their startup clients

Instead of David's solutions, they implemented the team's solutions. Close rates hit 38% within two quarters. Why? Because the people closest to the problem owned the solution.

Creating Cultures of Innovation

Innovation doesn't happen because someone decided "let's be innovative." It happens when people feel safe to experiment, fail, learn, and try again. Most organizations kill innovation with two phrases: "That's not how we do things here" and "What if it doesn't work?"

The Innovation Environment has four pillars:

Psychological Safety - People can voice ideas without fear of ridicule or punishment.

Resource Slack - Time, money, and energy for experimentation beyond immediate deadlines.

Learning Orientation - Failure is data, not grounds for termination.

Decision Authority - People can act on ideas without seventeen layers of approval.

Maya, a customer service manager, wanted to create an innovation culture but had zero budget for formal innovation programs. Her solution was brilliant in its simplicity:

"Experiment Fridays" - Last Friday of each month, anyone could spend two hours trying something new to improve customer experience.

"Failure Parties" - Monthly celebrations of experiments that didn't work. Pizza, stories, and lessons learned.

"Try-It Tuesday" - Any team member could propose a week-long experiment. If two people supported it, they could try it.

"Customer Spotlight" - Weekly stories of customers who benefited from team innovations.

Result? Her team generated 47 process improvements in the first year. Customer satisfaction increased 28%. Employee engagement scores were the highest in the company. All because she created space for people to think, try, and improve.

The Art of Empowering Questions

Not all questions empower. Some diminish, some confuse, some manipulate. Empowering questions have specific characteristics:

Open-ended, not leading: "What's your recommendation?" not "Don't you think we should do X?"

Future-focused, not blame-focused: "What can we do differently next time?" not "Why did this fail?"

Capability-assuming, not competence-questioning: "How would you solve this?" not "Do you even understand the problem?"

Growth-oriented, not gotcha-oriented: "What would help you succeed?" not "What's your excuse this time?"

Collaborative, not competitive: "How can we make this work?" not "Whose fault is this?"

Lisa, a project manager, transformed her team dynamics by changing one weekly question. Instead of "What roadblocks are you facing?" (which invited complaints), she asked "What would help you accelerate?" The shift from problems to possibilities changed everything. People started coming to meetings with solutions, not just status updates.

Digital Age Empowerment Tools

Technology can either centralize control or distribute it. Choose wisely:

Decision-Making Tools: Loom for async decision sharing, Miro for collaborative planning, Slack polls for quick consensus-building.

Autonomy Platforms: Calendly for self-scheduling, Notion for self-organizing workflows, GitHub for distributed code review.

Learning Systems: Internal wikis for knowledge sharing, Coursera for skill development, mentorship matching platforms.

Recognition Networks: Peer-to-peer recognition tools, internal social networks, project showcase platforms.

Feedback Loops: Regular pulse surveys, anonymous suggestion boxes, customer feedback dashboards visible to all teams.

The key is choosing tools that push authority down, not pull information up.

Common Empowerment Mistakes

The Abandonment Trap: Saying "figure it out" without providing context, resources, or guardrails. Empowerment isn't abandonment.

The False Choice: Offering options that all lead to your preferred outcome. "Would you like to implement solution A on Monday or Tuesday?" isn't empowerment.

The Micromanagement Yo-Yo: Empowering people, then swooping in at the first sign of struggle. Trust takes time to build and seconds to destroy.

The Perfectionism Prison: Expecting empowered teams to never make mistakes. If they're not failing occasionally, they're not taking enough risks.

The Credit Theft: Taking credit for successes that came from empowered teams. Nothing kills initiative faster than invisible contribution.

Building Your Empowerment Practice

The Question Journal: Track the ratio of questions to statements in your conversations. Aim for 60% questions.

The Assumption Audit: Before every meeting, list what you assume needs to happen. Then ask questions to test those assumptions.

The Solution Delay: When someone brings you a problem, resist the urge to solve it immediately. Ask three questions first.

The Decision Handoff: Identify three decisions you make regularly that could be made by others. Hand them off with clear success criteria.

The Innovation Investment: Dedicate 10% of your team's time to their own improvement ideas. Yes, 10% feels like a lot. Yes, it's worth it.

The Long Game of Empowerment

Empowerment is an investment that pays compound interest. Initially, it's slower. You could make the decision faster than facilitating the team to make it. You could solve the problem quicker than coaching them to solve it. You could implement the solution more efficiently than waiting for them to figure it out.

But month by month, quarter by quarter, the returns compound:

- Decisions get better because they're informed by diverse perspectives
- Implementation gets faster because people understand and own the solution
- Problems get solved before they reach you because people have authority to act
- Innovation accelerates because people feel safe to experiment
- Talent retention improves because people feel valued and developed

Most importantly, you scale yourself. Instead of being the bottleneck for every decision, you become the multiplier for every person.

When Empowerment Goes Wrong

Sometimes, empowered teams make bad decisions. Sometimes, distributed authority leads to chaos. Sometimes, people abuse the trust you've given them. This doesn't mean empowerment failed, it means your implementation needs refinement.

Clear Boundaries: Empowerment without guardrails is anarchy. Be explicit about what people can and cannot decide.

Progressive Empowerment: Start with small decisions and expand authority as competence and trust build.

Feedback Loops: Regular check-ins ensure empowerment isn't becoming isolation.

Skill Development: Authority without capability is unfair to everyone. Provide the training and support needed for success.

Cultural Alignment: Ensure empowered decisions align with organizational values and goals.

Chapter Summary

The Empowerment Equation isn't about giving up control—it's about multiplying your impact through others. When we lead through questions instead of commands, build ownership instead of compliance, and create cultures where innovation flourishes, we don't just get better results—we develop better people. In our complex, fast-changing world, the leaders who try to have all the answers will be overwhelmed. The leaders who help others find answers will be unstoppable. Master this, and you transform from manager to multiplier, from decision-maker to capability-builder, from leader to leader-creator.

Reflection

- Where do you default to giving answers instead of asking questions? What drives that impulse?
- Think of a time someone empowered you to solve a problem. How did it feel different from being told what to do?
- What decisions are you making that could be made by others? What stops you from delegating them?
- How does your current leadership style encourage or discourage initiative in others?

Action

This week, practice the "Empowerment Triple":

1. Replace three "Here's what we should do..." statements with "What do you think we should do?" questions
2. Give someone decision-making authority over something you normally control (with clear success criteria)
3. When someone brings you a problem, ask "What solutions have you considered?" before offering any suggestions

Notice how these shifts change both the quality of solutions and the energy of your team.

PRINCIPLE: LEAD THROUGH QUESTIONS

What's Next?

Empowerment creates the conditions for growth, but growth requires intentional cultivation. In our next chapter, Growth Catalyst, we'll explore how to make challenges feel conquerable, coach for continuous improvement, and build resilient teams that don't just survive change—they thrive because of it. Because empowered people without growth opportunities become frustrated people. And frustrated people don't stick around.

Chapter 11: Growth Catalyst

PRINCIPLE: MAKE THE IMPOSSIBLE FEEL INEVITABLE

I once watched a manager destroy someone's confidence with a single sentence. Jake, a promising analyst, had just presented a complex financial model to the leadership team. It wasn't perfect—there were gaps in the data, some assumptions needed refinement—but it was solid work that moved the project forward.

After the presentation, his manager said: "Good effort, Jake, but you're just not quite ready for this level of analysis yet."

I watched Jake's shoulders slump. The light in his eyes dimmed. Six months later, he transferred to another department. Two years later, he left the company entirely. That manager had meant to be helpful, to manage expectations, to be "realistic." Instead, he'd planted a seed of limitation that grew into a forest of self-doubt.

Contrast this with Sarah, who inherited Jake's replacement, Maya. Maya's first major presentation was equally imperfect. Sarah's response: "Maya, you've tackled something really complex here, and I can see the solid thinking behind it. The core framework is strong. Now, what if we could make this airtight? What additional data would help? Which assumptions should we stress-test? Let's turn this from good to bulletproof."

Maya's face lit up. She saw challenges, not limitations. Opportunities, not obstacles. That project became the foundation for a promotion, and Maya is now one of the company's top strategists.

The difference? One manager saw potential. The other saw deficits. One made growth feel possible. The other made it feel out of reach.

Making Challenges Feel Conquerable

The human brain is wired to avoid difficulty. When we perceive something as too hard, we don't just struggle with it—we avoid it entirely. This is why traditional "stretch goals" often backfire. Instead of inspiring people to reach higher, they trigger the brain's threat detection system, leading to paralysis, not performance.

But here's what neuroscience teaches us: we can rewire how people perceive challenges. The key is making the impossible feel inevitable through progressive revelation and systematic confidence-building.

The Confidence Staircase Method:

Step 1: Connect to Previous Success "Remember when you figured out that customer segmentation problem? This uses the same analytical thinking, just applied to a different dataset."

Step 2: Break Down the Mountain Instead of "Increase sales by 50%," try "Let's find 10% more prospects, convert 10% more of them, and get 10% more revenue per customer. Three focused improvements that compound."

Step 3: Make the First Step Ridiculously Easy "For this week, just gather the baseline data. Don't analyze it, don't draw conclusions, just collect it. Can you do that?"

Step 4: Celebrate Early Wins "Look at this data quality—this is exactly what we need for the analysis. You're already succeeding."

Step 5: Expand the Challenge Incrementally "Now that we have clean data, what patterns do you notice? Don't worry about being right—just share what you see."

Watch this in action: When Lisa's team was tasked with implementing a new CRM system—something none of them had done before—she could have said "This will be challenging, but I believe in you." Instead, she said:

"You know how you revamped our filing system last year? You identified what people needed, found the gaps, and created something that actually worked? This is the same process, just digital. We're going to start by spending one week just watching how we currently manage customer information. Not changing anything, not judging anything, just observing. Think you can handle being a detective for a week?"

By the end of that week, the team was excited to fix what they'd observed. The "impossible" CRM implementation became an obvious next step.

Coaching for Continuous Improvement

Traditional performance management happens in annual reviews—too late to matter and too infrequent to create change. Growth happens in the moments between moments, in the micro-conversations that compound over time.

The Daily Growth Practice:

Morning Questions:
- "What's one thing you want to get better at today?"
- "What would success look like for you today?"
- "What support do you need to make that happen?"

Evening Reflections:
- "What went well today? Why do you think that happened?"
- "What would you do differently? What did you learn?"
- "What's one small improvement you could make tomorrow?"

This isn't micromanagement—it's micro-development. Five minutes of intentional growth conversation daily beats three hours of annual performance review every time.

Marcus, a engineering manager, discovered this when his team's velocity plateaued. Instead of quarterly retrospectives, he introduced "Daily Tiny Improvements"—a two-minute standup addition where each person shared one thing they'd learned or improved since yesterday.

The results were startling:

- Code quality improved steadily instead of in dramatic bursts
- Knowledge sharing became natural, not forced
- People started seeking out learning opportunities
- Team velocity increased 35% over six months

Why? Because growth became a daily habit, not an annual event.

Building Resilient Teams

Resilience isn't about being tough enough to weather storms—it's about building systems and mindsets that help teams bounce back faster and stronger from inevitable setbacks.

The Four Pillars of Team Resilience:

Pillar 1: Psychological Safety People need to know they can fail without being fired, ask questions without being judged, and voice concerns without being labeled as "negative."

Pillar 2: Adaptive Capacity Teams need both deep expertise and broad flexibility—specialists who can learn new domains when needed.

Pillar 3: Sense-Making Ability When chaos hits, resilient teams can quickly understand what's happening and why, rather than just reacting emotionally.

Pillar 4: Recovery Rituals Structured ways to process setbacks, extract learning, and rebuild momentum.

Amy's customer service team exemplified this during a major system outage that left them unable to access customer accounts for three days. Instead of panic and blame, here's what happened:

Day 1: Team gathered virtually within two hours. Instead of "Who screwed up?" the question was "What do our customers need right now, and how can we deliver it without the system?"

Day 2: They created manual workarounds, proactive communication scripts, and a customer update system using basic tools.

Day 3: System restored, but they kept several of their manual innovations because they worked better than the original process.

Week 2: Full retrospective not on what went wrong, but on what they'd learned about their own capabilities and how to prepare for future disruptions.

The team didn't just survive the crisis, they grew stronger because of it. Customer satisfaction actually increased during the outage because of the personal attention customers received.

The Growth Mindset in Practice

Carol Dweck's research on growth mindset has been revolutionary, but it's often misapplied. Simply telling people "you can grow" isn't enough. You have to create systematic experiences that prove growth is possible.

Fixed Mindset Triggers:

- "You're so smart" (implies intelligence is static)
- "That's just how you are" (suggests personality is permanent)
- "Some people are naturally good at this" (creates learned helplessness)
- "This should be easy for you" (makes struggle feel like failure)

Growth Mindset Builders:

- "I can see how hard you worked on this" (celebrates effort over ability)
- "What strategies did you use?" (focuses on process over talent)
- "This is challenging, which means you're learning" (reframes difficulty as growth)
- "What would you try differently next time?" (assumes improvement is possible)

David, a sales director, transformed his team's relationship with rejection by changing one phrase. Instead of "Don't take it personally" (which implies rejection reflects on you), he started saying "That's one step closer to yes" (which reframes rejection as progress toward success).

The shift was profound. Sales calls went from scary tests of worth to learning opportunities. People started taking bigger risks because "failure" became "data." Monthly sales increased 28%, but more importantly, team confidence skyrocketed.

Digital Tools for Growth and Development

Technology can accelerate growth when used intentionally:

Micro-Learning Platforms: Duolingo for languages, LinkedIn Learning for skills, internal wiki for institutional knowledge. Growth happens in 15-minute chunks, not 8-hour workshops.

Progress Tracking Apps: Habitica for habit formation, Strava for fitness goals, custom dashboards for skill development. Visible progress motivates continued effort.

Peer Learning Networks: Slack channels for skill sharing, internal mentorship platforms, cross-functional project teams. People learn faster from peers than from formal training.

Reflection Tools: Journey for daily reflections, Notion for learning logs, simple spreadsheets for tracking what works. Growth requires intentional processing of experience.

Feedback Platforms: 15Five for regular check-ins, anonymous suggestion tools, customer feedback loops. Real-time feedback beats delayed feedback every time.

The key is creating systems that make growth visible, social, and rewarding.

Creating Learning from Failure

Most organizations say they embrace failure but punish it in practice. True growth cultures don't just tolerate failure—they mine it for gold.

The Failure Forensics Process:

Step 1: Rapid Response Address immediate consequences without blame. Fix the problem, support the people affected, stabilize the situation.

Step 2: Timeline Construction Create a factual timeline of what happened when. No interpretations, no blame, just facts.

Step 3: System Analysis Look for systemic issues that contributed to the failure. What processes, policies, or structures made this mistake more likely?

Step 4: Learning Extraction What specific lessons can be applied to prevent similar failures? What new capabilities do we need to develop?

Step 5: Knowledge Distribution Share learnings broadly so the entire organization benefits from the failure.

Step 6: Process Improvement Update systems, training, and procedures based on what you learned.

When Rachel's product team accidentally released a feature that crashed the mobile app for 12 hours, they could have fired someone, tightened control, and moved on. Instead, they used their Failure Forensics Process:

Rapid Response: Rolled back the feature, communicated with affected users, restored service.

Timeline: Documented exactly when each decision was made and by whom.

System Analysis: Discovered that testing protocols hadn't kept up with development speed, and junior developers felt pressure to ship without asking questions.

Learning Extraction: Need for automated testing, clearer escalation procedures, psychological safety for voicing concerns.

Knowledge Distribution: Company-wide engineering meeting to share lessons, updated onboarding for new developers.

Process Improvement: New CI/CD pipeline, mentor assignment for junior developers, regular "concerns and questions" sessions.

Result? Similar failures dropped 89% across all teams. The failure became the foundation for a more robust development culture.

Stretch Projects vs. Snap Projects

Not all challenging assignments build capability. Some destroy confidence. The difference lies in calibration.

Snap Projects (break people):

- No clear success criteria
- Insufficient resources or support
- Timeline pressure that prevents learning
- Stakes so high that failure isn't acceptable
- Skills gap too large to bridge

Stretch Projects (grow people):

- Clear definition of success
- Adequate resources and support
- Timeline that allows for learning cycles
- Failure is learning, not career death
- Skills gap is bridgeable with effort

The sweet spot is projects that require people to grow by 10-20%, not 100-200%.

Lisa wanted to develop her marketing coordinator's strategic thinking skills. Instead of throwing him into campaign strategy for their biggest client (snap project), she asked him to develop the social media strategy for their smallest client (stretch project). Clear scope, manageable stakes, direct mentorship available, and skills that built on his existing capabilities.

Six months later, he was ready for bigger strategic challenges because he'd built confidence and capability incrementally.

The Compound Effect of Growth Investment

Investing in people's growth doesn't just improve their current performance—it transforms their future potential. But most managers focus on immediate returns rather than compound growth.

Immediate Returns: Better performance in current role, higher engagement, reduced turnover.

Compound Returns: Increased capacity for future challenges, enhanced problem-solving ability, improved resilience, multiplier effect as they develop others.

The math is compelling: A 1% improvement in capability compounded over time creates exponential differences in impact. The manager who invests 30 minutes weekly in each team member's growth will, over two years, have a fundamentally different team than the manager who focuses only on immediate deliverables.

Maya discovered this when she started "Growth Fridays"—every Friday afternoon, each team member spent two hours on skill development of their choice, with results shared monthly. Initial productivity dropped 10% (30 minutes per week out of 40 hours). But within six months, overall team productivity was 25% higher because people were working smarter, not just harder.

Building Your Growth Catalyst Practice

Weekly Growth Conversations: 15 minutes per person focused entirely on their development. What's challenging them? What do they want to improve? How can you help?

Challenge Calibration: Before assigning stretch projects, ask: "What would make this feel challenging but achievable?" Adjust accordingly.

Learning Documentation: Keep notes on what each person is learning and how. Look for patterns and accelerants.

Failure Celebration: Monthly "Beautiful Failures" sessions where people share what they tried, what didn't work, and what they learned.

Progress Visualization: Create dashboards or simple tracking systems that make growth visible to the individual and the team.

Chapter Summary

Being a Growth Catalyst isn't about pushing people harder—it's about making growth irresistible. When we make challenges feel conquerable, create systems for continuous improvement, and build resilience into our teams, we don't just develop better performers—we develop better humans. In our rapidly changing world, the ability to grow and adapt isn't just nice to have—it's essential for survival. Master this, and you become the leader people seek out not just for opportunity, but for transformation. Because at the end of the day, people don't just want to succeed—they want to become.

Reflection

- Think of a time someone helped you tackle something that felt impossible. What specifically did they do that made it feel achievable?
- Where do you currently assign challenges that might be "snap projects" rather than true stretch opportunities?
- How do you personally process and learn from failures? How could you model this better for your team?
- What growth opportunities are you not pursuing because they feel too difficult? How could you apply the Confidence Staircase Method?

Action

This week, practice the "Growth Catalyst Triple":

1. Take one challenge facing your team and break it down using the Confidence Staircase Method
2. Have one growth-focused conversation with each team member—ask what they want to develop and how you can help
3. Share one of your own recent failures or learning experiences and what it taught you

Notice how focusing on growth changes both performance and engagement.

PRINCIPLE: MAKE THE IMPOSSIBLE FEEL INEVITABLE

What's Next?

Growth is powerful, but without purpose, it becomes empty self-improvement. In our next chapter, Purpose-Driven Leadership, we'll explore how to connect work to meaning, inspire through values alignment, and create movements that transcend individual achievement. Because when people understand not just how to grow, but why their growth matters, they don't just perform—they transform the world around them.

Chapter 12: Purpose-Driven Leadership

In 1962, President Kennedy visited NASA and encountered a janitor mopping the floor. When asked what he was doing, the janitor didn't say "I'm cleaning the building" or "I'm mopping floors." He said, "I'm helping put a man on the moon."

That janitor understood something that most organizations have forgotten: every job, no matter how small, contributes to something larger. The question isn't whether your work has purpose—it's whether you can see it, feel it, and share it with others.

I learned this lesson the hard way when I was leading a data entry team. Twenty people, eight hours a day, entering insurance claims into a system. Turnover was 80% annually. People called in sick constantly. The work felt meaningless because, honestly, I thought it was meaningless too.

Then I met Patricia, a claims processor whose house had burned down the year before. She told me how the insurance payout had saved her family, how the quick processing had meant the difference between rebuilding and bankruptcy, how someone in our company had treated her claim with urgency and care.

I realized we weren't just entering data. We were helping families rebuild their lives after disasters. We were the bridge between tragedy and recovery. We were hope made digital.

I started bringing customer stories to our team meetings. I showed them photos of rebuilt homes, letters of gratitude, families back on their feet. Suddenly, accuracy wasn't just about avoiding errors—it was about getting families the help they needed faster. Speed wasn't just about meeting quotas—it was about reducing the time between disaster and relief.

Turnover dropped to 15%. Sick days decreased 40%. Quality scores hit all-time highs. Same work, same people, completely different meaning.

Connecting Work to Meaning

Purpose isn't about finding the perfect job or working for a cause you're passionate about. Purpose is about understanding how your daily actions contribute to outcomes that matter to real people. It's about connecting the micro (what you do) to the macro (why it matters).

Every job has three levels of meaning:
Level 1: Task Purpose - What am I doing?

Level 2: Role Purpose - Why does my role exist?

Level 3: Impact Purpose - How does this help real people?

Most people never get past Level 1. They know their tasks but not their impact. Purpose-driven leaders help people climb to Level 3.

Watch this transformation: Marcus managed a software testing team. His people saw themselves as "bug finders"—not exactly inspiring. Marcus reframed it:
Level 1: "We test software applications"

Level 2: "We ensure product quality and user experience"

Level 3: "We protect customers from frustration, data loss, and security breaches. We're the guardians of trust."

He started showing them user feedback about bugs they'd caught: "Thank you for fixing this—it would have crashed during my daughter's video call with grandma." "Your team saved my presentation—I didn't even know there was a problem."

The team started calling themselves "Customer Guardians." They became more thorough, more creative, more proud of their work. Bug detection rates improved 45% because people understood they weren't just finding errors—they were protecting users.

Inspiring Through Values Alignment

Values aren't wall decorations. They're decision-making frameworks. When people's personal values align with organizational values—and they see those values lived out, not just posted—purpose becomes personal.

But here's what most leaders miss: values alignment isn't about finding people who already share your values. It's about helping people discover how their values can be expressed through your mission.

The Values Bridge Process:
Step 1: Discover Personal Values What matters most to you in life? What principles guide your decisions? When are you most proud of your actions?

Step 2: Identify Organizational Values Not the ones on the poster—the ones actually practiced. What behaviors get rewarded? What decisions reflect true priorities?

Step 3: Find the Connection Points Where do personal and organizational values intersect? How can the work express what matters to the person?

Step 4: Create Value Expression Opportunities Design roles, projects, and recognition systems that let people live their values through their work.

Sarah discovered this leading a sales team where people felt conflicted about "pushing products on customers." Through values conversations, she learned:

- Jennifer valued helping others and hated feeling manipulative
- Marcus valued honesty and struggled with "selling"
- Lisa valued problem-solving and felt like an order-taker

Sarah reframed sales through their values:

- Jennifer became a "customer success advocate" who helped clients find solutions
- Marcus became a "trusted advisor" who gave honest recommendations
- Lisa became a "problem diagnostic specialist" who solved business challenges

Same job, same company, but now their personal values were the driving force behind their professional success. Sales increased 32%, but more importantly, job satisfaction skyrocketed.

Creating Movements, Not Just Teams

Teams accomplish tasks. Movements change worlds. The difference is purpose that transcends individual benefit and creates collective identity around shared meaning.

Characteristics of Purpose-Driven Movements:
Bigger Than the Organization: The mission matters beyond profit or growth. It's about contribution to something larger.

Personal Investment: People don't just work for the mission—they own it, shape it, advocate for it.

Shared Language: Common vocabulary, stories, and symbols that create identity and belonging.

Ripple Effect: The purpose extends beyond immediate team members to customers, partners, and communities.

Sustainable Passion: Not dependent on charismatic leadership or external motivation—the purpose itself fuels continued commitment.

David saw this in action when his customer service team evolved into what they called "The Customer Happiness Movement." It started with a simple question: "What if we measured success not by call resolution time, but by customer delight?"

They created their own metrics: "Surprise and Delight" scores, "Problem Prevention" tracking, "Life Made Better" stories. They started proactively reaching out to customers with tips and resources. They created user guides that were actually helpful and enjoyable to read.

Other departments started asking to join. Engineering wanted to build features that created customer happiness. Marketing wanted to tell happiness stories. Sales wanted to sell happiness, not just products.

Within a year, customer retention was up 43%, referrals had doubled, and the company's Net Promoter Score was industry-leading. But the real transformation was internal: people couldn't wait to come to work because they were part of something meaningful.

The Language of Purpose

Purpose isn't communicated through mission statements and PowerPoints. It's communicated through stories, rituals, symbols, and daily language that makes meaning tangible.

Purpose Stories have three elements:

1. **Challenge:** What problem were we trying to solve?
2. **Action:** What specific actions did we take?
3. **Impact:** How did it change someone's life?

Instead of "We increased efficiency by 20%," try: "Maria was spending three hours every morning pulling reports for her team. Now she gets them automatically and uses that time to coach her people. Her team's performance has improved, and she goes home less stressed."

Purpose Rituals embed meaning into routine:

- Starting meetings with customer impact stories
- Celebrating solutions that help people, not just hit metrics
- Recognition that connects individual contribution to larger purpose
- Regular "Why We Do This" conversations

Purpose Language shifts focus from internal to external:

- Not "We need to hit our numbers" but "Our customers are counting on us"
- Not "This is company policy" but "This is how we protect people"
- Not "Let's be more efficient" but "Let's help people faster"

Lisa transformed her accounting team's relationship with their work through language alone. Instead of "processing invoices," they were "enabling business partnerships." Instead of "accounts receivable," they were "helping cash flow so our clients can grow." Instead of "expense reports," they were "supporting people who serve customers."

Same spreadsheets, same calculations, completely different sense of purpose.

Digital Age Purpose Communication

In our distributed, digital-first world, purpose communication faces new challenges:

Challenge 1: Attention Fragmentation People consume information in micro-bursts across multiple platforms. Purpose messages must be designed for mobile consumption and social sharing.

Challenge 2: Authenticity Detection Digital natives can spot corporate BS instantly. Purpose communication must be genuine, specific, and backed by real action.

Challenge 3: Personalization at Scale Different people connect to purpose differently. Digital tools allow for personalized purpose experiences.

Digital Purpose Strategies:

Micro-Stories: 60-second videos of real customers sharing real impact. Post them everywhere—Slack, email signatures, lobby screens.

Impact Dashboards: Real-time displays showing how today's work is helping real people. Not just revenue metrics, but human impact metrics.

Virtual Reality Experiences: Let people see the impact of their work firsthand. Customer visits, facility tours, before-and-after walkthroughs.

User-Generated Content: Encourage team members to share their own purpose stories. People trust peer communication more than corporate communication.

Interactive Purpose Mapping: Digital tools that help individuals connect their specific role to organizational impact.

When Purpose Goes Wrong

Purpose can be powerful, but it can also be manipulative, overwhelming, or hollow. Avoid these common mistakes:

Purpose Washing: Claiming noble purpose while making decisions that contradict it. People can smell hypocrisy from space.

Purpose Overwhelming: Making every task feel life-or-death important. Purpose should energize, not exhaust.

Purpose Mandating: Forcing people to find their work meaningful instead of helping them discover meaning that already exists.

Purpose Replacing: Using purpose as a substitute for fair compensation, good management, or healthy culture. Purpose doesn't pay rent.

Purpose Monopolizing: Insisting everyone find the same meaning in the work. Different people connect to purpose differently.

Maria learned this when her "Purpose Initiative" backfired. She mandated that every team meeting start with purpose statements, required people to write purpose essays, and constantly asked "How does this connect to our mission?"

Instead of inspiration, she created eye-rolls and cynicism. People felt manipulated, not motivated. The initiative died within three months.

Her successful second attempt was different: she simply started sharing customer impact stories naturally in conversations, celebrated team members who went above and beyond for customers, and asked "What made you proud of your work this week?" during one-on-ones.

Purpose emerged organically because people felt it, not because they were told to feel it.

Building Your Purpose-Driven Practice

Daily Purpose Connection: Start each day by connecting your work to its impact. How will today's tasks help real people?

Weekly Impact Inventory: Track stories, feedback, and evidence of how your team's work made a difference. Share these stories regularly.

Monthly Purpose Conversations: Ask team members: "When did your work feel most meaningful this month? What made it feel that way?"

Quarterly Values Alignment: Review decisions and priorities against stated values. Where are you aligned? Where are you drifting?

Annual Purpose Evolution: Purpose isn't static. How has your understanding of impact deepened? How has the mission evolved?

The Measurement Challenge

How do you measure purpose? Traditional metrics don't capture meaning, and meaning without measurement can become mere sentiment.

Purpose Indicators:

- Employee engagement scores specifically related to meaning and impact
- Voluntary turnover rates (people who find purpose stay longer)
- Quality of discretionary effort (do people go above and beyond?)
- Internal referral rates (do people recommend working here?)
- Customer feedback about team passion and care
- Innovation rates (purpose-driven people create more solutions)

Purpose Stories:

- Collect and categorize stories of impact
- Track how often these stories are shared and referenced
- Measure the emotional response to purpose communications
- Document how purpose influences decision-making

The key is measuring both the quantitative impact (performance) and qualitative experience (meaning) of purpose-driven work.

Chapter Summary

Purpose-Driven Leadership isn't about finding meaning in meaningless work—it's about revealing the meaning that already exists. When we connect daily tasks to real human impact, align personal values with organizational mission, and create movements that transcend individual achievement, we tap into the deepest source of human motivation. In our purpose-hungry world, leaders who can help others see why their work matters don't just get better performance—they get better humans. Master this, and you transform from manager to meaning-maker, from boss to belief-builder, from leader to legacy-creator.

Reflection

- What's the real impact of your work beyond the immediate tasks and metrics? Who benefits from what you do?
- How do your personal values align with your current role? Where are the strongest connections?
- Think of a time when your work felt deeply meaningful. What made it feel that way?
- What stories of impact could you be sharing with your team that you're currently keeping to yourself?

Action

This week, practice the "Purpose Connection Triple":

1. Share one specific story of how your team's work helped a real person (with details and human impact)
2. Have one conversation with a team member about what makes their work feel meaningful
3. Connect one routine task to its larger purpose—help someone see beyond the immediate activity

Notice how purpose conversations change energy, engagement, and performance.

PRINCIPLE: CONNECT WORK TO WHY

What's Next?

Purpose provides the foundation, but in our hyperconnected world, we face new challenges that threaten to undermine even the strongest sense of meaning. In our next chapter, Digital Wellness and Boundaries, we'll explore how to maintain humanity in digital spaces, set healthy communication boundaries, and balance efficiency with empathy.

Because purpose without boundaries leads to burnout, and connection without limits leads to disconnection from what matters most.

Chapter 13: Digital Wellness and Boundaries

PRINCIPLE: PROTECT YOUR HUMANITY

At 11:47 PM on a Tuesday, my phone buzzed with a Slack message from my boss: "Quick question about tomorrow's presentation." I was in bed, finally relaxing after a long day. But I looked. Of course I looked. And once I looked, I had to respond, because leaving a boss hanging felt rude. Which led to a 20-minute exchange about slide formatting and font choices.

The next morning, I was exhausted. Not because I'd stayed up late working on something important, but because I'd allowed the boundary between work and life to dissolve completely. I'd traded my peace of mind for the illusion of being responsive.

Six months later, I was burned out, my family felt neglected, and my actual work performance was suffering. I'd confused being always available with being valuable. I'd mistaken digital connectivity for human connection.

That's when I learned the hardest lesson of modern leadership: in our hyperconnected world, the most radical act is occasionally disconnecting.

Maintaining Humanity in Digital Spaces

We're conducting an unprecedented experiment: trying to maintain human relationships through digital interfaces designed for efficiency, not empathy. The results are predictable—we're becoming more connected and less human simultaneously.

The symptoms are everywhere:

- Zoom fatigue from staring at screens all day
- Email anxiety from constant notification pressure
- Slack stress from never-ending chat streams
- Social media comparison from curated highlight reels
- Decision paralysis from information overload

But here's what I've discovered: digital wellness isn't about rejecting technology. It's about using technology intentionally, in ways that enhance rather than erode our humanity.

The Humanity Test: Before engaging with any digital communication, ask:

- Does this make me feel more or less human?
- Am I connecting with a person or performing for an audience?
- Would this interaction be better face-to-face?
- Am I choosing efficiency over empathy?

Sarah, a customer service manager, applied this test when her team started using chatbots for initial customer interactions. The efficiency gains were impressive—response times dropped 60%. But customer satisfaction scores started declining.

The problem? The bot interactions were stripping away humanity. Customers felt processed, not heard. Sarah's solution: program the bot to offer human handoffs early and often, train agents to acknowledge the customer's digital experience ("I know you just spoke with our bot—let me give you the personal attention you deserve"), and create "humanity moments" where agents could break script to address the person, not just the problem.

Result: Efficiency stayed high, but humanity returned. Customer satisfaction scores not only recovered but reached new heights.

Setting Healthy Communication Boundaries

The biggest lie of the digital age is that being available equals being valuable. We've confused responsiveness with responsibility, presence with productivity. But research shows the opposite: people with healthy boundaries are more creative, more strategic, and ultimately more valuable than those who are always "on."

The Boundary Framework:
Response Time Expectations:

- Immediate (under 1 hour): True emergencies only
- Same day (within 8 hours): Urgent but not emergency
- 24-48 hours: Normal business communication
- Weekly: Strategic planning and development

Channel Hierarchy:

- Phone call: Emergency (someone needs help now)
- Text message: Urgent (today matters)
- Email: Important (this week matters)
- Slack/Teams: Collaborative (when you're available)
- Project tools: Reference (when needed)

Time Boundaries:

- Core hours: Fully available and responsive
- Flex hours: Available but not immediate response
- Off hours: Emergency contact only
- Vacation/weekend: Complete disconnection

Marcus, an engineering director, discovered the power of explicit boundaries when his team was struggling with burnout. Instead of asking people to work less (which felt impossible given deadlines), he asked them to work more intentionally.

His team co-created a "Communication Charter":

9 AM - 5 PM: Full responsiveness expected

5 PM - 8 PM: Personal time, but urgent items OK with context

8 PM - 9 AM: Emergency only (and they defined emergency)

Weekends: No work communication unless server is on fire

Vacation: Complete blackout, no exceptions

The results shocked him: productivity increased 25% because people weren't constantly context-switching between work and life. Creativity improved because people's brains had time to rest and recharge. Most surprisingly, the quality of communication improved because people became more thoughtful about what truly needed immediate attention.

Balancing Efficiency with Empathy

The efficiency trap is real: digital tools can make us faster at the expense of making us colder. We optimize for throughput over connection, speed over understanding, scale over soul.

But empathy isn't the enemy of efficiency—it's the foundation of sustainable efficiency. When people feel heard and valued, they communicate more clearly, collaborate more effectively, and require less back-and-forth clarification.

The Empathy-Efficiency Matrix:

High Empathy, High Efficiency: The sweet spot

- Video calls for complex discussions
- Voice messages for nuanced feedback
- Synchronous collaboration for creative work
- Clear documentation with personal context

High Empathy, Low Efficiency: Relationship-rich but time-poor

- Endless video calls without clear outcomes
- Over-explaining simple decisions
- Too much personal checking in meetings
- Emotional processing in work channels

Low Empathy, High Efficiency: Fast but cold

- Curt emails with no context
- Meetings that skip relationship building
- Feedback without emotional consideration
- Processes that ignore human needs

Low Empathy, Low Efficiency: The worst of both worlds

- Unclear digital communication requiring multiple clarifications
- Avoiding difficult conversations until they explode
- Impersonal tools for personal situations
- No investment in relationship or systems

Lisa's marketing team was stuck in Low Empathy, High Efficiency mode. They communicated through brief emails, had agenda-only meetings, and measured success purely through output metrics. It worked until it didn't—collaboration broke down, people felt isolated, and creative work suffered.

Her solution was the "5-Minute Human Rule": every meeting started with five minutes of personal check-in, every email included one personal note, and every project included a celebration moment when completed.

This 10% investment in empathy created a 30% improvement in overall efficiency because people communicated more clearly, collaborated more willingly, and stayed engaged longer.

Digital Detox Strategies

Complete digital detox isn't realistic for most people, but strategic disconnection is both possible and necessary. Think of it like interval training for your attention span.

Micro-Detoxes (Daily):

- First hour of the day phone-free
- Last hour before bed screen-free
- Lunch break with no digital devices
- Walking meetings without phones
- One meal per day with full presence

Mini-Detoxes (Weekly):

- Saturday morning digital sabbath
- Sunday afternoon offline time
- One evening per week device-free
- One hobby that requires no screens
- Weekly nature time without phones

Major Detoxes (Monthly/Quarterly):

- Full weekend offline retreats
- Vacation time with minimal connectivity
- Digital sabbatical days
- Device-free social gatherings
- Analog vacation days

David, a busy CEO, implemented "Analog Sundays"—no work devices, no social media, no news. Just books, conversations, walks, and rest. He was terrified the business would fall apart without his constant oversight.

Instead, he discovered two things: first, his team was more capable than he'd realized when he wasn't hovering over every decision. Second, his Monday performance was dramatically better after a day of mental rest. He started encouraging his entire leadership team to take their own analog time.

Creating Digital Wellness Cultures

Individual wellness is important, but cultural wellness is transformative. When organizations intentionally design for human wellbeing in digital spaces, everyone benefits.

Digital Wellness Culture Elements:

Response Time Norms: Explicitly stated expectations about when people should respond to different types of communication.

Meeting Hygiene: Default 25/50-minute meetings (buffer time), agenda requirements, cameras optional policies.

Notification Management: Guidelines for when to use @everyone, when to DM vs. channel post, how to mark true urgency.

Asynchronous Respect: Designing workflows that don't require immediate responses, documenting decisions for timezone differences.

Rest and Recovery: Encouraging actual vacation time, modeling digital boundaries at leadership levels, celebrating offline achievements.

Amy implemented "Digital Wellness Wednesdays" at her startup—one day per week with modified communication norms:

- No meetings before 10 AM or after 4 PM
- No Slack messages marked as urgent unless truly emergency
- Encouraged 1-hour lunch breaks away from screens
- Optional video for all calls (audio-only encouraged)
- No emails after 6 PM

The weekly reset day helped everyone recognize how much digital stress they'd normalized. Team members started implementing their own mini-wellness practices throughout the week.

The Attention Economy and Your Wellbeing

Every digital platform is designed to capture and hold your attention. Your attention is literally the product being sold to advertisers. Understanding this isn't paranoia—it's digital literacy.

Attention Hijacking Techniques:

- Infinite scroll designs that eliminate natural stopping points
- Push notifications designed to trigger fear of missing out
- Variable reward schedules that create addiction-like responses
- Social comparison features that trigger status anxiety
- Urgency indicators that make everything feel important

Attention Protection Strategies:

- Turn off non-essential notifications
- Use airplane mode for focused work
- Create physical phone-free zones
- Delete apps that don't add genuine value
- Use website blockers during deep work
- Practice single-tasking instead of multitasking

Marcus discovered his productivity secret when he tracked his attention patterns. He was checking email 47 times per day, switching between apps every 3 minutes, and had 23 browser tabs open on average. No wonder he felt scattered.

His intervention was simple but radical: he checked email only at 9 AM, 1 PM, and 5 PM. He kept only essential apps on his phone. He worked with single browser tabs and single applications open.

The result: his deep work capacity increased 300%. Projects that used to take all day were completed in 2-3 focused hours. His stress levels dropped dramatically because he wasn't constantly reacting to digital demands.

Technology Mindfulness

Mindfulness isn't just for meditation—it's essential for healthy technology use. Most of our digital interactions are unconscious habits that happen below the level of awareness.

Digital Mindfulness Practices:

Intention Setting: Before opening any app or device, pause and ask "What am I hoping to accomplish here?"

Notification Meditation: When you hear a notification, pause for three breaths before responding. This breaks the instant reaction cycle.

Transition Rituals: Create small ceremonies between digital activities—close your laptop fully before dinner, put your phone in a drawer when you arrive home, take three deep breaths before opening email.

Digital Gratitude: End each day by identifying one positive digital interaction that made you feel more connected to someone.

Screen Time Awareness: Use built-in screen time tracking not for judgment, but for awareness of your actual usage patterns.

Lisa started each workday with a two-minute intention-setting practice: "How do I want to show up digitally today? What kind of presence do I want to bring to my online interactions?" This simple pause helped her approach her digital work more consciously rather than reactively.

Building Digital Empathy

In our rush toward efficiency, we often forget that there's a human on the other side of every screen. Digital empathy requires intentional cultivation.

Digital Empathy Practices:

The Human Reminder: Before sending any message, pause and picture the actual person who will receive it. How might they interpret it? What's their current context?

Emotional Labeling: In digital communication, explicitly name emotions when they're relevant. "I'm excited about this" or "I'm feeling overwhelmed by this timeline."

Assume Positive Intent: When someone's digital communication seems harsh or dismissive, imagine three positive explanations before assuming negative intent.

Video When It Matters: For complex, emotional, or sensitive topics, default to video or phone calls instead of text-based communication.

Follow-Up Check-ins: After difficult digital conversations, follow up personally to ensure the relationship is intact.

Chapter Summary

Digital Wellness and Boundaries isn't about becoming a digital hermit—it's about being intentional with technology so it serves your humanity rather than consuming it. When we set healthy boundaries, practice digital mindfulness, and create cultures that prioritize wellbeing over constant connectivity, we don't just protect ourselves from burnout—we model sustainable success for others. In our hyperconnected world, the most radical act isn't being always available—it's being fully present when you choose to connect. Master this, and you transform from a reactive responder to an intentional connector, from a digital slave to a technology master.

Reflection

- What digital habits are serving your wellbeing, and which are draining you?
- Where have you confused being available with being valuable?
- How might your digital communication style be affecting others' wellbeing?
- What boundaries do you need to set to protect your most important relationships and activities?

Action

This week, practice the "Digital Wellness Triple":

1. Implement one clear boundary around response times or offline hours—communicate this boundary to your team
2. Replace one digital interaction with a face-to-face or voice conversation
3. Take one daily micro-detox (30 minutes completely disconnected from devices)

Notice how these changes affect your energy, focus, and relationships.

PRINCIPLE: PROTECT YOUR HUMANITY

What's Next?

Individual wellness is crucial, but in our interconnected world, we're called to something larger: building communities that thrive across digital and physical spaces. In our next chapter, Building Communities, we'll explore how to create belonging in virtual environments, foster genuine engagement across distances, and practice the art of digital hospitality. Because wellness without community is just sophisticated isolation, and the future belongs to those who can build bridges, not just boundaries.

Chapter 14: Building Communities

The loneliest I've ever felt was in a room with 500 people. It was a virtual conference—hundreds of faces in tiny squares, chat messages flying by faster than I could read, breakout rooms filled with awkward silence and people waiting for someone else to speak first. We were all connected, but nobody was connecting.

Then something remarkable happened. The facilitator said, "I want everyone to turn off their cameras for sixty seconds and think about why you're here—not the official reason, but the real reason. What are you hoping will be different in your life after today?"

When cameras came back on, something had shifted. A therapist from Portland shared that she was burning out and needed to remember why she loved her work. A startup founder from Mumbai admitted he felt like he was failing his team and needed new ideas. A teacher from São Paulo said she missed feeling excited about education.

Suddenly, the chat wasn't full of corporate buzzwords and networking pitches. It was full of "me too" and "I felt that" and "let's talk after this session." People started connecting in breakout rooms, sharing contact information, forming genuine relationships that lasted long after the conference ended.

The difference between a crowd and a community isn't technology—it's intention. It's the deliberate creation of space where people can be real, vulnerable, and human with each other.

Creating Belonging in Virtual Spaces

Belonging isn't about being included in a group—it's about feeling valued for who you are within that group. In physical spaces, belonging emerges from shared experiences, casual interactions, and nonverbal cues that say "you matter here." In virtual spaces, belonging must be intentionally designed.

The Four Pillars of Virtual Belonging:

Pillar 1: Psychological Safety People need to know they can speak without being judged, ask questions without being dismissed, and make mistakes without being shamed.

Pillar 2: Shared Identity Communities form around common experiences, values, or goals that create an "us" feeling stronger than individual interests.

Pillar 3: Meaningful Contribution Everyone needs to feel that their presence adds value—that the community is different because they're part of it.

Pillar 4: Connection Rituals Regular practices that bring people together and reinforce community bonds.

Maria discovered this when she took over a remote customer success team that was functioning but not flourishing. People did their jobs competently but didn't collaborate, innovate, or really know each other. Team meetings were efficient and lifeless.

Her intervention was simple but transformative:
Monthly "Origin Stories": Each team member shared the story of how they came to customer success work—not their resume, but their journey.

Weekly "Customer Wins": Celebrating not just metrics, but stories of how they'd made customers' lives better.

Quarterly "Challenge Solutions": Collaborative problem-solving sessions where the team tackled real customer issues together.

Daily "Weather Check": Two-minute team check-ins where people shared their emotional and energy state, not just task updates.

Within six months, the team had transformed. They started collaborating spontaneously, sharing resources without being asked, and covering for each other during busy periods. Customer satisfaction scores improved 34%, but more importantly, team satisfaction skyrocketed.

Fostering Engagement Across Distances

Distance doesn't kill engagement—indifference does. The challenge isn't that people are physically apart; it's that traditional engagement strategies were designed for physical proximity. Virtual engagement requires new approaches.

The Engagement Equation: Frequency × Intimacy × Purpose = Connection

Frequency: How often do people interact? But not just any interaction—meaningful contact that builds relationships.

Intimacy: How deeply do people know each other? Not personal details, but understanding what matters to each person.

Purpose: Why does the community exist beyond its official function? What shared meaning brings people together?

David, a project manager leading a global software development team across five time zones, struggled with engagement until he applied this equation:

Increased Frequency: Instead of weekly all-hands meetings, he created daily async check-ins where people shared one thing they were working on and one thing they needed help with.

Deepened Intimacy: Monthly "Life Outside Work" show-and-tells where people shared hobbies, family moments, or interesting experiences—completely optional but surprisingly popular.

Clarified Purpose: Regular reminders of how their code was helping real users, with specific customer stories and usage data that showed impact.

The transformation was remarkable. Bug reports became collaborative problem-solving sessions. Code reviews became learning opportunities. People started reaching out to help each other proactively. The team's velocity increased 40%, but the real win was that people genuinely enjoyed working together.

The Art of Digital Hospitality

Hospitality is the art of making people feel welcome, comfortable, and valued. In physical spaces, we do this naturally—offering coffee, asking about the drive, making introductions. In digital spaces, hospitality requires intentional design.

Digital Hospitality Principles:

The Welcome Experience: How do new people learn the community's culture, norms, and unwritten rules?

The Onboarding Journey: What support do people need to become contributing members, not just observers?

The Ongoing Care: How do you check in on community members and ensure they continue to feel valued?

The Graceful Exit: How do you honor people's contributions when they leave the community?

Lisa created a masterclass in digital hospitality when launching an internal innovation community at her company. Instead of just creating a Slack channel and hoping people would engage, she designed a hospitality experience:

Week 1 - Personal Welcome: New members got a personal video message from Lisa explaining why she was excited they'd joined and what they might contribute.

Week 2 - Introduction Ritual: New members shared their "innovation superpower" and one project they were curious about.

Week 3 - Pairing Connection: New members were paired with established community members for virtual coffee chats.

Week 4 - First Contribution: New members were invited to share a small innovation they'd implemented, however simple.

Ongoing - Community Care: Monthly check-ins with less active members, celebration of community achievements, and regular "community health" conversations.

The community grew from 12 founding members to 347 active participants over eighteen months. More importantly, it generated 23 successful innovation projects and became the model for other internal communities.

Building Rituals That Bind

Rituals create shared meaning and predictable connection points. They don't have to be elaborate—simple, consistent practices often work better than complex ceremonies.

Types of Community Rituals:

Opening Rituals: How does the community begin interactions? A specific greeting, moment of recognition, or shared intention-setting.

Transition Rituals: How does the community mark important changes? New member welcomes, role changes, project completions.

Celebration Rituals: How does the community acknowledge achievements? Individual recognition, team victories, milestone moments.

Reflection Rituals: How does the community learn and grow? Regular retrospectives, story-sharing, wisdom exchanges.

Closing Rituals: How does the community end interactions? Appreciation rounds, commitment statements, or gratitude expressions.

Marcus built one of the most engaged remote engineering teams I've ever seen through simple but consistent rituals:

Monday Morning "Weekend Wins": Three-minute sharing of something good from the weekend—personal or professional.

Wednesday "Wisdom Wednesdays": One team member shared a technical tip, tool, or learning that helped them.

Friday "Failure Fridays": Celebrating something that didn't work and what they learned from it.

Monthly "Demo Days": Showcasing not just completed work, but interesting problems, creative solutions, or cool experiments.

Quarterly "Team Time Capsules": Recording video messages to themselves about current challenges, goals, and hopes, then watching previous quarters' messages.

These rituals created anticipation, shared language, and inside jokes that bonded the team across continents. People started scheduling vacation around Demo Days because they didn't want to miss them.

Scaling Intimacy

The biggest challenge in community building is maintaining intimacy as you grow. Small communities feel personal; large communities feel institutional. But some communities manage to feel intimate even at scale.

Intimacy Scaling Strategies:

Nested Communities: Large community with smaller sub-groups based on interests, roles, or geography.

Rotating Leadership: Different community members take turns facilitating, hosting, or organizing.

Personal Storytelling: Regular opportunities for individuals to share their experiences and perspectives.

Direct Connection: Systems that help community members find and connect with specific others.

Local Chapters: Geographic or functional groups that meet more frequently or intimately.

Sarah's customer advocacy community grew from 50 beta users to 5,000 active members while maintaining an intimate feel through intentional scaling:

Industry Circles: Smaller groups organized by industry vertical (healthcare, finance, education) with monthly focused discussions.

Mentorship Matching: Experienced users paired with newcomers for quarterly check-ins and ongoing support.

Regional Meetups: Local in-person gatherings in major cities, supported by the larger virtual community.

Customer Advisory Board: Rotating group of 12 members who provided direct input on product development.

Success Story Spotlights: Weekly features of individual customer achievements, shared across the entire community.

The community maintained 73% monthly active engagement even at 5,000 members because people felt known and valued, not just counted.

Digital Community Tools and Platforms

The platform doesn't make the community, but the wrong platform can kill it. Different tools enable different types of interaction and belonging.

Platform Considerations:

Slack/Discord: Great for real-time chat, quick collaboration, and casual interaction. Can become overwhelming with growth.

Circle/Mighty Networks: Designed specifically for community building with features like member directories, event hosting, and content libraries.

Facebook Groups: High adoption rates since people already use Facebook, but limited customization and platform dependency.

LinkedIn Groups: Professional focus, good for industry-specific communities, but limited engagement features.

Custom Platforms: Maximum customization and control, but higher development costs and adoption barriers.

Hybrid Approaches: Combining multiple platforms for different community functions.

The key is choosing platforms that match your community's communication patterns and technical comfort levels, not just the newest or flashiest options.

Managing Community Challenges

Every community faces predictable challenges. Preparing for them prevents them from becoming community-killers.

Common Community Challenges:

The Ghost Town: Low engagement, people join but don't participate. Usually solved by better onboarding and early engagement strategies.

The Echo Chamber: Only a few people participate while others lurk. Requires intentional inclusion of quieter voices.

The Drama Zone: Conflicts, personality clashes, or toxic behavior. Needs clear community guidelines and consistent enforcement.

The Content Chaos: Too much information, poor organization, or off-topic discussions. Requires structure and moderation.

The Burnout Leader: Community dependent on one person who gets overwhelmed. Needs distributed leadership and sustainability planning.

David's developer community faced the classic "90-9-1 rule"—90% lurkers, 9% occasional contributors, 1% active creators. His solution was systematic:

Lurker Activation: Monthly "Ask Me Anything" sessions where lurkers could ask questions anonymously.

Contribution Ladders: Easy ways for people to contribute without major time investment—sharing links, answering simple questions, giving feedback.

Recognition Systems: Highlighting helpful community members, not just the most vocal ones.

Content Curation: Weekly digests of the best community discussions for people who couldn't keep up with daily activity.

Personal Invitations: Direct, personal invitations for specific people to contribute their expertise on relevant topics.

Within a year, active participation increased from 1% to 23% of community members.

Measuring Community Health

Communities aren't just about numbers—they're about relationships. But measuring relationship quality requires different metrics than measuring engagement quantity.

Community Health Metrics:
Quantitative Measures:

- Active participation rates
- Retention and return rates
- Cross-connections (how many members interact with each other)
- Content quality scores
- Response times to questions or requests

Qualitative Measures:

- Member satisfaction surveys
- Exit interviews with departing members
- Story collection about community impact
- Observation of interaction quality
- Assessment of community culture alignment

Leading Indicators:

- New member onboarding completion rates
- Question-to-answer ratios
- Spontaneous appreciation expressions
- Cross-community collaboration instances
- Member-initiated content creation

The healthiest communities track both numbers and stories, measuring not just how much activity they generate but how much value they create for members' lives and work.

Chapter Summary

Building Communities isn't about creating more digital spaces—it's about creating spaces where people genuinely belong, contribute, and thrive together. When we intentionally design for belonging, foster engagement through purpose and intimacy, practice digital hospitality, and create rituals that bind people together, we transform collections of individuals into communities of connection. In our increasingly isolated world, the ability to build genuine community across digital spaces isn't just valuable—it's vital. Master this, and you become more than a community builder—you become a belonging creator, a connection catalyst, a force for human flourishing in digital spaces.

Reflection

- What communities do you belong to that make you feel truly valued? What specific practices create that sense of belonging?
- Where in your professional life could stronger community improve collaboration, innovation, or satisfaction?
- How might you apply digital hospitality principles to make newcomers feel more welcome in your existing groups?
- What rituals could you create to strengthen the bonds in your current team or community?

Action

This week, practice the "Community Building Triple":

1. Design one small ritual for a group you're part of (could be as simple as starting meetings with appreciation)
2. Practice digital hospitality by personally welcoming someone new to your team or community
3. Create one opportunity for deeper connection among people in your professional network

Notice how these community-building practices change the quality of relationships and collaboration.

PRINCIPLE: CREATE BELONGING

What's Next?

Community provides the foundation, but in our rapidly changing world, both individuals and communities must continuously adapt to stay relevant and effective. In our next chapter, Adaptive Communication, we'll explore how to stay agile in evolving conversations, continuously learn and grow your communication skills, and prepare for future communication challenges we can't yet imagine. Because the future belongs not to those who communicate perfectly today, but to those who can adapt their communication for tomorrow's world.

Chapter 15: Adaptive Communication

PRINCIPLE: EVOLVE WITH THE WORLD

In 2019, my communication toolkit was perfectly calibrated for success. I knew how to work a room at conferences, read body language in negotiations, build rapport over business dinners, and close deals with firm handshakes. I was a master of in-person influence.

Then March 2020 happened. Overnight, my entire communication skill set became obsolete. Conferences moved to Zoom. Negotiations happened through screens. Business dinners became awkward virtual coffee chats. Handshakes became... nothing.

I watched colleagues who'd thrived in the old world struggle to adapt. Senior executives who commanded rooms couldn't figure out how to command attention through a camera. Sales stars who read micro-expressions couldn't close deals when they could only see people's foreheads. Network builders who thrived on serendipitous connections withered when networking became scheduled Zoom rooms.

But I also watched others who not only adapted but flourished. They didn't just translate their old skills to new mediums—they developed entirely new capabilities. They learned to read energy through audio cues, build trust through asynchronous communication, and create intimacy through intentional digital design.

The difference wasn't talent or experience. It was adaptability—the willingness to let go of what worked yesterday and learn what works today.

Staying Relevant in Changing Times

The only constant in communication is change. Every generation develops new channels, norms, and expectations. What felt cutting-edge five years ago feels outdated today. What seems impossible today will be routine tomorrow.

But here's what I've learned: adaptability isn't about chasing every new trend or mastering every new platform. It's about understanding the unchanging human needs that drive all communication, then learning how to meet those needs through evolving channels.

The Unchanging Needs:

- To be seen and understood
- To feel valued and respected
- To belong to something larger than ourselves
- To have our voices heard and our ideas considered
- To build trust and meaningful relationships

The Ever-Changing Channels:

- From letters to emails to instant messages to voice notes
- From face-to-face to phone calls to video to virtual reality
- From broadcast to social to algorithmic to AI-curated
- From formal to casual to visual to interactive

Sarah, a marketing director, exemplified this principle when TikTok emerged as a business communication platform. Instead of dismissing it as "kid stuff" or trying to replicate exactly what teenagers were doing, she asked: "How can we use this medium to help our customers feel seen and understood?"

Her approach wasn't to go viral with dance videos. Instead, she created "Behind the Problems" series—short, authentic videos showing the real challenges their customer service team solved each day, the process behind product improvements, and genuine reactions to customer feedback.

The content performed exceptionally well, not because she mastered TikTok's algorithms, but because she understood how to translate timeless communication principles into a new medium.

Continuous Learning and Growth

Adaptive communication requires a growth mindset applied specifically to how we connect with others. This means treating every communication failure as a learning opportunity and every successful interaction as a data point for future adaptation.

The Communication Learning Loop:

Step 1: Experiment Try new approaches, channels, or techniques. Small experiments, not major overhauls.

Step 2: Observe Pay attention to what works and what doesn't. What generates engagement? What creates confusion? What builds or breaks trust?

Step 3: Analyze Look for patterns across different situations and audiences. Why did something work in one context but not another?

Step 4: Adjust Modify your approach based on what you've learned. Keep what works, discard what doesn't, improve what shows promise.

Step 5: Scale Once you've refined an approach, teach it to others and incorporate it into your standard practices.

Marcus, a team leader, applied this when his remote team struggled with decision-making. Traditional approaches—email chains and video meetings—led to either paralysis or uninformed choices.

Experiment: He tried asynchronous decision-making using shared documents where team members could add input, questions, and recommendations over several days.

Observe: Decisions took longer initially, but they were higher quality and had broader buy-in. People who rarely spoke up in meetings contributed thoughtful analysis in writing.

Analyze: The asynchronous format gave introverts time to process, allowed for research and reflection, and created a paper trail that prevented revisiting settled decisions.

Adjust: He refined the process with templates, clear deadlines, and guidelines for when decisions needed synchronous discussion vs. asynchronous input.

Scale: The approach spread to other teams and became the company's standard for non-urgent strategic decisions.

Preparing for Future Communication Challenges

The future of communication will bring challenges we can't fully predict, but we can prepare by developing meta-skills that transfer across any medium or technology.

Future-Ready Communication Skills:

Digital Fluency: The ability to quickly learn and adapt to new communication platforms and tools. Not just technical skills, but understanding how different mediums affect human psychology and relationship building.

Cultural Agility: As global remote work becomes standard, the ability to communicate effectively across cultures, time zones, and communication styles becomes essential.

Attention Management: In an increasingly distracting world, the ability to capture, hold, and direct attention becomes a core leadership skill.

Empathy Scaling: The ability to maintain human connection and understanding even as communication becomes more automated and efficient.

Information Curation: The skill of finding, filtering, and synthesizing relevant information from overwhelming data streams.

Authenticity Authentication: As AI becomes better at mimicking human communication, the ability to be genuinely, recognizably human becomes more valuable.

Lisa, a customer success manager, demonstrated future-ready thinking when her company began integrating AI chatbots into customer service. Instead of viewing this as a threat to human connection, she asked: "How can we use AI to enhance rather than replace human empathy?"

Her team developed a hybrid approach:

- AI handled routine questions and gathered initial context
- Human agents received comprehensive customer background before engaging
- AI suggested empathy prompts based on customer emotion detection
- Humans focused on complex problem-solving and relationship building

Result: Customer satisfaction increased 28% because customers got faster initial responses plus more personalized human attention when it mattered most.

The Evolution of Professional Communication

Professional communication is evolving rapidly, driven by generational changes, technological advancement, and shifting work cultures.

Current Trends:

Formality Flattening: Traditional hierarchical communication styles are giving way to more casual, direct approaches across all levels.

Visual Communication: Information increasingly shared through images, videos, and interactive media rather than text-only formats.

Asynchronous Preference: Especially among younger workers, preference for communication that doesn't require immediate response or scheduled meetings.

Authenticity Premium: Genuine, personal communication valued over polished, corporate messaging.

Micro-Interactions: Brief, frequent check-ins replacing longer, formal communication sessions.

Context Collapse: Professional and personal communication styles blending as work-life boundaries blur.

David, a finance director, initially resisted these trends. His training emphasized formal protocols, detailed documentation, and hierarchical respect. But when his team's engagement scores plummeted, he realized his communication style was creating barriers, not clarity.

His evolution was gradual but transformative:

- Replaced formal email updates with brief video messages
- Started team meetings with personal check-ins, not just agenda items
- Used collaborative documents instead of one-way presentations
- Encouraged questions and challenges during his presentations
- Shared his own learning journey and mistakes openly

The change didn't happen overnight, but within a year, his team's engagement scores were among the highest in the company. More importantly, their financial insights became more accurate because people felt safe sharing concerns and asking clarifying questions.

Building Adaptive Communication Skills

Adaptability isn't a trait you're born with—it's a skill you develop through practice and intention.

Adaptability Practices:

Platform Experimentation: Regularly try new communication tools, even if they seem irrelevant to your current work. Understanding their strengths and limitations prepares you for future adoption.

Generation Learning: Spend time understanding how different age groups prefer to communicate. Shadow younger colleagues, ask for reverse mentoring, observe communication patterns.

Cultural Immersion: Engage with communication styles from different cultures, industries, and backgrounds. What feels natural to others that seems strange to you?

Feedback Seeking: Regularly ask how your communication is being received. What's working? What's confusing? What would be more effective?

Trend Monitoring: Follow communication technology developments, not to adopt everything, but to understand what's coming and how it might affect human connection.

Failure Recovery: When communication breaks down, analyze what went wrong and what you could do differently. Treat failures as learning laboratories.

Amy, a project manager, built her adaptability systematically. She dedicated one hour weekly to "communication experiments"—trying new tools, techniques, or approaches with low-stakes interactions. She kept a simple log of what worked, what didn't, and why.

Over two years, these small experiments compounded into significant capability growth. She became known as someone who could communicate effectively with anyone— technical teams, executive leadership, external partners, global colleagues—because she'd systematically developed adaptability as a core skill.

The AI Communication Revolution

Artificial intelligence is transforming communication in ways we're just beginning to understand. Rather than replacing human communication, AI is augmenting it in unprecedented ways.

Current AI Communication Applications:

- Real-time language translation breaking down global barriers
- Sentiment analysis helping leaders understand team emotional states
- Personalized communication recommendations based on recipient preferences
- Automated meeting summaries and action item extraction
- Voice cloning and deepfake detection for authenticity verification

Future Possibilities:

- AI coaches providing real-time communication feedback
- Personality-matched communication style suggestions
- Predictive conflict detection and resolution recommendations
- Virtual reality presence that feels indistinguishable from physical presence
- Thought-to-text communication bypassing traditional interfaces

The key isn't to master every AI tool, but to understand how AI can enhance your human communication capabilities while preserving the authenticity that makes you uniquely valuable.

Rachel, a sales leader, embraced AI augmentation thoughtfully. She used AI tools to:

- Analyze customer communication patterns to personalize her approach
- Receive real-time feedback on presentation engagement levels
- Generate initial drafts of routine communications that she then personalized
- Track emotional patterns in team communications to identify support needs

But she was careful to maintain her human edge: genuine curiosity about customer needs, authentic relationship building, and intuitive reading of interpersonal dynamics that AI couldn't replicate.

Cross-Generational Communication Bridges

One of the biggest adaptive challenges is communicating effectively across generational divides, especially as four generations work together for the first time in history.

Generational Communication Preferences:

Traditionalists (born before 1945): Formal, hierarchical, face-to-face or phone preferred

Baby Boomers (1946-1964): Professional but personal, phone calls and formal emails

Generation X (1965-1980): Direct, efficient, email and structured meetings

Millennials (1981-1996): Collaborative, informal, instant messaging and video calls

Generation Z (1997-2012): Visual, authentic, social platforms and voice messages

The adaptive communicator doesn't stereotype but understands these general preferences while recognizing individual variations.

Marcus discovered this leading a multi-generational engineering team. Initial team communications failed because he used one-size-fits-all approaches. His solution was communication optionality:

- Important announcements delivered through multiple channels
- Meeting formats that included both structured presentation and open discussion
- Documentation available in both detailed written form and visual summaries
- Feedback opportunities through various mediums—face-to-face, anonymous surveys, group discussions

This inclusive approach improved engagement across all generations while teaching team members to adapt their own communication styles.

Building Your Adaptive Practice

Weekly Adaptation Ritual: Dedicate time each week to trying one new communication approach, tool, or technique.

Quarterly Skill Assessment: Evaluate which communication skills are becoming more or less relevant in your context. What should you develop? What can you deprioritize?

Annual Communication Audit: Review how your communication style has evolved over the year. What's working better? What needs continued development?

Feedback Loop Creation: Establish regular mechanisms for receiving honest feedback about your communication effectiveness from diverse perspectives.

Future Learning: Stay informed about emerging communication trends, but focus on understanding underlying human needs rather than chasing every new platform.

Chapter Summary

Adaptive Communication isn't about becoming a communication chameleon who changes with every trend. It's about maintaining your authentic core while continuously evolving how you express it through changing mediums and contexts. When we stay curious about new approaches, build bridges across generational and cultural differences, and prepare for future challenges while honoring timeless human needs, we become communication leaders who thrive in any era. In our rapidly changing world, the most valuable communicators aren't those who've perfected yesterday's methods—they're those who can learn tomorrow's while remaining genuinely human. Master this, and you become not just an effective communicator, but a communication evolution catalyst.

Reflection

- What communication skills that served you well in the past might be becoming less relevant?
- Where do you feel resistant to new communication trends? What might you be protecting?
- How has your communication style evolved over the past five years? What drove those changes?
- What future communication challenges excite you? Which ones concern you?

Action

This week, practice the "Adaptive Communication Triple":

1. Experiment with one communication method you've been avoiding or dismissing
2. Ask someone from a different generation how they prefer to communicate about work topics
3. Identify one communication skill you want to develop and take one concrete step toward building it

Notice how stepping outside your communication comfort zone reveals new possibilities.

PRINCIPLE: EVOLVE WITH THE WORLD

What's Next?

Adaptation prepares us for the future, but all of our communication skills ultimately serve one purpose: creating a lasting positive impact that extends beyond ourselves. In our final chapter, Your Connection Legacy, we'll explore how to define your communication values, build relationships that endure, and create ripple effects that make the world more connected and humane. Because the ultimate measure of communication mastery isn't how well you connect—it's how many others you inspire to connect more deeply.

Chapter 16: Your Connection Legacy

PRINCIPLE: LEAVE THE WORLD MORE CONNECTED

Maya Angelou once said, "People will forget what you said, people will forget what you did, but people will never forget how you made them feel." She was talking about personal encounters, but I think about this quote differently now. I think about the ripple effects of how we make people feel about connection itself.

I learned this from watching my mentor, Dr. Janet Williams, a pediatric surgeon who somehow made everyone around her feel more capable, more valued, more human. It wasn't just that she was kind—plenty of people are kind. It was that being around her made you want to be kinder to others. Watching her listen deeply made you a better listener. Seeing her assume positive intent made you more generous in your own assumptions.

Twenty years after her retirement, I still meet people who say, "I had this amazing doctor once who changed how I think about treating people." But the real magic wasn't just in her direct impact—it was in how she inspired hundreds of medical students, residents, and colleagues to approach human connection differently. Her influence multiplied exponentially because she didn't just connect well with people; she made them better at connecting with others.

That's what I call a connection legacy—the way your approach to human relationships ripples outward long after you've left the room, creating waves of more thoughtful, empathetic, and effective communication throughout the world.

Defining Your Communication Values

Your connection legacy starts with clarity about what you stand for in human relationships. Not your professional brand or your networking strategy, but the core values that guide how you show up with other human beings.

The Values Clarity Process:

Step 1: Reflect on Peak Connection Moments Think of times when your communication created real breakthrough, healing, or transformation. What values were you expressing? What principles guided your behavior?

Step 2: Identify Your Communication Non-Negotiables What lines will you never cross in how you treat people? What behaviors feel fundamentally wrong to you, regardless of potential benefit?

Step 3: Examine Your Communication Triggers What communication styles or behaviors frustrate you most? Often our triggers reveal our values—we get upset when others violate principles we hold dear.

Step 4: Envision Your Ideal Impact If people described your communication style to others, what would you want them to say? How would you want to be remembered?

Step 5: Create Your Communication Constitution Write 3-5 core principles that will guide your communication choices, regardless of situation or audience.

Sarah went through this process after a difficult period where she felt she'd lost herself in corporate communication games—saying what people wanted to hear instead of what needed to be said, networking transactionally instead of connecting authentically.

Her Communication Constitution emerged as:

1. **Curiosity Over Certainty**: Ask better questions rather than give quick answers
2. **Courage Over Comfort**: Address difficult topics with care but not avoidance
3. **Connection Over Impression**: Focus on understanding others rather than managing their perception of me
4. **Growth Over Perfection**: Share learning and vulnerability rather than polished expertise
5. **Service Over Self**: Use communication to help others succeed, not just advance my own agenda

These principles became her North Star, guiding decisions from daily email responses to major presentation opportunities. Colleagues started seeking her out not because she always said the right thing, but because they trusted her intentions and approach.

Building Relationships That Endure

Transactional relationships end when the transaction is complete. Legacy relationships compound over time, becoming more valuable and meaningful as they mature.

Characteristics of Legacy Relationships:

Mutual Growth: Both people are different—and better—because of the relationship.

Weathered Storms: The relationship has survived disagreements, disappointments, or difficult seasons.

Generous Exchange: More giving than getting, with trust that reciprocity will balance over time.

Authentic Foundation: Built on genuine compatibility and respect, not just professional utility.

Future Orientation: Focused on who both people are becoming, not just who they are today.

Marcus, a technology executive, realized that most of his professional relationships were functional but not foundational. When he changed companies, most connections faded. When he retired, few relationships continued.

He decided to intentionally build different kinds of relationships:

The Investment Approach: Instead of networking broadly, he focused on deepening relationships with 20 people who shared his values and interests.

The Growth Partnership: He proposed mutual mentoring relationships where he and colleagues committed to each other's development.

The Legacy Project: He started an informal "wisdom exchange" where experienced professionals shared lessons with emerging leaders—not one-way mentoring, but mutual learning.

The Service Commitment: He identified ways to use his expertise to help others succeed, regardless of direct benefit to himself.

Five years later, Marcus had built a network that felt more like a community—people who genuinely cared about each other's success and wellbeing, not just professional advancement.

Creating Positive Ripple Effects

Your connection legacy isn't just about the relationships you build directly—it's about how your approach to connection influences others to connect more thoughtfully themselves.

Ripple Effect Strategies:

Model the Behavior: Be the example of the communication you want to see in the world. People learn more from what they observe than what they're taught.

Teach Through Stories: Share examples of great communication you've witnessed or experienced. Stories spread behaviors more effectively than principles.

Create Connection Opportunities: Design situations where others can practice better communication skills and experience the benefits firsthand.

Celebrate Connection: Recognize and appreciate instances when you see others communicating with empathy, authenticity, or courage.

Facilitate Growth: Help others develop their own communication skills through feedback, coaching, or resource sharing.

Lisa discovered her ripple effect power during a team retreat when she introduced "appreciation rounds"—structured time for team members to share specific gratitudes for each other. The practice felt awkward initially, but the impact was profound. People shared vulnerabilities, acknowledged contributions they'd never mentioned, and left feeling more connected.

Six months later, she learned that three team members had introduced similar practices in their own families. One had started weekly appreciation dinners with his teenagers. Another had implemented gratitude practices in her volunteer organization. The third had taught the technique to her book club.

Lisa's simple facilitation of connection had rippled into dozens of other relationships and communities. Her investment in her team's communication skills had multiplied far beyond her immediate influence.

The Mentorship Multiplier Effect

One of the most powerful ways to create a connection legacy is through intentional mentorship—not just sharing expertise, but developing others' capacity for meaningful relationships.

Connection Mentorship Focus Areas:

Empathy Development: Helping others see situations from multiple perspectives and understand the emotions behind behaviors.

Communication Courage: Supporting others in having difficult conversations they've been avoiding.

Authentic Leadership: Encouraging others to lead with vulnerability and genuine care rather than performance and control.

Conflict Resolution: Teaching others to transform disagreement into deeper understanding and stronger relationships.

Community Building: Helping others create environments where people feel valued, heard, and connected.

David, a senior manager, realized that traditional mentorship focused on career advancement and skill development, but rarely addressed relationship and communication capabilities. He started what he called "Connection Mentorship"—focusing specifically on helping emerging leaders build stronger relationships.

His approach included:

- Monthly conversations about communication challenges and opportunities
- Real-time coaching during difficult relationship situations
- Introduction to his own network with context about each person's communication strengths
- Shared reading and discussion of books about human connection and leadership
- Collaborative projects that required relationship building and collaboration skills

The results exceeded his expectations. His mentees not only advanced in their careers but became known as leaders who brought out the best in others. Several started their own mentorship programs focused on relationship building. The approach spread throughout the organization and influenced hiring and promotion criteria.

Technology and Human Connection Legacy

In our digital age, your connection legacy includes how you use technology to enhance rather than diminish human relationships.

Digital Legacy Principles:

Humanity First: Use technology to amplify human connection, not replace it. When efficiency comes at the cost of empathy, choose empathy.

Presence Over Performance: Focus on being fully present in digital interactions rather than managing your online image.

Bridge Building: Use digital tools to connect people who should know each other, facilitate meaningful conversations, and break down barriers.

Learning and Growth: Share knowledge, resources, and opportunities that help others develop their own relationship skills.

Sustainable Practices: Model healthy boundaries and digital wellness that others can emulate.

Maria, a remote team leader, consciously built her digital legacy through:

- Creating video messages for important communications instead of emails when tone mattered
- Facilitating virtual coffee chats between team members who didn't normally interact
- Sharing articles and resources about remote relationship building with her network
- Teaching other leaders how to create psychological safety in virtual environments
- Advocating for policies that prioritized human connection in digital-first organizations

Her influence spread as other leaders adopted her practices and shared them with their own teams and networks.

The Global Connection Challenge

We live in an interconnected world facing enormous challenges that require unprecedented cooperation, understanding, and collaboration. Your connection legacy contributes to humanity's capacity to work together across differences.

Global Connection Opportunities:

Cultural Bridge-Building: Developing and sharing skills for cross-cultural communication and collaboration.

Empathy Expansion: Helping others understand perspectives and experiences different from their own.

Conflict Transformation: Teaching approaches that turn division into dialogue and competition into collaboration.

Community Resilience: Building local and digital communities that can support people through challenges and change.

Next Generation Development: Preparing emerging leaders with the relationship skills needed for an interconnected world.

Rachel, an international business consultant, realized her work gave her unique opportunities to model and teach global connection skills:

- She created a "Cultural Intelligence Toolkit" that helped teams work effectively across cultures
- She facilitated "empathy exchanges" where people from different backgrounds shared their experiences and perspectives
- She mentored young professionals from underrepresented communities, focusing on relationship-building skills
- She advocated for inclusive communication practices in every organization she worked with
- She used her platform to amplify voices and perspectives that were often marginalized in business settings

Her legacy extended far beyond her consulting work to influence how hundreds of people approached cross-cultural relationships and global collaboration.

Measuring Your Connection Legacy

Legacy isn't something you can measure in real-time, but there are indicators that your approach to relationships is creating positive ripple effects:

Observable Indicators:

- People seek you out for advice about relationship challenges
- Others adopt communication practices they've learned from you
- Your former team members are known for strong relationship skills
- People describe feeling more confident or capable after interactions with you
- Others credit you with helping them navigate difficult relationship situations

Story Indicators:

- You hear secondhand about positive impacts you've had on relationships you're not directly involved in
- People share examples of how they've applied something they learned from you
- Others mention that your approach influenced how they handle similar situations
- You see your communication practices spread to new contexts and relationships

System Indicators:

- Organizations or communities you've been part of maintain healthier communication cultures after you leave
- Policies or practices you've advocated for continue to benefit relationships long-

term
- People you've mentored go on to mentor others using similar principles and approaches

The most meaningful legacy indicators are often the stories you never hear—the conversation someone had with courage because you modeled authenticity, the conflict someone resolved peacefully because you taught them empathy, the community someone built because you showed them what belonging looks like.

Your Legacy Action Plan

Daily Practices:

- Approach each interaction with intention about the impact you want to have
- Look for opportunities to help others connect more effectively
- Practice the communication values you want to model for others
- Share resources, insights, or connections that could benefit someone else's relationships

Weekly Reflection:

- Consider what ripple effects your communication might be creating
- Identify one person you could mentor or support in their relationship development
- Evaluate whether your digital communication is enhancing or diminishing human connection
- Plan one action that could strengthen the relationship culture in your community or organization

Monthly Investment:

- Have deeper conversations with people about what matters most to them
- Introduce people who should know each other
- Share a story about excellent communication you've witnessed
- Take on a project or role that requires building stronger relationships

Annual Evolution:

- Review and refine your communication values based on what you've learned
- Assess the quality and depth of your most important relationships
- Consider how your approach to connection has influenced others
- Set intentions for the legacy you want to build in the coming year

Chapter Summary

Your Connection Legacy isn't about being remembered as a great communicator—it's about leaving the world more connected because you were in it. When we clarify our communication values, build relationships that endure, create positive ripple effects, and use our influence to help others connect more deeply, we contribute to humanity's capacity for understanding, cooperation, and care. In our divided world, every person who commits to building bridges instead of walls, who chooses empathy over indifference, who models authentic connection over performative networking, becomes a force for healing and hope. Your legacy isn't what you achieve for yourself—it's how many others you inspire to connect more courageously, communicate more authentically, and love more fully. That's how we change the world: one connection at a time, one conversation at a time, one relationship at a time.

Reflection

- How do you want to be remembered in terms of how you treated people and built relationships?
- What communication values feel most important to you, regardless of external expectations?
- Where have you already created positive ripple effects through your approach to relationships?
- What would the world look like if everyone communicated the way you do at your best?

Action

This week, practice the "Connection Legacy Triple":

1. Clarify one core communication value that will guide your interactions going forward
2. Invest in deepening one relationship that has legacy potential—move beyond transaction to transformation
3. Create one opportunity for others to experience better connection (facilitate an

introduction, teach a skill, model vulnerable leadership)

Remember: your legacy isn't built in grand gestures but in daily choices to connect with authenticity, courage, and care.

PRINCIPLE: LEAVE THE WORLD MORE CONNECTED

Conclusion

We began this journey acknowledging that we live in an age of unprecedented connection yet profound loneliness, endless communication options yet frequent misunderstanding, infinite networking opportunities yet genuine relationship scarcity.

But we've also discovered something hopeful: in this digital age, the fundamentals of human connection haven't changed—they've simply found new expressions. The need to be seen, heard, valued, and understood remains constant. The desire for authentic relationships, meaningful community, and purposeful contribution endures. The power of empathy, curiosity, and genuine care to transform relationships is as strong as ever.

What has changed is the skill required to create these connections intentionally, consistently, and across the various mediums of modern life. The leaders, professionals, and humans who thrive in this new world aren't necessarily the most technically savvy or digitally native—they're the ones who've learned to be authentically, empathetically, and courageously human through any channel.

The principles in this book—from authenticity to adaptability, from curiosity to courage—aren't just communication techniques. They're choices about the kind of person you want to be and the kind of world you want to create. Every interaction is an opportunity to model the connection you want to see, to practice the empathy the world needs, to build the bridges our divided times demand.

Your connection legacy starts now, with your next conversation, your next meeting, your next message. Make it count. Make it real. Make it human.

The world is waiting for leaders who can connect across any divide, communicate through any medium, and create communities where everyone belongs.

That leader is you.

Acknowledgments

This book exists because of the countless people who taught me that authentic connection is both the means and the end of meaningful work.

To Dale Carnegie, whose foundational insights about human nature created the template for relationship-focused leadership. Your work proved that investing in people isn't just nice, it's necessary. This book is a grateful update of your timeless wisdom for our digital age.

To my mentors who modeled authentic leadership before it was a buzzword: Dr. Janet Williams, who showed me that competence without compassion is incomplete; Sarah Chen, who taught me that vulnerability is a strength, not a weakness; and Marcus Rodriguez, who demonstrated that the best leaders are those who create more leaders.

To my global community of collaborators, colleagues, and friends who helped me understand connection across cultures, time zones, and digital platforms. Special thanks to Priya Sharma for insights on cross-cultural communication, Lin Zhang for lessons on asynchronous collaboration, Amy Johnson for wisdom on digital wellness, and David Thompson for perspective on building virtual communities.

To the remote teams, distributed organizations, and online communities who served as living laboratories for these principles. Your willingness to experiment, share failures, and iterate on connection practices made this book possible.

To my early readers and feedback providers: Lisa Park, Rachel Williams, Tom Anderson, and Maria Santos. Your honest critiques and enthusiastic encouragement shaped every chapter.

To my family, who patiently listened to countless stories about digital empathy over dinner and who reminded me that the best communication principles start at home.

To my editor, who helped transform rambling thoughts about modern relationships into coherent frameworks for human connection.

And to everyone who has ever felt lonely in a crowded digital space, confused by conflicting communication channels, or frustrated by the gap between technological connection and human understanding. This book is for you, and it exists because of you.

The principles in these pages work because they're built on a simple truth: in our rush toward digital efficiency, we must never forget our fundamental humanity. Thank you to everyone who helped me remember that, practice that, and hopefully pass that wisdom along.

Appendix A: Quick Reference Frameworks

The 16 Core Principles

Part One: The Connection Code

1. **Be Real** (The Authenticity Advantage)
2. **Feel First** (Digital Empathy)
3. **Ask Better** (The Curiosity Principle)
4. **Honor Differences** (Cultural Intelligence)

Part Two: The Communication Compass

5. **Lift While You Shift** (The Feedback Framework)
6. **Find the Gold** (Conflict Alchemy)
7. **Own It All** (The Accountability Advantage)
8. **Make It Stick** (Story Power)

Part Three: The Leadership Legacy

9. **Fuel the Fire** (Motivation Mastery)
10. **Lead Through Questions** (The Empowerment Equation)
11. **Make the Impossible Feel Inevitable** (Growth Catalyst)
12. **Connect Work to Why** (Purpose-Driven Leadership)

Part Four: The Future of Connection

13. **Protect Your Humanity** (Digital Wellness and Boundaries)
14. **Create Belonging** (Building Communities)
15. **Evolve With the World** (Adaptive Communication)
16. **Leave the World More Connected** (Your Connection Legacy)

Essential Digital Communication Templates

The Difficult Conversation Email

Subject: [Specific Topic] - Let's Talk

Hi [Name],

I've been thinking about [specific situation], and I'd like to discuss it with you. I value our [relationship/partnership/collaboration] and want to make sure we're aligned.

Would you have 30 minutes this week for a conversation? I'm hoping we can understand each other's perspectives and find a path forward that works for everyone.

I'm available [specific times] or happy to work around your schedule.

Thanks, [Your name]

The Appreciation Message

Hi [Name],

I wanted to take a moment to acknowledge [specific action/behavior]. [Specific impact it had].

This is exactly the kind of [value/behavior] that makes our team stronger. Thank you for [specific behavior].

Best, [Your name]

The Boundary-Setting Message

Hi [Name],

Thanks for your message about [topic]. To give this the attention it deserves, I'll respond by [specific time/date].

For urgent matters, please [specific escalation process].

Thanks for understanding, [Your name]

The Conflict Resolution Follow-Up

Hi [Name],

Thank you for the conversation earlier about [topic]. I appreciated your willingness to [specific positive behavior during conversation].

To make sure I understood correctly: [summary of key points and agreements].

I'm committed to [specific action you'll take] by [date]. Please let me know if I missed anything or if you have other thoughts.

Looking forward to [positive future outcome]. [Your name]

Cultural Communication Guidelines

High-Context Cultures (Japan, Korea, Arab countries, Latin America)

- Allow for longer relationship-building phases
- Pay attention to what's not said
- Use indirect communication styles
- Provide face-saving opportunities
- Build consensus slowly and thoroughly

Low-Context Cultures (Germany, Scandinavia, US, Australia)

- Be direct and explicit
- Focus on tasks alongside relationships
- Provide clear action items and deadlines
- Address conflicts directly but respectfully
- Appreciate efficiency and clarity

Individualistic Cultures (US, UK, Australia, Netherlands)

- Recognize individual contributions publicly
- Support personal achievement and autonomy
- Encourage direct feedback and debate
- Focus on personal accountability
- Celebrate individual innovation

Collectivistic Cultures (China, Mexico, India, many African countries)

- Emphasize group harmony and consensus
- Recognize team achievements

- Provide feedback privately
- Build group identity and shared purpose
- Support collective decision-making

Appendix B: Digital Wellness Tools and Resources

Recommended Apps and Tools

Focus and Attention Management

- **Freedom**: Block distracting websites and apps across devices
- **Forest**: Gamified focus sessions with tree-planting rewards
- **RescueTime**: Automatic time tracking and productivity insights
- **Momentum**: Browser extension for mindful internet use

Communication and Collaboration

- **Calendly**: Eliminate back-and-forth scheduling
- **Loom**: Quick video messages for complex communication
- **Notion**: All-in-one workspace for teams
- **Miro**: Visual collaboration for remote teams

Relationship Management

- **HubSpot CRM**: Free relationship tracking for professionals
- **Clay**: Personal CRM for networking and relationships
- **Google Keep**: Simple note-taking for conversation follow-ups
- **Calendars**: Schedule regular check-ins with important relationships

Digital Wellness

- **Screen Time** (iOS) / **Digital Wellbeing** (Android): Built-in usage tracking
- **Moment**: Mindful phone usage tracking
- **Headspace**: Meditation and mindfulness training
- **Do Not Disturb** settings: Customize notification schedules

Digital Detox Strategies

Daily Micro-Detoxes (5-60 minutes)

- First hour phone-free morning routine
- Device-free meals
- Walking meetings without phones

- Last hour before bed screen-free
- Commute without digital entertainment

Weekly Mini-Detoxes (2-8 hours)

- Saturday morning offline time
- Sunday afternoon digital sabbath
- One evening per week device-free
- Analog hobby time
- Nature time without phones

Monthly Major Detoxes (24-72 hours)

- Full weekend offline retreats
- Vacation days with minimal connectivity
- Digital sabbatical experiments
- Device-free social gatherings
- Reading retreats with physical books

Boundary-Setting Scripts

Response Time Expectations

"I typically respond to emails within 24 hours during business days. For urgent matters, please call or text."

Off-Hours Communication

"I maintain work-life boundaries by not checking messages after 7 PM or on weekends. For true emergencies, please call."

Meeting-Free Times

"I block 9-11 AM daily for deep work. Please schedule meetings outside this window when possible."

Vacation Boundaries

"I'll be completely offline from [dates]. [Colleague name] can assist with urgent matters. I'll respond to messages when I return."

Appendix C: Building Your Personal Communication System

Monthly Communication Audit Questions

Relationship Quality Assessment

1. Which relationships in my life feel most energizing? What makes them work?
2. Which relationships feel draining or stagnant? What might need to change?
3. Where am I investing too much energy for the return? Too little energy for the importance?
4. What relationships am I neglecting that matter to my values and goals?
5. How has my communication style helped or hindered my most important relationships?

Digital Communication Effectiveness

1. Which digital channels serve my communication goals best? Which create more problems than they solve?
2. Where am I communicating efficiently but not effectively?
3. What digital habits are serving my relationships? Which are harming them?
4. How do I show up differently online vs. in person? Is that alignment serving me?
5. What boundaries do I need to strengthen to protect my best communication?

Growth and Development Focus

1. What communication skills do I want to develop in the coming month?
2. Where did I handle a difficult conversation well recently? What can I learn from that success?
3. What communication mistake did I make recently? What would I do differently?
4. Who could I learn from? Who might I mentor?
5. How can I use my communication skills to serve others better?

Annual Communication Planning

Vision Setting

- How do I want to be described as a communicator and relationship-builder?
- What kind of community do I want to create around myself?
- How do I want my communication style to evolve in the coming year?
- What legacy do I want to build through my relationships?

Skill Development Priorities

- Which communication skills would have the highest impact on my goals?
- What cultural intelligence do I need to develop for my context?
- How can I better leverage technology for authentic connection?
- Where do I need to build more courage in my communication?

Relationship Investment Strategy

- Which relationships deserve more intentional investment?
- How will I maintain connection with people who matter most?
- What new relationships do I want to build this year?
- How will I contribute to others' success and development?

System and Habit Design

- What communication rituals will support my relationship goals?
- How will I track progress on relationship building and communication skills?
- What tools and resources will support my communication development?
- How will I maintain accountability for my communication values?

Bibliography

Carnegie, Dale. *How to Win Friends and Influence People*. New York: Simon & Schuster, 1936.

- The seminal work on interpersonal relationships and influence.

Newport, Cal. *Digital Minimalism: Choosing a Focused Life in a Noisy World*. New York: Portfolio/Penguin, 2019.

- Explores strategies for thriving amidst digital distractions.

Sinek, Simon. *Leaders Eat Last: Why Some Teams Pull Together and Others Don't*. New York: Portfolio, 2014.

- Insights on building trust and lasting teams in modern workplaces.

Grant, Adam. *Give and Take: A Revolutionary Approach to Success*. New York: Viking, 2013.

- Examines reciprocity and authentic connection in professional relationships.

Turkle, Sherry. *Reclaiming Conversation: The Power of Talk in a Digital Age*. New York: Penguin Press, 2015.

- Looks at the impact of technology on our ability to communicate.

Goleman, Daniel. *Emotional Intelligence: Why It Can Matter More Than IQ*. New York: Bantam Books, 1995.

- A foundational text on the role of EQ in relationships and leadership.

Brown, Brené. *Dare to Lead: Brave Work. Tough Conversations. Whole Hearts*. New York: Random House, 2018.

- Explores vulnerability, authenticity, and courage as keys to connection.

Ferriss, Timothy. *The 4-Hour Workweek: Escape 9-5, Live Anywhere, and Join the New Rich*. New York: Crown, 2007.

- Early vision of remote work and lifestyle design.

Friedman, Thomas L. *The World Is Flat: A Brief History of the Twenty-First Century*. New York: Farrar, Straus and Giroux, 2005.

- On globalization, digital connectivity, and distributed teams.

Clark, Dorie. *Entrepreneurial You: Monetize Your Expertise, Create Multiple Income Streams, and Thrive*. Boston: Harvard Business Review Press, 2017.

Building authentic brands and influence in crowded digital markets.

PART 2 - PROCRASTINATION

To everyone standing at the crossroads of action and hesitation, may this book be the spark that turns hope into momentum. For the dreamers haunted by unfinished chapters, and the fighters who refuse to let yesterday define tomorrow. Dedicated to all who struggle, strive, and still dare to begin again. Your persistence writes the story of success.

"Never put off till tomorrow what you can do today."—**Benjamin Franklin**

Procrastination
BREAKING FREE FROM THE DREAM KILLER

About Things That Matter

A SELF-IMPROVEMENT SERIES FOR SUCCESS

Book 10

JC Ryan

About This Book

Are you frustrated by endless to-do lists, abandoned goals, and the nagging feeling that you could accomplish so much more if only procrastination wasn't holding you back? You're not alone—and you're not powerless.

"Procrastination: Breaking Free from the Dream Killer" is more than just a self-help guide; it's a transformative toolkit designed for real people facing real struggles with momentum, motivation, and productivity. Drawing from scientific research, personal development strategies, and actionable insights, this book unpacks the roots of procrastination and shows you how to reclaim control over your day, your mind, and your future.

Inside, you'll find:

- Cutting-edge psychology and proven frameworks for understanding why we procrastinate.
- Practical, hands-on worksheets and time audit tools to help you track and optimize your energy and productivity.
- Inspiration and wisdom from classic thinkers and contemporary coaches, giving you a well-rounded approach to change.
- Straightforward advice for dealing with resistance—whether it comes from within, or from those around you.
- Real stories and candid answers to common challenges, so you're never left wondering, "Is it just me?"

No matter where you are on your journey, each chapter is crafted to support your progress from stuck to unstoppable. If you've ever "started strong but lost momentum," this book is your invitation to begin again—and finish what matters most.

Unlock the satisfaction of progress, experience the joy of accomplishment, and discover the freedom that comes when procrastination no longer calls the shots.

Chapter 1: The True Face of Procrastination

Procrastination is not simply about being lazy or having poor time management skills. It's a complex psychological phenomenon that affects millions of people across all walks of life, from students struggling with assignments to executives avoiding crucial business decisions. At its core, procrastination is the voluntary delay of an intended course of action despite expecting to be worse off for the delay.

What Procrastination Really Is

The word "procrastination" comes from the Latin "procrastinatus," meaning "to put off until tomorrow." But this definition barely scratches the surface of what procrastination truly represents. Procrastination is fundamentally about emotional regulation, not time management. When we procrastinate, we're prioritizing our current emotional state over our future well-being.

Procrastination manifests as a behavioral pattern where individuals consistently delay tasks they know they should complete. This delay isn't accidental or due to external circumstances—it's a deliberate choice made in the moment, often followed by feelings of guilt, anxiety, and regret. The procrastinator knows what needs to be done and often knows how to do it, yet still chooses to delay action.

The Procrastination Epidemic

Research indicates that procrastination has reached epidemic proportions in modern society. Studies show that approximately 20% of adults are chronic procrastinators, while up to 95% of people admit to procrastinating at least occasionally. Among college students, the numbers are even more staggering, with some studies suggesting that 80-95% of students engage in procrastination, and approximately 50% procrastinate consistently and problematically.

The digital age has only exacerbated this problem. Social media, streaming services, and instant entertainment options provide endless opportunities for distraction and delay. The constant availability of immediate gratification makes it increasingly difficult to focus on tasks that require sustained effort or don't provide instant rewards.

Distinguishing Normal Delays from Chronic Procrastination

Not all delays constitute procrastination. Sometimes we postpone tasks for legitimate reasons: we're waiting for more information, we need to prioritize more urgent matters, or we're strategically timing our actions. The key distinction lies in the intention and outcome.

Normal delay occurs when:
- You consciously choose to postpone a task for strategic reasons
- The delay serves a purpose and improves the outcome
- You feel in control of your schedule and decisions
- The postponement doesn't cause significant stress or negative consequences

Procrastination occurs when:
- You delay despite knowing it will make things worse
- The delay is driven by emotional avoidance rather than strategy
- You feel out of control and guilty about the delay
- The postponement creates stress, anxiety, and negative consequences

The Hidden Costs

Procrastination exacts a heavy toll that extends far beyond missed deadlines. The costs are multifaceted and compound over time:

Financial Impact: Procrastination can cost thousands of dollars annually through late fees, missed opportunities, rushed work that requires corrections, and career stagnation. Late tax filings, delayed bill payments, and postponed financial planning all carry direct monetary costs.

Emotional Toll: The psychological burden of procrastination includes chronic stress, anxiety, guilt, and shame. These emotions create a vicious cycle where the negative feelings about procrastinating make it even harder to take action, leading to more procrastination and more negative emotions.

Relationship Damage: Procrastination erodes trust and reliability in personal and professional relationships. When we consistently fail to follow through on commitments, others lose confidence in our dependability. This can lead to damaged friendships, strained family relationships, and missed career opportunities.

Health Consequences: Chronic procrastination is linked to various health problems, including increased stress levels, poor sleep quality, weakened immune system, and higher rates of depression and anxiety. The constant state of stress from looming deadlines and unfinished tasks takes a physical toll on the body.

Why This Matters

Understanding procrastination matters because it's not a character flaw or a sign of laziness—it's a learned behavior that can be unlearned. Procrastination represents a fundamental conflict between our present and future selves. Our present self wants comfort, ease, and immediate gratification, while our future self needs us to do difficult, sometimes unpleasant work now to achieve long-term goals.

This internal conflict is at the heart of the human condition. We all struggle with the tension between what we want to do and what we need to do. Recognizing procrastination as a normal human challenge rather than a personal failing is the first step toward overcoming it.

The Connection Between Procrastination and Life Satisfaction

Research consistently shows that people who procrastinate less report higher levels of life satisfaction, better relationships, and greater achievement of their goals. They experience less stress, better health, and more opportunities for growth and success. Conversely, chronic procrastinators often feel stuck, overwhelmed, and disappointed with their progress in life.

The relationship between procrastination and life satisfaction isn't just correlational—it's causal. Procrastination directly undermines our ability to achieve our goals, maintain relationships, and feel good about ourselves. When we consistently delay important tasks, we rob ourselves of the satisfaction that comes from accomplishment and progress.

Breaking the Procrastination Myth

One of the most damaging myths about procrastination is that some people "work better under pressure." While it's true that deadlines can motivate action, the quality of work produced under last-minute pressure is typically inferior to work completed with adequate time and preparation. The stress of rushing also takes a toll on health and well-being.

Another common myth is that procrastination is simply a time management problem. While time management skills can help, procrastination is fundamentally an emotional regulation issue. People procrastinate not because they don't know how to manage their time, but because they're avoiding negative emotions associated with the task.

The Path Forward

Recognizing procrastination for what it truly is—a complex but conquerable challenge—is the first step toward change. Procrastination isn't about being lazy, undisciplined, or lacking willpower. It's about being human and struggling with the universal challenge of doing difficult things now for future benefit.

The good news is that procrastination is a learned behavior, which means it can be unlearned. With the right strategies, mindset, and commitment, anyone can overcome procrastination and reclaim control over their time and life. The journey begins with understanding—understanding what procrastination really is, why it happens, and what it costs us.

As we move forward in this book, we'll explore the science behind procrastination, help you identify your personal procrastination patterns, and provide you with proven strategies to overcome this challenge once and for all. The power to change is in your hands, and the time to start is now.

Chapter 2: The Science Behind Procrastination

For decades, procrastination was dismissed as a character flaw or moral failing. However, modern neuroscience and psychology have revealed that procrastination is a complex phenomenon rooted in brain structure, evolutionary psychology, and learned behavioral patterns. Understanding the science behind procrastination is crucial for developing effective strategies to overcome it.

Psychological Foundations

Research has identified several key psychological mechanisms that drive procrastination. At its core, procrastination represents a failure of self-regulation—the ability to control our thoughts, emotions, and behaviors in service of long-term goals.

Temporal Discounting: One of the primary psychological drivers of procrastination is our tendency to value immediate rewards more highly than future benefits. This phenomenon, known as temporal discounting or present bias, means that the pain of doing a difficult task now feels more significant than the future consequences of not doing it. Our brains are wired to prioritize immediate gratification, a trait that served our ancestors well in survival situations but creates challenges in modern life where long-term planning is essential.

Mood Regulation: Procrastination is fundamentally about mood regulation rather than time management. When faced with a task that triggers negative emotions—boredom, anxiety, frustration, or fear—we naturally seek to avoid those feelings. Procrastination provides temporary relief from negative emotions, making it a form of emotional avoidance.

The Intention-Action Gap: Psychologists have identified a significant gap between our intentions and our actions. We may genuinely intend to complete a task, but when the time comes to act, various psychological barriers prevent us from following through. This gap is influenced by factors such as task aversiveness, self-efficacy beliefs, and competing motivations.

The Brain's Role

Neuroimaging studies have revealed specific brain regions and networks involved in procrastination. Understanding these neural mechanisms helps explain why procrastination feels so automatic and why it's challenging to overcome through willpower alone.

The Limbic System vs. Prefrontal Cortex: Procrastination represents a battle between two brain systems. The limbic system, which includes structures like the amygdala and nucleus accumbens, is responsible for immediate emotional responses and reward-seeking behavior. This system is ancient, powerful, and operates largely below conscious awareness.

In contrast, the prefrontal cortex is responsible for executive functions like planning, decision-making, and impulse control. This region is evolutionarily newer and requires more energy to operate effectively. When we're tired, stressed, or emotionally depleted, the prefrontal cortex's ability to override limbic impulses diminishes, making procrastination more likely.

Default Mode Network: Recent research has identified the default mode network (DMN) as playing a crucial role in procrastination. The DMN is active when we're not focused on specific tasks and is associated with mind-wandering, self-referential thinking, and mental time travel. Overactivity in the DMN is linked to procrastination, as it represents the brain's tendency to drift away from demanding tasks toward more pleasant mental activities.

Dopamine and Motivation: The neurotransmitter dopamine plays a crucial role in motivation and reward-seeking behavior. Procrastination is often associated with dysregulated dopamine systems, where the brain fails to generate sufficient motivation for long-term goals while being hypersensitive to immediate rewards and distractions.

Psychological Distance Theory

One of the most significant scientific insights into procrastination comes from Psychological Distance Theory, developed by researchers Yaacov Trope and Nira Liberman. This theory explains how our perception of tasks affects our likelihood to procrastinate.

According to this theory, we perceive events as psychologically distant along four dimensions:

- **Temporal distance**: How far in the future the task or its consequences seem

- **Social distance**: How relevant the task is to people we care about
- **Spatial distance**: How physically close or far the task feels
- **Hypothetical distance**: How certain or uncertain the task and its outcomes seem

The greater the psychological distance, the more likely we are to procrastinate. When tasks feel distant, abstract, or irrelevant, our brains don't generate the urgency needed for action. Conversely, when tasks feel immediate, concrete, and personally relevant, we're more likely to take action.

Research has demonstrated this principle in practice. In one study, students who were asked to think about a task in concrete, specific terms (the "how" of doing it) were much more likely to complete it promptly than students who thought about it in abstract terms (the "why" of doing it).

The Procrastination-Perfectionism Connection

Scientific research has revealed a strong link between perfectionism and procrastination. Perfectionism creates procrastination through several mechanisms:

Fear of Failure: Perfectionists often have an intense fear of producing work that doesn't meet their impossibly high standards. This fear can be so paralyzing that they avoid starting tasks altogether, reasoning that not trying is better than trying and failing.

All-or-Nothing Thinking: Perfectionists tend to view outcomes in binary terms—either perfect or worthless. This cognitive distortion makes it difficult to appreciate progress and leads to abandoning tasks at the first sign of imperfection.

Analysis Paralysis: The perfectionist's desire to find the "perfect" approach can lead to endless planning and research without ever taking action. They become stuck in preparation mode, always seeking more information or a better strategy before beginning.

Cultural and Environmental Factors

While procrastination has biological and psychological roots, cultural and environmental factors significantly influence its expression and prevalence.

Cultural Values: Cultures that emphasize long-term thinking, delayed gratification, and collective responsibility tend to have lower rates of procrastination. Conversely, cultures that prioritize immediate gratification and individual achievement may inadvertently encourage procrastination.

Technology and Distraction: The modern digital environment has created unprecedented opportunities for distraction and procrastination. Social media, streaming services, and mobile devices provide constant access to immediate gratification, making it increasingly difficult to focus on demanding tasks.

Educational Systems: Traditional educational approaches that emphasize external motivation, punishment for failure, and rigid deadlines may inadvertently foster procrastination by creating negative associations with learning and achievement.

The Stress-Procrastination Cycle

Research has identified a vicious cycle between stress and procrastination. Procrastination creates stress through looming deadlines and unfinished tasks, while stress impairs the cognitive functions needed to overcome procrastination.

When we're stressed, our prefrontal cortex—the brain region responsible for executive control—functions less effectively. This makes it harder to resist immediate temptations and focus on long-term goals. Simultaneously, stress activates the limbic system, making us more reactive to immediate rewards and more likely to seek comfort through procrastination.

Individual Differences

Not everyone procrastinates equally. Research has identified several individual differences that influence procrastination tendency:

Personality Traits: People high in conscientiousness and self-discipline tend to procrastinate less, while those high in impulsivity and neuroticism procrastinate more. However, personality isn't destiny—even highly impulsive individuals can learn to manage procrastination effectively.

Cognitive Styles: Some people are naturally more concrete thinkers, while others are more abstract. Concrete thinkers tend to procrastinate less because they naturally focus on specific actions and immediate steps, while abstract thinkers may get caught up in big-picture concerns without taking action.

Attachment Styles: Research suggests that people with secure attachment styles procrastinate less than those with anxious or avoidant attachment styles. This may be because secure attachment is associated with better emotional regulation and more realistic self-assessment.

The Neuroscience of Change

Understanding the science behind procrastination also reveals why change is possible. The brain's neuroplasticity—its ability to form new neural connections throughout life—means that procrastination patterns can be rewired through consistent practice and the right strategies.

Habit Formation: Procrastination often becomes an automatic habit loop: cue (difficult task) → routine (avoidance behavior) → reward (temporary relief). Breaking this loop requires conscious intervention to create new, more productive habits.

Cognitive Behavioral Mechanisms: The most effective interventions for procrastination work by addressing the cognitive and behavioral patterns that maintain it. This includes changing thought patterns, developing better emotional regulation skills, and creating environmental supports for desired behaviors.

Implications for Treatment

The scientific understanding of procrastination has important implications for how we approach overcoming it:

1. **It's Not About Willpower**: Since procrastination involves automatic brain processes, simply trying harder rarely works. Effective strategies must address the underlying psychological and neurological mechanisms.
2. **Emotional Regulation is Key**: Since procrastination is fundamentally about avoiding negative emotions, developing better emotional regulation skills is crucial for long-term success.
3. **Environmental Design Matters**: Given the brain's susceptibility to distraction and immediate rewards, creating environments that support desired behaviors is essential.
4. **Practice and Consistency**: Changing deeply ingrained neural patterns requires consistent practice over time. Quick fixes rarely work for chronic procrastination.

The science of procrastination reveals that this challenge is both universal and conquerable. By understanding the psychological and neurological mechanisms involved, we can develop more effective strategies for change. The key is working with our brain's natural tendencies rather than against them, creating conditions that make productive action more likely than procrastination.

Chapter 3: Identifying Your Procrastination Profile

Not all procrastination is created equal. While the underlying mechanisms may be similar, the specific triggers, patterns, and manifestations of procrastination vary significantly from person to person. Understanding your unique procrastination profile is essential for developing targeted strategies that work for your specific situation. This chapter will help you identify your personal procrastination patterns, triggers, and the specific costs it has imposed on your life.

Common Procrastinator Types

Research has identified several distinct procrastination profiles, each with unique characteristics, triggers, and optimal intervention strategies. Most people exhibit characteristics of multiple types, but usually have one dominant pattern.

The Perfectionist Procrastinator

Perfectionist procrastinators delay starting or completing tasks because they fear the work won't meet their impossibly high standards. They often spend excessive time planning, researching, and preparing, but struggle to actually begin or finish projects.

Characteristics:
- Sets unrealistically high standards
- Fears making mistakes or producing imperfect work
- Spends excessive time in preparation phases
- Often abandons projects when they don't meet expectations
- Experiences intense anxiety about being judged

Common thoughts: "If I can't do it perfectly, why bother?" "I need to research more before I start." "This isn't good enough yet."

The Overwhelmed Procrastinator

This type becomes paralyzed when faced with large, complex tasks or multiple competing demands. They often feel like they don't know where to start and become overwhelmed by the scope of what needs to be done.

Characteristics:
- Feels paralyzed by large or complex tasks

- Struggles with prioritization and decision-making
- Often takes on too many commitments
- Experiences anxiety about having "too much to do"
- May work frantically on small, less important tasks to avoid big ones

Common thoughts: "There's too much to do." "I don't know where to start." "I'll never get all this done."

The Rebel Procrastinator

Rebel procrastinators delay tasks as a form of resistance to authority or external control. They may procrastinate more when they feel coerced or when tasks are imposed by others rather than chosen freely.

Characteristics:
- Resents external deadlines and authority
- Procrastinates more on tasks imposed by others
- Values autonomy and freedom highly
- May deliberately delay to assert independence
- Often performs better on self-chosen tasks

Common thoughts: "Nobody can tell me what to do." "I'll do it when I'm ready." "Why should I rush just because they say so?"

The Dreamer Procrastinator

Dreamer procrastinators are great at generating ideas and making plans but struggle with execution and follow-through. They often get excited about new projects but lose interest when the work becomes routine or difficult.

Characteristics:
- Excellent at generating ideas and making plans
- Struggles with execution and follow-through
- Gets bored with routine or detail-oriented tasks
- Often starts multiple projects but finishes few
- Prefers creative, big-picture thinking to implementation

Common thoughts: "I have so many great ideas." "The details are boring." "I'll figure out the implementation later."

The Worrier Procrastinator

Worrier procrastinators delay because they're anxious about potential negative outcomes. They may fear failure, success, judgment, or making the wrong decision. This anxiety becomes so overwhelming that avoidance seems like the safer option.

Characteristics:
- Experience high anxiety about potential outcomes
- Catastrophizes about what might go wrong
- Seeks excessive reassurance from others
- May procrastinate on decisions as well as tasks
- Often has physical symptoms of anxiety

Common thoughts: "What if I fail?" "What if I make the wrong choice?" "Everyone will think I'm incompetent."

The Crisis-Maker Procrastinator

Crisis-maker procrastinators consistently wait until the last minute, claiming they "work better under pressure." While they may meet deadlines, the quality of their work and their stress levels suffer.

Characteristics:
- Consistently waits until the last minute
- Claims to "work better under pressure"
- Creates artificial urgency and drama
- Often produces lower-quality work due to time constraints
- May enjoy the adrenaline rush of deadline pressure

Common thoughts: "I work better under pressure." "I still have time." "The deadline isn't until tomorrow."

Self-Assessment Tools

To identify your procrastination profile, complete the following comprehensive assessment. Be honest in your responses—this information is for your benefit alone.

Procrastination Intensity Scale

Rate each statement from 1 (never) to 5 (always):
1. I put off tasks until the last minute
2. I feel overwhelmed by large projects
3. I spend too much time planning and not enough time doing

4. I avoid tasks that might result in failure or criticism
5. I procrastinate more on tasks imposed by others
6. I start many projects but finish few
7. I work better under pressure
8. I feel anxious when thinking about certain tasks
9. I get distracted easily when trying to work
10. I make excuses for not completing tasks on time
11. I feel guilty about my procrastination
12. My procrastination has negatively affected my relationships
13. I miss deadlines regularly
14. I avoid tasks that seem boring or unpleasant
15. I procrastinate even on things I want to do

Scoring:
- 15-30: Minimal procrastination
- 31-45: Moderate procrastination
- 46-60: Significant procrastination
- 61-75: Severe procrastination

Trigger Identification Exercise

Identify your specific procrastination triggers by completing these statements:

Task-Related Triggers:
- I procrastinate most on tasks that are: _____
- I avoid tasks that make me feel: _____
- The types of projects I delay most are: _____

Emotional Triggers:
- I procrastinate when I'm feeling: _____
- The emotions I most want to avoid are: _____
- I use procrastination to cope with: _____

Environmental Triggers:
- I procrastinate most when I'm in: _____
- The time of day I procrastinate most is: _____
- I'm most likely to procrastinate when: _____

Social Triggers:
- I procrastinate more on tasks assigned by: _____
- I avoid tasks when I'm worried about: _____
- I procrastinate more when I feel: _____

Recognizing Your Patterns

Once you've completed the assessments, look for patterns in your responses. Most people have a primary procrastination type with secondary characteristics from other types.

Pattern Recognition Questions:

1. What types of tasks do you consistently avoid or delay?
2. What emotions do you experience before, during, and after procrastinating?
3. What time of day or circumstances make procrastination more likely?
4. How do you typically justify or rationalize your procrastination?
5. What are the immediate "benefits" you get from procrastinating?
6. What are the long-term costs of your procrastination patterns?

The Procrastination Cycle

Understanding how procrastination perpetuates itself is crucial for breaking the cycle. Most procrastination follows a predictable pattern:

Stage 1: Task Presentation. A task or deadline is presented, either by others or self-imposed.

Stage 2: Initial Avoidance. The task triggers negative emotions (anxiety, boredom, overwhelm), leading to initial avoidance.

Stage 3: Rationalization. The mind creates justifications for the delay: "I work better under pressure," "I need more information," "I'll do it tomorrow."

Stage 4: Distraction and Relief. Engaging in alternative activities provides temporary relief from negative emotions.

Stage 5: Mounting Pressure. As deadlines approach, anxiety and guilt increase, but the task now feels even more overwhelming.

Stage 6: Crisis Mode. Last-minute panic leads to rushed completion or complete avoidance.

Stage 7: Negative Consequences. Poor quality work, missed deadlines, or abandoned projects create negative outcomes.

Stage 8: Self-Criticism and Shame. Negative self-talk reinforces the belief that "I'm a procrastinator," setting up the next cycle.

Measuring the Impact

To fully understand your procrastination profile, you need to honestly assess its impact on your life. This assessment serves both as motivation for change and as a baseline for measuring progress.

Life Areas Assessment

Rate how procrastination has affected each area of your life (1 = no impact, 5 = severe impact):

- Career/Work: ___
- Education/Learning: ___
- Finances: ___
- Health: ___
- Relationships: ___
- Personal Goals: ___
- Self-Esteem: ___
- Stress Levels: ___
- Overall Life Satisfaction: ___

Calculating the Costs

Complete this comprehensive cost analysis:

Financial Costs:

- Late fees paid in the last year: $_____
- Missed opportunities (estimate): $_____
- Career impact (promotions, raises missed): $_____
- Health costs from stress: $_____
- Total estimated financial cost: $_____

Relationship Costs:

- Relationships damaged by unreliability: _____
- Trust lost due to missed commitments: _____
- Opportunities for connection missed: _____
- Family/friend disappointments caused: _____

Personal Costs:

- Goals abandoned due to procrastination: _____
- Dreams deferred or given up: _____
- Skills not developed: _____
- Experiences missed: _____

Emotional Costs:

- Days spent feeling guilty or anxious: _____
- Self-esteem damage: _____
- Stress-related health issues: _____
- Sleep lost to worry: _____

Your Procrastination Profile Summary

Based on your assessments, create a summary of your procrastination profile:

Primary Type: _____

Secondary Characteristics: _____

Main Triggers: _____

Typical Patterns: _____

Primary Costs: _____

Motivation for Change: _____

Using Your Profile for Change

Understanding your procrastination profile is the foundation for developing an effective change strategy. Different types of procrastinators need different approaches:

- **Perfectionists** need to focus on "good enough" standards and progress over perfection
- **Overwhelmed** types need better task breakdown and prioritization skills
- **Rebels** need more autonomy and self-chosen goals
- **Dreamers** need better implementation and follow-through systems
- **Worriers** need anxiety management and cognitive restructuring
- **Crisis-makers** need to challenge their "pressure" beliefs and develop consistent work habits

Your procrastination profile isn't fixed—it can change as you develop new skills and awareness. The key is to start with strategies that match your current patterns while gradually building new, more productive habits.

Remember, identifying your procrastination profile isn't about labeling yourself or accepting limitations. It's about understanding your starting point so you can chart the most effective path forward. With this self-knowledge, you're ready to begin implementing the targeted strategies that will help you overcome procrastination once and for all.

The journey from procrastination to productivity begins with self-awareness. Now that you understand your unique patterns and triggers, you're equipped to tackle the root causes of your procrastination and build a more productive, fulfilling life.

The Root Causes

Chapter 4: Fear-Based Procrastination

Fear is one of the most powerful drivers of procrastination, yet it often operates beneath our conscious awareness. When we procrastinate out of fear, we're not simply being lazy or disorganized—we're protecting ourselves from perceived threats to our self-worth, identity, or emotional well-being. Understanding the different types of fear that fuel procrastination is essential for breaking free from this paralyzing cycle.

Fear of Failure: The Paralysis of Possibility

Fear of failure is perhaps the most common fear-based cause of procrastination. This fear manifests as an intense anxiety about not meeting expectations, making mistakes, or producing work that falls short of standards. The procrastinator reasons, often unconsciously, that if they don't try, they can't truly fail.

The Logic of Avoidance. The fear-of-failure procrastinator operates on a twisted but understandable logic: "If I don't complete this task, I can always tell myself (and others) that I could have done well if I had really tried." This preserves their self-image and protects them from the devastating blow of genuine failure. However, this protection comes at an enormous cost—the complete abandonment of potential success.

Manifestations in Daily Life. Fear of failure procrastination appears in countless ways:
- The student who doesn't study for an exam because "at least then I'll know why I failed"
- The entrepreneur who endlessly researches business ideas but never launches
- The writer who has "great ideas" but never puts pen to paper
- The job seeker who doesn't apply for positions they really want because "I probably wouldn't get them anyway"

The Perfectionism Connection. Fear of failure often intertwines with perfectionism, creating a double bind. The individual sets impossibly high standards, then becomes paralyzed by the fear that they cannot meet these standards. This creates a vicious cycle where the fear of imperfection prevents any action at all.

Breaking Free from Failure Fear. Overcoming fear-of-failure procrastination requires a fundamental shift in how we view failure itself. Instead of seeing failure as a reflection of our worth, we must learn to view it as information, feedback, and an inevitable part of growth. This involves:
- **Redefining failure** as a learning opportunity rather than a judgment

- **Setting "good enough" standards** that allow for progress over perfection
- **Celebrating attempts** regardless of outcome
- **Developing self-compassion** for mistakes and setbacks
- **Focusing on process goals** rather than only outcome goals

Fear of Success: The Surprising Anxiety of Achievement

While fear of failure is widely understood, fear of success is often overlooked yet equally paralyzing. This counterintuitive fear stems from anxiety about the changes, responsibilities, and expectations that come with success.

Why Success Feels Threatening. Fear of success can arise from several sources:

- **Increased expectations**: Success often leads to higher expectations from others and ourselves
- **Imposter syndrome**: Feeling unworthy of success and fearing exposure as a "fraud"
- **Loss of identity**: Success might conflict with how we see ourselves or how others see us
- **Guilt and responsibility**: Success can bring guilt about surpassing others or responsibility for maintaining achievements
- **Fear of change**: Success inevitably brings change, which can feel threatening even when positive

The Self-Sabotage Pattern. Those with fear of success often engage in self-sabotage just as they're on the verge of achievement. They might:

- Procrastinate on the final steps of important projects
- Make "careless" mistakes that undermine their work
- Avoid opportunities that could lead to advancement
- Downplay their abilities and achievements
- Create crises that distract from potential success

Cultural and Social Factors. Fear of success is often reinforced by cultural messages about humility, not "getting too big for your britches," or the belief that success comes at others' expense. Some individuals fear that success will alienate them from their family, friends, or community.

Overcoming Success Anxiety. Addressing fear of success requires:

- Examining beliefs about success and where they originated
- **Visualizing positive outcomes** of success rather than only focusing on potential downsides
- **Building a support network** that celebrates rather than undermines achievement

- **Developing a growth mindset** that sees success as expandable rather than limited
- **Practicing receiving** compliments, recognition, and opportunities

Fear of Judgment: The Paralyzing Power of Others' Opinions

The fear of being judged, criticized, or rejected by others is a powerful procrastination trigger. This fear can be so intense that individuals avoid taking action entirely rather than risk negative evaluation.

The Social Nature of Fear. Humans are inherently social beings, and our survival has historically depended on acceptance by our group. This evolutionary programming makes the fear of social rejection particularly powerful. In modern life, this fear can become disproportionate and paralyzing.

Common Judgment Fears

- Fear of being seen as incompetent or stupid
- Fear of being criticized or ridiculed
- Fear of standing out or being different
- Fear of disappointing others
- Fear of being rejected or abandoned

The Perfectionism-Judgment Connection. Fear of judgment often drives perfectionism, as individuals believe that only perfect work will be immune from criticism. This creates an impossible standard that leads to procrastination, as the person delays action until they can guarantee a perfect outcome.

Social Media and Modern Judgment. The digital age has amplified fear of judgment through social media platforms where every action can be publicly scrutinized, commented upon, and permanently recorded. This has created new forms of performance anxiety and procrastination.

Strategies for Overcoming Judgment Fear

- **Recognizing that criticism is inevitable** and not necessarily meaningful
- **Developing internal validation** rather than relying solely on external approval
- **Practicing vulnerability** in safe relationships to build tolerance for judgment
- **Focusing on your values** rather than others' opinions
- **Building self-worth** independent of others' evaluations

Imposter Syndrome: Feeling Unworthy of Success

Imposter syndrome—the persistent feeling that you're a fraud who doesn't deserve success—is a specific type of fear that drives procrastination. Those experiencing imposter syndrome live in constant fear of being "found out" as incompetent or unqualified.

The Imposter's Dilemma. Individuals with imposter syndrome often procrastinate because:

- They fear their work will reveal their "true" incompetence
- They believe they don't deserve opportunities or success
- They worry that others will discover they're not as capable as they appear
- They feel like they're constantly fooling people about their abilities

High Achievers and Imposter Syndrome. Paradoxically, imposter syndrome often affects high achievers most severely. The more successful they become, the more they fear being exposed as frauds. This creates a cycle where success increases rather than decreases their anxiety.

The Procrastination Connection. Imposter syndrome leads to procrastination through several mechanisms:

- **Over-preparation**: Spending excessive time preparing to compensate for perceived inadequacy
- **Avoidance**: Avoiding tasks that might reveal "incompetence"
- **Perfectionism**: Setting impossibly high standards to prove worthiness
- **Self-sabotage**: Unconsciously undermining success to avoid the anxiety of maintaining it

Overcoming Imposter Syndrome

- Recognizing the universality of imposter feelings
- Documenting achievements and positive feedback
- **Reframing thoughts** about competence and worthiness
- **Seeking mentorship** and support from others who've experienced similar feelings
- Accepting that learning is ongoing and that no one knows everything

Strategies for Confronting Fear-Based Delays

Overcoming fear-based procrastination requires a multi-faceted approach that addresses both the emotional and practical aspects of fear.

Cognitive Strategies

- **Identify and challenge fearful thoughts**: Recognize catastrophic thinking patterns and replace them with more realistic assessments
- **Use the "worst-case scenario" technique**: Fully explore what would actually happen if your fears came true—often the reality is far less catastrophic than imagined
- **Practice thought stopping**: When fearful thoughts arise, consciously redirect attention to the present moment and the task at hand

Behavioral Approaches

- **Start with small steps**: Break feared tasks into tiny, manageable pieces that feel less threatening
- **Use the "two-minute rule"**: Commit to working on a feared task for just two minutes—often this is enough to overcome initial resistance
- **Create accountability**: Share your goals with others who can provide support and gentle pressure

Emotional Regulation Techniques

- **Practice mindfulness**: Learn to observe fears without being controlled by them
- **Use relaxation techniques**: Deep breathing, progressive muscle relaxation, and meditation can help manage fear-based anxiety
- **Develop self-compassion**: Treat yourself with the same kindness you would show a good friend facing similar fears

Environmental Modifications

- **Create safe spaces**: Establish environments where you feel secure enough to take risks and make mistakes
- **Limit exposure to judgment**: Initially work on feared tasks in private or with supportive people
- **Build supportive relationships**: Surround yourself with people who encourage growth rather than perfection

Gradual Exposure

Like treating phobias, overcoming fear-based procrastination often requires gradual exposure to the feared situation:

- Start with less threatening versions of the feared task
- Gradually increase the stakes or visibility of your work
- Celebrate small victories and progress along the way
- Build confidence through repeated successful experiences

Fear-based procrastination is not a character flaw or a sign of weakness—it's a natural human response to perceived threats. By understanding the specific fears that drive your procrastination and implementing targeted strategies to address them, you can break free from the paralysis of fear and begin taking meaningful action toward your goals.

The key is to remember that courage isn't the absence of fear—it's action in the presence of fear. Every time you act despite your fears, you weaken their power over you and strengthen your capacity for future action.

Chapter 5: Perfectionism and Procrastination

Perfectionism and procrastination form one of the most destructive partnerships in human behavior. While perfectionism might seem like a positive trait—after all, who doesn't want to do excellent work?—it often becomes a prison that prevents any work from being completed at all. Understanding the complex relationship between perfectionism and procrastination is crucial for anyone seeking to break free from this paralyzing cycle.

The Perfectionist's Dilemma: When "Good Enough" Feels Impossible

Perfectionism is not simply having high standards or striving for excellence. True perfectionism is characterized by setting unrealistically high standards and being overly critical of one's performance. Perfectionists often believe that anything less than perfect is worthless, creating an all-or-nothing mentality that makes starting tasks feel overwhelming and completing them feel impossible.

The Perfectionist Mindset. Perfectionists operate under several problematic beliefs:

- "If I can't do it perfectly, there's no point in doing it at all"
- "My worth as a person depends on my performance"
- "Others will judge me harshly if my work isn't flawless"
- "Mistakes are unacceptable and reflect fundamental inadequacy"
- "There is always a perfect solution if I just think hard enough"

These beliefs create a psychological trap where the perfectionist becomes paralyzed by the impossibility of meeting their own standards. The fear of producing imperfect work becomes so overwhelming that they avoid starting altogether.

Types of Perfectionism

Research has identified different types of perfectionism, each with its own relationship to procrastination:

Self-Oriented Perfectionism: Setting impossibly high standards for oneself. These individuals procrastinate because they fear their work won't meet their internal standards.

Other-Oriented Perfectionism: Expecting perfection from others. While this doesn't directly cause personal procrastination, it can lead to delegation difficulties and relationship problems that create additional stress.

Socially Prescribed Perfectionism: Believing that others expect perfection from you. This type is most strongly linked to procrastination, as individuals feel paralyzed by the perceived expectations of others.

All-or-Nothing Thinking: Breaking Free from Binary Mindsets

At the heart of perfectionist procrastination lies all-or-nothing thinking—the cognitive distortion that views outcomes in absolute terms. For the perfectionist, work is either perfect or worthless, success is either complete or failure, and performance is either flawless or inadequate.

The Binary Trap. All-or-nothing thinking creates several problems:

- **Impossible standards**: If only perfection is acceptable, most efforts will be deemed failures
- **Motivation paralysis**: Why start something that's destined to be "worthless"?
- **Progress blindness**: Incremental improvements are invisible when only perfection matters
- **Abandonment tendency**: Projects are abandoned at the first sign of imperfection

Real-World Consequences. This binary thinking manifests in various ways:

- The writer who deletes entire chapters because they're not "perfect"
- The student who doesn't submit assignments because they're not completely satisfied with them
- The entrepreneur who endlessly revises business plans without ever launching
- The artist who destroys work that doesn't meet impossible standards

Breaking the Binary Pattern. Overcoming all-or-nothing thinking requires developing what psychologists call "cognitive flexibility"—the ability to see situations in shades of gray rather than black and white. This involves:

- **Recognizing the spectrum**: Understanding that quality exists on a continuum, not as a binary
- **Valuing progress over perfection**: Celebrating incremental improvements and learning
- **Embracing "good enough"**: Recognizing that good enough is often actually excellent
- **Understanding diminishing returns**: Recognizing when additional effort yields minimal improvement

Setting Realistic Standards: The Art of "Good Enough"

One of the most crucial skills for overcoming perfectionist procrastination is learning to set realistic, achievable standards. This doesn't mean lowering your standards to mediocrity—it means setting standards that allow for progress, learning, and completion.

The 80/20 Rule in Practice. The Pareto Principle suggests that 80% of results come from 20% of efforts. For perfectionists, this means recognizing that the final 20% of "perfection" often requires 80% of the time and effort—time that could be better spent on other valuable activities.

Defining Good Enough. "Good enough" doesn't mean sloppy or careless. Instead, it means:

- Meeting the essential requirements of the task or goal
- Serving the intended purpose effectively
- Being appropriate for the context and audience
- Allowing for future improvement if necessary
- Balancing quality with other priorities like time and resources

Context-Dependent Standards. Different situations require different standards. A rough draft should be held to different standards than a final presentation. An internal memo requires different attention than a client proposal. Learning to calibrate standards to context is essential for productive perfectionism.

The Minimum Viable Product Approach. Borrowed from the startup world, the concept of a "minimum viable product" can be applied to any task. This involves creating the simplest version that serves the core purpose, then iterating and improving based on feedback and results.

Learning from Mistakes: Reframing Failure as Feedback

Perfectionists often have a deeply problematic relationship with mistakes and failure. They view errors as catastrophic reflections of their inadequacy rather than natural parts of the learning process. This fear of making mistakes becomes a major driver of procrastination.

The Growth Mindset Alternative. Psychologist Carol Dweck's research on growth mindset provides a powerful alternative to perfectionist thinking. A growth mindset views abilities as developable through effort and learning, while a fixed mindset sees them as static traits. Perfectionists typically operate from a fixed mindset, believing that mistakes reveal fundamental inadequacy.

Reframing Mistakes. Instead of viewing mistakes as failures, they can be reframed as:

- **Learning opportunities**: Each mistake teaches something valuable
- **Feedback mechanisms**: Errors provide information about what doesn't work
- **Progress indicators**: Mistakes often signal that you're pushing boundaries and growing
- **Humanity markers**: Mistakes remind us that we're human, not machines
- **Innovation catalysts**: Many breakthroughs come from "happy accidents"

The Scientific Method Approach. Scientists don't view failed experiments as personal failures—they view them as data points that inform future research. Adopting this scientific approach to personal projects can help perfectionists see setbacks as valuable information rather than devastating failures.

Building Mistake Tolerance. Developing tolerance for mistakes requires:

- **Starting with low-stakes situations**: Practice making and accepting mistakes in less important contexts
- **Documenting lessons learned**: Keep track of what mistakes teach you
- **Celebrating attempts**: Acknowledge effort and courage regardless of outcome
- **Seeking feedback actively**: View criticism as valuable input rather than personal attack
- **Sharing mistakes**: Talking about errors with others normalizes the experience

Progressive Excellence: Building Quality Incrementally

Rather than demanding perfection from the start, progressive excellence involves building quality incrementally through multiple iterations and refinements. This approach allows for immediate action while still achieving high standards over time.

The Iterative Process.

Progressive excellence follows a cycle:

1. **Create a basic version**: Focus on getting something complete rather than perfect
2. **Evaluate and identify improvements**: Assess what works and what doesn't
3. **Make targeted refinements**: Improve specific aspects rather than starting over
4. **Repeat the cycle**: Continue refining until the work meets appropriate standards

Benefits of the Iterative Approach

- **Reduces initial overwhelm**: Starting is easier when perfection isn't required immediately
- **Provides early feedback**: You can get input and course-correct early in the process
- **Builds momentum**: Completing iterations creates positive momentum

- **Allows for learning**: Each iteration teaches you something new about the project
- **Manages scope creep**: Iterations help maintain focus on essential elements

Version Control Mentality. Software developers use version control systems that track changes and improvements over time. Adopting this mentality for any project helps normalize the idea that work evolves through versions rather than emerging perfect from the start.

The Draft Concept. Writers understand that first drafts are meant to be imperfect—their purpose is to get ideas down on paper, not to create finished prose. This concept can be applied to any work:

- **First draft**: Get the basic structure and content in place
- **Second draft**: Refine organization and flow
- **Third draft**: Polish language and presentation
- **Final draft**: Make final adjustments and corrections

Practical Strategies for Perfectionist Procrastinators

Overcoming perfectionist procrastination requires specific strategies that address both the thinking patterns and behaviors that maintain the cycle.

Time-Boxing Techniques. Set strict time limits for tasks to prevent endless refinement:

- **Pomodoro Technique**: Work in focused 25-minute intervals
- **Time budgets**: Allocate specific amounts of time to different aspects of a project
- **Deadline pressure**: Use external deadlines to force completion
- **Good enough timers**: Set a timer for when something becomes "good enough"

The 70% Rule. Military strategists often use the 70% rule: when you have 70% of the information you need and are 70% confident in your plan, it's time to act. Waiting for 100% certainty often means missing opportunities entirely.

Prototype Thinking. Approach projects as prototypes rather than final products:

- **Rapid prototyping**: Create quick, rough versions to test ideas
- **Feedback loops**: Get input early and often
- **Iteration planning**: Build improvement into the process from the start
- **Learning objectives**: Focus on what you want to learn from each version

The "Shitty First Draft" Permission. Give yourself explicit permission to create imperfect first attempts. Writer Anne Lamott popularized the concept of "shitty first drafts"—the idea that all good writing begins with terrible first attempts. This permission can be liberating for perfectionists.

Quality Calibration Exercises. Practice calibrating your quality standards:

- **Compare examples**: Look at work you consider "good enough" versus "perfect"
- **Time tracking**: Track how much time you spend on the last 10% of perfection
- **Feedback collection**: Ask others to evaluate work at different quality levels
- **Cost-benefit analysis**: Calculate the true cost of perfectionist standards

The Perfectionism Audit. Regularly assess whether your perfectionist standards are serving you:

- **Identify perfectionist triggers**: What situations activate your perfectionist tendencies?
- **Evaluate costs**: What opportunities are you missing due to perfectionist delays?
- **Assess benefits**: When does high attention to detail actually add value?
- **Adjust standards**: Consciously choose appropriate standards for different contexts

Support Systems. Build support systems that counter perfectionist tendencies:

- **Accountability partners**: Work with others who can provide perspective on "good enough"
- **Feedback groups**: Join groups that provide constructive criticism and support
- **Mentorship**: Learn from others who have overcome perfectionist procrastination
- **Professional help**: Consider therapy if perfectionism significantly impairs functioning

The Perfectionist's Recovery Plan

Overcoming perfectionist procrastination is a gradual process that requires patience and self-compassion. Here's a structured approach to recovery:

Phase 1: Awareness Building

- Recognize perfectionist thoughts and behaviors
- Identify the costs of perfectionist procrastination
- Understand the difference between healthy striving and perfectionism

Phase 2: Standard Recalibration

- Practice setting "good enough" standards
- Experiment with time limits and deadlines
- Learn to recognize diminishing returns

Phase 3: Action Taking

- Start projects with explicit permission to be imperfect
- Focus on completion rather than perfection
- Celebrate progress and effort over outcomes

Phase 4: Iteration Mastery

- Develop comfort with multiple drafts and versions
- Build feedback-seeking into your process
- Learn to refine rather than restart

Phase 5: Integration

- Apply anti-perfectionist strategies consistently
- Help others overcome similar challenges
- Maintain vigilance against perfectionist relapses

Remember, the goal isn't to eliminate all standards or stop caring about quality. The goal is to develop a healthier relationship with excellence—one that allows for progress, learning, and completion. Perfectionism promises perfect results but delivers procrastination and paralysis. Progressive excellence promises continuous improvement and delivers both high-quality work and personal satisfaction.

The journey from perfectionist procrastination to productive excellence is challenging but ultimately liberating. It requires courage to be imperfect, wisdom to know when something is good enough, and faith that iteration leads to improvement. Most importantly, it requires the understanding that done is often better than perfect, and that perfect is often the enemy of good.

Chapter 6: Overwhelm and Task Avoidance

Overwhelm is one of the most common yet misunderstood causes of procrastination. When faced with tasks that seem too large, complex, or numerous, our natural response is often to avoid them entirely. This avoidance provides temporary relief but ultimately makes the situation worse, creating a vicious cycle of increasing overwhelm and decreasing action. Understanding the psychology of overwhelm and developing strategies to manage it is essential for breaking free from this paralyzing pattern.

When Tasks Feel Too Big: Breaking Down Overwhelming Projects

The human brain is remarkably capable, but it has limitations when it comes to processing complex, multi-faceted tasks. When we encounter a project that seems too large or complicated, our cognitive systems can become overloaded, triggering a stress response that makes us want to avoid the task entirely.

The Overwhelm Response

When faced with overwhelming tasks, several psychological processes occur:

- **Cognitive overload**: The brain struggles to process all the components simultaneously
- **Stress activation**: The sympathetic nervous system triggers fight-or-flight responses
- **Analysis paralysis**: Too many options or considerations prevent decision-making
- **Avoidance motivation**: The brain seeks to escape the uncomfortable feelings of overwhelm

Why Big Tasks Feel Impossible

Large projects trigger overwhelm for several reasons:

- **Lack of clear structure**: Without obvious starting points, tasks feel amorphous and unmanageable
- **Unknown variables**: Uncertainty about requirements, resources, or timelines creates anxiety
- **Multiple skill requirements**: Tasks requiring diverse abilities can feel beyond our capabilities
- **High stakes**: Important projects carry emotional weight that amplifies overwhelm
- **Time pressure**: Deadlines can make large tasks feel impossible to complete adequately

The Swiss Cheese Method Revisited

Alan Lakein's Swiss Cheese Method, mentioned in the original procrastination research, offers a powerful solution to overwhelming tasks. The method involves making random "holes" in a large project by working on whatever small piece you can tackle in the moment, regardless of sequence or logic.

How the Swiss Cheese Method Works:
- **Identify any small component** of the large task that you can complete quickly
- **Work on that component** for 5-15 minutes without worrying about the overall project
- **Repeat this process** whenever you have small pockets of time
- **Gradually create "holes"** throughout the project until it becomes manageable
- **Eventually connect the pieces** into a coherent whole

This method is particularly effective because it:
- Reduces the psychological weight of the entire project
- Creates momentum through small completions
- Provides a sense of progress and control
- Makes use of small time windows that might otherwise be wasted

The Project Breakdown Strategy

A more systematic approach to overwhelming tasks involves breaking them down into manageable components:

Level 1: Major Phases. Divide the project into 3-7 major phases or sections. Each phase should represent a significant milestone or deliverable.

Level 2: Specific Tasks. Break each phase into specific, actionable tasks. Each task should be completable in 1-4 hours of focused work.

Level 3: Next Actions. For each task, identify the very next physical action required. This should be something you can do immediately without further planning.

Example Breakdown: Project: Write a Business Plan

Phase 1: Market Research
- Task: Analyze competitor websites
- Next Action: Open browser and list top 5 competitors
- Task: Survey potential customers
- Next Action: Draft three survey questions

Phase 2: Financial Projections
- Task: Create revenue forecasts
- Next Action: Open spreadsheet software

Decision Paralysis: Too Many Choices, Too Little Action

Modern life presents us with an unprecedented number of choices, and this abundance of options can become paralyzing. When faced with too many alternatives, our decision-making systems can become overwhelmed, leading to procrastination as we attempt to avoid making the "wrong" choice.

The Paradox of Choice

Psychologist Barry Schwartz identified the "paradox of choice"—the phenomenon where having more options actually decreases satisfaction and increases anxiety. This paradox affects procrastination in several ways:

- **Analysis paralysis**: Spending excessive time evaluating options without making decisions
- **Perfectionist pressure**: Believing there's one "perfect" choice among many alternatives
- **Regret anticipation**: Fear of making the wrong choice and experiencing regret
- **Opportunity cost anxiety**: Worrying about what you'll miss by choosing one option over others

Types of Decision Paralysis

Different types of decisions create different forms of paralysis:

Option Paralysis: Too many similar choices (e.g., choosing from hundreds of potential topics for a research paper)

Priority Paralysis: Multiple important tasks competing for attention (e.g., deciding which urgent project to tackle first)

Method Paralysis: Multiple ways to approach the same task (e.g., choosing between different software tools or methodologies)

Timing Paralysis: Uncertainty about when to act (e.g., waiting for the "perfect" moment to start)

Strategies for Overcoming Decision Paralysis

- **Set decision deadlines**: Give yourself a specific time limit for making choices

- **Use satisficing instead of maximizing**: Choose the first option that meets your criteria rather than searching for the perfect choice
- **Limit options**: Artificially restrict your choices to 3-5 alternatives
- **Use decision frameworks**: Apply consistent criteria for evaluating options
- **Embrace "good enough"**: Accept that most decisions can be adjusted later if needed

Information Overload: When Research Becomes Procrastination

In the digital age, access to information is virtually unlimited. While this can be beneficial, it can also become a form of procrastination when research and planning become substitutes for action. Many procrastinators fall into the trap of endless information gathering, convincing themselves they need "just a little more research" before they can begin.

The Research Trap. Information gathering becomes procrastination when:
- **Research has no clear endpoint**: You keep looking for more information without defining what constitutes "enough"
- **Information seeking replaces action**: Reading about doing something substitutes for actually doing it
- **Perfectionist standards apply**: You believe you need to know everything before starting
- **Analysis substitutes for synthesis**: You collect information without organizing or applying it
- **Research becomes entertainment**: Information consumption becomes a form of distraction

Signs of Information Overload Procrastination
- Having dozens of bookmarked articles you "need to read"
- Constantly seeking new methods, tools, or approaches
- Feeling overwhelmed by conflicting advice or information
- Spending more time learning about a task than doing it
- Using phrases like "I just need to research this a bit more"

The 70% Rule for Information. Military strategists often use the 70% rule: when you have 70% of the information you need, it's time to act. Waiting for 100% of the information often means never acting at all, as complete information is rarely available.

Strategies for Managing Information Overload

- **Set research limits**: Define specific time limits or information quotas for research phases
- **Use the "good enough" principle**: Seek sufficient information rather than complete information
- **Focus on actionable information**: Prioritize information that directly supports your next actions
- **Create information filters**: Develop criteria for what information is truly necessary
- **Schedule regular "information fasts"**: Take breaks from consuming new information to focus on application

Energy Management: Understanding Your Natural Rhythms

Overwhelm is often exacerbated by poor energy management. When we try to tackle demanding tasks during our low-energy periods or fail to account for our natural rhythms, even manageable tasks can feel overwhelming.

The Energy-Overwhelm Connection. Energy levels affect our perception of task difficulty:

- **High energy periods**: Tasks feel more manageable and approachable
- **Low energy periods**: The same tasks can feel overwhelming and impossible
- **Energy depletion**: As energy decreases throughout the day, overwhelm increases
- **Recovery needs**: Without adequate rest, everything feels more difficult

Types of Energy.

Understanding different types of energy helps optimize task scheduling:

Physical Energy: The body's capacity for activity and movement

- Highest: Usually morning for most people
- Affected by: Sleep, nutrition, exercise, health
- Best for: Physical tasks, exercise, active work

Mental Energy: The brain's capacity for focused thinking and problem-solving

- Highest: Varies by individual (morning larks vs. night owls)
- Affected by: Sleep, stress, mental fatigue, blood sugar
- Best for: Complex analysis, creative work, decision-making

Emotional Energy: The capacity to deal with interpersonal interactions and emotional challenges

- Highest: When feeling positive and supported
- Affected by: Relationships, stress, life events, mood
- Best for: Difficult conversations, networking, collaborative work

Creative Energy: The capacity for innovation, imagination, and original thinking

- Highest: Often during relaxed, unstructured time
- Affected by: Pressure, routine, inspiration, environment
- Best for: Brainstorming, artistic work, problem-solving

Energy Audit Process

Conduct an energy audit to understand your patterns:

1. **Track energy levels** hourly for one week
2. **Note activities** that increase or decrease energy
3. Identify peak performance times for different types of work
4. Recognize energy drains and energy sources
5. **Design your schedule** around your energy patterns

Energy-Based Task Scheduling

- **Match tasks to energy**: Schedule demanding work during high-energy periods
- **Batch similar activities**: Group tasks that require similar types of energy
- **Plan recovery time**: Build in breaks and restoration activities
- **Protect peak hours**: Guard your highest-energy time for most important work
- **Use low-energy time wisely**: Handle routine tasks when energy is lower

The Power of Simplification

Simplification is one of the most powerful tools for overcoming overwhelm. By reducing complexity, eliminating non-essentials, and focusing on core elements, we can make overwhelming tasks manageable and approachable.

The Simplification Mindset. Simplification involves:

- **Identifying the essential**: What are the core elements that truly matter?
- **Eliminating the non-essential**: What can be removed without significant impact?
- **Reducing complexity**: How can processes be streamlined or simplified?
- **Focusing on fundamentals**: What are the basic building blocks of success?

Simplification Strategies

The 80/20 Analysis. Apply the Pareto Principle to identify the 20% of efforts that produce 80% of results:

- **List all components** of the overwhelming task
- **Evaluate impact**: Which components contribute most to the desired outcome?
- **Prioritize ruthlessly**: Focus on high-impact elements first
- **Eliminate or defer**: Remove or postpone low-impact components

The Minimum Viable Approach. Borrowed from startup methodology, this involves creating the simplest version that serves the core purpose:

- **Define core purpose**: What is the task really trying to accomplish?
- **Identify minimum requirements**: What's the least that must be done to achieve the purpose?
- **Create basic version**: Build the simplest functional version
- **Iterate and improve**: Add complexity only as needed

The Single Focus Principle. Instead of trying to accomplish multiple objectives simultaneously:

- Choose one primary goal for each work session
- Eliminate competing priorities during focused work time
- **Complete one thing fully** before moving to the next
- **Resist multitasking** which increases overwhelm

Environmental Simplification. Reduce overwhelm by simplifying your environment:

- **Clear physical space**: Remove clutter and distractions from work areas
- **Organize tools**: Keep necessary resources easily accessible
- **Limit options**: Reduce choices in your immediate environment
- **Create systems**: Develop simple, repeatable processes

Digital Simplification

- **Limit information sources**: Choose 2-3 primary sources for information
- **Unsubscribe ruthlessly**: Remove unnecessary emails and notifications
- **Organize files systematically**: Create simple, logical filing systems
- **Use single-purpose tools**: Choose tools that do one thing well rather than complex multi-purpose solutions

Building Overwhelm Resistance

Developing resilience to overwhelm is crucial for long-term productivity and well-being. This involves building both practical skills and psychological resources that help you handle complex situations without becoming paralyzed.

Practical Skills for Overwhelm Management

- **Project management**: Learn basic skills for organizing and tracking complex work
- **Time estimation**: Develop better ability to estimate how long tasks will take
- **Resource planning**: Understand what resources you need before starting
- **Contingency planning**: Prepare for potential obstacles and setbacks

Psychological Resources

- **Stress tolerance**: Build capacity to handle uncertainty and pressure
- **Self-efficacy**: Develop confidence in your ability to handle challenges
- **Growth mindset**: View overwhelm as a learning opportunity rather than a threat
- **Self-compassion**: Treat yourself kindly when feeling overwhelmed

The Overwhelm Recovery Protocol

When overwhelm strikes, use this systematic approach:

1. **Stop and breathe**: Take several deep breaths to activate the parasympathetic nervous system
2. **Acknowledge the feeling**: Recognize that overwhelm is a normal response to complexity
3. **Brain dump**: Write down everything that's contributing to the overwhelm
4. **Categorize and prioritize**: Group related items and identify what's most important
5. **Choose one small action**: Select the smallest possible next step
6. **Take that action**: Focus solely on completing that one small step
7. **Reassess**: After completing the action, evaluate the situation again

Building Long-Term Overwhelm Resilience

- **Regular practice**: Consistently apply overwhelm management techniques
- **Skill development**: Continuously improve your ability to handle complexity
- **Support systems**: Build relationships with people who can help during overwhelming periods
- **Self-care**: Maintain physical and emotional resources through good habits
- **Boundary setting**: Learn to say no to additional commitments when already overwhelmed

Overwhelm and task avoidance create a vicious cycle that can trap even the most capable individuals. By understanding the psychological mechanisms behind overwhelm and developing systematic approaches to manage it, you can break free from this cycle and tackle even the most complex challenges with confidence. Remember, the goal isn't to eliminate overwhelm entirely—it's to develop the skills and resilience to work effectively even when facing complex, demanding situations.

The key insight is that overwhelm is often more about perception than reality. By changing how we approach and think about complex tasks, we can transform overwhelming challenges into manageable projects. This transformation requires practice, patience, and persistence, but the payoff—in terms of both productivity and peace of mind—is immense.

The EMS Framework for Change

Chapter 7: Establish Priorities (The E in EMS)

The foundation of overcoming procrastination lies in establishing clear, meaningful priorities. Without a solid understanding of what truly matters, we become reactive rather than proactive, constantly putting out fires instead of building the life we want. The "E" in the EMS framework—Establish Priorities—is your first line of defense against the chaos that breeds procrastination.

The Time Management Matrix: Urgent vs. Important Quadrants

Stephen Covey's Time Management Matrix provides one of the most powerful frameworks for understanding and establishing priorities. This matrix divides all activities into four quadrants based on two criteria: urgency and importance.

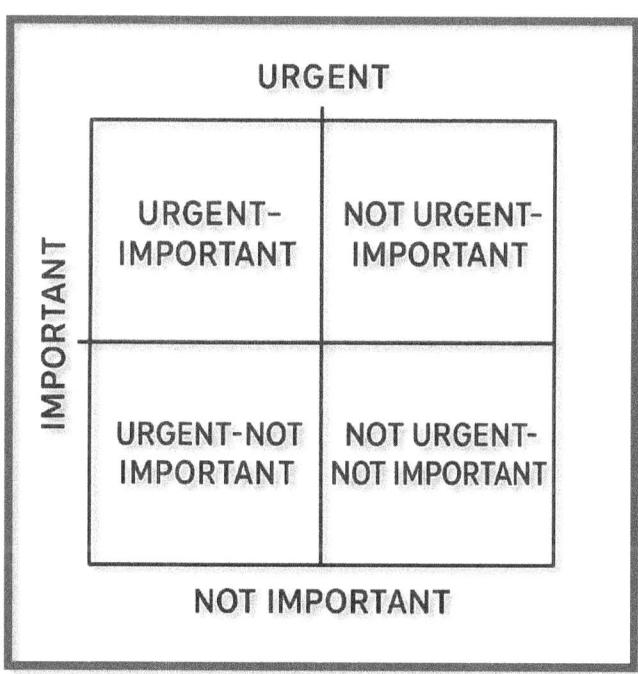

Quadrant I: Urgent and Important (Crisis Management). These are the fires that demand immediate attention:

- Medical emergencies
- Crisis situations at work
- Last-minute deadlines

- Pressing problems

While these activities are necessary, living primarily in Quadrant I leads to stress, burnout, and reactive behavior. Chronic procrastinators often find themselves trapped here, constantly dealing with crises that could have been prevented.

Quadrant II: Important but Not Urgent (Prevention and Preparation). This is where highly effective people spend most of their time:

- Planning and preparation
- Relationship building
- Personal development
- Exercise and health maintenance
- Skill development

Quadrant II activities are the key to breaking the procrastination cycle. By investing time here, you prevent many Quadrant I crises from occurring.

Quadrant III: Urgent but Not Important (Deception). These activities feel important because they're urgent, but they don't contribute to your long-term goals:

- Interruptions and distractions
- Some phone calls and emails
- Certain meetings
- Popular activities that don't align with your values

Many procrastinators mistake Quadrant III activities for priorities, staying busy but not productive.

Quadrant IV: Neither Urgent nor Important (Waste). These are time-wasters that provide no value:

- Mindless social media scrolling
- Excessive television watching
- Gossip and trivial conversations
- Addictive games or activities

Procrastinators often retreat to Quadrant IV when avoiding important tasks.

The Priority Shift Strategy. To overcome procrastination, gradually shift your time allocation:

1. **Minimize Quadrant IV**: Eliminate or drastically reduce time-wasting activities
2. **Reduce Quadrant III**: Learn to say no to urgent but unimportant demands
3. **Manage Quadrant I**: Handle crises efficiently without letting them dominate your schedule

4. **Maximize Quadrant II**: Invest heavily in prevention, preparation, and growth activities

Values-Based Priority Setting: Aligning Tasks with What Matters Most

True priorities emerge from your core values—the fundamental beliefs and principles that guide your decisions and define who you are. When your daily activities align with your values, you naturally feel more motivated and less likely to procrastinate.

Identifying Your Core Values

Complete this values clarification exercise:

Life Review: Think about moments when you felt most fulfilled and energized. What values were you honoring?

Peak Experiences: Recall times when you felt proud of your actions. What principles guided those decisions?

Values Inventory: From the following list, select your top 5-7 core values:

1. Achievement
2. Adventure
3. Authenticity
4. Balance
5. Compassion
6. Creativity
7. Excellence
8. Family
9. Freedom
10. Growth
11. Health
12. Integrity
13. Knowledge
14. Leadership
15. Security
16. Service
17. Spirituality
18. Wealth

Priority Ranking: Rank your selected values in order of importance.

The Values-Tasks Alignment Process.

Once you've identified your core values, use this process to set priorities:

1. **Task Evaluation**: For each major task or commitment, ask: "How does this align with my core values?"
2. **Values Scoring**: Rate each task on a scale of 1-10 for how well it supports your top three values.
3. **Priority Assignment**: Tasks that score highest become your top priorities.
4. **Regular Review**: Weekly, assess whether your time allocation matches your values priorities.

Example Values-Based Priority Setting. If your top three values are Family, Health, and Growth:

- **High Priority**: Family dinner time, exercise routine, professional development course
- **Medium Priority**: Networking events, home organization projects
- **Low Priority**: Optional work meetings, social media management, excessive entertainment

The 80/20 Rule Applied

Focusing on High-Impact Activities.

The Pareto Principle, commonly known as the 80/20 rule, states that 80% of results come from 20% of efforts. This principle is particularly powerful for overcoming procrastination because it helps you identify and focus on the activities that produce the greatest impact.

Identifying Your High-Impact 20%. Use these strategies to discover your most productive activities:

The Results Analysis Method

1. **Track Your Activities**: For one week, record how you spend your time in 30-minute blocks
2. **Measure Outcomes**: At the end of each day, identify which activities produced the most significant results
3. **Pattern Recognition**: Look for patterns in your high-impact activities
4. **Priority Adjustment**: Allocate more time to activities that consistently produce results

The Energy-Impact Matrix. Create a matrix with four quadrants:

- **High Energy, High Impact**: Your sweet spot—prioritize these activities
- **High Energy, Low Impact**: Enjoyable but not productive—limit these
- **Low Energy, High Impact**: Important but draining—schedule during peak energy times

- **Low Energy, Low Impact**: Eliminate or delegate these activities

Common High-Impact Activities. While everyone's 20% is different, these activities often provide disproportionate returns:

- Strategic planning and goal setting
- Skill development in your core competencies
- Building key relationships
- Automating or systematizing routine tasks
- Focusing on your most important clients or projects
- Health and energy management

The 80/20 Procrastination Breakthrough. Apply the 80/20 rule to overcome procrastination:

1. **Identify the 20% of tasks** that create 80% of your procrastination stress
2. Focus on completing these high-impact tasks first
3. **Use the momentum** from completing important tasks to tackle smaller ones
4. **Eliminate or delegate** the 80% of tasks that produce minimal results

Daily, Weekly, and Monthly Priority Systems

Effective priority management requires systems that work at different time horizons. Here's how to create integrated priority systems for maximum effectiveness.

Daily Priority System: The Rule of Three. Each morning, identify three priorities that will make the day successful:

The Three-Priority Framework

1. **One Big Priority**: The most important task that moves you toward your major goals
2. **One Relationship Priority**: An action that strengthens an important relationship
3. **One Personal Priority**: Something that maintains your health, energy, or well-being

Daily Priority Implementation

- **Morning Planning**: Spend 5-10 minutes each morning identifying your three priorities
- **Time Blocking**: Schedule specific times for each priority
- **Progress Tracking**: At day's end, assess completion and plan adjustments
- **Flexibility**: Allow for urgent matters while protecting priority time

Weekly Priority System: The Weekly Review

Conduct a weekly review every Sunday or Monday to maintain perspective and alignment:

The Weekly Review Process

Previous Week Assessment:

- What were your biggest accomplishments?

- What priorities were missed and why?
- What patterns do you notice?

Coming Week Planning:

- What are your 3-5 most important outcomes for the week?
- How do these align with your monthly and quarterly goals?
- What obstacles might you face, and how will you handle them?

Schedule Integration:

- Block time for your weekly priorities
- Identify potential conflicts and resolve them in advance
- Build in buffer time for unexpected demands

Monthly Priority System: The Strategic Focus

Monthly planning provides the strategic context for your daily and weekly priorities:

Monthly Priority Planning

1. **Goal Review**: Assess progress toward quarterly and annual goals
2. **Priority Themes**: Identify 2-3 major themes or focus areas for the month
3. **Project Planning**: Break down major projects into weekly milestones
4. **Resource Allocation**: Ensure you have the time, energy, and resources needed
5. **Accountability Setup**: Establish check-ins and accountability measures

Integration Across Time Horizons

Create alignment between your different priority systems:

- **Monthly priorities** inform weekly planning
- **Weekly priorities** guide daily choices
- **Daily actions** accumulate to achieve monthly goals
- **Regular reviews** ensure continued alignment and adjustment

Saying No Effectively: Protecting Your Priorities

One of the biggest challenges in maintaining priorities is learning to say no to requests, opportunities, and demands that don't align with your goals. Effective boundary setting is essential for overcoming procrastination because it prevents priority dilution.

The Cost of Not Saying No. When you don't protect your priorities by saying no:

- **Priority dilution**: Your attention gets scattered across too many commitments
- **Increased stress**: Overcommitment leads to overwhelm and procrastination
- **Reduced quality**: Trying to do everything means doing nothing well
- **Resentment**: Saying yes when you mean no creates internal conflict
- **Goal failure**: Important objectives get pushed aside for urgent requests

The Yes/No Decision Framework. Use this framework to make better decisions about requests and opportunities:

The Priority Filter Questions. Before saying yes to any request, ask:

1. **Alignment**: Does this align with my core values and priorities?
2. **Capacity**: Do I have the time and energy to do this well?
3. **Opportunity Cost**: What will I have to give up to say yes to this?
4. **Timing**: Is this the right time for this commitment?
5. **Uniqueness**: Am I the only person who can do this?

The POWER Method for Saying No

- **P**ause: Don't respond immediately; ask for time to consider
- **O**ffer alternatives: Suggest other solutions or people who might help
- **W**hy: Briefly explain your reasoning without over-justifying
- **E**mpathy: Acknowledge the importance of their request
- **R**ecommit: Reaffirm your commitment to your current priorities

Saying No Scripts. Practice these responses for common situations:

- **For Work Requests**: "I appreciate you thinking of me for this project. Given my current commitments to [specific priorities], I won't be able to give this the attention it deserves. Have you considered [alternative solution]?"
- **For Social Invitations**: "Thank you for the invitation. I'm focusing on [priority area] right now, so I need to pass. I hope you have a wonderful time."
- **For Volunteer Opportunities**:"This sounds like a meaningful cause. I'm currently committed to [existing priority], but I'd be happy to help you think through other people who might be interested."

The Graceful No Principles

- **Be prompt**: Respond quickly rather than avoiding the conversation
- **Be honest**: Give genuine reasons without elaborate excuses
- **Be kind**: Maintain relationships while protecting boundaries
- **Be consistent**: Apply your criteria fairly across all requests
- **Be helpful**: When possible, suggest alternatives or other resources

Building Your No Muscle. Saying no effectively is a skill that improves with practice:

1. **Start small**: Practice saying no to low-stakes requests
2. **Prepare responses**: Have standard phrases ready for common situations
3. **Review decisions**: Regularly assess whether your nos align with your priorities
4. **Celebrate boundaries**: Acknowledge when saying no protects your priorities
5. **Adjust as needed**: Refine your approach based on results and feedback

Priority Maintenance Strategies

Establishing priorities is only the beginning; maintaining them requires ongoing attention and systematic approaches.

The Priority Drift Problem

Over time, priorities naturally drift due to:

- **New opportunities** that seem attractive but don't align with goals
- **Urgent demands** that crowd out important activities
- **Changing circumstances** that require priority adjustments
- **Success** that brings new responsibilities and requests
- **Fatigue** that makes it easier to default to easier, less important tasks

Priority Maintenance Systems

Weekly Priority Reviews. Every week, spend 15-20 minutes reviewing:

- Which priorities received appropriate attention?
- What caused priority drift or distraction?
- How can you better protect your priorities next week?
- Do any priorities need adjustment based on new information?

The Priority Dashboard. Create a visual system to track priority attention:

- List your top 5 priorities
- Track daily time spent on each priority
- Use color coding (green = adequate attention, yellow = some attention, red = neglected)
- Review weekly patterns and adjust accordingly

Environmental Design for Priorities

Structure your environment to support your priorities:

- **Physical space**: Organize your workspace to facilitate priority work
- **Digital environment**: Set up systems and tools that support your priorities
- **Social environment**: Surround yourself with people who support your goals
- **Temporal environment**: Schedule your day to protect priority time

The Priority Protection Protocol

When facing requests or opportunities that might derail your priorities:

1. **Pause**: Don't decide immediately
2. **Assess**: Use your priority filter questions
3. **Consult**: If uncertain, discuss with a trusted advisor
4. **Decide**: Make a clear yes or no decision

5. **Communicate**: Respond promptly and clearly
6. **Follow through**: Honor your decision consistently

Establishing priorities is the cornerstone of overcoming procrastination. When you know what truly matters and have systems to protect and maintain those priorities, you create a foundation for consistent action and meaningful progress. The clarity that comes from well-established priorities eliminates much of the confusion and overwhelm that fuel procrastination, replacing them with focus, direction, and motivation.

Remember, priorities aren't just about what you choose to do—they're equally about what you choose not to do. The power to say no to good opportunities in service of great ones is what separates those who overcome procrastination from those who remain trapped by it.

Chapter 8: Manage Time (The M in EMS)

Time management is not about managing time itself—time moves at a constant rate regardless of what we do. Instead, it's about managing ourselves within time, making conscious choices about how we allocate our most precious and finite resource. For procrastinators, poor time management often stems from a lack of awareness about where time actually goes and unrealistic expectations about how long tasks will take.

Time Audit Techniques: Understanding Where Your Time Actually Goes

The first step in effective time management is developing an accurate understanding of how you currently spend your time. Most people have significant blind spots about their time usage, which contributes to procrastination and poor planning.

The Time Tracking Foundation

Before you can improve your time management, you need data. Time tracking reveals:

- **Time leaks**: Small activities that consume more time than you realize
- **Energy patterns**: When you're most and least productive
- **Distraction sources**: What pulls you away from important tasks
- **Realistic baselines**: How long tasks actually take versus estimates
- **Priority alignment**: Whether your time allocation matches your stated priorities

The Seven-Day Time Audit

Conduct a comprehensive time audit using this systematic approach:

Week 1: Baseline Tracking. For seven consecutive days, track your time in 15-30 minute increments:

- **Record everything**: Work, personal activities, meals, breaks, transitions
- **Be specific**: Instead of "work," write "email," "meeting," or "project X"
- **Note energy levels**: Rate your energy from 1-10 for each time block
- **Track interruptions**: Record what interrupted you and for how long
- **Include transitions**: Account for time spent switching between activities

Time Tracking Tools. Choose a method that you'll actually use consistently:

- **Digital apps**: RescueTime, Toggl, or smartphone time tracking features
- **Spreadsheets**: Simple, customizable, and easy to analyze
- **Paper logs**: Portable and don't require technology
- **Hybrid approach**: Digital for automatic tracking, manual for detailed analysis

Time Audit Analysis Framework. After collecting one week of data, analyze your findings:

Time Allocation Analysis

Category Totals: How much time did you spend on:

- Work/career activities
- Personal/family time
- Health and self-care
- Learning and development
- Entertainment and leisure
- Administrative tasks

Priority Alignment: Compare time spent with stated priorities:

- Do your time allocations match your values?
- Which priorities received inadequate attention?
- What activities consumed time without providing value?

Efficiency Patterns: Identify:

- Your most productive hours
- Times when you're prone to distraction
- Activities that energize versus drain you
- Optimal work session lengths

The Time Leak Investigation

Focus on identifying and quantifying time leaks:

Common Time Leaks

- **Social media and web browsing**: Often underestimated by 200-300%
- **Email and messaging**: Frequent checking creates constant interruption
- **Meetings**: Many meetings are longer than necessary or poorly focused
- **Commuting and transitions**: Dead time that could be optimized
- **Decision-making**: Spending too long on minor decisions
- **Searching and organizing**: Time lost due to poor systems

Time Leak Calculation

For each identified time leak:

1. **Daily impact**: How many minutes per day does this leak consume?
2. **Weekly total**: Multiply daily impact by 7
3. **Annual projection**: Multiply weekly total by 52
4. **Opportunity cost**: What could you accomplish with this reclaimed time?

Example Time Leak Analysis

Social media checking:

- Daily impact: 20 minutes (often underestimated)

- Weekly total: 140 minutes (2.3 hours)
- Annual projection: 121 hours (3 full work weeks)
- Opportunity cost: Complete a significant course, write a book, or develop a new skill

The Pomodoro Technique and Time Blocking

Two of the most effective time management techniques for overcoming procrastination are the Pomodoro Technique and time blocking. Both create structure that makes it easier to start and maintain focus on important tasks.

The Pomodoro Technique: Focused Work Sessions. Developed by Francesco Cirillo, the Pomodoro Technique uses timed work sessions to improve focus and reduce procrastination.

Basic Pomodoro Process

1. Choose a task to work on
2. **Set a timer** for 25 minutes
3. **Work on the task** until the timer rings
4. Take a short break (5 minutes)
5. Repeat the cycle 3-4 times
6. Take a longer break (15-30 minutes)

Why Pomodoros Work for Procrastinators

- **Reduces overwhelm**: 25 minutes feels manageable for any task
- **Creates urgency**: The timer provides gentle pressure to stay focused
- **Builds momentum**: Completing one Pomodoro makes starting the next easier
- **Prevents burnout**: Regular breaks maintain energy and focus
- **Provides data**: You can track how many Pomodoros different tasks require

Advanced Pomodoro Strategies

Task-Specific Timing. Adjust Pomodoro length based on task type:

- **Creative work**: 45-90 minutes for deep creative flow
- **Administrative tasks**: 15-25 minutes for routine activities
- **Learning**: 25-50 minutes depending on complexity
- **Planning**: 15-30 minutes for focused planning sessions

The Pomodoro Planning Method

1. **Daily planning**: Estimate how many Pomodoros each task will require
2. **Priority sequencing**: Tackle high-priority tasks during peak energy Pomodoros
3. **Buffer Pomodoros**: Include extra Pomodoros for unexpected tasks or overruns
4. **Review and adjust**: Track actual versus estimated Pomodoros to improve planning

Pomodoro Troubleshooting

Common challenges and solutions:

- **Interruptions**: Note interruptions but return to the current Pomodoro
- **Task completion**: If you finish early, use remaining time for review or preparation
- **Resistance**: Start with shorter intervals (10-15 minutes) if 25 feels overwhelming
- **Flow states**: If you're in deep flow when the timer rings, consider extending the session

Time Blocking: Strategic Schedule Design

Time blocking involves scheduling specific time periods for different types of activities, creating a structured approach to time management that prevents procrastination.

Time Blocking Fundamentals

1. **Block similar activities**: Group related tasks together
2. **Protect deep work time**: Schedule uninterrupted blocks for important work
3. **Include buffer time**: Add extra time between blocks for transitions
4. **Plan breaks**: Schedule rest and renewal activities
5. **Review and adjust**: Regularly refine your time blocking approach

Types of Time Blocks

Deep Work Blocks

- **Duration**: 90-180 minutes
- **Purpose**: Complex, high-concentration tasks
- **Protection**: No interruptions, notifications off
- **Timing**: During your peak energy hours
- **Examples**: Writing, strategic planning, complex problem-solving

Administrative Blocks

- **Duration**: 30-60 minutes
- **Purpose**: Routine tasks that require less concentration
- **Batching**: Group similar activities together
- **Timing**: During lower energy periods
- **Examples**: Email, scheduling, filing, routine communications

Communication Blocks

- **Duration**: 60-120 minutes
- **Purpose**: Meetings, calls, and collaborative work
- **Scheduling**: Cluster meetings to minimize context switching
- **Preparation**: Include prep time before and follow-up time after

- **Examples**: Team meetings, client calls, one-on-ones

Learning Blocks

- **Duration**: 45-90 minutes
- **Purpose**: Skill development and knowledge acquisition
- **Consistency**: Regular, recurring blocks work best
- **Environment**: Distraction-free learning environment
- **Examples**: Reading, online courses, skill practice

The Weekly Time Blocking Process

1. **Sunday planning**: Design your weekly time block schedule
2. **Daily adjustments**: Make minor tweaks based on changing priorities
3. **Block protection**: Treat time blocks as important appointments
4. **Transition rituals**: Develop routines for moving between different types of blocks
5. **Weekly review**: Assess what worked and what needs adjustment

Energy-Based Scheduling

Matching Tasks to Your Natural Energy Cycles. Traditional time management focuses on hours and minutes, but energy management recognizes that not all hours are created equal. Your capacity for different types of work varies throughout the day based on natural biological rhythms.

Understanding Your Chronotype

Your chronotype determines your natural energy patterns:

Morning Larks (25% of population)

- **Peak energy**: 6 AM - 10 AM
- **Good energy**: 10 AM - 2 PM
- **Declining energy**: 2 PM - 6 PM
- **Low energy**: 6 PM - 10 PM

Night Owls (25% of population)

- **Low energy**: 6 AM - 10 AM
- **Building energy:** 10 AM - 2 PM
- **Good energy**: 2 PM - 6 PM
- **Peak energy**: 6 PM - 10 PM

Third Birds (50% of population)

- **Moderate energy**: 6 AM - 10 AM
- **Peak energy**: 10 AM - 2 PM
- **Good energy**: 2 PM - 6 PM

- **Declining energy:** 6 PM - 10 PM

Identifying Your Personal Energy Patterns

Track your energy levels for two weeks:

1. **Hourly ratings**: Rate your energy from 1-10 every hour you're awake
2. **Activity correlation**: Note what activities increase or decrease your energy
3. **Pattern recognition**: Look for consistent patterns across days
4. **External factors**: Consider how sleep, food, and exercise affect your patterns

Energy-Task Matching Strategy

Align different types of tasks with appropriate energy levels:

High Energy Tasks *(Your peak 2-3 hours)*

- Complex problem-solving
- Creative work
- Important decision-making
- Challenging conversations
- Learning new skills

Medium Energy Tasks *(Your good energy hours)*

- Routine work that requires focus
- Planning and organizing
- Regular meetings
- Administrative tasks requiring accuracy

Low Energy Tasks *(Your declining energy hours)*

- Email and routine communication
- Filing and organizing
- Simple, repetitive tasks
- Research and information gathering
- Planning for the next day

Energy Management Strategies

Energy Protection

- **Guard peak hours**: Never waste high-energy time on low-value activities
- **Minimize energy drains**: Identify and reduce activities that deplete you unnecessarily
- **Energy boundaries**: Protect your best hours from interruptions and meetings
- **Recovery planning**: Schedule restoration activities after energy-intensive work

Energy Optimization

- **Ultradian rhythms**: Work with natural 90-120 minute cycles of alertness

- **Strategic breaks**: Take breaks before energy crashes, not after
- **Environment design**: Optimize lighting, temperature, and space for energy
- **Nutrition timing**: Eat to support stable energy throughout the day

The Energy-Based Weekly Schedule

Design your weekly schedule around energy optimization:

Monday: Often lower energy due to weekend transition

- Schedule routine tasks and planning
- Avoid scheduling the most challenging work
- Use the day to build momentum for the week

Tuesday-Thursday: Typically peak energy days

- Schedule your most important and challenging work
- Block time for deep work and complex projects
- Handle difficult conversations and decisions

Friday: Often declining energy as the week progresses

- Focus on completion and wrap-up activities
- Schedule lighter, more social activities
- Plan and prepare for the following week

Eliminating Time Wasters: Social Media, Unnecessary Meetings, and Distractions

Time wasters are activities that consume time without providing proportional value. For procrastinators, time wasters often serve as escape mechanisms from important but challenging tasks.

The Time Waster Audit

Identify your personal time wasters using your time tracking data:

Digital Time Wasters

- **Social media**: Scrolling, commenting, sharing
- **News consumption**: Excessive reading of news and opinion pieces
- **Entertainment**: Streaming, gaming, YouTube rabbit holes
- **Email**: Constant checking and unnecessary correspondence
- **Web browsing**: Aimless surfing and information consumption

Social Time Wasters

- **Gossip and small talk**: Conversations that don't build relationships or provide value
- **Unnecessary meetings**: Meetings without clear agendas or outcomes

- **Social obligations**: Events attended out of obligation rather than genuine interest
- **Interruptions**: Allowing others to derail your focus unnecessarily

Mental Time Wasters

- **Overthinking**: Spending excessive time on decisions that don't warrant it
- **Perfectionism**: Polishing work beyond the point of diminishing returns
- **Worry**: Mental energy spent on things outside your control
- **Regret**: Dwelling on past mistakes instead of learning and moving forward

Strategic Time Waster Elimination

The 80/20 Elimination Process

1. List all time wasters from your audit
2. **Calculate total time** spent on each per week
3. **Identify the 20%** that consume 80% of your wasted time
4. **Focus elimination efforts** on the biggest time wasters first
5. Implement specific strategies for each major time waster

Social Media Management

- **Time limits**: Use app timers to limit daily usage
- **Scheduled checking**: Check social media only at predetermined times
- **Notification management**: Turn off all non-essential notifications
- **Purpose-driven usage**: Define specific purposes for social media use
- **Alternative activities**: Replace social media time with more valuable activities

Meeting Optimization

- **Meeting audit**: Question the necessity of every recurring meeting
- **Agenda requirements**: Attend only meetings with clear agendas and objectives
- **Time limits**: Advocate for shorter, more focused meetings
- **Alternative formats**: Suggest emails or brief calls instead of full meetings
- **Preparation standards**: Come prepared to make meetings more efficient

Distraction Management

- **Environment design**: Create physical spaces that minimize distractions
- **Technology boundaries**: Use website blockers and app restrictions during focused work
- **Communication protocols**: Establish specific times for checking and responding to messages
- **Interruption handling**: Develop polite but firm ways to defer non-urgent interruptions
- **Focus rituals**: Create routines that signal the start of focused work time

Creating Productive Environments

Your environment significantly influences your ability to manage time effectively and avoid procrastination. A well-designed environment makes productive behavior easier and procrastination harder.

Physical Environment Design

Workspace Optimization

- **Dedicated space**: Have a specific area designated for focused work
- **Minimal distractions**: Remove or minimize visual and auditory distractions
- **Ergonomic setup**: Ensure comfort to maintain focus for extended periods
- **Tool accessibility**: Keep necessary tools and resources easily accessible
- **Inspiration elements**: Include items that motivate and inspire you

Environmental Psychology Principles

- **Lighting**: Natural light improves alertness and mood
- **Temperature**: Slightly cool temperatures (68-72°F) optimize cognitive performance
- **Color**: Blue and green promote focus, while red can increase urgency
- **Sound**: Consider background noise preferences (silence, white noise, or instrumental music)
- **Plants**: Indoor plants can improve air quality and reduce stress

Digital Environment Design

Computer and Device Setup

- **Desktop organization**: Keep digital desktops clean and organized
- **Bookmark management**: Organize bookmarks for quick access to important resources
- **App organization**: Arrange apps to support productive behaviors
- **Notification settings**: Turn off all non-essential notifications during work time
- **Distraction blocking**: Use software to block distracting websites during focused work

Information Management Systems

- **File organization**: Create logical, consistent filing systems
- **Cloud storage**: Use cloud services for easy access across devices
- **Task management**: Implement digital systems for tracking tasks and projects
- **Calendar integration**: Sync calendars across all devices and platforms
- **Backup systems**: Ensure important information is backed up and accessible

Social Environment Design

Boundary Setting

- **Communication expectations**: Establish clear expectations about availability and response times
- **Interruption protocols**: Train others on when and how to interrupt you appropriately
- **Support network**: Surround yourself with people who support your productivity goals
- **Accountability partners**: Work with others who can help you stay on track
- **Professional relationships**: Cultivate relationships that enhance rather than drain your productivity

Time Blocking for Environment Transitions

- **Setup time**: Include time for preparing your environment before focused work
- **Cleanup time**: Schedule time for organizing and preparing for the next session
- **Transition rituals**: Develop routines for moving between different types of work
- **Environment switching**: Use different environments for different types of activities

Time management is ultimately about making conscious choices about how you spend your finite time and energy. By conducting regular time audits, implementing structured techniques like Pomodoros and time blocking, aligning tasks with your natural energy patterns, eliminating time wasters, and creating supportive environments, you build a comprehensive system that supports consistent action and reduces procrastination.

Remember that effective time management isn't about perfection—it's about progress. Start with one or two techniques that resonate with you, implement them consistently, and gradually build a more comprehensive time management system. The goal is to create sustainable habits that support your priorities and help you take consistent action toward your most important goals.

Chapter 9: Set Goals (The S in EMS)

Goal setting is the final component of the EMS framework, but it's far from the least important. Without clear, compelling goals, even the best priorities and time management systems lack direction and motivation. For procrastinators, vague or overwhelming goals often contribute to avoidance and delay. This chapter will teach you how to set goals that inspire action rather than paralysis.

BRILLIANT Goal Setting

Bull's-eye Specific, Realistic, Inherently Measurable Goals

The original procrastination document introduced the BRILLIANT goal-setting framework, which provides a comprehensive approach to creating goals that overcome the common pitfalls that lead to procrastination.

B - Bull's-eye Specific

Vague goals create procrastination because they don't provide clear direction for action. Bull's-eye specific goals hit the center of the target with precision.

Vague Goal Examples:
- "Get in better shape"
- "Improve my career"
- "Be more organized"
- "Learn something new"

Bull's-eye Specific Examples:
- "Run a 5K race in under 30 minutes by June 15th"
- "Earn a promotion to Senior Manager in my current company by December 31st"
- "Implement a daily filing system and clear all paper clutter from my desk by March 1st"
- "Complete a 40-hour online course in data analysis and earn the certificate by August 30th"

The Specificity Test. Your goal passes the specificity test if:
- A stranger could understand exactly what you want to achieve
- You can visualize the specific end result
- You know exactly what the first step should be
- There's no ambiguity about what "done" looks like

R – Realistic

Unrealistic goals create procrastination because they feel impossible, leading to avoidance and eventual abandonment. Realistic goals stretch you without breaking you.

Realistic vs. Easy. Realistic doesn't mean easy—it means achievable with effort and commitment. Consider:

- **Your current situation**: What resources, skills, and time do you actually have?
- **Your track record**: What have you successfully accomplished in the past?
- **External constraints**: What limitations do you need to work within?
- **Growth potential**: How much can you reasonably expect to improve?

The Goldilocks Principle. Your goals should be "just right":

- **Too easy**: Won't motivate you or create meaningful progress
- **Too hard**: Will overwhelm you and trigger procrastination
- **Just right**: Challenging enough to be meaningful, achievable enough to maintain motivation

I - Inherently Measurable

Measurable goals provide clear feedback on progress, which is essential for maintaining motivation and overcoming procrastination.

Quantitative Measures

- Numbers: "Increase sales by 25%"
- Time: "Complete the project in 6 weeks"
- Frequency: "Exercise 4 times per week"
- Percentages: "Improve test scores by 15%"

Qualitative Measures

- Completion: "Finish writing the first draft"
- Achievement: "Earn the certification"
- Implementation: "Launch the new system"
- Mastery: "Demonstrate proficiency in the skill"

L – Legitimate

Legitimate goals align with your values, priorities, and authentic desires. Goals imposed by others or based on "shoulds" often trigger resistance and procrastination.

The Legitimacy Check

Ask yourself:

- **Why do I want this?** Is the motivation internal or external?

- **Does this align with my values?** Will achieving this goal honor what's important to me?
- **Is this my goal or someone else's?** Am I pursuing this for myself or to please others?
- **Will I be proud of achieving this?** Does this goal represent something meaningful to me?

L - Logical

Logical goals make sense within the context of your life, resources, and other commitments. Illogical goals create internal conflict and procrastination.

Logic Assessment

- **Sequence**: Does this goal follow logically from your current situation?
- **Resources**: Do you have or can you obtain the necessary resources?
- **Timing**: Does the timeline make sense given your other commitments?
- **Dependencies**: Are there prerequisite goals that need to be achieved first?

I - Impeccably Clear

Clear goals eliminate confusion and decision paralysis. Every aspect of the goal should be crystal clear.

Clarity Components

- **Outcome**: Exactly what will be achieved
- **Timeline**: When it will be completed
- **Standards**: What constitutes success
- **Context**: Where and how it will be accomplished
- **Resources**: What will be needed to achieve it

A - Action-Oriented

Action-oriented goals focus on what you will do, not just what you want to have or be. This orientation naturally leads to implementation.

Action vs. Outcome Focus

- **Outcome-focused**: "Lose 20 pounds"
- **Action-focused**: "Follow a structured meal plan and exercise routine for 12 weeks"
- **Outcome-focused**: "Get promoted"
- **Action-focused**: "Complete leadership training and take on two high-visibility projects"

N – Noteworthy

Noteworthy goals are significant enough to justify the effort required and create lasting satisfaction when achieved.

The Significance Test

- **Impact**: Will achieving this goal make a meaningful difference in your life?
- **Growth**: Will pursuing this goal help you develop as a person?
- **Legacy**: Will you be glad you achieved this goal five years from now?
- **Effort justification**: Is the potential reward worth the required effort?

T - Time-Based

Time-based goals create urgency and prevent indefinite postponement. Deadlines activate our natural tendency to complete tasks as deadlines approach.

Effective Deadline Setting

- **Specific dates**: Use exact dates, not vague timeframes
- **Realistic timelines**: Allow adequate time without being too generous
- **Milestone deadlines**: Break longer goals into shorter deadline segments
- **Buffer time**: Include some extra time for unexpected challenges
- **External accountability**: Share deadlines with others when possible

Breaking Down Large Goals: The Swiss Cheese Method

Large goals often trigger procrastination because they feel overwhelming and unclear. The Swiss Cheese Method, mentioned in the original procrastination research, provides a powerful approach to making progress on large goals without feeling overwhelmed.

Understanding the Swiss Cheese Method

The Swiss Cheese Method involves making random "holes" in a large project by working on whatever small piece you can tackle in the moment, regardless of sequence or logic. Like making holes in Swiss cheese, you gradually work through the project until it becomes manageable.

Why the Swiss Cheese Method Works

- **Reduces overwhelm**: You only focus on small, manageable pieces
- **Creates momentum**: Each small completion builds confidence and energy
- **Provides flexibility**: You can work on whatever piece feels most accessible
- **Reveals structure**: As you create holes, the overall structure becomes clearer
- **Builds familiarity**: Regular contact with the project reduces anxiety and avoidance

Implementing the Swiss Cheese Method

Step 1: Project Mapping. Create a rough map of your large goal:

- **List major components**: What are the main parts of this goal?
- **Identify small tasks**: What small actions could you take within each component?
- **Note dependencies**: Which tasks must be completed before others can begin?
- **Estimate time**: How long might each small task take?

Step 2: Hole-Making Sessions. Schedule regular "hole-making" sessions:

- **Frequency**: Daily 15-30 minute sessions work well
- **Flexibility**: Work on whatever piece feels most accessible that day
- **No pressure**: Don't worry about perfect sequence or completion
- **Progress tracking**: Keep a simple record of holes made

Step 3: Pattern Recognition. As you make holes, patterns will emerge:

- **Natural sequences**: Some tasks will naturally follow others
- **Skill requirements**: You'll identify what skills or resources you need
- **Time estimates**: You'll get better at estimating how long tasks take
- **Motivation patterns**: You'll discover what types of tasks energize or drain you

Step 4: Strategic Assembly. Eventually, begin connecting the holes:

- **Link related tasks**: Connect tasks that naturally flow together
- **Fill remaining gaps**: Identify and complete missing pieces
- **Polish and refine**: Improve the quality of completed sections
- **Final integration**: Bring all pieces together into the completed goal

Swiss Cheese Method Examples

Writing a Book. Instead of trying to write from beginning to end:

- Write random scenes or chapters that interest you
- Research topics as they occur to you
- Develop character profiles when inspired
- Create outlines for different sections
- Write dialogue snippets
- Gradually connect and organize the pieces

Starting a Business. Rather than following a linear business plan:

- Research one aspect of your market
- Design a simple logo or business card
- Write one section of your business plan
- Interview one potential customer

- Research one competitor
- Test one small aspect of your product or service

Home Organization Project. Instead of trying to organize everything at once:

- Sort through one drawer
- Organize one shelf
- Create a filing system for one category of papers
- Declutter one small area
- Research organization solutions for one room
- Gradually expand and connect organized areas

Milestone Creation: Celebrating Progress Along the Way

Long-term goals can feel abstract and distant, making it easy to procrastinate. Creating meaningful milestones breaks large goals into smaller, more immediate targets that provide regular opportunities for progress and celebration.

The Psychology of Milestones

Milestones work because they:

- **Create urgency**: Shorter deadlines feel more immediate and actionable
- **Provide feedback**: Regular check-ins show whether you're on track
- **Build momentum**: Achieving milestones creates positive reinforcement
- **Enable adjustment**: You can modify your approach based on milestone results
- **Maintain motivation**: Regular progress prevents discouragement and abandonment

Milestone Design Principles

The 25% Rule

Create milestones at roughly 25% intervals of your goal:

- **25% milestone**: Early progress that builds confidence
- **50% milestone**: Midpoint assessment and potential course correction
- **75% milestone**: Final push motivation as the end comes into view
- **100% milestone**: Goal completion and celebration

SMART Milestone Criteria

Each milestone should be:

- **Specific**: Clear about what will be accomplished
- **Measurable**: Quantifiable progress indicators
- **Achievable**: Realistic given the timeframe
- **Relevant**: Meaningful progress toward the larger goal

- **Time-bound**: Specific deadline for completion

Milestone Types

Progress Milestones

Measure advancement toward the final goal:

- "Complete 25% of required coursework"
- "Lose first 5 pounds of 20-pound goal"
- "Save $2,500 of $10,000 target"
- "Write 25 pages of 100-page document"

Skill Milestones

Mark development of necessary capabilities:

- "Master basic techniques before advancing"
- "Complete foundational training module"
- "Demonstrate proficiency in core skills"
- "Pass prerequisite certification exam"

System Milestones

Establish supporting structures and processes:

- "Implement daily practice routine"
- "Set up tracking and measurement system"
- "Create accountability partnership"
- "Establish workspace and tools"

Milestone Celebration Strategy

Celebrating milestones is crucial for maintaining motivation:

Celebration Principles

- **Proportional rewards**: Match celebration size to milestone significance
- **Immediate recognition**: Celebrate as soon as possible after achievement
- **Personal meaning**: Choose rewards that are personally meaningful
- **Shared celebration**: Include others who support your goals
- **Forward momentum**: Use celebration to build energy for the next milestone

Celebration Ideas by Milestone Size

Small Milestones (Weekly progress)

- Special meal or treat
- Favorite activity or hobby time
- Small purchase you've been wanting
- Extra leisure time

- Sharing progress with a friend

Medium Milestones (Monthly progress)

- Day trip or special outing
- Meaningful purchase related to your goal
- Celebration dinner with family or friends
- Weekend getaway
- Professional development opportunity

Major Milestones (Quarterly progress)

- Vacation or extended break
- Significant purchase or investment
- Public recognition or announcement
- Professional celebration or networking event
- Major experience or adventure

Accountability Systems

External Support for Internal Motivation

Accountability systems provide external structure and support that help overcome the internal resistance that leads to procrastination. When you know others are tracking your progress, you're more likely to follow through on commitments.

Types of Accountability Systems

Accountability Partners. Work with one other person who shares similar goals or commitment to growth:

Partner Selection Criteria

- **Reliability**: Someone who will consistently follow through
- **Honesty**: Willing to provide honest feedback and gentle confrontation
- **Support**: Genuinely wants to see you succeed
- **Availability**: Has time for regular check-ins
- **Complementary goals**: Working on similar or related objectives

Accountability Partnership Structure

- **Regular meetings**: Weekly or bi-weekly check-ins
- **Progress reporting**: Share specific progress on goals
- **Challenge discussion**: Talk through obstacles and setbacks
- **Strategy brainstorming**: Help each other problem-solve
- **Celebration sharing**: Acknowledge and celebrate successes

Accountability Groups

Work with a small group (3-5 people) focused on goal achievement:

Group Benefits

- **Diverse perspectives**: Multiple viewpoints on challenges and solutions
- **Peer learning**: Learn from others' experiences and strategies
- **Social support**: Encouragement from multiple sources
- **Healthy competition**: Motivation from seeing others' progress
- **Shared resources**: Access to group knowledge and connections

Group Structure

- **Regular meetings**: Monthly or bi-weekly group sessions
- **Individual updates**: Each person reports on progress and challenges
- **Group problem-solving**: Collective brainstorming on obstacles
- **Resource sharing**: Exchange helpful tools, techniques, and contacts
- **Group celebrations**: Acknowledge individual and collective achievements

Professional Accountability

Work with coaches, mentors, or consultants who specialize in accountability:

Professional Benefits

- **Expertise**: Specialized knowledge in goal achievement and behavior change
- **Objectivity**: Neutral perspective without personal relationships complications
- **Structure**: Systematic approaches and proven methodologies
- **Availability**: Dedicated time and attention to your goals
- **Results focus**: Professional commitment to helping you achieve outcomes

Digital Accountability Systems

Use technology to create accountability structures:

Apps and Platforms

- **Goal tracking apps**: Visual progress tracking and reminder systems
- **Social accountability**: Share goals and progress on social platforms
- **Habit tracking**: Daily tracking of goal-supporting behaviors
- **Calendar integration**: Automated reminders and scheduling
- **Progress photography**: Visual documentation of progress over time

Public Accountability

Make your goals public to create social pressure for follow-through:

- **Social media announcements**: Share goals and regular progress updates
- **Blog or vlog documentation**: Create content about your goal journey
- **Community involvement**: Join groups related to your goals
- **Professional networking**: Share goals within professional circles
- **Family and friends**: Involve your personal network in your goal pursuit

Accountability System Design

Create a comprehensive accountability system:

System Components

1. **Primary accountability**: Choose your main accountability source (partner, group, or professional)
2. **Secondary support**: Add additional accountability layers for reinforcement
3. **Progress tracking**: Implement systems for measuring and recording progress
4. **Regular reporting**: Establish consistent communication about progress
5. **Consequence structure**: Create meaningful consequences for not following through

Accountability Agreements

Formalize your accountability relationships:

Agreement Elements

- **Goal specification**: Clearly defined goals and milestones
- **Meeting schedule**: Regular check-in times and formats
- **Progress metrics**: How progress will be measured and reported
- **Support expectations**: What kind of support each party will provide
- **Consequence agreements**: What happens if commitments aren't met
- **Celebration plans**: How successes will be acknowledged

Goal Adjustment: When and How to Modify Objectives

Goals are not set in stone. As circumstances change and you learn more about yourself and your objectives, goal adjustment becomes necessary. The key is knowing when and how to modify goals without abandoning them entirely.

When to Adjust Goals

Legitimate Reasons for Goal Adjustment

- **Changed circumstances**: Significant life changes that affect goal relevance or feasibility
- **New information**: Learning something that changes your understanding of the goal

- **Resource changes**: Significant changes in available time, money, or support
- **Priority shifts**: Changes in values or life priorities that affect goal importance
- **Skill development**: Discovering you're capable of more (or less) than originally thought

Warning Signs of Necessary Adjustment

- **Consistent failure**: Repeatedly missing milestones despite good effort
- **Loss of motivation**: Goal no longer feels meaningful or exciting
- **Overwhelming stress**: Goal pursuit is causing unsustainable stress or harm
- **Conflicting priorities**: Goal conflicts with other important life areas
- **Changed relevance**: Goal no longer serves your current life situation

Illegitimate Reasons for Goal Adjustment

Distinguish between necessary adjustments and procrastination-driven abandonment:

- **Temporary setbacks**: Short-term obstacles that can be overcome
- **Fear-based resistance**: Anxiety about success or failure
- **Perfectionist standards**: Unrealistic expectations about the process
- **Comparison discouragement**: Feeling behind compared to others
- **Impatience**: Wanting results faster than realistic timelines allow

How to Adjust Goals Effectively

The Goal Review Process

1. **Honest assessment**: Objectively evaluate your current situation and progress
2. **Root cause analysis**: Identify why adjustment seems necessary
3. **Option exploration**: Consider different ways to modify the goal
4. **Stakeholder consultation**: Discuss with accountability partners or advisors
5. **Decision and commitment**: Make a clear decision and recommit to the adjusted goal

Types of Goal Adjustments

Timeline Adjustments

- **Extension**: Give yourself more time to achieve the goal
- **Acceleration**: Speed up the timeline if you're ahead of schedule
- **Milestone redistribution**: Adjust milestone timing while keeping the end date
- **Seasonal adjustments**: Align timeline with natural cycles or life rhythms

Scope Adjustments

- **Scaling up**: Increase the goal if you're exceeding expectations
- **Scaling down**: Reduce the scope to match realistic capacity

- **Focus narrowing**: Concentrate on the most important aspects
- **Breadth expansion**: Add related objectives that support the main goal

Method Adjustments

- **Strategy changes**: Modify your approach while keeping the same outcome
- **Resource reallocation**: Change how you use time, money, or energy
- **Support system changes**: Adjust accountability or help systems
- **Skill development**: Add learning objectives to support goal achievement

Standards Adjustments

- **Quality standards**: Adjust expectations about perfection or excellence
- **Success criteria**: Modify what constitutes successful completion
- **Measurement methods**: Change how you track and evaluate progress
- **Celebration thresholds**: Adjust when and how you acknowledge progress

Goal Adjustment Best Practices

Documentation

- **Record changes**: Keep a written record of goal adjustments and reasons
- **Version control**: Maintain clarity about current versus previous goal versions
- **Learning capture**: Document what you learned that led to the adjustment
- **Pattern recognition**: Look for patterns in your goal adjustment needs

Communication

- **Stakeholder updates**: Inform accountability partners about goal changes
- **Reasoning explanation**: Share why adjustments were necessary
- **Renewed commitment**: Clearly commit to the adjusted goal
- **Support requests**: Ask for help with the modified objectives

Recommitment Process

After adjusting a goal:

1. **Rewrite the goal**: Create a new, clear statement of the adjusted goal
2. **Update systems**: Modify tracking, accountability, and support systems
3. **Renewed visualization**: Imagine achieving the adjusted goal
4. **Fresh start mentality**: Approach the adjusted goal with renewed energy
5. **Learning integration**: Apply lessons learned to improve your approach

Setting effective goals is both an art and a science. The BRILLIANT framework provides a systematic approach to creating goals that inspire action rather than procrastination. By breaking large goals into manageable pieces using methods like the Swiss Cheese approach, creating meaningful milestones, establishing accountability systems, and knowing when and how to adjust goals, you create a comprehensive goal-setting system that supports consistent progress.

Remember that goals are tools for growth and achievement, not rigid contracts that can't be modified. The key is to maintain the balance between commitment and flexibility, staying true to your deeper purposes while adapting to changing circumstances and new learning. When your goals are clear, compelling, and supported by effective systems, they become powerful antidotes to procrastination and catalysts for meaningful achievement.

Context-Specific Solutions

Chapter 10: Conquering Home Procrastination

Home procrastination presents unique challenges that differ significantly from workplace or academic procrastination. The home environment, while offering comfort and relaxation, can become a procrastination trap filled with distractions, competing priorities, and the absence of external accountability structures. Understanding and addressing these specific challenges is essential for creating a productive and fulfilling home life.

The Home Environment Challenge: Distractions and Comfort Zones

The home environment creates a perfect storm for procrastination through several interconnected factors that make it particularly challenging to maintain focus and motivation on important tasks.

The Comfort Paradox

While comfort is generally positive, it can become counterproductive when it comes to tackling challenging or unpleasant tasks. The home environment signals relaxation and leisure to our brains, making it difficult to shift into productive work mode. This comfort paradox manifests in several ways:

- **Physical comfort**: Soft furniture, familiar surroundings, and casual dress can reduce alertness and motivation
- **Psychological comfort**: The absence of external pressure and supervision can lead to complacency
- **Emotional comfort**: Home feels safe, making it easier to avoid tasks that trigger anxiety or stress
- **Social comfort**: Family members and roommates may not understand or respect work boundaries

Distraction Abundance

Homes are filled with potential distractions that compete for attention:

Entertainment Distractions

- Television with endless streaming options
- Gaming systems and mobile games
- Social media and internet browsing
- Books, magazines, and other leisure reading

- Chores and maintenance tasks that seem urgent
- Organizing and cleaning projects
- Cooking and meal preparation
- Pet care and interaction

Social Distractions

- Family members seeking attention or assistance
- Friends calling or visiting
- Neighbors and community interactions
- Social obligations and events

The Blurred Boundaries Problem

Home environments often lack clear boundaries between work, leisure, and personal time. This boundary blur creates several challenges:

- **Space confusion**: Using the same space for work and relaxation sends mixed signals to the brain
- **Time confusion**: Without clear start and end times, tasks can expand indefinitely or be postponed indefinitely
- **Role confusion**: Switching between family member, homeowner, and productive worker roles can be mentally exhausting
- **Priority confusion**: Competing demands from different life areas make it difficult to focus on any single task

Household Management: Chores, Maintenance, and Family Responsibilities

Household management represents one of the most common areas of home procrastination. Unlike work projects with clear deadlines, household tasks often seem less urgent, leading to chronic postponement that eventually creates overwhelming backlogs.

The Household Procrastination Cycle

Household procrastination typically follows a predictable pattern:

1. **Task Recognition**: Noticing something needs to be done (cleaning, organizing, maintenance)
2. **Postponement**: Deciding it can wait until later
3. **Accumulation**: Multiple postponed tasks pile up
4. **Overwhelm**: The accumulated tasks feel too big to tackle

5. **Avoidance**: Continuing to postpone due to overwhelm
6. **Crisis**: Tasks become urgent due to health, safety, or social concerns
7. **Rushed Completion**: Frantically addressing tasks under pressure
8. **Exhaustion**: Feeling drained and vowing to stay on top of things
9. **Cycle Restart**: Gradually falling back into postponement patterns

Common Household Procrastination Areas

Cleaning and Organization

- Regular cleaning tasks (vacuuming, dusting, bathroom cleaning)
- Seasonal deep cleaning projects
- Decluttering and organizing spaces
- Laundry and clothing maintenance

Maintenance and Repairs

- Routine maintenance (changing filters, checking smoke detectors)
- Minor repairs (fixing leaky faucets, squeaky doors)
- Seasonal preparations (winterizing, spring cleaning)
- Appliance maintenance and servicing

Financial Management

- Bill paying and budget tracking
- Tax preparation and filing
- Insurance reviews and updates
- Investment and retirement planning

Administrative Tasks

- Medical appointments and health maintenance
- Vehicle registration and maintenance
- Home insurance and warranty management
- Important document organization

Strategies for Household Management

The 15-Minute Rule

Commit to spending 15 minutes daily on household tasks. This small commitment prevents accumulation and makes tasks feel manageable:

- Set a timer for 15 minutes
- Choose one area or type of task
- Work until the timer rings
- Stop and celebrate the progress made

- Gradually increase time as the habit strengthens

Task Batching for Households

Group similar household tasks together to improve efficiency:

- **Cleaning batches**: Do all bathroom cleaning at once
- **Administrative batches**: Handle all bills and paperwork in one session
- **Maintenance batches**: Complete all seasonal maintenance tasks together
- **Shopping batches**: Combine all errands into one trip

The One-Touch Rule

Handle household items and tasks only once when possible:

- Open mail immediately and file, act on, or discard it
- Put items away immediately after use
- Complete small tasks (under 2 minutes) immediately
- Make decisions quickly rather than repeatedly reconsidering

Work-from-Home Strategies: Maintaining Productivity in Personal Spaces

The rise of remote work has created new challenges for maintaining productivity in home environments. Success requires intentional strategies to create professional boundaries and maintain focus despite domestic distractions.

Creating Physical Boundaries

Dedicated Workspace Design

Establish a specific area exclusively for work:

- **Physical separation**: Use a separate room or clearly defined area
- **Visual boundaries**: Use screens, curtains, or furniture to create separation
- **Ergonomic setup**: Invest in proper desk, chair, and lighting
- **Professional atmosphere**: Decorate to feel more like an office than a home

Environmental Optimization

- **Lighting**: Ensure adequate, preferably natural lighting
- **Temperature**: Maintain comfortable temperature for alertness
- **Noise control**: Use noise-canceling headphones or white noise
- **Technology setup**: Reliable internet, proper equipment, and backup systems

Establishing Temporal Boundaries

Structured Schedule Creation

- **Fixed start and end times**: Treat home work like office work
- **Break scheduling**: Plan specific times for meals and breaks
- **Transition rituals**: Create routines that signal work start and end
- **Weekend protection**: Maintain clear boundaries between work and personal time

Time-Blocking for Home Workers

- **Deep work blocks**: Schedule uninterrupted time for complex tasks
- **Communication blocks**: Designated times for emails and calls
- **Administrative blocks**: Time for planning, organizing, and routine tasks
- **Personal blocks**: Protected time for household and family needs

Managing Home-Specific Distractions

Family and Household Member Management

- **Communication**: Clearly explain work requirements and boundaries
- **Visual signals**: Use signs or signals to indicate when not to disturb
- **Scheduled interaction**: Plan specific times for family interaction
- **Childcare arrangements**: Secure appropriate childcare during work hours

Household Task Temptation

- **Task scheduling**: Assign household tasks to specific non-work times
- **Visual barriers**: Keep household projects out of sight during work
- **Reward systems**: Use household tasks as rewards after completing work
- **Boundary enforcement**: Resist the urge to "quickly" do household tasks during work time

Creating Productive Home Routines

Successful home productivity requires intentional routine development that supports both personal and professional goals while preventing procrastination.

Morning Routine Design

Energy and Focus Optimization

- **Consistent wake time**: Maintain regular sleep schedule even without commute
- **Physical activation**: Include exercise or movement to increase alertness
- **Nutritious breakfast**: Fuel the body and brain for productive work
- **Mental preparation**: Review goals and priorities for the day

Transition Rituals

Create rituals that signal the shift from personal to productive time:

- **Dress change**: Change from sleepwear to work-appropriate clothing
- **Space preparation**: Set up workspace and organize materials
- **Technology activation**: Boot up systems and check essential communications
- **Intention setting**: Review daily goals and priorities

Workday Structure

Time-Blocking Implementation

- **Priority blocks**: Schedule most important tasks during peak energy times
- **Routine blocks**: Handle regular tasks (email, calls) at consistent times
- **Break blocks**: Plan specific times for rest and renewal
- **Flexibility blocks**: Leave time for unexpected tasks or opportunities

Productivity Rhythms

Align tasks with natural energy patterns:

- **High-energy tasks**: Complex projects, creative work, important decisions
- **Medium-energy tasks**: Routine work, meetings, administrative tasks
- **Low-energy tasks**: Organizing, planning, simple communications

Evening Routine Development

Work Completion Rituals

- **Task review**: Assess daily accomplishments and plan for tomorrow
- **Workspace cleanup**: Organize space for next day's productivity
- **Technology shutdown**: Close work applications and devices
- **Transition activity**: Engage in activity that signals work end

Personal Time Protection

- **Family time**: Dedicated time for relationships and personal connections
- **Self-care activities**: Exercise, hobbies, relaxation, or personal development
- **Household management**: Planned time for necessary home tasks
- **Preparation for tomorrow**: Organize for next day's success

Balancing Rest and Productivity

One of the biggest challenges in home environments is finding the right balance between productivity and rest. Both are essential for long-term success and well-being.

Understanding Rest vs. Procrastination

- **Intentional**: Consciously chosen for specific purposes
- **Rejuvenating**: Actually restores energy and motivation
- **Time-bounded**: Has clear start and end times
- **Guilt-free**: Doesn't create anxiety or regret
- **Balanced**: Proportionate to work and other responsibilities

Procrastination Characteristics

- **Avoidant**: Used to escape from important tasks
- **Depleting**: Leaves you feeling worse than before
- **Open-ended**: Continues indefinitely without clear stopping point
- **Guilt-inducing**: Creates anxiety about avoided responsibilities
- **Disproportionate**: Takes time away from important priorities

Strategic Rest Planning

Active Rest Activities

Choose rest activities that genuinely restore energy:

- **Physical activities**: Walking, stretching, light exercise
- **Creative pursuits**: Art, music, crafts, gardening
- **Social connection**: Quality time with family and friends
- **Learning activities**: Reading, documentaries, skill development
- **Mindfulness practices**: Meditation, deep breathing, nature observation

Passive Rest Management

When choosing passive rest, do so intentionally:

- **Time limits**: Set specific durations for activities like TV watching
- **Quality selection**: Choose content that aligns with your values and goals
- **Comfort optimization**: Create truly restful environments
- **Transition planning**: Plan how to move from rest back to productivity

Energy Management Strategies

Ultradian Rhythm Awareness

Work with natural 90-120 minute cycles of alertness:

- **Peak periods**: Schedule most demanding tasks during natural high-energy times
- **Valley periods**: Use for routine tasks or planned rest
- **Transition management**: Allow time for natural energy shifts
- **Individual variation**: Discover your personal energy patterns

- **Micro-recoveries**: Brief 2-5 minute breaks every 25-50 minutes
- **Mini-recoveries**: 15-30 minute breaks every 2-3 hours
- **Macro-recoveries**: Longer breaks, evenings, and weekends for full restoration
- **Seasonal recoveries**: Longer vacations and sabbaticals for deep renewal

Home Productivity Systems

Task Management for Home

- **Capture systems**: Reliable methods for recording tasks and ideas
- **Categorization**: Organize tasks by context, energy level, and priority
- **Scheduling**: Assign tasks to specific times and days
- **Review systems**: Regular assessment of progress and priorities

Accountability Structures

Create accountability in the absence of external supervision:

- **Self-monitoring**: Track progress and productivity patterns
- **External accountability**: Share goals with family, friends, or coaches
- **Public commitment**: Use social media or blogs to create public accountability
- **Professional support**: Work with coaches, consultants, or productivity groups

Technology Integration

- **Productivity apps**: Use tools that support rather than distract from goals
- **Automation**: Automate routine tasks where possible
- **Communication management**: Set boundaries around email, social media, and messaging
- **Digital organization**: Maintain organized digital files and systems

Troubleshooting Common Home Procrastination Issues

The "I'll Do It Later" Trap

- **Immediate action rule**: If a task takes less than 2 minutes, do it now
- **Specific scheduling**: Assign vague "later" tasks to specific times
- **Deadline creation**: Set artificial deadlines for tasks without natural ones
- **Accountability partners**: Share commitments with others who will follow up

The Perfectionism Paralysis

- **Good enough standards**: Define what constitutes acceptable completion
- **Time boxing**: Set maximum time limits for tasks
- **Progressive improvement**: Focus on making things better, not perfect
- **Done is better than perfect**: Embrace completion over perfection

The Overwhelm Shutdown

- **Task breakdown**: Divide overwhelming projects into smaller pieces
- **Priority focus**: Choose one thing to focus on at a time
- **Support seeking**: Ask for help when tasks feel too big
- **Stress management**: Use relaxation techniques to manage overwhelm

Home procrastination is conquerable with the right strategies, systems, and mindset. The key is recognizing that home environments require different approaches than other settings. By creating clear boundaries, establishing productive routines, managing distractions intentionally, and balancing productivity with genuine rest, you can transform your home from a procrastination trap into a productivity sanctuary.

Remember that conquering home procrastination is not about turning your home into a sterile office environment. It's about creating a space and lifestyle that supports both your productivity goals and your personal well-being. The goal is to feel energized, accomplished, and at peace in your home environment.

Chapter 11: Academic Procrastination Solutions

Academic procrastination is one of the most common and destructive forms of procrastination, affecting students at all levels from elementary school through graduate studies. The unique pressures of academic life—multiple deadlines, complex projects, high stakes, and often abstract or distant rewards—create perfect conditions for procrastination to flourish. However, with targeted strategies and systematic approaches, academic procrastination can be overcome.

Study Procrastination Patterns: Homework, Papers, and Exam Preparation

Academic procrastination manifests in predictable patterns that vary by task type and individual student characteristics. Understanding these patterns is the first step toward developing effective countermeasures.

Homework Procrastination Patterns

The Daily Avoidance Cycle

Many students fall into a daily pattern of homework avoidance:

1. **After-school decompression**: "I need to relax after a long day"
2. **Activity prioritization**: "I'll do homework after dinner/TV/games"
3. **Energy depletion**: "I'm too tired now, I'll do it in the morning"
4. **Morning panic**: "I don't have time now, I'll do it at lunch/study hall"
5. **Last-minute scramble**: Rushing through assignments just before class
6. **Quality compromise**: Submitting work that doesn't reflect true capability
7. **Guilt and stress**: Feeling bad about the pattern but repeating it

Subject-Specific Avoidance

Students often procrastinate more on certain subjects:

- **Disliked subjects**: Avoiding subjects they find boring or difficult
- **Abstract subjects**: Postponing work in subjects that seem less concrete or practical
- **Cumulative subjects**: Avoiding subjects where current work builds on previous knowledge
- **High-stakes subjects**: Procrastinating on work for classes that significantly impact GPA or future plans

Paper and Project Procrastination Patterns

The Research Rabbit Hole. Many students get stuck in endless research without beginning to write:

- **Over-researching**: Collecting far more sources than necessary
- **Perfectionist preparation**: Waiting until they know "everything" about the topic
- **Analysis paralysis**: Becoming overwhelmed by the amount of information available
- **Procrastination disguised as productivity**: Feeling busy while avoiding actual writing

The Outline Obsession

Some students create elaborate outlines as a form of procrastination:

- **Over-planning**: Spending excessive time on detailed outlines
- **Revision loops**: Continuously revising outlines without writing
- **Structure perfectionism**: Believing the outline must be perfect before writing begins
- **False progress**: Feeling productive while avoiding the actual writing task

The Last-Minute Marathon

The classic pattern of waiting until the last possible moment:

- **Deadline denial**: Ignoring approaching deadlines until they become urgent
- **All-nighter culture**: Romanticizing last-minute work sessions
- **Adrenaline addiction**: Becoming dependent on deadline pressure for motivation
- **Quality sacrifice**: Producing work that doesn't reflect true ability due to time constraints

Exam Preparation Procrastination Patterns

The Cramming Cycle. Many students rely on last-minute cramming despite its ineffectiveness:

- **Early dismissal**: "The exam is weeks away, I have plenty of time"
- **Gradual anxiety**: Growing awareness of approaching exam without action
- **Panic point**: Sudden realization that the exam is imminent
- **Cramming session**: Intensive, often ineffective last-minute studying
- **Performance anxiety**: Increased stress due to inadequate preparation
- **Poor performance**: Results that don't reflect true knowledge or ability

The Study Avoidance Shuffle

Students often engage in pseudo-studying activities:

- **Organizational procrastination**: Spending excessive time organizing notes and materials
- **Passive reviewing**: Reading notes without active engagement or testing

- **Social studying**: Group study sessions that become social gatherings
- **Technology distraction**: Using digital tools that become sources of distraction

The Student's Toolkit: Time-Blocking for Academic Success

Time-blocking is particularly effective for students because it provides structure in environments that often lack external organization. Academic time-blocking requires adaptation to the unique rhythms and demands of student life.

Academic Time-Blocking Fundamentals

Class Schedule Integration. Build time blocks around fixed class schedules:

- **Pre-class preparation**: Block time before classes for review and preparation
- **Post-class processing**: Schedule immediate review and note organization
- **Inter-class optimization**: Use gaps between classes for specific tasks
- **Daily wrap-up**: End each day with planning for the next

Energy-Based Academic Scheduling. Align different types of academic work with appropriate energy levels:

High-Energy Blocks (Peak mental performance times)

- Complex problem-solving (mathematics, physics, programming)
- Creative writing and original thinking
- Difficult reading and comprehension
- Exam preparation for challenging subjects

Medium-Energy Blocks (Good focus but not peak performance)

- Routine homework and assignments
- Research and information gathering
- Note-taking and organization
- Group study sessions

Low-Energy Blocks (Tired but still functional)

- Reading assignments (especially lighter material)
- Organizing and filing
- Planning and scheduling
- Simple, repetitive tasks

Weekly Academic Time-Blocking Structure

Sunday Planning Sessions. Use Sundays for comprehensive weekly planning:

- **Syllabus review**: Check all syllabi for upcoming assignments and exams
- **Priority assessment**: Identify the most important tasks for the week
- **Time allocation**: Assign specific time blocks to major assignments

- **Resource preparation**: Ensure all necessary materials are available

Daily Time-Blocking Implementation

- **Morning review**: Start each day by reviewing the day's time blocks
- **Transition rituals**: Develop routines for moving between different types of work
- **Block protection**: Treat time blocks as important appointments
- **Evening assessment**: Review the day's productivity and adjust tomorrow's plan

Flexible Time-Blocking for Students

Buffer Time Integration

Students need more flexibility than traditional workers:

- **Assignment buffers**: Add extra time for assignments that might run long
- **Social buffers**: Include time for spontaneous social interactions
- **Crisis buffers**: Leave time for unexpected academic emergencies
- **Rest buffers**: Ensure adequate time for sleep and relaxation

Seasonal Adjustments

Adapt time-blocking to academic calendar rhythms:

- **Semester beginnings**: Lighter academic loads, more time for organization
- **Mid-semester**: Heavier workloads, more structured time-blocking
- **Finals periods**: Intensive study schedules with minimal other commitments
- **Breaks**: Recovery time and preparation for upcoming semesters

Research and Writing Strategies: Overcoming Blank Page Syndrome

Research and writing tasks are particularly prone to procrastination because they're often ambiguous, creative, and subject to perfectionist tendencies. Specific strategies can help students overcome these challenges.

Research Strategy Development

The Research Roadmap Method

Create a clear plan before beginning research:

1. **Question formulation**: Define specific research questions
2. **Source identification**: Identify types and numbers of sources needed
3. **Search strategy**: Plan specific databases, keywords, and search methods
4. **Time allocation**: Set time limits for different research phases
5. **Organization system**: Establish methods for organizing and citing sources

The Swiss Cheese Research Approach

Apply the Swiss Cheese Method to research projects:

- **Random source gathering**: Collect sources whenever you encounter them
- **Opportunistic reading**: Read sources when you have small pockets of time
- **Incremental note-taking**: Take notes in small sessions rather than marathon sessions
- **Gradual synthesis**: Slowly build understanding through repeated exposure

Research Time Management

- **Pomodoro research**: Use 25-minute focused research sessions
- **Source quotas**: Set specific numbers of sources to find in each session
- **Quality over quantity**: Focus on finding highly relevant sources rather than many sources
- **Research deadlines**: Set artificial deadlines for completing research phases

Writing Strategy Implementation

Overcoming Blank Page Syndrome

The Brain Dump Method

Start by writing everything you know about the topic:

- **Stream of consciousness**: Write continuously without editing or organizing
- **No judgment**: Don't worry about quality, grammar, or organization
- **Time limits**: Set a timer and write until it goes off
- **Raw material creation**: Generate content that can be organized and refined later

The Question-Answer Approach

Structure writing around specific questions:

- **Question generation**: Create a list of questions your paper should answer
- **Individual responses**: Write responses to each question separately
- **Gradual integration**: Combine individual responses into coherent sections
- **Iterative refinement**: Improve organization and flow through multiple revisions

The Outline-to-Draft Method

Create detailed outlines that naturally evolve into drafts:

- **Detailed outlining**: Create outlines with complete sentences rather than phrases
- **Expansion writing**: Expand each outline point into full paragraphs
- **Connection creation**: Add transitions and connections between sections
- **Refinement process**: Polish the expanded outline into a finished draft

Writing Process Management

Daily Writing Habits

Establish consistent writing routines:

- **Minimum daily writing**: Commit to writing at least 15-30 minutes daily
- **Same time, same place**: Write at consistent times and locations
- **Progress tracking**: Keep records of daily writing progress
- **Momentum maintenance**: Never end a writing session without knowing what comes next

Draft Management

Develop healthy relationships with imperfect drafts:

- **Permission to write badly**: Accept that first drafts are meant to be imperfect
- **Revision planning**: Build revision time into project timelines
- **Feedback seeking**: Share drafts with others for input and accountability
- **Version control**: Keep track of different draft versions

Self-Reinforcement Systems: Rewarding Academic Progress

Academic work often lacks immediate rewards, making self-reinforcement systems crucial for maintaining motivation and overcoming procrastination.

Immediate Reward Systems

Task-Completion Rewards

Create immediate positive consequences for completing academic tasks:

- **Small treats**: Favorite snacks, drinks, or small purchases
- **Entertainment rewards**: Episodes of favorite shows, games, or social media time
- **Activity rewards**: Walks, exercise, or other enjoyable activities
- **Social rewards**: Time with friends or family

Progress-Based Rewards

Reward progress rather than just completion:

- **Page-count rewards**: Reward writing specific numbers of pages
- **Time-based rewards**: Reward sustained work periods regardless of output
- **Effort rewards**: Acknowledge hard work even when results aren't perfect
- **Improvement rewards**: Celebrate getting better rather than being perfect

The Academic Token System

Create a point-based reward system:

- **Point earning**: Assign points to different academic activities

- **Point banking**: Save points for larger rewards
- **Reward menu**: Create a list of rewards with different point costs
- **Bonus points**: Award extra points for particularly challenging tasks

Long-Term Motivation Systems

Goal-Linked Rewards. Connect rewards to meaningful academic goals:

- **Grade-based rewards**: Celebrate achieving target grades
- **Skill-development rewards**: Acknowledge mastering new abilities
- **Completion rewards**: Celebrate finishing major projects or courses
- **Growth rewards**: Recognize improvement and development

Identity-Based Reinforcement. Reinforce your identity as a successful student:

- **Success journaling**: Record academic achievements and progress
- **Skill inventory**: Keep track of developing abilities and knowledge
- **Story creation**: Develop narratives about your academic growth
- **Future visioning**: Connect current work to future goals and aspirations

Social Reinforcement Systems

Accountability Partnerships. Work with others to create mutual accountability:

- **Study buddies**: Partner with classmates for mutual support
- **Progress sharing**: Regularly report progress to accountability partners
- **Goal witnessing**: Have others witness your commitment to academic goals
- **Celebration sharing**: Include others in celebrating academic achievements

Family and Friend Integration. Involve your support network in academic success:

- **Goal communication**: Share academic goals with family and friends
- **Progress updates**: Regularly update supporters on your progress
- **Support requests**: Ask for specific types of help and encouragement
- **Achievement celebration**: Include loved ones in celebrating successes

Building Study Habits That Stick

Sustainable academic success requires developing study habits that become automatic and require minimal willpower to maintain.

The Academic Habit Loop. Apply habit formation principles to studying:

- **Cue identification**: Establish clear triggers for study behavior
- **Routine development**: Create consistent study procedures
- **Reward integration**: Build satisfying rewards into study sessions
- **Tracking systems**: Monitor habit development and maintenance

Keystone Study Habits. Focus on developing habits that naturally lead to other positive behaviors:

- **Daily planning**: Spending 10 minutes each morning planning the day
- **Immediate note review**: Reviewing notes within 24 hours of taking them
- **Weekly planning**: Conducting comprehensive weekly planning sessions
- **Regular sleep schedule**: Maintaining consistent sleep and wake times

Study Space Optimization. Create environments that support rather than hinder study habits:

- **Dedicated study areas**: Establish specific locations for different types of study
- **Distraction elimination**: Remove or minimize potential distractions
- **Resource accessibility**: Keep necessary materials easily available
- **Comfort optimization**: Ensure physical comfort without encouraging sleepiness

Technology Integration. Use technology to support rather than undermine study habits:

- **App selection**: Choose productivity apps that genuinely help rather than distract
- **Notification management**: Turn off non-essential notifications during study time
- **Website blocking**: Use tools to block distracting websites during study sessions
- **Digital organization**: Maintain organized digital files and systems

Consistency Over Perfection. Focus on maintaining habits rather than performing them perfectly:

- **Minimum viable habits**: Establish habits that are easy to maintain even on difficult days
- **Flexibility planning**: Develop strategies for maintaining habits during disruptions
- **Recovery protocols**: Create plans for getting back on track after breaking habits
- **Progress celebration**: Acknowledge consistency even when performance isn't perfect

Habit Stacking for Students. Link new study habits to existing routines:

- **Morning stacking**: Add study habits to existing morning routines
- **Class transition stacking**: Use transitions between classes as habit triggers
- **Evening stacking**: Integrate study habits into evening routines
- **Weekend stacking**: Connect study habits to weekend activities

Advanced Academic Procrastination Solutions

The Pomodoro Technique for Students. Adapt the Pomodoro Technique for academic work:

- **Subject-specific Pomodoros**: Use different timer lengths for different subjects
- **Task-appropriate timing**: Adjust intervals based on task complexity

- **Break optimization**: Use breaks for physical movement and mental rest
- **Progress tracking**: Keep records of Pomodoros completed for different subjects

The Two-Minute Rule for Academics. Apply the two-minute rule to academic tasks:

- **Immediate action**: Complete any academic task that takes less than two minutes immediately
- **Task breakdown**: Break larger tasks into two-minute components when possible
- **Momentum building**: Use quick completions to build motivation for larger tasks
- **Procrastination prevention**: Prevent small tasks from becoming procrastination triggers

Academic Procrastination Emergency Protocols

Crisis Management. When procrastination has created academic emergencies:

- **Damage assessment**: Honestly evaluate the situation and available time
- **Priority triage**: Focus on the most important and achievable tasks
- **Help seeking**: Reach out to professors, tutors, or academic support services
- **Minimum viable completion**: Focus on completing work to minimum acceptable standards

Recovery and Prevention. After managing academic crises:

- **Pattern analysis**: Identify what led to the crisis situation
- **System improvement**: Modify planning and organization systems
- **Early warning systems**: Develop methods for recognizing procrastination patterns early
- **Support system activation**: Engage help before reaching crisis points

Academic procrastination is a complex challenge that requires multifaceted solutions. By understanding common patterns, implementing effective time management strategies, developing strong research and writing processes, creating self-reinforcement systems, and building sustainable study habits, students can overcome procrastination and achieve their academic potential.

The key to success is recognizing that academic procrastination is not a character flaw but a set of behaviors that can be changed through consistent application of proven strategies. Start with one or two techniques that resonate most strongly with your situation, implement them consistently, and gradually build a comprehensive system for academic success.

Remember that overcoming academic procrastination is not about becoming a perfect student overnight. It's about making consistent progress toward better habits, more effective strategies, and ultimately, academic success that reflects your true capabilities and aspirations.

Chapter 12: Workplace Procrastination Mastery

Workplace procrastination presents unique challenges that can significantly impact career advancement, professional relationships, and job satisfaction. Unlike academic or home environments, the workplace involves complex interpersonal dynamics, competing priorities, external pressures, and often unclear or changing expectations. Mastering workplace procrastination requires understanding these professional dynamics and developing strategies that work within organizational contexts.

Professional Procrastination Patterns: Meetings, Emails, and Project Deadlines

Workplace procrastination manifests in distinct patterns that reflect the unique pressures and structures of professional environments. Recognizing these patterns is essential for developing targeted interventions.

Email and Communication Procrastination

The Email Avoidance Trap. Many professionals fall into patterns of email avoidance that create mounting pressure:

- **Inbox overwhelm**: Allowing emails to accumulate until the volume feels unmanageable
- **Difficult conversation avoidance**: Postponing responses to challenging or confrontational emails
- **Decision paralysis**: Avoiding emails that require decisions or commitments
- **Perfectionist drafting**: Spending excessive time crafting "perfect" responses
- **Priority confusion**: Treating all emails as equally urgent or equally unimportant

Communication Procrastination Consequences

- **Relationship damage**: Delayed responses can harm professional relationships
- **Missed opportunities**: Important opportunities may pass while avoiding communication
- **Increased pressure**: Delayed responses often require more complex explanations
- **Reputation impact**: Consistent communication delays can damage professional reputation
- **Escalation effects**: Minor issues can become major problems when communication is delayed

Meeting-Related Procrastination

Pre-Meeting Procrastination

- **Preparation avoidance**: Failing to prepare adequately for meetings
- **Agenda neglect**: Not reviewing meeting agendas or materials in advance
- **Research postponement**: Delaying necessary research or data gathering
- **Presentation procrastination**: Waiting until the last minute to prepare presentations

Post-Meeting Procrastination

- **Follow-up delays**: Postponing promised actions or communications
- **Note organization**: Failing to organize or distribute meeting notes promptly
- **Task implementation**: Delaying work on tasks assigned during meetings
- **Feedback provision**: Avoiding giving or seeking feedback on meeting outcomes

Project and Deadline Procrastination

The Project Procrastination Cycle. Large workplace projects often trigger predictable procrastination patterns:

1. **Initial optimism**: Feeling confident about timeline and scope
2. **Planning postponement**: Delaying detailed project planning
3. **False starts**: Beginning work but not sustaining effort
4. **Scope creep anxiety**: Becoming overwhelmed as project complexity becomes clear
5. **Avoidance escalation**: Increasing avoidance as deadline pressure mounts
6. **Crisis mode**: Last-minute scrambling to meet deadlines
7. **Quality compromise**: Delivering work that doesn't reflect true capability
8. **Stress and exhaustion**: Physical and emotional toll of crisis-mode work

Deadline Procrastination Patterns

- **Soft deadline dismissal**: Ignoring deadlines that seem flexible or negotiable
- **Multiple deadline juggling**: Becoming overwhelmed by competing deadlines
- **Buffer time elimination**: Failing to build buffer time into project schedules
- **Dependency chain disruption**: Procrastination that affects others' ability to complete their work

Managing Workplace Distractions: Colleagues, Technology, and Interruptions

The modern workplace is filled with distractions that can derail productivity and contribute to procrastination. Effective distraction management requires both personal strategies and environmental modifications.

Colleague and Social Distractions

Interruption Management. Colleagues can be significant sources of distraction, but managing these interruptions requires diplomatic approaches:

The Polite Boundary System

- **Visual signals**: Use headphones, closed doors, or desk arrangements to signal focus time
- **Scheduled availability**: Establish specific times when you're available for questions and conversations
- **Redirection techniques**: Politely redirect non-urgent interruptions to appropriate times
- **Collaboration balance**: Maintain helpful relationships while protecting productive time

Office Politics and Social Dynamics

- **Gossip avoidance**: Minimize participation in unproductive workplace gossip
- **Social obligation management**: Balance relationship building with productivity needs
- **Meeting culture navigation**: Participate appropriately in meeting culture without over-committing
- **Networking optimization**: Engage in professional networking without letting it consume productive time

Technology Distraction Management

Email and Messaging Systems

- **Batch processing**: Check and respond to emails at designated times rather than continuously
- **Notification control**: Turn off non-essential notifications during focused work periods
- **Response time expectations**: Set realistic expectations for email response times
- **Priority filtering**: Develop systems for identifying and prioritizing important communications

Digital Distraction Control

- **Website blocking**: Use software to block distracting websites during work hours
- **App management**: Remove or restrict access to distracting applications
- **Phone management**: Keep personal phones out of sight during focused work periods

- **Social media boundaries**: Establish clear boundaries around social media use during work

Meeting and Calendar Distractions

Meeting Optimization

- **Meeting necessity evaluation**: Question whether meetings are necessary or if alternatives exist
- **Agenda requirements**: Insist on clear agendas for meetings you attend
- **Time boundary enforcement**: Start and end meetings on time
- **Participation optimization**: Contribute meaningfully while avoiding meeting overload

Calendar Management

- **Focus time protection**: Block calendar time for important work
- **Meeting clustering**: Group meetings together to create longer periods of uninterrupted work
- **Buffer time scheduling**: Include transition time between meetings and tasks
- **Priority-based scheduling**: Schedule important work during peak energy times

Project Management for Procrastinators: Breaking Down Complex Work Tasks

Complex workplace projects are particularly susceptible to procrastination because they often lack clear structure, have distant deadlines, and require sustained effort over extended periods.

Project Breakdown Strategies

The Work Breakdown Structure (WBS). Adapt project management principles for personal productivity:

1. **Project definition**: Clearly define the project scope and objectives
2. **Major phase identification**: Break the project into 3-7 major phases
3. **Task decomposition**: Break each phase into specific, actionable tasks
4. **Subtask creation**: Further break down complex tasks into subtasks
5. **Dependency mapping**: Identify which tasks depend on others
6. **Resource identification**: Determine what resources each task requires

The Swiss Cheese Method for Projects. Apply the Swiss Cheese Method to complex workplace projects:

- **Opportunistic task completion**: Work on whatever project components are accessible
- **Small time window utilization**: Use brief periods for project progress

250

- **Momentum building**: Create progress through small, consistent actions
- **Anxiety reduction**: Reduce project anxiety through familiarity and progress

Timeline and Milestone Development

Backward Planning

Start with the deadline and work backward:

1. **Final deadline identification**: Establish the absolute deadline
2. **Buffer time allocation**: Reserve time for unexpected issues
3. **Major milestone setting**: Identify key project milestones
4. **Task duration estimation**: Estimate realistic time requirements for each task
5. **Schedule creation**: Create a detailed project schedule
6. **Contingency planning**: Develop plans for potential delays or obstacles

Milestone Management

- **Meaningful milestones**: Create milestones that represent significant progress
- **Celebration planning**: Plan appropriate celebrations for milestone achievements
- **Progress tracking**: Develop systems for monitoring progress toward milestones
- **Adjustment protocols**: Create processes for adjusting milestones when necessary

Resource and Dependency Management

Resource Planning

- **Skill assessment**: Identify skills needed for different project components
- **Resource availability**: Determine when resources will be available
- **External dependency management**: Coordinate with others whose work affects your project
- **Tool and technology needs**: Ensure necessary tools and technology are available

Dependency Chain Management

- **Critical path identification**: Identify the sequence of tasks that determines project duration
- **Bottleneck prevention**: Identify and address potential bottlenecks early
- **Communication protocols**: Establish clear communication with people whose work affects yours
- **Contingency planning**: Develop backup plans for critical dependencies

Communication and Deadline Management

Effective communication and deadline management are crucial for preventing workplace procrastination and maintaining professional relationships.

Proactive Communication Strategies

Expectation Management

- **Deadline negotiation**: Negotiate realistic deadlines based on actual capacity and priorities
- **Progress reporting**: Provide regular updates on project progress
- **Challenge communication**: Communicate obstacles and challenges early rather than at deadline
- **Capacity transparency**: Be honest about workload and availability

Stakeholder Communication

- **Regular check-ins**: Schedule regular communication with project stakeholders
- **Status reporting**: Provide clear, concise status reports
- **Issue escalation**: Communicate problems early and suggest solutions
- **Feedback seeking**: Actively seek feedback to ensure alignment with expectations

Deadline Management Systems

Personal Deadline Tracking

- **Comprehensive calendar**: Maintain a complete calendar of all deadlines and commitments
- **Priority ranking**: Rank deadlines by importance and consequences
- **Buffer time integration**: Build buffer time into all deadline planning
- **Review systems**: Regularly review upcoming deadlines and adjust plans accordingly

Team Deadline Coordination

- **Shared calendars**: Use shared calendars for team deadline visibility
- **Dependency communication**: Clearly communicate how your deadlines affect others
- **Collaborative planning**: Involve team members in deadline planning when appropriate
- **Conflict resolution**: Address deadline conflicts proactively

Crisis Communication

When Deadlines Are at Risk

- **Early warning**: Communicate potential deadline issues as soon as they become apparent
- **Solution focus**: Present problems along with potential solutions
- **Impact assessment**: Clearly communicate the implications of deadline changes
- **Alternative proposals**: Suggest alternative approaches or modified deliverables

Damage Control

When deadlines are missed:

- **Immediate communication**: Notify affected parties immediately
- **Responsibility acceptance**: Take responsibility without making excuses
- **Recovery planning**: Present clear plans for completing the work
- **Prevention measures**: Explain what you'll do differently to prevent future occurrences

Career Advancement Through Consistent Action

Overcoming workplace procrastination is not just about completing tasks—it's about building a reputation for reliability and excellence that supports career advancement.

Building Professional Reputation

Reliability Development

- **Consistent delivery**: Build a track record of meeting commitments
- **Quality maintenance**: Maintain high standards even under pressure
- **Proactive communication**: Keep stakeholders informed about progress and challenges
- **Solution orientation**: Focus on solving problems rather than explaining them

Skill Development Integration

- **Continuous learning**: Integrate skill development into regular work routines
- **Stretch assignments**: Volunteer for challenging projects that build capabilities
- **Feedback seeking**: Actively seek feedback to improve performance
- **Knowledge sharing**: Share knowledge and skills with colleagues

Leadership Through Example

Modeling Productive Behaviors

- **Time management demonstration**: Show others effective time management in action
- **Stress management**: Maintain composure and effectiveness under pressure
- **Collaboration enhancement**: Improve team productivity through your example
- **Innovation encouragement**: Demonstrate creative problem-solving approaches

Mentoring and Support

- **Colleague assistance**: Help colleagues overcome their own procrastination challenges
- **Knowledge transfer**: Share effective strategies and techniques

- **Team productivity**: Contribute to overall team effectiveness
- **Organizational culture**: Help create a culture that supports productivity and achievement

Strategic Career Planning

Goal-Oriented Work
- **Career objective alignment**: Ensure daily work supports long-term career goals
- **Skill gap identification**: Identify and address skills needed for career advancement
- **Network building**: Build professional relationships that support career growth
- **Opportunity recognition**: Stay alert to opportunities for advancement and growth

Performance Optimization
- **Strength utilization**: Focus on work that leverages your natural strengths
- **Weakness management**: Address weaknesses that could limit career advancement
- **Value demonstration**: Consistently demonstrate your value to the organization
- **Results documentation**: Keep records of achievements and contributions

Workplace Procrastination Prevention Systems

Daily Management Systems
- **Morning planning**: Start each day with clear priorities and plans
- **Energy management**: Align tasks with natural energy patterns
- **Progress tracking**: Monitor daily progress toward goals and deadlines
- **Evening review**: End each day by assessing progress and planning tomorrow

Weekly and Monthly Systems
- **Weekly reviews**: Conduct comprehensive weekly planning and review sessions
- **Monthly assessment**: Evaluate monthly progress toward larger goals
- **Quarterly planning**: Align quarterly objectives with annual career goals
- **Annual evaluation**: Conduct thorough annual reviews of career progress and goals

Organizational Integration
- **System alignment**: Ensure personal productivity systems align with organizational systems
- **Tool utilization**: Effectively use organizational tools and technologies
- **Culture adaptation**: Adapt productivity approaches to organizational culture
- **Change management**: Adjust systems as organizational needs change

Troubleshooting Workplace Procrastination

Common Workplace Procrastination Triggers

- **Unclear expectations**: Seek clarification when expectations are ambiguous
- **Overwhelming workload**: Negotiate priorities when workload becomes unmanageable
- **Boring or repetitive tasks**: Find ways to make routine tasks more engaging
- **Difficult relationships**: Address interpersonal challenges that affect productivity

Recovery Strategies

- **Honest assessment**: Accurately assess the impact of procrastination
- **Stakeholder communication**: Communicate with affected parties about recovery plans
- **System modification**: Adjust systems and approaches based on what you've learned
- **Prevention focus**: Implement measures to prevent similar issues in the future

Mastering workplace procrastination requires a comprehensive approach that addresses the unique challenges of professional environments. By understanding common procrastination patterns, managing distractions effectively, breaking down complex projects, communicating proactively, and focusing on career advancement, you can transform procrastination from a career liability into a source of competitive advantage.

The key to success is recognizing that workplace procrastination affects not just your own productivity, but also your relationships with colleagues, your reputation within the organization, and your long-term career prospects. By developing strong anti-procrastination systems and consistently applying them, you can build a reputation for reliability, effectiveness, and leadership that opens doors to new opportunities and career advancement.

Remember that overcoming workplace procrastination is an ongoing process that requires continuous attention and refinement. As your career evolves and your responsibilities change, your anti-procrastination strategies must evolve as well. The investment you make in mastering workplace procrastination will pay dividends throughout your entire career.

Relationships and Personal Growth

Chapter 13: Procrastination's Impact on Relationships

Procrastination is rarely a solitary problem. While we often think of it as a personal struggle with productivity and time management, procrastination has profound effects on our relationships with family, friends, romantic partners, and colleagues. Understanding these relational impacts is crucial not only for maintaining healthy connections but also for finding the motivation to overcome procrastination itself.

Trust and Reliability: How Delays Affect Personal Connections

Trust forms the foundation of all meaningful relationships, and procrastination systematically erodes this foundation through patterns of unreliability and broken commitments. When we consistently delay or avoid following through on our promises, we send a clear message to others that they cannot depend on us, regardless of our intentions.

The Trust Erosion Process

Trust erosion through procrastination follows a predictable pattern that can devastate even the strongest relationships:

Initial Disappointment: The first instances of procrastination-related delays create minor disappointment. Partners, friends, or family members may excuse these lapses as isolated incidents or temporary stress responses.

Pattern Recognition: As delays become more frequent, others begin to recognize a pattern. What initially seemed like occasional forgetfulness or busy schedules now appears to be a consistent behavior pattern that affects their lives.

Expectation Adjustment: People begin to lower their expectations and plan around the procrastinator's unreliability. They may stop counting on commitments or begin to build buffer time into their own schedules to accommodate expected delays.

Emotional Withdrawal: As trust continues to erode, emotional investment in the relationship decreases. People become less willing to share important matters or rely on the procrastinator for significant responsibilities.

Relationship Deterioration: In the final stages, the relationship may become superficial or end entirely as the cost of maintaining connection with an unreliable person becomes too high.

The Reliability Paradox

Procrastinators often experience a painful paradox: they genuinely care about their relationships and want to be reliable, yet their behavior consistently demonstrates the opposite. This creates internal conflict and shame that can actually worsen procrastination patterns, creating a vicious cycle of good intentions followed by disappointing outcomes.

Trust Rebuilding Strategies

Rebuilding trust after procrastination has damaged relationships requires consistent action over time:

- **Acknowledge the impact**: Recognize and validate how your procrastination has affected others
- **Make smaller commitments**: Start with commitments you can reliably keep to rebuild credibility
- **Communicate proactively**: Update others about your progress rather than waiting for them to ask
- **Accept consequences**: Allow natural consequences to occur rather than making excuses
- **Demonstrate change**: Show through actions, not words, that you're addressing the underlying issues

Communication About Procrastination: Honest Conversations with Loved Ones

Open communication about procrastination can be challenging because it requires vulnerability and often involves admitting to behaviors that have hurt others. However, honest conversations are essential for healing relationships and creating supportive environments for change.

Initiating Difficult Conversations

Starting conversations about procrastination requires courage and careful preparation:

Choose the Right Time and Place: Select a time when both parties are calm and have adequate time to talk without interruptions. Avoid bringing up the topic during stressful periods or in public settings.

Take Responsibility: Begin by acknowledging your role in creating problems rather than focusing on how others have responded to your procrastination. Use "I" statements to own your behavior and its impacts.

Be Specific: Instead of vague apologies, identify specific instances where your procrastination affected the other person. This demonstrates awareness and genuine understanding of the impact.

Express Genuine Remorse: Show that you understand how your behavior has affected others emotionally, not just practically. Acknowledge feelings of frustration, disappointment, or hurt that your procrastination has caused.

Present a Change Plan: Come to the conversation with concrete steps you're taking to address the procrastination, not just promises to "do better."

Conversation Framework for Procrastinators

Use this structure for discussing procrastination with loved ones:

1. **Acknowledgment**: "I want to talk about how my procrastination has affected our relationship."
2. **Specific Examples**: "I realize that when I delayed [specific situation], it caused you [specific impact]."
3. **Emotional Recognition**: "I can see that this made you feel [frustrated/disappointed/unimportant]."
4. **Responsibility**: "This is my problem to solve, and I take full responsibility for the impact it's had on you."
5. **Action Plan**: "Here's what I'm doing to change: [specific steps]."
6. **Support Request**: "I would appreciate your support in [specific way], but I understand if you need time to see changes first."

Responding to Others' Concerns

When others bring up concerns about your procrastination:

- **Listen without defending**: Allow them to express their feelings without immediately explaining or justifying your behavior
- **Validate their experience**: Acknowledge that their frustrations are legitimate and understandable

- **Ask clarifying questions**: Understand specifically how your procrastination has affected them
- **Avoid making immediate promises**: Focus on understanding rather than rushing to make commitments you might not keep
- **Thank them for their honesty**: Appreciate their willingness to address a difficult topic

Supporting Others Without Enabling: Helping Procrastinating Partners or Family

When someone you care about struggles with procrastination, finding the balance between support and enabling can be challenging. Effective support helps them develop their own capacity to overcome procrastination rather than compensating for their delays.

Understanding the Difference Between Support and Enabling

Supportive Behaviors:

- Encouraging their efforts to change
- Celebrating small victories and progress
- Providing emotional support during setbacks
- Helping them identify resources or strategies
- Maintaining your own boundaries and responsibilities

Enabling Behaviors:

- Completing their responsibilities for them
- Making excuses for their procrastination to others
- Rescuing them from natural consequences
- Taking over their commitments without discussion
- Adjusting your life entirely around their procrastination patterns

Strategies for Supportive Relationships

Set Clear Boundaries: Establish what you will and won't do to accommodate their procrastination. Communicate these boundaries clearly and maintain them consistently.

Focus on Natural Consequences: Allow procrastination to have its natural consequences rather than protecting them from the results of their choices.

Encourage Professional Help: Support them in seeking professional assistance if procrastination significantly impacts their life or relationships.

Maintain Your Own Well-being: Don't sacrifice your own mental health, goals, or responsibilities to manage their procrastination.

Celebrate Progress: Acknowledge improvements and efforts, even if they're small or inconsistent.

Avoid Nagging or Controlling: Resist the urge to constantly remind, check up on, or manage their responsibilities.

Social Procrastination: Avoiding Social Obligations and Commitments

Social procrastination involves delaying or avoiding social interactions, commitments, and relationship maintenance activities. This form of procrastination can be particularly damaging because it directly impacts the quantity and quality of our social connections.

Common Forms of Social Procrastination

Communication Delays: Postponing responses to texts, emails, or phone calls, often leading to awkward delays that make communication more difficult over time.

Event Avoidance: Consistently canceling or avoiding social gatherings, celebrations, or planned activities, often at the last minute.

Relationship Maintenance Neglect: Failing to invest time and energy in maintaining friendships and family relationships through regular contact and shared activities.

Conflict Avoidance: Postponing difficult conversations or avoiding addressing relationship problems, allowing issues to fester and grow.

Commitment Phobia: Avoiding making social commitments or consistently backing out of plans due to anxiety or fear of obligation.

The Social Isolation Cycle

Social procrastination often creates a self-reinforcing cycle:

1. **Initial Avoidance**: Postponing social activities due to anxiety, overwhelm, or other priorities
2. **Guilt and Shame**: Feeling bad about avoiding social connections
3. **Increased Anxiety**: Worrying about how others perceive the avoidance
4. **Further Avoidance**: Using continued avoidance to manage the anxiety and guilt

5. **Relationship Deterioration**: Experiencing weakened relationships due to lack of investment
6. **Increased Isolation**: Finding oneself with fewer social connections and support
7. **Heightened Avoidance**: Feeling even more anxious about social situations due to decreased practice and confidence

Breaking the Social Procrastination Pattern

Start Small: Begin with low-stakes social interactions that feel manageable, such as brief text responses or short phone calls.

Schedule Social Time: Treat social activities as important appointments rather than optional activities that can be postponed indefinitely.

Use the Two-Minute Rule: Respond to social communications immediately if they can be handled in two minutes or less.

Practice Vulnerability: Share your struggles with trusted friends or family members who can provide support and accountability.

Set Social Goals: Establish specific, measurable goals for social connection, such as reaching out to one friend per week or attending one social event per month.

Rebuilding Damaged Relationships

When procrastination has significantly damaged relationships, rebuilding requires patience, consistency, and often professional support. The process is gradual and requires sustained effort over time.

Assessment and Acknowledgment

Before attempting to rebuild relationships, conduct an honest assessment of the damage:

Relationship Inventory: List the relationships that have been affected by your procrastination and assess the current state of each relationship.

Impact Assessment: For each relationship, identify specific ways your procrastination has caused harm, including broken promises, missed events, or emotional hurt.

Responsibility Acceptance: Take full responsibility for your role in the relationship damage without blaming others for their responses to your behavior.

Motivation Clarification: Understand why you want to rebuild each relationship and ensure your motivations are genuine rather than guilt-driven.

The Rebuilding Process

Phase 1: Foundation Repair (Months 1-3)

- Focus on consistent, small actions that demonstrate reliability
- Avoid making large promises or commitments during this phase
- Communicate regularly about your progress and setbacks
- Accept that others may remain skeptical during this period

Phase 2: Trust Building (Months 3-12)

- Gradually take on larger commitments as you prove reliability
- Proactively address any setbacks or lapses honestly
- Invest time and energy in understanding the other person's needs and perspectives
- Celebrate small victories together while maintaining realistic expectations

Phase 3: Relationship Renewal (12+ Months)

- Work together to create new patterns and traditions
- Address any remaining resentment or hurt through continued communication
- Establish new agreements and boundaries that support both parties
- Focus on building positive new memories and experiences

Professional Support for Relationship Repair

Sometimes professional help is necessary for rebuilding severely damaged relationships:

Individual Therapy: Work with a therapist to address the underlying causes of procrastination and develop healthier relationship patterns.

Couples Counseling: For romantic relationships, professional guidance can help both partners communicate effectively and rebuild trust.

Family Therapy: When procrastination has affected family dynamics, family therapy can help all members understand and address the patterns.

Support Groups: Join groups for people dealing with procrastination or those affected by others' procrastination to gain perspective and strategies.

Maintaining Rebuilt Relationships

Once relationships begin to heal, maintaining progress requires ongoing attention:

Regular Check-ins: Schedule periodic conversations about how the relationship is progressing and address any concerns early.

Continued Growth: Keep working on personal development and procrastination management to prevent relapse.

Patience with Setbacks: Understand that rebuilding trust is not linear and that occasional setbacks are normal.

Appreciation and Gratitude: Regularly express appreciation for others' patience and support during the rebuilding process.

Boundary Respect: Honor the boundaries others have established as a result of past hurt, even if they feel restrictive.

The impact of procrastination on relationships is profound and far-reaching, affecting trust, communication, and emotional connection[4]. However, with awareness, commitment, and appropriate strategies, it's possible to repair damaged relationships and build stronger, more honest connections. The key is recognizing that relationship repair, like overcoming procrastination itself, requires consistent action over time rather than dramatic gestures or empty promises.

Remember that some relationships may not be repairable, and that's a natural consequence of prolonged procrastination patterns. Focus your energy on the relationships that matter most and where both parties are willing to invest in rebuilding. The process of addressing procrastination's impact on relationships often becomes a catalyst for deeper personal growth and more authentic connections with others.

Chapter 14: The Psychology of Change

Understanding the psychology of change is crucial for anyone seeking to overcome procrastination permanently. Change is not simply a matter of willpower or motivation—it involves complex psychological processes that, when understood and leveraged properly, can make the difference between temporary improvement and lasting transformation. This chapter explores the mental and emotional aspects of change that are essential for breaking free from procrastination patterns.

Understanding Resistance: Why Change Feels Difficult

Human beings are naturally resistant to change, even when that change would clearly benefit them. This resistance isn't a character flaw or sign of weakness—it's a fundamental aspect of how our brains and psychological systems work. Understanding this resistance is the first step toward working with it rather than against it.

The Neuroscience of Resistance

Our brains are prediction machines designed to keep us safe and conserve energy. When we attempt to change established patterns like procrastination, several neurological processes create resistance:

The Default Mode Network: This network of brain regions becomes active when we're not focused on specific tasks. For procrastinators, the default mode often includes patterns of avoidance, distraction, and delay. Changing these patterns requires conscious effort to override automatic responses.

Cognitive Load: Learning new behaviors and breaking old habits requires significant mental energy. Our brains naturally resist activities that demand high cognitive load, especially when we're tired, stressed, or overwhelmed.

Neural Pathway Strength: Procrastination patterns become deeply ingrained neural pathways that fire automatically in response to certain triggers. These pathways have been strengthened through repetition over months or years, making them feel natural and comfortable despite their negative consequences.

Threat Detection Systems: The brain's threat detection systems can interpret change as danger, even when the change is positive. This triggers stress responses that make us want to return to familiar patterns, even if those patterns are problematic.

Psychological Sources of Resistance

Beyond neurological factors, several psychological mechanisms create resistance to change:

Identity Protection: We develop identities around our behaviors, including procrastination. Changing these behaviors can feel like losing part of ourselves, triggering identity-protection mechanisms that resist change.

Fear of Failure: Attempting to change opens us up to the possibility of failure, which can feel more threatening than maintaining the status quo. Some people prefer the familiar discomfort of procrastination to the uncertain discomfort of trying and potentially failing to change.

Fear of Success: Success can feel threatening because it brings new responsibilities, expectations, and potential for future failure. Some procrastinators unconsciously resist change because they fear the consequences of actually becoming more productive and successful.

Secondary Gains: Procrastination often provides hidden benefits, such as avoiding difficult emotions, maintaining control, or getting attention from others. Giving up these secondary gains can feel like a loss, even when the overall change is positive.

Perfectionist Standards: Perfectionists often resist change because they want to implement changes perfectly from the start. This all-or-nothing thinking can prevent them from beginning the change process at all.

Working with Resistance Rather Than Against It

Effective change strategies acknowledge and work with resistance rather than trying to overcome it through force:

Gradual Implementation: Start with small changes that don't trigger strong resistance. As these small changes become comfortable, gradually expand them.

Compassionate Self-Talk: Treat resistance with curiosity and kindness rather than judgment. Resistance often contains important information about fears or concerns that need to be addressed.

Identify Secondary Gains: Explore what benefits procrastination might be providing and find healthier ways to meet those needs.

Address Underlying Fears: Work directly with fears about failure, success, or identity change rather than trying to ignore them.

Celebrate Small Wins: Acknowledge and celebrate small changes to build positive associations with the change process.

Motivation vs. Discipline: Building Systems That Don't Rely on Feeling Motivated

One of the biggest misconceptions about overcoming procrastination is that it requires constant motivation. In reality, motivation is unreliable and temporary, while sustainable change comes from building systems and habits that function regardless of how we feel in the moment.

The Motivation Myth

Motivation is often misunderstood as the primary driver of behavior change. However, research shows that motivation has several significant limitations:

Temporary Nature: Motivation naturally fluctuates based on mood, energy levels, circumstances, and other factors. Relying on motivation means your progress will be inconsistent and vulnerable to external influences.

Emotional Dependence: Motivation is closely tied to emotions, which are inherently variable. When we feel good, motivation is high; when we feel bad, motivation disappears.

Decision Fatigue: Making decisions about whether to act based on motivation levels depletes mental energy and makes procrastination more likely as the day progresses.

External Dependency: Motivation often depends on external factors like praise, deadlines, or consequences, making it unreliable for self-directed change.

The Discipline Advantage

Discipline, properly understood, is not about forcing yourself to do things through willpower. Instead, it's about creating systems and structures that make desired behaviors easier and more automatic:

Consistency Over Intensity: Discipline focuses on consistent, sustainable actions rather than intense bursts of effort followed by burnout.

System-Dependent: Disciplined approaches rely on systems, habits, and environmental design rather than internal states.

Energy Conservation: Well-designed disciplined systems actually conserve mental energy by reducing the number of decisions required.

Momentum Building: Discipline creates positive momentum that makes continued action easier over time.

Building Motivation-Independent Systems

Environmental Design: Structure your environment to support desired behaviors and make procrastination more difficult. This might include removing distractions, organizing your workspace, or placing important items in visible locations.

Habit Stacking: Link new behaviors to existing habits so they become automatic. For example, "After I pour my morning coffee, I will review my daily priorities."

Implementation Intentions: Create specific if-then plans that remove decision-making from the equation. "If it's 9 AM on a weekday, then I will work on my most important project for 25 minutes."

Minimum Viable Habits: Establish habits that are so small they can be maintained even on difficult days. Focus on consistency rather than intensity.

Accountability Systems: Create external accountability that doesn't depend on your internal motivation levels.

The Role of Motivation in Sustainable Change

While motivation shouldn't be the primary driver of change, it still plays important roles:

Initiation: Motivation often provides the initial energy needed to start the change process and design better systems.

Course Correction: Periodic motivation can help you reassess and adjust your systems when they're not working effectively.

Celebration and Reinforcement: Motivation often increases after successful actions, creating positive feedback loops that support continued change.

Vision and Purpose: Connecting with deeper motivations—your values, long-term goals, and sense of purpose—can provide sustained energy for change efforts.

Identity Shifts: From "I'm a Procrastinator" to "I Take Action"

One of the most powerful aspects of lasting change involves shifting your identity from someone who procrastinates to someone who takes action. This identity shift goes beyond changing behaviors to changing how you see yourself at a fundamental level.

The Power of Identity-Based Change

Traditional approaches to overcoming procrastination focus on changing behaviors or outcomes. Identity-based change focuses on becoming the type of person who naturally engages in desired behaviors:

Behavior-Based Approach: "I want to stop procrastinating on my projects."

Identity-Based Approach: "I want to become the type of person who takes consistent action toward their goals."

Outcome-Based Approach: "I want to complete this project on time."

Identity-Based Approach: "I want to become someone who reliably delivers high-quality work."

The Identity-Behavior Loop

Identity and behavior reinforce each other in a continuous loop:

1. **Identity influences behavior**: How you see yourself determines what actions feel natural and consistent with who you are.
2. **Behavior reinforces identity**: Each action you take provides evidence about what type of person you are.
3. **Identity becomes stronger**: Repeated behaviors strengthen your identity, making future similar behaviors more likely.
4. **Behavior becomes more automatic**: As identity strengthens, desired behaviors require less conscious effort.

Shifting from Procrastinator Identity

Many people who struggle with procrastination have incorporated it into their identity: "I'm just a procrastinator," "I work better under pressure," or "I'm not good with deadlines." These identity statements become self-fulfilling prophecies that maintain procrastination patterns.

Identifying Current Identity Statements

Examine the stories you tell yourself about procrastination:

- What do you say about yourself when you procrastinate?
- How do you explain your procrastination to others?
- What beliefs do you hold about your ability to change?
- How do you describe your work style or personality?

Develop new identity statements that support the person you want to become:

- "I am becoming someone who takes consistent action"
- "I am developing into a reliable person who follows through on commitments"
- "I am learning to be someone who starts tasks promptly"
- "I am growing into someone who manages time effectively"

Evidence-Based Identity Building

Build new identity through small, consistent actions that provide evidence of change:

Start with Tiny Behaviors: Choose behaviors so small that you can do them consistently, providing regular evidence of your new identity.

Track Your Actions: Keep records of actions that align with your desired identity to make the evidence visible and concrete.

Celebrate Identity-Consistent Actions: Acknowledge when you act in ways that align with your new identity, even if the actions are small.

Use Identity-Based Language: When you take action, reinforce it with identity-based self-talk: "This is what someone who takes action does."

Reframe Setbacks: When you experience setbacks, frame them as temporary lapses rather than evidence of your "true" identity.

Handling Setbacks: When Old Patterns Resurface

Setbacks are a normal and expected part of the change process, not signs of failure or evidence that change is impossible. Understanding how to handle setbacks effectively can mean the difference between temporary lapses and complete abandonment of change efforts.

The Nature of Setbacks

Setbacks occur for several predictable reasons:

Stress and Overwhelm: During periods of high stress, people naturally revert to familiar coping mechanisms, including procrastination.

Cognitive Overload: When mental resources are depleted, it becomes harder to maintain new behaviors that require conscious effort.

Environmental Changes: Changes in environment, routine, or circumstances can disrupt new habits and trigger old patterns.

Emotional Triggers: Strong emotions can override rational decision-making and trigger automatic procrastination responses.

Overconfidence: Sometimes early success leads to overconfidence, causing people to relax their systems and structures prematurely.

The Setback Recovery Protocol

When setbacks occur, use this systematic approach to get back on track:

1. Pause and Assess

- Stop and acknowledge that a setback has occurred without judgment
- Assess the scope and impact of the setback objectively
- Identify what triggered the return to old patterns

2. Learn and Adjust

- Extract lessons from the setback about vulnerabilities in your system
- Identify what you could do differently in similar situations
- Adjust your strategies based on what you've learned

3. Recommit and Restart

- Recommit to your goals and identity-based change process
- Start again immediately rather than waiting for the "perfect" time
- Focus on your very next action rather than trying to make up for lost time

4. Strengthen Your System

- Modify your environment or systems to prevent similar setbacks
- Add additional support or accountability if needed
- Simplify your approach if it was too complex or demanding

Common Setback Traps to Avoid

All-or-Nothing Thinking: Viewing setbacks as complete failures rather than temporary lapses.

Shame Spirals: Using setbacks as evidence of personal inadequacy rather than normal parts of the change process.

Perfectionist Restart: Waiting for the "perfect" time to restart rather than beginning again immediately.

System Abandonment: Throwing out entire systems because they didn't prevent setbacks rather than making adjustments.

Isolation: Withdrawing from support systems when setbacks occur rather than reaching out for help.

Building Self-Compassion: Treating Yourself Kindly During the Change Process

Self-compassion is one of the most important factors in successful long-term change. People who treat themselves with kindness during the change process are more likely to persist through difficulties and maintain progress over time.

Understanding Self-Compassion

Self-compassion involves treating yourself with the same kindness and understanding you would offer a good friend facing similar challenges. It includes three key components:

Self-Kindness: Being gentle and understanding with yourself rather than harshly critical when you experience setbacks or difficulties.

Common Humanity: Recognizing that struggle and imperfection are part of the human experience rather than personal failings.

Mindful Awareness: Observing your thoughts and feelings without being overwhelmed by them or pushing them away.

Self-Compassion vs. Self-Indulgence

Many people worry that self-compassion will make them soft or less motivated to change. Research shows the opposite is true:

Self-Compassion Supports Change:

- Reduces shame and self-criticism that often trigger procrastination
- Increases resilience and ability to bounce back from setbacks
- Provides emotional safety that makes it easier to acknowledge problems
- Supports sustainable motivation based on care rather than criticism

Self-Indulgence Undermines Change:

- Makes excuses for problematic behaviors
- Avoids taking responsibility for actions and their consequences
- Prioritizes immediate comfort over long-term well-being
- Enables continued harmful patterns

Developing Self-Compassion Practices

Self-Compassion Breaks: When experiencing difficulty or setbacks, pause and offer yourself compassion using phrases like:

- "This is a moment of struggle"
- "Struggle is part of the human experience"
- "May I be kind to myself in this moment"

Compassionate Self-Talk: Replace harsh self-criticism with kind, encouraging internal dialogue:

- Instead of: "I'm such a failure for procrastinating again"
- Try: "I'm learning to change a difficult pattern, and setbacks are part of the process"

Friend Perspective: Ask yourself how you would respond to a good friend experiencing the same challenges, then offer yourself the same compassion.

Loving-Kindness Meditation: Practice sending kind wishes to yourself and others to develop the capacity for compassion.

Self-Compassion Journaling: Write about difficult experiences from a compassionate perspective, acknowledging your pain while offering yourself kindness.

The Long-Term Benefits of Self-Compassion

Research consistently shows that self-compassionate people are more successful at making lasting changes:

- They're more likely to persist through difficulties
- They experience less anxiety and depression during change processes
- They're more willing to acknowledge mistakes and learn from them
- They maintain better relationships with others during stressful periods
- They're more resilient in the face of setbacks and challenges

The psychology of change is complex, involving neurological, emotional, and social factors that can either support or undermine our efforts to overcome procrastination. By understanding resistance, building motivation-independent systems, shifting identity, handling setbacks effectively, and practicing self-compassion, we create the psychological conditions necessary for lasting change.

Remember that change is not a linear process—it involves cycles of progress, setbacks, learning, and growth. The key is developing the psychological skills and perspectives that support you through this natural process rather than expecting perfect, uninterrupted progress. With patience, understanding, and the right psychological tools, anyone can overcome procrastination and create lasting positive change in their life.

Advanced Strategies and Long-Term Success

Chapter 15: Advanced Anti-Procrastination Techniques

Having mastered the fundamentals of overcoming procrastination through the EMS framework and context-specific solutions, it's time to explore advanced techniques that can elevate your productivity to new levels. These sophisticated strategies go beyond basic time management to address the deeper psychological and behavioral patterns that sustain procrastination. They represent the cutting edge of productivity science and have been proven effective for those ready to make a serious commitment to transformation.

The Two-Minute Rule: Immediate Action for Small Tasks

The Two-Minute Rule, popularized by productivity expert David Allen in his "Getting Things Done" methodology, is deceptively simple yet profoundly effective: if a task takes less than two minutes to complete, do it immediately rather than adding it to your task list or postponing it for later.

The Psychology Behind the Two-Minute Rule

This technique works because it addresses several key psychological barriers to action:

Decision Fatigue Prevention: By eliminating the need to decide when to do small tasks, you preserve mental energy for more important decisions. Each time you encounter a two-minute task and postpone it, you create a small but cumulative drain on your cognitive resources.

Momentum Building: Completing small tasks immediately creates positive momentum that carries over to larger projects. Success breeds success, and the satisfaction of quick completions can energize you for more challenging work.

Cognitive Load Reduction: Unfinished tasks occupy mental space through what psychologists call the "Zeigarnik Effect"—our tendency to remember incomplete tasks more vividly than completed ones. By finishing small tasks immediately, you free up mental bandwidth for more important work.

Implementation Strategies

Task Identification: Learn to quickly assess whether a task truly takes two minutes or less. Common two-minute tasks include:
- Responding to simple emails

- Filing documents
- Making quick phone calls
- Updating calendar entries
- Clearing small areas of clutter
- Sending brief text messages

Boundary Setting: Be strict about the two-minute limit. If a task will take longer, add it to your task management system rather than extending the rule. This prevents the technique from becoming a procrastination tool itself.

Context Awareness: Apply the rule when you have the appropriate context and energy. Don't interrupt deep work sessions for two-minute tasks, but use transition periods and lower-energy times effectively.

Advanced Applications

The Five-Minute Extension: Once you've mastered the two-minute rule, you can carefully extend it to five-minute tasks during specific times of day when you have energy but not enough time for major projects.

Batch Processing: Group related two-minute tasks together for even greater efficiency. For example, process all quick emails at once rather than handling them individually throughout the day.

Energy Matching: Use two-minute tasks strategically to match your energy levels. Handle administrative two-minute tasks during low-energy periods and save creative or complex quick tasks for when you're more alert.

Temptation Bundling: Pairing Unpleasant Tasks with Enjoyable Activities

Temptation bundling, a concept developed by behavioral economist Katherine Milkman, involves pairing activities you should do but often avoid with activities you want to do but perhaps shouldn't indulge in freely. This technique leverages the power of immediate gratification to motivate action on important but less appealing tasks.

The Science of Temptation Bundling

This approach works by hijacking your brain's reward system:

Immediate Gratification: By linking delayed rewards (the benefits of completing important tasks) with immediate rewards (enjoyable activities), you create a more compelling motivation structure.

Habit Stacking: Temptation bundling creates strong associative links between behaviors, making it easier to maintain consistency over time.

Reduced Resistance: When you know that completing an unpleasant task will be paired with something enjoyable, your psychological resistance decreases significantly.

Practical Implementation

Entertainment Bundling

- Listen to favorite podcasts only while doing household chores
- Watch engaging TV shows only while exercising
- Enjoy special music playlists only while working on difficult projects
- Read pleasure books only while commuting to work

Social Bundling

- Schedule challenging work sessions with accountability partners you enjoy spending time with
- Combine networking events with learning opportunities
- Plan difficult conversations during pleasant activities like walks

Sensory Bundling

- Use special candles or aromatherapy only during focused work sessions
- Enjoy premium coffee or tea only while tackling important projects
- Create pleasant work environments that you access only when being productive

Advanced Bundling Strategies

Variable Ratio Reinforcement: Don't bundle every instance of an unpleasant task with a reward. Sometimes provide the reward, sometimes don't, creating a more powerful psychological incentive similar to gambling mechanics.

Graduated Bundling: Start with highly appealing rewards for difficult tasks, then gradually reduce the intensity of rewards as the tasks become more habitual.

Reverse Bundling: Occasionally, require yourself to complete unpleasant tasks before engaging in routine enjoyable activities, creating negative reinforcement for procrastination.

Implementation Intentions

If-Then Planning for Automatic Responses

Implementation intentions, developed by psychologist Peter Gollwitzer, involve creating specific if-then plans that automate responses to common procrastination triggers. This technique transforms conscious decision-making into automatic behavior, reducing the cognitive load required to take action.

The Structure of Implementation Intentions

Every implementation intention follows the same basic format: "If [situation X occurs], then I will [perform behavior Y]." This simple structure creates powerful behavioral programming that bypasses conscious deliberation.

Neurological Basis

Implementation intentions work by:

Pre-Commitment: By deciding in advance how you'll respond to specific situations, you eliminate the need for in-the-moment decision-making when willpower might be low.

Automatic Activation: The brain treats if-then plans as automatic responses, similar to habits, requiring less conscious effort to execute.

Cue Recognition: The "if" component trains your brain to recognize specific situations as triggers for action, increasing the likelihood that you'll notice opportunities to act.

Procrastination-Specific Applications

Trigger Management

- "If I feel the urge to check social media during work time, then I will take three deep breaths and return to my current task."
- "If I start feeling overwhelmed by a large project, then I will write down the smallest possible next step and do it immediately."
- "If I catch myself making excuses to avoid a task, then I will set a timer for 10 minutes and work on it anyway."

Time-Based Intentions

- "If it's 9 AM on a weekday, then I will immediately begin working on my most important project."
- "If I finish eating lunch, then I will spend 15 minutes organizing my workspace."
- "If it's Sunday evening, then I will plan my priorities for the upcoming week."

- "If I sit down at my desk, then I will review my daily priorities before checking email."
- "If I feel tired in the afternoon, then I will take a 10-minute walk before deciding whether to continue working."
- "If I receive a difficult email, then I will wait 24 hours before responding unless it's urgent."

Advanced Implementation Strategies

Nested Intentions: Create chains of if-then statements that guide you through complex scenarios:

- "If I start procrastinating on a project, then I will break it into smaller tasks."
- "If I break a project into smaller tasks, then I will choose the easiest one to start with."
- "If I complete the easiest task, then I will immediately begin the next one."

Emotional Intentions: Address the emotional aspects of procrastination:

- "If I feel anxious about a task, then I will remind myself of three previous successes I've had with similar challenges."
- "If I feel perfectionist pressure, then I will set a 'good enough' standard and commit to meeting only that level initially."

Recovery Intentions: Plan for setbacks:

- "If I procrastinate for more than a day on an important task, then I will ask for help or accountability from someone I trust."
- "If I miss a self-imposed deadline, then I will immediately reschedule the task rather than abandoning it."

Environmental Design: Setting Up Your Surroundings for Success

Environmental design involves deliberately structuring your physical and digital environments to make productive behaviors easier and procrastination more difficult. This approach recognizes that willpower is limited and that changing your environment is often more effective than trying to change your behavior through force alone.

Principles of Environmental Design

Friction Reduction: Make desired behaviors as easy as possible by removing obstacles and streamlining processes.

Friction Addition: Make undesired behaviors more difficult by adding obstacles and inconveniences.

Visual Cues: Use environmental cues to remind yourself of your goals and priorities.

Context Optimization: Create specific environments that support specific types of work or behavior.

Physical Environment Optimization

Workspace Design

- Position your most important work materials in the most accessible locations
- Remove or hide distracting items from your immediate work area
- Use lighting that promotes alertness during work hours
- Maintain a clutter-free environment that reduces cognitive load

Tool Preparation

- Keep all necessary tools for important tasks readily available
- Create "stations" for different types of work (writing station, planning station, etc.)
- Use visual reminders and checklists to guide behavior
- Organize supplies so that starting work requires minimal setup time

Distraction Management

- Place phones and other distracting devices out of sight and reach
- Use physical barriers to separate work and leisure areas
- Create dedicated spaces for specific activities
- Remove or minimize visual clutter that can trigger procrastination

Digital Environment Optimization

Technology Configuration

- Set up website blockers during focused work periods
- Organize digital files and folders for easy access to important materials
- Use apps and tools that support rather than hinder productivity
- Configure notifications to minimize interruptions during deep work

Information Architecture

- Create simple, logical systems for organizing digital information
- Use consistent naming conventions for files and folders
- Implement search strategies that help you find information quickly
- Maintain clean, organized digital workspaces

Automation Implementation

- Automate routine tasks wherever possible
- Use templates and systems to reduce decision-making requirements

- Set up automatic reminders for important deadlines and commitments
- Create workflows that guide you through complex processes

Advanced Environmental Strategies

Context Switching: Create distinct environments for different types of work to help your brain shift into appropriate modes more quickly.

Progressive Enhancement: Gradually improve your environment over time rather than trying to create the perfect setup immediately.

Seasonal Adjustments: Modify your environment based on changing seasons, energy levels, and life circumstances.

Technology Tools and Apps: Digital Assistance for Organization

While technology can be a source of distraction, when used strategically, it can become a powerful ally in overcoming procrastination. The key is choosing tools that genuinely support your productivity goals rather than adding complexity to your life.

Categories of Productivity Technology

Task Management Systems. Modern task management apps go far beyond simple to-do lists:

- **Project Breakdown**: Tools that help you break large projects into manageable components
- **Priority Management**: Systems that help you identify and focus on high-impact activities
- **Deadline Tracking**: Applications that provide visual representations of upcoming deadlines
- **Progress Monitoring**: Tools that track your progress over time and identify patterns

Time Tracking and Management

- **Automatic Tracking**: Applications that monitor how you spend time on digital devices
- **Manual Logging**: Tools for recording time spent on various activities
- **Analysis and Reporting**: Systems that provide insights into your productivity patterns
- **Goal Setting**: Applications that help you set and track time-based objectives

Focus and Concentration Tools

- **Website Blocking**: Applications that restrict access to distracting websites during work periods
- **Ambient Sound**: Tools that provide background noise conducive to concentration

- **Break Reminders**: Systems that encourage regular breaks to maintain productivity
- **Deep Work Timers**: Applications that guide you through focused work sessions

Selection Criteria for Productivity Tools

Simplicity Over Complexity: Choose tools that are intuitive and don't require extensive setup or maintenance. Complex systems often become procrastination tools themselves.

Integration Capabilities: Select applications that work well with your existing tools and workflows rather than requiring you to completely change your systems.

Reliability and Stability: Use tools that are dependable and won't lose your data or fail when you need them most.

Customization Options: Look for applications that can be adapted to your specific needs and working style.

Implementation Best Practices

Gradual Introduction: Implement new tools one at a time rather than trying to revolutionize your entire system at once.

Trial Periods: Test tools thoroughly before committing to them long-term. Many productivity applications offer free trials or basic versions.

Regular Evaluation: Periodically assess whether your tools are still serving your needs or have become sources of distraction themselves.

Backup Systems: Maintain non-digital backup systems for critical information and processes.

Advanced Technology Strategies

Automation Workflows: Create automated sequences that handle routine tasks without your intervention.

Data Analysis: Use the data collected by productivity tools to identify patterns and optimize your approaches.

Cross-Platform Synchronization: Ensure your tools work seamlessly across all your devices and platforms.

Privacy and Security: Choose tools that protect your data and respect your privacy, especially for sensitive information.

The advanced techniques presented in this chapter represent sophisticated approaches to overcoming procrastination that go beyond basic time management. They require commitment and practice to master, but they offer the potential for dramatic improvements in productivity and life satisfaction. The key to success with these techniques is to implement them gradually, allowing each one to become natural before adding the next. Remember that the goal is not to use every technique, but to find the combination that works best for your unique situation and personality.

As you experiment with these advanced strategies, pay attention to which ones resonate with you and produce the best results. Some people thrive with highly structured environmental design, while others prefer the flexibility of implementation intentions. The most effective approach is the one you'll actually use consistently over time.

Chapter 16: Building Lasting Habits

The ultimate goal of overcoming procrastination is not just to complete individual tasks more efficiently, but to fundamentally change your relationship with action and productivity. This transformation happens through the development of lasting habits that make productive behavior automatic and effortless. This chapter explores the science of habit formation and provides practical strategies for building habits that will serve you for a lifetime.

The Habit Loop: Cue, Routine, Reward Cycles

Understanding the neurological basis of habits is crucial for anyone seeking to build lasting behavioral change. Habits operate through what researchers call the "habit loop"—a three-part neurological pattern that governs all habitual behavior.

The Three Components of the Habit Loop

Cue (Trigger): The cue is the environmental or internal signal that triggers the habitual behavior. Cues can be:

- **Environmental**: Specific locations, times of day, or objects in your environment
- **Emotional**: Particular feelings or moods that trigger behavior
- **Social**: Interactions with specific people or groups
- **Preceding Actions**: Other behaviors that naturally lead to the habit
- **Physical Sensations**: Hunger, fatigue, or other bodily signals

Routine (Behavior): The routine is the actual behavior or sequence of actions that you perform. This can be:

- **Physical**: Actions involving movement or manipulation of objects
- **Mental**: Thought patterns, decision-making processes, or cognitive routines
- **Emotional**: Patterns of feeling or emotional regulation strategies

Reward (Benefit): The reward is the benefit you gain from performing the routine. Rewards can be:

- **Intrinsic**: Internal satisfaction, sense of accomplishment, or emotional relief
- **Extrinsic**: External benefits like money, recognition, or tangible outcomes
- **Neurochemical**: The release of dopamine and other feel-good chemicals in the brain

The Neuroscience of Habit Formation

When you first learn a new behavior, your brain's prefrontal cortex—responsible for conscious decision-making—is highly active. However, as the behavior becomes more automatic, activity shifts to the basal ganglia, a more primitive part of the brain that handles automatic behaviors. This shift is what makes habits feel effortless once they're established.

Habit Strength and Automaticity: The strength of a habit is determined by how automatically it's triggered by its cue. Strong habits require minimal conscious thought or willpower to execute, while weak habits still require deliberate effort.

Neural Pathway Development: Each time you complete the habit loop, you strengthen the neural pathways associated with that behavior. This is why consistency is so important in habit formation—each repetition literally rewires your brain.

Craving and Anticipation: Over time, the cue begins to trigger not just the routine, but also a craving for the reward. This craving is what makes habits powerful and self-reinforcing.

Designing Effective Habit Loops for Productivity

Cue Design Strategies

- **Make cues obvious**: Place visual reminders in your environment where you'll encounter them regularly
- **Stack habits**: Use existing habits as cues for new ones
- **Use time-based cues**: Link habits to specific times of day when you're naturally alert and motivated
- **Create environmental cues**: Modify your environment to trigger desired behaviors automatically

Routine Optimization

- **Start small**: Begin with the smallest possible version of the desired behavior
- **Focus on consistency**: Prioritize performing the routine regularly over performing it perfectly
- **Remove friction**: Eliminate obstacles that make the routine difficult to perform
- **Create clear procedures**: Develop step-by-step processes that guide you through the routine

Reward Enhancement

- **Immediate gratification**: Ensure that rewards come immediately after completing the routine
- **Intrinsic motivation**: Connect routines to deeper values and long-term goals
- **Celebration rituals**: Develop specific ways to acknowledge and celebrate completion
- **Progress tracking**: Use visual indicators of progress as rewards

Keystone Habits: Small Changes That Create Big Transformations

Keystone habits are small changes or habits that people introduce into their routines that unintentionally carry over into other aspects of their lives. These habits have the power to start a chain reaction, changing other habits as they move through an organization or individual's life.

Characteristics of Keystone Habits

Widespread Impact: Keystone habits influence multiple areas of life simultaneously. For example, regular exercise often leads to better eating habits, improved sleep, increased productivity, and better mood regulation.

Identity Reinforcement: These habits reinforce a positive self-image that supports other good habits. When you see yourself as "someone who exercises regularly," you're more likely to make other health-conscious choices.

Skill Development: Keystone habits often teach valuable skills that transfer to other areas. Planning and executing a daily exercise routine develops discipline, time management, and goal-setting skills.

Momentum Creation: Success with keystone habits creates positive momentum that makes other changes feel more achievable.

Common Keystone Habits for Overcoming Procrastination

Daily Planning and Review

- **Morning Planning**: Spending 10-15 minutes each morning identifying priorities and planning the day
- **Evening Review**: Reflecting on the day's accomplishments and planning for tomorrow
- **Weekly Planning**: Conducting comprehensive weekly planning sessions

This keystone habit impacts:

- Time management skills
- Priority clarity
- Goal achievement
- Stress reduction
- Decision-making quality

Regular Exercise

- **Daily Movement**: Incorporating some form of physical activity into each day
- **Scheduled Workouts**: Maintaining a consistent exercise schedule
- **Active Commuting**: Walking, biking, or using active transportation when possible

This keystone habit impacts:

- Energy levels
- Mental clarity
- Stress management
- Sleep quality
- Self-discipline

Consistent Sleep Schedule

- **Regular Bedtime**: Going to bed at the same time each night
- **Morning Routine**: Waking up at the same time each day
- **Sleep Hygiene**: Maintaining practices that support quality sleep

This keystone habit impacts:

- Cognitive function
- Emotional regulation
- Physical health
- Productivity levels
- Decision-making ability

Meditation or Mindfulness Practice

- **Daily Meditation**: Regular mindfulness or meditation practice
- **Mindful Moments**: Incorporating brief mindfulness exercises throughout the day
- **Stress Awareness**: Developing awareness of stress and emotional states

This keystone habit impacts:

- Emotional regulation
- Focus and concentration
- Stress management
- Self-awareness
- Impulse control

Implementing Keystone Habits

Identification Process

1. **Assess Current Challenges**: Identify the areas of your life where procrastination is most problematic

2. **Look for Connections**: Find habits that could positively impact multiple problem areas
3. **Consider Your Personality**: Choose keystone habits that align with your natural preferences and strengths
4. **Start Small**: Begin with the smallest possible version of the keystone habit

Implementation Strategy

1. **Focus on One Habit**: Implement only one keystone habit at a time
2. **Perfect the Basics**: Master the fundamental routine before adding complexity
3. **Track Progress**: Monitor both the keystone habit and its ripple effects
4. **Be Patient**: Allow time for the habit to establish before expecting widespread changes

Monitoring Ripple Effects

- **Keep a Journal**: Record changes you notice in other areas of your life
- **Regular Assessment**: Periodically evaluate how the keystone habit is affecting other behaviors
- **Celebrate Connections**: Acknowledge and celebrate when you notice positive spillover effects
- **Adjust as Needed**: Modify the keystone habit if it's not producing the desired ripple effects

Habit Stacking: Linking New Behaviors to Established Routines

Habit stacking, popularized by James Clear in "Atomic Habits," is a strategy that involves linking a new habit to an existing habit. This technique leverages the power of established neural pathways to make new habits more likely to stick.

The Science Behind Habit Stacking

Neural Pathway Utilization: Existing habits have well-established neural pathways that fire automatically in response to specific cues. By linking new behaviors to these established pathways, you can "piggyback" on the existing automaticity.

Reduced Cognitive Load: Because the existing habit requires minimal conscious thought, you have more mental resources available to focus on establishing the new behavior.

Contextual Cueing: The completion of the existing habit serves as a powerful and consistent cue for the new habit, eliminating the need to remember to perform the new behavior.

The Habit Stacking Formula

The basic formula for habit stacking is: "After I [existing habit], I will [new habit]."

Examples:

- "After I pour my morning coffee, I will write down my three priorities for the day."
- "After I sit down at my desk, I will take three deep breaths and review my task list."
- "After I finish eating lunch, I will spend five minutes organizing my workspace."
- "After I close my laptop at the end of the workday, I will plan tomorrow's most important task."

Advanced Habit Stacking Strategies

Chain Stacking: Create chains of habits that flow naturally from one to the next:

- "After I wake up, I will make my bed."
- "After I make my bed, I will do 10 push-ups."
- "After I do 10 push-ups, I will meditate for 5 minutes."
- "After I meditate, I will review my daily priorities."

Context Stacking: Link habits to specific contexts or environments rather than just other habits:

- "When I enter my office, I will immediately review my task list."
- "When I sit in my car, I will take three deep breaths before starting the engine."
- "When I open my laptop, I will check my calendar before checking email."

Time-Based Stacking: Combine habit stacking with specific times:

- "After I eat breakfast at 8 AM, I will work on my most important project for 30 minutes."
- "After I finish my 2 PM meeting, I will take a 10-minute walk."

Implementation Guidelines

Choose Strong Anchor Habits: Select existing habits that are:

- **Highly consistent**: Performed almost every day without fail
- **Well-established**: Habits you've been doing for months or years
- **Naturally occurring**: Behaviors that happen automatically without reminders

Match Habit Intensity: Pair new habits with anchor habits of similar intensity:

- **High-energy anchors**: Link challenging new habits to energizing existing habits
- **Low-energy anchors**: Link simple new habits to calm, routine existing habits
- **Cognitive matching**: Pair mentally demanding new habits with cognitively light anchor habits

Consider Timing and Context: Ensure that the new habit makes sense in the context of the anchor habit:

- **Logical flow**: The new habit should feel like a natural next step
- **Appropriate timing**: Consider whether you'll have time and energy for the new habit
- **Environmental compatibility**: Ensure you'll be in the right place to perform the new habit

Troubleshooting Common Stacking Problems

Weak Anchor Habits: If your anchor habit isn't consistent enough, the stack will fail. Choose more reliable anchors or strengthen existing habits before stacking.

Incompatible Contexts: If the new habit doesn't fit naturally with the anchor habit's context, the stack will feel forced and be difficult to maintain.

Overambitious New Habits: If the new habit is too challenging or time-consuming, it will disrupt the flow of the anchor habit and be abandoned.

Tracking Progress: Measurement Systems That Motivate

What gets measured gets managed, and this principle is especially important when building lasting habits. Effective tracking systems provide motivation, accountability, and valuable data about your progress and patterns.

The Psychology of Progress Tracking

Visual Progress: Seeing tangible evidence of your progress activates the brain's reward system and provides motivation to continue.

Accountability: Tracking creates a form of self-accountability that makes it harder to ignore or rationalize missed days.

Pattern Recognition: Data from tracking helps you identify patterns in your behavior, including what helps and what hinders your habit formation.

Momentum Building: Visible streaks and progress create psychological momentum that makes habits easier to maintain.

Types of Tracking Systems

Binary Tracking: Simple yes/no tracking of whether you performed the habit:
- **Habit calendars**: Mark an X for each day you complete the habit
- **Streak counters**: Track consecutive days of habit completion
- **Checkbox lists**: Simple daily checklists of habits to complete

Quantitative Tracking: Measuring specific metrics related to your habits:
- **Time tracking**: Recording how long you spend on habit-related activities

- **Repetition counting**: Tracking the number of times you perform a behavior
- **Quality metrics**: Rating the quality or intensity of your habit performance

Qualitative Tracking: Recording subjective experiences and observations:

- **Mood tracking**: Recording how habits affect your emotional state
- **Energy levels**: Noting how habits impact your energy throughout the day
- **Reflection notes**: Writing brief observations about your habit experiences

Digital vs. Analog Tracking

Digital Tracking Advantages:

- **Automation**: Some aspects can be tracked automatically
- **Data analysis**: Easy to analyze patterns and trends
- **Reminders**: Built-in notification systems
- **Accessibility**: Available on multiple devices

Analog Tracking Advantages:

- **Tactile satisfaction**: Physical act of marking progress
- **Visual prominence**: Always visible without opening apps
- **Simplicity**: No technology dependencies
- **Customization**: Easy to adapt to personal preferences

Designing Effective Tracking Systems

Keep It Simple: The tracking system should take minimal time and effort to maintain. Complex systems are more likely to be abandoned.

Make It Visible: Place tracking tools where you'll see them regularly and be reminded to update them.

Focus on Leading Indicators: Track behaviors you can control rather than outcomes you can't directly influence.

Include Recovery Tracking: Track not just successes but also how quickly you recover from missed days.

Tracking Best Practices

Start Small: Begin by tracking just one or two habits rather than trying to monitor everything at once.

Be Consistent: Update your tracking system at the same time each day to make it habitual.

Review Regularly: Periodically review your tracking data to identify patterns and make adjustments.

Celebrate Milestones: Use your tracking data to identify and celebrate important milestones and achievements.

Adjust as Needed: Modify your tracking system if it becomes burdensome or stops providing value.

Maintaining Momentum: Strategies for Long-Term Consistency

Building lasting habits requires more than just initial motivation—it requires strategies for maintaining momentum through the inevitable challenges, setbacks, and changes that life brings.

Understanding Momentum in Habit Formation

The Plateau Effect: After initial progress, habit formation often reaches plateaus where progress feels slow or non-existent. Understanding this is normal helps maintain motivation during these periods.

Motivation Fluctuation: Motivation naturally fluctuates over time. Sustainable habits must be designed to survive periods of low motivation.

Life Changes: Major life changes (moves, job changes, relationship changes) can disrupt established habits. Building flexibility into your habit systems helps them survive these transitions.

Strategies for Long-Term Maintenance

The Never Miss Twice Rule: When you miss a day of your habit, make it a priority to get back on track the next day. This prevents single missed days from becoming abandoned habits.

Minimum Viable Habits: Establish "emergency" versions of your habits that you can maintain even on difficult days:

- **Full habit**: 30-minute morning workout
- Minimum version: 5 push-ups
- **Emergency version**: Put on workout clothes

Seasonal Adjustments: Modify your habits to account for seasonal changes in energy, schedule, and motivation:

- **Winter adaptations**: Indoor alternatives for outdoor habits
- **Holiday modifications**: Simplified versions during busy periods
- **Schedule changes**: Adjusted timing for different life phases

Identity-Based Maintenance: Focus on becoming the type of person who naturally performs these habits rather than just trying to achieve specific outcomes.

Building Anti-Fragile Habits

Redundancy: Create multiple pathways to maintain your habits so that disruption in one area doesn't derail everything.

Flexibility: Build adaptability into your habit systems so they can evolve with changing circumstances.

Recovery Protocols: Develop specific plans for getting back on track after disruptions or setbacks.

Support Systems: Cultivate relationships and environments that support your habits even when your personal motivation is low.

Long-Term Habit Evolution

Progressive Enhancement: Gradually improve and expand your habits over time rather than trying to achieve perfection immediately.

Habit Retirement: Recognize when habits have served their purpose and can be retired to make room for new ones.

System Integration: Over time, integrate individual habits into comprehensive systems that support your overall life goals.

Continuous Learning: Stay curious about new approaches and techniques that can enhance your existing habit systems.

Building lasting habits is one of the most powerful ways to overcome procrastination permanently. By understanding the science of habit formation and implementing proven strategies for habit development and maintenance, you can create automatic systems that support productivity and achievement without requiring constant willpower or motivation.

Remember that habit formation is a gradual process that requires patience and persistence. Focus on consistency over perfection, and celebrate small wins along the way. The habits you build today will compound over time, creating a foundation for lifelong productivity and success.

The key to success with habit formation is to start small, be consistent, and gradually build complexity over time. Don't try to transform your entire life overnight—instead, focus on building one solid habit at a time, allowing each one to become automatic before adding the next. With patience and persistence, you can create a life where productive action becomes as natural and automatic as breathing.

Chapter 17: Creating Your Personal Action Plan

The journey from chronic procrastination to consistent productivity requires more than just understanding concepts and techniques—it demands a personalized, systematic approach that transforms knowledge into action. This chapter will guide you through creating a comprehensive action plan tailored to your specific situation, challenges, and goals. By the end of this chapter, you'll have a clear roadmap for implementing everything you've learned in a way that creates lasting change.

Comprehensive Self-Assessment: Where You Are Now

Before you can chart a course to where you want to be, you must have a clear understanding of your current situation. This comprehensive self-assessment will help you identify your specific procrastination patterns, strengths, challenges, and readiness for change.

Procrastination Pattern Analysis

Frequency and Intensity Assessment

Rate yourself on the following scale for each area of your life:

- 1 = Never procrastinate in this area
- 2 = Rarely procrastinate (less than once per month)
- 3 = Sometimes procrastinate (1-3 times per month)
- 4 = Often procrastinate (1-3 times per week)
- 5 = Constantly procrastinate (daily)

Life Areas to Assess:

- **Work/Career Tasks**: Projects, deadlines, meetings, emails
- **Personal Finance**: Bill paying, budgeting, tax preparation, investment decisions
- **Health and Fitness**: Exercise, medical appointments, healthy eating, sleep hygiene
- **Relationships**: Communication, conflict resolution, quality time, commitments
- **Home Management**: Cleaning, organizing, maintenance, repairs
- **Personal Development**: Learning, skill building, goal pursuit, creative projects
- **Social Obligations**: Events, gatherings, community involvement, volunteer work

Trigger Identification Exercise

For each area where you scored 3 or higher, identify:

Emotional Triggers: What feelings typically precede procrastination?

- Anxiety or fear
- Overwhelm or confusion
- Boredom or lack of interest
- Perfectionist pressure
- Resentment or resistance

Situational Triggers: What circumstances make procrastination more likely?

- Time of day
- Physical environment
- Presence of distractions
- Energy levels
- Social context

Task Characteristics: What types of tasks do you most often avoid?

- Large, complex projects
- Unfamiliar or challenging tasks
- Boring or repetitive activities
- Tasks with unclear requirements
- High-stakes or important work

Current Coping Strategies Assessment

Existing Strengths: Identify areas where you already manage procrastination well:

- What strategies have worked for you in the past?
- In which contexts are you naturally more productive?
- What motivates you most effectively?
- When do you feel most confident and capable?

Current Challenges: Honestly assess your biggest obstacles:

- What consistently derails your productivity efforts?
- Which environments or situations trigger procrastination?
- What excuses do you most commonly make?
- Where do you feel most stuck or helpless?

Resource Inventory: Catalog your available resources:

- **Time**: How much time can you realistically dedicate to change efforts?
- **Energy**: When are your peak energy periods for implementing new strategies?
- **Support**: Who in your life can provide encouragement and accountability?

- **Tools**: What productivity tools, apps, or systems do you already have access to?
- **Knowledge**: What relevant skills or knowledge do you already possess?

Readiness for Change Assessment

Motivation Level: On a scale of 1-10, rate your motivation to overcome procrastination:

- 1-3: Low motivation, change feels overwhelming or unnecessary
- 4-6: Moderate motivation, willing to try but not fully committed
- 7-10: High motivation, ready to make significant changes

Confidence Level: Rate your confidence in your ability to change:

- 1-3: Low confidence, doubt your ability to change
- 4-6: Moderate confidence, believe change is possible but challenging
- 7-10: High confidence, believe you can successfully overcome procrastination

Priority Level: Rate how important overcoming procrastination is compared to other life priorities:

- 1-3: Low priority, other concerns are more pressing
- 4-6: Moderate priority, important but competing with other goals
- 7-10: High priority, one of your most important current objectives

Barrier Analysis: Identify potential obstacles to implementing change:

- **Internal barriers**: Fear, perfectionism, low self-efficacy, competing priorities
- **External barriers**: Lack of time, unsupportive environment, competing demands
- **Systemic barriers**: Organizational culture, family dynamics, financial constraints

Goal Setting Workshop: Defining Your Procrastination-Free Future

With a clear understanding of your current situation, it's time to define what success looks like for you. This goal-setting workshop will help you create compelling, achievable objectives that will guide your transformation journey.

Vision Creation Exercise

Future Self Visualization: Imagine yourself one year from now, having successfully overcome procrastination. Write detailed descriptions of:

Daily Life: How does your typical day look different?

- What time do you wake up and how do you start your day?
- How do you approach work tasks and deadlines?
- What does your workspace look like and how do you use it?
- How do you handle interruptions and distractions?
- How do you end your workday and transition to personal time?

Emotional State: How do you feel about yourself and your capabilities?

- What emotions do you experience when facing challenging tasks?
- How confident do you feel about meeting commitments?
- What is your relationship with deadlines and time pressure?
- How do you handle setbacks and unexpected challenges?

Relationships: How have your relationships changed?

- How do others perceive your reliability and trustworthiness?
- What kinds of commitments are you able to make and keep?
- How do you handle requests and expectations from others?
- What role do you play in group projects and collaborations?

Achievements: What have you accomplished?

- What projects have you completed that you're proud of?
- What opportunities have opened up due to your increased productivity?
- What skills have you developed through consistent action?
- What goals have you achieved that previously seemed impossible?

BRILLIANT Goal Framework Application

Using the BRILLIANT framework from the original procrastination document, create specific goals for your transformation:

Bull's-eye Specific Goals: Define exactly what you want to achieve:

- "Complete all work projects by their original deadlines without last-minute rushing"
- "Maintain a clean and organized home environment through daily 15-minute maintenance sessions"
- "Exercise for 30 minutes, 5 days per week, for 6 consecutive months"

Realistic and Achievable: Ensure your goals are challenging but attainable:

- Consider your current situation and constraints
- Build on existing strengths and successful patterns
- Allow adequate time for habit formation and skill development
- Include contingency plans for potential obstacles

Inherently Measurable: Create clear metrics for success:

- **Behavioral measures**: Frequency of desired actions
- **Outcome measures**: Results achieved through consistent action
- **Time-based measures**: Deadlines met, time saved, efficiency gains
- **Quality measures**: Standards maintained, satisfaction levels

Legitimate and Personal: Ensure goals align with your values and desires:

- Connect goals to your deeper motivations and values

- Distinguish between goals you want and goals others expect
- Consider how achieving these goals will impact other areas of your life
- Ensure goals feel personally meaningful and worthwhile

Logical and Sequential: Create goals that build on each other:

- **Foundation goals**: Basic habits and systems that support everything else
- **Development goals**: Skills and capabilities that enable higher-level achievements
- **Achievement goals**: Specific outcomes you want to accomplish
- **Maintenance goals**: Systems for sustaining progress over time

Impeccably Clear: Remove any ambiguity from your goals:

- Define exactly what success looks like
- Specify the conditions under which goals will be considered achieved
- Clarify any assumptions or dependencies
- Create detailed action steps for each goal

Action-Oriented: Focus on behaviors you can control:

- Emphasize what you will do rather than what you hope will happen
- Break goals down into specific, actionable steps
- Identify the first action you'll take toward each goal
- Create implementation plans that specify when and how you'll act

Noteworthy and Meaningful: Ensure goals are worth the effort required:

- Connect goals to larger life purposes and values
- Consider the impact achieving these goals will have on your life
- Ensure goals are significant enough to sustain motivation through challenges
- Celebrate the importance of the changes you're making

Time-Based: Set specific deadlines and milestones:

- **Short-term goals** (1-3 months): Habit establishment and initial changes
- **Medium-term goals** (3-12 months): Skill development and system refinement
- **Long-term goals** (1+ years): Major achievements and lifestyle transformation

30-60-90 Day Implementation Plans: Gradual, Sustainable Change

Sustainable change happens gradually, through consistent small steps rather than dramatic overnight transformations. This phased approach allows you to build momentum, learn from experience, and adjust your strategies based on what works best for you.

30-Day Foundation Phase: Building Basic Systems

The first 30 days focus on establishing fundamental habits and systems that will support all future progress. This phase is about creating a solid foundation rather than achieving dramatic results.

Week 1: Assessment and Preparation

- Complete comprehensive self-assessment
- Choose one keystone habit to focus on
- Set up basic tracking system
- Prepare environment for success
- Identify and remove obvious obstacles

Week 2: Habit Initiation

- Begin daily practice of chosen keystone habit
- Implement basic time-blocking system
- Start daily planning routine (5-10 minutes each morning)
- Practice the Two-Minute Rule for small tasks
- Begin tracking progress daily

Week 3: System Refinement

- Adjust keystone habit based on initial experience
- Add one implementation intention for common procrastination trigger
- Expand time-blocking to include personal activities
- Implement weekly review process
- Address any emerging obstacles or challenges

Week 4: Consolidation and Planning

- Solidify gains from first three weeks
- Conduct comprehensive review of progress
- Plan for 60-day phase based on lessons learned
- Celebrate successes and learn from setbacks
- Prepare for next level of implementation

30-Day Success Metrics:

- Keystone habit performed at least 20 out of 30 days
- Daily planning routine established and maintained
- Basic time-blocking system in place and functioning
- Tracking system providing useful data and motivation
- Increased awareness of procrastination patterns and triggers

60-Day Development Phase: Expanding and Deepening

The second month focuses on expanding your anti-procrastination toolkit and deepening the habits established in the foundation phase.

Week 5-6: Habit Expansion

- Add second keystone habit or expand existing habit
- Implement temptation bundling for difficult tasks
- Create environmental modifications to support productivity
- Develop more sophisticated time management systems
- Begin using advanced techniques like the Swiss Cheese Method

Week 7-8: System Integration

- Integrate multiple productivity techniques into cohesive system
- Develop context-specific strategies (home, work, social situations)
- Create accountability partnerships or support systems
- Implement more advanced tracking and analysis methods
- Address relationship impacts of behavior changes

60-Day Success Metrics:

- Multiple habits functioning smoothly together
- Noticeable improvement in at least one major life area
- Consistent use of multiple anti-procrastination techniques
- Strong tracking system providing insights and motivation
- Positive feedback from others about increased reliability

90-Day Mastery Phase: Optimization and Sustainability

The third month focuses on optimizing your systems, addressing remaining challenges, and building long-term sustainability.

Week 9-10: Advanced Implementation

- Implement most challenging or sophisticated techniques
- Address persistent procrastination patterns
- Optimize systems based on 60 days of experience
- Develop strategies for handling setbacks and disruptions
- Create plans for maintaining progress during stressful periods

Week 11-12: Sustainability Planning

- Develop long-term maintenance strategies
- Create systems for continuous improvement
- Plan for handling major life changes or disruptions

- Establish ongoing accountability and support systems
- Celebrate achievements and plan for continued growth

90-Day Success Metrics:

- Significant improvement in all major procrastination areas
- Robust systems that function even during stressful periods
- Strong sense of identity as someone who takes consistent action
- Positive impact on relationships, career, and personal satisfaction
- Clear plans for continued growth and development

Building Your Support Network: Friends, Family, and Professional Help

Overcoming procrastination is challenging work that's much easier with support from others. Building a strong support network provides encouragement, accountability, and practical assistance when you need it most.

Types of Support You Need

Emotional Support: People who provide encouragement, understanding, and motivation:

- **Family members** who understand your goals and cheer your progress
- **Friends** who celebrate your successes and provide comfort during setbacks
- **Mentors** who have overcome similar challenges and can provide perspective
- **Support groups** where you can connect with others facing similar challenges

Practical Support: People who provide concrete assistance and accountability:

- **Accountability partners** who check in on your progress regularly
- **Colleagues** who can help with work-related procrastination challenges
- **Professional organizers** who can help optimize your environment
- **Coaches or therapists** who provide specialized guidance and support

Informational Support: People who provide knowledge, advice, and resources:

- **Experts** in productivity, time management, or behavior change
- **Peers** who have successfully overcome procrastination
- **Professionals** who can address underlying issues like ADHD or anxiety
- **Authors and educators** whose work provides ongoing learning and inspiration

Building Your Support Network

Family and Friends

- **Communicate your goals**: Share your procrastination-fighting goals with people close to you

- **Ask for specific support**: Be clear about what kind of help you need
- **Set boundaries**: Protect your productivity time while maintaining relationships
- **Express gratitude**: Acknowledge and appreciate the support you receive

Professional Support

- **Therapists or counselors**: For addressing underlying emotional or psychological issues
- **Coaches**: For ongoing guidance and accountability
- **Medical professionals**: For addressing potential ADHD, depression, or other conditions
- **Productivity consultants**: For help with systems and environmental design

Peer Support

- **Accountability partners**: Find someone with similar goals for mutual support
- **Study groups or work groups**: Join or create groups focused on productivity
- **Online communities**: Participate in forums or social media groups about overcoming procrastination
- **Local meetups**: Find in-person groups focused on productivity or personal development

Maintaining Your Support Network

Regular Communication: Stay in touch with your support network consistently, not just when you need help.

Reciprocal Support: Offer support to others in your network, creating mutually beneficial relationships.

Appreciation and Gratitude: Regularly express thanks for the support you receive.

Boundary Respect: Honor the boundaries and limitations of your support network members.

Network Evolution: Allow your support network to evolve as your needs and circumstances change.

Emergency Protocols: What to Do When Procrastination Strikes

Despite your best efforts and systems, there will be times when procrastination strikes. Having emergency protocols in place helps you respond quickly and effectively, minimizing the impact and getting back on track as soon as possible.

Immediate Response Protocol (First 5 Minutes)

Step 1: Pause and Acknowledge

- Stop what you're doing and take three deep breaths
- Acknowledge that procrastination is happening without judgment
- Remind yourself that this is temporary and manageable

Step 2: Assess the Situation

- Identify what triggered the procrastination
- Assess your current emotional and physical state
- Determine the urgency and importance of the avoided task

Step 3: Choose Your Response

- Select the most appropriate emergency technique based on the situation
- Commit to trying the technique for at least 10 minutes
- Set a timer to create urgency and focus

Emergency Technique Menu

For Overwhelm: The Brain Dump Method

- Write down everything that's overwhelming you
- Categorize items by urgency and importance
- Choose the smallest, most manageable item to start with
- Focus on just that one item for 10 minutes

For Perfectionism: The "Good Enough" Standard

- Define what "good enough" looks like for this task
- Set a timer for a specific amount of time
- Work toward the "good enough" standard only
- Remind yourself that done is better than perfect

For Lack of Motivation: The Two-Minute Start

- Commit to working on the task for just two minutes
- Set a timer and begin immediately
- Focus only on starting, not on finishing
- Often momentum will carry you beyond the two minutes

For Fear or Anxiety: The Worst-Case Scenario Analysis

- Write down what you're afraid will happen
- Assess how likely these outcomes really are
- Develop plans for handling worst-case scenarios
- Remind yourself of past successes in similar situations

For Boredom: Temptation Bundling Emergency

- Pair the boring task with something enjoyable
- Listen to favorite music or podcasts while working
- Work in a pleasant environment
- Promise yourself a reward after completion

Recovery Protocol (First 24 Hours)

Hour 1-2: Immediate Action

- Use emergency techniques to take some action on the avoided task
- Focus on momentum rather than perfection
- Celebrate any progress made, no matter how small

Hour 2-6: System Analysis

- Identify what led to the procrastination episode
- Assess whether your current systems need adjustment
- Plan specific modifications to prevent similar episodes
- Reach out to accountability partners if needed

Day 1: Recommitment

- Recommit to your goals and systems
- Adjust plans based on lessons learned
- Strengthen weak points in your anti-procrastination system
- Plan for continued progress tomorrow

Prevention Protocol (Ongoing)

Daily Prevention

- Start each day with clear priorities and plans
- Use your tracking system to maintain awareness
- Practice stress management and self-care
- End each day with reflection and planning for tomorrow

Weekly Prevention

- Conduct weekly reviews to identify potential problems early
- Adjust systems and strategies based on what's working
- Plan for challenging periods or high-stress situations
- Maintain connection with your support network

Monthly Prevention

- Assess overall progress and system effectiveness
- Make larger adjustments to goals or strategies if needed
- Celebrate successes and learn from setbacks

- Plan for seasonal changes or life transitions

Creating your personal action plan is the bridge between knowledge and transformation. By conducting a thorough self-assessment, setting clear goals, implementing gradual change, building strong support networks, and preparing for challenges, you create a comprehensive roadmap for overcoming procrastination permanently.

Remember that your action plan is a living document that should evolve as you grow and change. Be willing to adjust your strategies based on what you learn about yourself and what works best in your unique situation. The key to success is not perfection, but persistence and continuous improvement.

Your journey from procrastination to productivity is unique to you, but you don't have to travel it alone. Use the frameworks and strategies in this chapter to create a plan that fits your life, your goals, and your circumstances. With commitment, patience, and the right support, you can transform procrastination from a persistent problem into a conquered challenge.

The power to change is in your hands. Your procrastination-free future begins with the first step you take today.

Living Procrastination-Free

Chapter 18: Maintaining Your Progress

The journey from chronic procrastination to consistent productivity doesn't end when you've successfully implemented your personal action plan. In many ways, it's just the beginning. The most challenging aspect of overcoming procrastination isn't the initial breakthrough—it's maintaining that progress over the long term. This chapter provides you with the tools, strategies, and mindset necessary to sustain your transformation and continue growing throughout your life.

Regular Review Systems: Monthly and Quarterly Check-ins

Maintaining progress requires systematic evaluation of your anti-procrastination systems and strategies. Without regular review, even the most effective systems can gradually deteriorate, allowing old patterns to creep back into your life.

The Power of Regular Reviews

Regular reviews serve multiple critical functions in maintaining your progress:

Progress Tracking: Reviews help you measure how far you've come and identify areas where you're still struggling. This objective assessment prevents you from falling into the trap of either overconfidence or unnecessary self-criticism.

System Optimization: What worked perfectly three months ago might need adjustment as your life circumstances change. Regular reviews allow you to fine-tune your approaches and eliminate strategies that are no longer serving you.

Early Warning Detection: Reviews help you spot the early signs of procrastination creeping back before it becomes a serious problem. This early detection allows for quick course corrections rather than major overhauls.

Motivation Renewal: Seeing concrete evidence of your progress during reviews can reignite motivation and commitment during challenging periods.

Monthly Review Framework

Conduct monthly reviews using this comprehensive framework:

Progress Assessment

- **Habit Tracking Review**: Analyze your habit tracking data for patterns and trends
- **Goal Achievement**: Assess progress toward your monthly and quarterly goals
- **Challenge Areas**: Identify areas where procrastination still occurs most frequently

- **Success Stories**: Document specific instances where you successfully overcame procrastination impulses

System Evaluation

- **Tool Effectiveness**: Evaluate which productivity tools and techniques are working best
- **Time Management**: Assess the effectiveness of your time-blocking and scheduling systems
- **Environmental Factors**: Review whether your physical and digital environments still support productivity
- **Energy Management**: Analyze how well you're managing your energy levels throughout the day

Adjustment Planning

- **Strategy Modifications**: Identify specific changes to make to your anti-procrastination strategies
- **New Challenges**: Plan how to address emerging procrastination triggers or situations
- **Skill Development**: Identify areas where you need to develop new skills or knowledge
- **Support System**: Evaluate and adjust your accountability and support systems

Quarterly Review Process

Quarterly reviews provide a broader perspective and allow for more significant strategic adjustments:

Comprehensive Life Assessment

- **Major Life Areas**: Evaluate progress in career, relationships, health, personal development, and other key areas
- **Values Alignment**: Assess whether your activities and goals still align with your core values
- **Identity Evolution**: Reflect on how your identity and self-concept have evolved
- **Long-term Vision**: Review and potentially adjust your long-term vision and goals

Deep System Analysis

- **Pattern Recognition**: Look for deeper patterns in your procrastination and productivity cycles
- **Seasonal Adjustments**: Plan for seasonal changes that might affect your productivity
- **Life Stage Considerations**: Adjust strategies based on changing life circumstances

- **Technology Evolution**: Evaluate new tools and technologies that might enhance your systems

Strategic Planning

- **Quarterly Objectives**: Set specific objectives for the next quarter
- **System Upgrades**: Plan major improvements to your productivity systems
- **Learning Goals**: Identify new skills or knowledge areas to develop
- **Relationship Goals**: Set objectives for improving or developing key relationships

Adjusting Strategies: Adapting Techniques as Life Changes

Life is dynamic, and your anti-procrastination strategies must be equally adaptable. What works during one phase of your life may need significant modification as circumstances change.

Common Life Changes Requiring Strategy Adjustments

Career Transitions

- **New Job Responsibilities**: Different roles may require different productivity approaches
- **Changing Work Environments**: Remote work, office work, or hybrid arrangements each have unique challenges
- **Increased Responsibilities**: Promotions or expanded roles may require more sophisticated time management
- **Industry Changes**: Evolving industries may demand new skills and approaches

Relationship Changes

- **Marriage or Partnership**: Shared living requires coordination and compromise in productivity systems
- **Parenthood**: Children dramatically change available time and energy patterns
- **Caregiving Responsibilities**: Caring for aging parents or family members requires schedule flexibility
- **Social Circle Evolution**: New relationships may bring different influences and expectations

Health and Aging

- **Energy Level Changes**: Natural aging or health conditions may require energy management adjustments
- **Physical Limitations**: Injuries or chronic conditions may necessitate new approaches

- **Mental Health Fluctuations**: Depression, anxiety, or other conditions may require specialized strategies
- **Medication Effects**: New medications may affect concentration, energy, or motivation

Life Stage Transitions

- **Student to Professional**: The transition from academic to work life requires significant strategy shifts
- **Mid-life Transitions**: Career changes, empty nest syndrome, or mid-life reassessment periods
- **Retirement Preparation**: Shifting from external structure to self-directed time management
- **Geographic Moves**: Relocations disrupt established routines and support systems

Adaptation Strategies

Flexible Core Principles. Maintain core anti-procrastination principles while adapting specific techniques:

- **Priority Management**: The need to establish priorities remains constant, but the criteria may change
- **Time Awareness**: Time management remains important, but the structure may need to be more or less rigid
- **Goal Setting**: Goal-setting principles stay the same, but the timeframes and types of goals may evolve
- **Self-Awareness**: Continued self-monitoring remains crucial regardless of life circumstances

Gradual Transition Approach. When major life changes occur, implement strategy adjustments gradually:

- **Assess New Requirements**: Understand what the new situation demands before making changes
- **Pilot New Approaches**: Test new strategies on a small scale before full implementation
- **Maintain Stability**: Keep some familiar elements while introducing new ones
- **Monitor and Adjust**: Pay close attention to what's working and what isn't during transition periods

Context-Specific Customization. Develop different approaches for different contexts:

- **Work Strategies**: Techniques optimized for your professional environment
- **Home Strategies**: Approaches that work well in your personal space

- **Travel Strategies**: Simplified systems that work when you're away from your usual environment
- **Crisis Strategies**: Emergency protocols for high-stress or unusual situations

Preventing Relapse: Recognizing and Addressing Warning Signs

Procrastination relapse is common and doesn't indicate failure—it's a normal part of the change process. The key is recognizing warning signs early and having strategies ready to address them before they become serious problems.

Early Warning Signs of Procrastination Relapse

Behavioral Indicators

- **Increased Task Avoidance**: Finding yourself avoiding tasks you previously handled well
- **Return to Old Patterns**: Reverting to familiar procrastination behaviors like excessive social media use
- **Deadline Pressure**: Feeling rushed or stressed about deadlines that previously felt manageable
- **Incomplete Tasks**: Leaving more tasks unfinished than usual
- **Excuse Making**: Increasing frequency of rationalization and excuse-making

Emotional Indicators

- **Guilt and Shame**: Feeling bad about your productivity levels
- **Overwhelm**: Feeling like you have too much to do and don't know where to start
- **Anxiety**: Increased worry about tasks, deadlines, or performance
- **Frustration**: Feeling annoyed with yourself or your systems
- **Apathy**: Losing interest in goals that previously motivated you

Cognitive Indicators

- **All-or-Nothing Thinking**: Returning to perfectionist or binary thinking patterns
- **Negative Self-Talk**: Increased criticism of yourself or your abilities
- **Future Discounting**: Difficulty connecting current actions with future consequences
- **Catastrophizing**: Imagining worst-case scenarios for minor setbacks
- **Rumination**: Spending excessive time thinking about problems rather than solving them

- **Sleep Disruption**: Changes in sleep patterns, often staying up late to catch up on work

- **Energy Depletion**: Feeling more tired or drained than usual

- **Stress Symptoms**: Physical manifestations of stress like headaches, muscle tension, or digestive issues

- **Neglected Self-Care**: Skipping exercise, poor eating habits, or ignoring health needs

- **Workspace Deterioration**: Allowing your work environment to become disorganized or cluttered

Relapse Prevention Strategies

Early Intervention Protocol. When you notice warning signs, implement this systematic response:

Step 1: Acknowledge Without Judgment

- Recognize that noticing warning signs is actually a success—it shows your self-awareness is working

- Avoid self-criticism or catastrophic thinking about the situation

- Remember that temporary setbacks are normal and don't erase your progress

Step 2: Assess the Situation

- Identify which specific warning signs you're experiencing

- Determine potential triggers or causes for the relapse

- Evaluate which of your systems or strategies have been neglected

- Consider whether external circumstances have changed

Step 3: Implement Immediate Interventions

- Return to your most basic, reliable anti-procrastination strategies

- Simplify your approach temporarily to reduce overwhelm

- Focus on completing one small task to rebuild momentum

- Reach out to your support network for accountability and encouragement

Step 4: Address Root Causes

- Modify your systems to address the identified triggers

- Adjust your strategies to accommodate any changed circumstances

- Strengthen the areas where you've been struggling most

- Consider whether you need additional support or resources

Resilience Building

Stress Inoculation. Gradually expose yourself to manageable levels of stress and challenge to build resilience:

- **Controlled Challenges**: Deliberately take on slightly challenging projects to maintain your skills
- **Stress Management Practice**: Regularly practice stress management techniques even when not stressed
- **Flexibility Training**: Intentionally vary your routines to build adaptability
- **Recovery Practice**: Develop and practice recovery strategies before you need them

Support System Maintenance. Keep your support systems active even when you're doing well:

- **Regular Check-ins**: Maintain contact with accountability partners and mentors
- **Peer Learning**: Continue learning from others who have overcome similar challenges
- **Professional Development**: Invest in ongoing learning about productivity and personal development
- **Community Involvement**: Participate in communities focused on personal growth and productivity

Continuous Improvement: Refining Your Anti-Procrastination Skills

Maintaining progress isn't just about preventing relapse—it's about continuously improving and refining your skills. The goal is to become increasingly effective and efficient while making productivity feel more natural and effortless.

The Continuous Improvement Mindset

Growth Orientation. Adopt a mindset that views challenges as opportunities for growth:

- **Learning from Setbacks**: Treat every procrastination episode as valuable data for improvement
- **Skill Development**: Continuously work on developing new productivity and life management skills
- **Innovation**: Experiment with new techniques and approaches
- **Mastery Pursuit**: Aim for increasing levels of mastery in your core productivity skills

Systems Thinking. View your anti-procrastination approach as an integrated system:

- **Interconnectedness**: Understand how different elements of your system affect each other
- **Optimization**: Look for ways to make your systems more efficient and effective

- **Integration**: Ensure all parts of your system work together harmoniously
- **Evolution**: Allow your systems to evolve and improve over time

Areas for Continuous Improvement

Skill Refinement

- **Time Estimation**: Become increasingly accurate at estimating how long tasks will take
- **Priority Assessment**: Develop more sophisticated ability to identify what's truly important
- **Energy Management**: Refine your understanding of your energy patterns and optimization strategies
- **Decision Making**: Improve your ability to make quick, effective decisions
- **Communication**: Enhance your ability to communicate boundaries and expectations to others

System Optimization

- **Tool Mastery**: Become more proficient with your productivity tools and technologies
- **Process Streamlining**: Continuously look for ways to make your processes more efficient
- **Automation**: Identify opportunities to automate routine tasks and decisions
- **Integration**: Better integrate your various productivity systems and tools
- **Customization**: Tailor your approaches more precisely to your unique needs and preferences

Knowledge Expansion

- **Industry Trends**: Stay current with developments in productivity research and techniques
- **Personal Insights**: Deepen your understanding of your own patterns and preferences
- **Best Practices**: Learn from others who have achieved high levels of productivity
- **Scientific Understanding**: Stay informed about research in psychology, neuroscience, and behavior change
- **Practical Application**: Continuously experiment with applying new knowledge to your situation

Improvement Implementation Strategies

Experimental Approach. Treat improvement efforts as experiments:

- **Hypothesis Formation**: Develop clear hypotheses about what might improve your productivity
- **Controlled Testing**: Test one change at a time to isolate its effects

- **Data Collection**: Gather objective data about the results of your experiments
- **Analysis and Conclusion**: Draw evidence-based conclusions about what works
- **Implementation or Abandonment**: Either implement successful changes or abandon unsuccessful ones

Incremental Enhancement. Make small, continuous improvements rather than dramatic overhauls:

- **1% Better**: Focus on being slightly better each day rather than seeking dramatic transformations
- **Compound Effects**: Understand that small improvements compound over time
- **Sustainable Pace**: Maintain a pace of improvement that doesn't create overwhelm
- **Patience**: Allow time for improvements to take effect before making additional changes
- **Consistency**: Prioritize consistent small improvements over sporadic large ones

Learning Integration. Systematically integrate new learning into your existing systems:

- **Regular Learning**: Dedicate time to learning about productivity and personal development
- **Practical Application**: Immediately look for ways to apply new learning
- **Reflection and Integration**: Reflect on how new learning fits with your existing knowledge
- **Teaching Others**: Reinforce your learning by teaching or sharing with others
- **Documentation**: Keep records of what you learn and how you apply it

Life-Long Learning: Staying Curious and Growing Beyond Procrastination

The most successful people in overcoming procrastination are those who maintain a commitment to life-long learning and growth. This extends far beyond just productivity techniques to encompass personal development, skill building, and continuous expansion of capabilities.

The Learning Mindset

Curiosity Cultivation. Maintain active curiosity about yourself and the world around you:

- **Self-Discovery**: Continue exploring your motivations, values, and aspirations
- **Skill Exploration**: Remain open to developing new skills and capabilities
- **Perspective Seeking**: Actively seek out different viewpoints and approaches
- **Question Asking**: Maintain the habit of asking thoughtful questions
- **Wonder Preservation**: Keep alive your sense of wonder and interest in learning

Growth Challenges. Regularly challenge yourself to grow in new ways:

- **Comfort Zone Expansion**: Deliberately step outside your comfort zone
- **Skill Stretching**: Take on projects that require you to develop new abilities
- **Perspective Broadening**: Expose yourself to different cultures, ideas, and ways of thinking
- **Leadership Development**: Look for opportunities to lead and influence others positively
- **Creative Expression**: Explore creative outlets that challenge different aspects of your mind

Learning Applications

Professional Development. Continue growing in your career and professional capabilities:

- **Industry Expertise**: Deepen your knowledge in your field of work
- **Leadership Skills**: Develop your ability to lead and influence others
- **Communication Enhancement**: Continuously improve your communication abilities
- **Strategic Thinking**: Develop your capacity for strategic and systems thinking
- **Innovation Capability**: Enhance your ability to innovate and solve complex problems

Personal Growth. Invest in your personal development beyond productivity:

- **Emotional Intelligence**: Develop greater self-awareness and interpersonal skills
- **Relationship Building**: Enhance your ability to build and maintain meaningful relationships
- **Health and Wellness**: Continuously learn about and improve your physical and mental health
- **Spiritual Development**: Explore questions of meaning, purpose, and connection
- **Life Skills**: Develop practical skills that enhance your quality of life

Contribution and Legacy. Use your growth to contribute to others and create a positive legacy:

- **Mentoring**: Share your knowledge and experience with others who are struggling with procrastination
- **Teaching**: Formally or informally teach others about productivity and personal development
- **Writing and Speaking**: Share your insights through writing, speaking, or content creation
- **Community Building**: Help build communities of people committed to growth and productivity

- **Social Impact**: Use your enhanced capabilities to make a positive impact on society

Learning Strategies for Life-Long Growth

Structured Learning. Engage in formal learning opportunities:

- **Courses and Workshops**: Regularly participate in educational programs
- **Reading Programs**: Maintain a consistent reading habit focused on growth
- **Conferences and Events**: Attend events related to your interests and professional development
- **Certification Programs**: Pursue relevant certifications and credentials
- **Degree Programs**: Consider formal education programs when appropriate

Experiential Learning. Learn through direct experience and practice:

- **Project-Based Learning**: Take on projects that require you to learn new skills
- **Travel and Exploration**: Use travel and new experiences as learning opportunities
- **Volunteer Work**: Engage in volunteer activities that challenge and develop you
- **Side Projects**: Pursue personal projects that interest and challenge you
- **Collaboration**: Work with others who can teach you new approaches and perspectives

Reflective Learning. Develop your capacity for learning from experience:

- **Journaling**: Maintain a regular practice of reflective writing
- **Meditation and Contemplation**: Use quiet time for deeper reflection and insight
- **Feedback Seeking**: Actively seek feedback from others about your growth and development
- **Self-Assessment**: Regularly assess your progress and areas for improvement
- **Integration Practice**: Consciously work to integrate new learning into your life and work

Maintaining progress in overcoming procrastination is a life-long journey that requires commitment, flexibility, and continuous growth. By implementing regular review systems, staying alert to warning signs, continuously improving your skills, and maintaining a learning mindset, you can not only sustain your progress but continue to grow and develop throughout your life.

Remember that the goal isn't perfection—it's progress. There will be setbacks, challenges, and periods of struggle. What matters is your commitment to getting back on track, learning from your experiences, and continuing to move forward. The skills you develop in overcoming procrastination will serve you well in all areas of life, creating a foundation for continuous growth and achievement.

Chapter 19: The Procrastination-Free Life

Living free from the grip of chronic procrastination represents more than just improved productivity—it's a fundamental transformation that touches every aspect of your existence. This final chapter explores what life looks like when procrastination no longer controls your decisions, relationships, and dreams. It's about understanding the profound changes that occur when you consistently take action toward your goals and live with intention and purpose.

What Changes: Improved Relationships, Career Advancement, Personal Satisfaction

The transformation from a procrastination-dominated life to one of consistent action creates ripple effects that extend far beyond simply completing tasks on time. These changes often surprise people with their depth and breadth, touching areas of life they never expected.

Relationship Transformation

Trust and Reliability. When you consistently follow through on commitments, people begin to see you differently. The transformation in how others perceive and interact with you can be profound:

- **Increased Respect**: Others begin to respect your word and value your commitments
- **Greater Responsibility**: People start entrusting you with more important tasks and decisions
- **Deeper Connections**: Relationships deepen when others know they can count on you
- **Leadership Opportunities**: Your reliability naturally positions you as someone others want to follow
- **Reduced Conflict**: Fewer broken promises mean fewer arguments and disappointments

Communication Improvements. Freedom from procrastination changes how you communicate:

- **Proactive Updates**: You communicate about progress rather than making excuses for delays
- **Honest Timelines**: You become more accurate in estimating and communicating realistic timeframes

- **Confident Commitments**: You make commitments with confidence because you know you'll follow through
- **Problem-Solving Focus**: Conversations shift from explaining delays to solving challenges
- **Future-Oriented Discussions**: You can engage in long-term planning because others trust your follow-through

Family Dynamics. The impact on family relationships is often the most meaningful:

- **Modeling Behavior**: Your children learn the value of commitment and follow-through
- **Reduced Stress**: Family stress decreases when everyone can rely on your commitments
- **Quality Time**: You have more genuine free time because you're not constantly catching up
- **Shared Goals**: You can work together on family goals because others trust your participation
- **Legacy Building**: You begin building a legacy of reliability and achievement for your family

Career Advancement

Professional Reputation. Your professional reputation undergoes a dramatic transformation:

- **Dependability**: Colleagues and supervisors see you as someone they can count on
- **Quality Work**: Without last-minute rushes, your work quality improves significantly
- **Innovation Opportunity**: You have time to think creatively rather than just react to deadlines
- **Leadership Potential**: Your reliability makes you a natural candidate for leadership roles
- **Network Expansion**: People want to work with reliable individuals, expanding your professional network

Opportunity Creation. Consistent action creates opportunities that weren't previously available:

- **Stretch Assignments**: Supervisors offer you challenging projects because they trust your delivery
- **Cross-Functional Collaboration**: Other departments seek you out for important initiatives
- **Client Relationships**: Clients specifically request to work with you
- **Speaking and Teaching**: Your expertise and reliability create opportunities to share knowledge

- **Entrepreneurial Ventures**: You have the confidence and track record to pursue independent ventures

Financial Impact. The financial benefits of overcoming procrastination compound over time:

- **Promotion Acceleration**: Reliable employees advance faster and earn more
- **Bonus Eligibility**: Consistent performance makes you eligible for performance bonuses
- **Opportunity Capture**: You're positioned to take advantage of financial opportunities
- **Reduced Costs**: Fewer late fees, rush charges, and missed opportunities
- **Investment Capability**: Better financial management creates investment opportunities

Personal Satisfaction and Well-being

Internal Peace. Perhaps the most significant change is the internal peace that comes from alignment between intentions and actions:

- **Reduced Anxiety**: No more constant worry about unfinished tasks and looming deadlines
- **Improved Sleep**: Your mind can rest because you're not mentally rehearsing tomorrow's catch-up activities
- **Increased Confidence**: Each completed commitment builds confidence in your capabilities
- **Authentic Self-Expression**: You can be genuine because you're not hiding behind excuses
- **Present Moment Awareness**: You can enjoy the present because you're not mentally stuck in past failures or future anxieties

Energy and Vitality. Living without procrastination dramatically increases your energy levels:

- **Physical Energy**: Less stress means more physical vitality and health
- **Mental Clarity**: Your mind is clearer when not cluttered with unfinished business
- **Emotional Stability**: Consistent action creates emotional equilibrium
- **Creative Flow**: You have mental space for creativity and innovation
- **Spiritual Connection**: Alignment between values and actions enhances spiritual well-being

Achievement and Growth. The compound effect of consistent action creates remarkable achievements:

- **Goal Attainment**: You actually achieve the goals you set rather than just hoping for them

- **Skill Development**: Consistent practice leads to genuine expertise and mastery
- **Learning Acceleration**: You learn faster because you apply knowledge immediately
- **Challenge Embrace**: You welcome challenges because you trust your ability to handle them
- **Legacy Creation**: Your consistent actions create a meaningful legacy

Unexpected Benefits: Increased Creativity, Better Health, Enhanced Self-Esteem

While the obvious benefits of overcoming procrastination are well-known, many people are surprised by the unexpected positive changes that emerge. These secondary benefits often prove to be as valuable as the primary improvements in productivity.

Increased Creativity and Innovation

Mental Space Liberation. When your mind isn't constantly occupied with unfinished tasks and looming deadlines, remarkable creative capacity emerges:

- **Cognitive Freedom**: Your brain has processing power available for creative thinking rather than anxiety management
- **Associative Thinking**: You can make connections between ideas because your mind isn't fragmented
- **Playful Exploration**: You have permission to explore ideas without the pressure of urgent tasks
- **Risk-Taking Ability**: Security in your productivity gives you freedom to take creative risks
- **Flow State Access**: You can enter flow states more easily when not distracted by procrastination guilt

Creative Confidence. Overcoming procrastination builds creative confidence:

- **Idea Implementation**: You trust yourself to follow through on creative ideas
- **Experimentation Freedom**: You can experiment because you know you'll complete what you start
- **Failure Tolerance**: You're more willing to risk creative failure because you trust your recovery ability
- **Collaborative Creativity**: Others seek your creative input because they trust your follow-through
- **Innovation Leadership**: You become known for both creative ideas and practical implementation

Artistic and Creative Pursuits. Many people discover or rediscover artistic talents:

- **Hobby Development**: You have time and energy for creative hobbies and interests
- **Skill Building**: Consistent practice leads to genuine artistic skill development
- **Creative Projects**: You can undertake and complete meaningful creative projects
- **Artistic Expression**: You find unique ways to express yourself creatively
- **Creative Community**: You connect with other creative individuals and communities

Better Physical and Mental Health

Stress Reduction. The health benefits of reduced procrastination-related stress are profound:

- **Cortisol Regulation**: Lower chronic stress leads to better hormonal balance
- **Immune Function**: Reduced stress improves immune system functioning
- **Cardiovascular Health**: Lower stress reduces risk of heart disease and hypertension
- **Digestive Health**: Stress reduction improves digestive function and gut health
- **Sleep Quality**: Better stress management leads to more restorative sleep

Lifestyle Improvements. Overcoming procrastination often catalyzes broader lifestyle improvements:

- **Exercise Consistency**: You're more likely to maintain regular exercise routines
- **Nutrition Planning**: You plan and prepare healthier meals rather than relying on convenience foods
- **Medical Care**: You keep up with preventive medical care and health screenings
- **Self-Care Practices**: You prioritize activities that support your physical and mental well-being
- **Work-Life Balance**: You create better boundaries between work and personal time

Mental Health Enhancement. The psychological benefits extend far beyond reduced anxiety:

- **Depression Resistance**: Consistent achievement provides natural protection against depression
- **Resilience Building**: Success in overcoming procrastination builds general resilience
- **Emotional Regulation**: You develop better skills for managing difficult emotions
- **Mindfulness Capacity**: Present-moment awareness improves when not distracted by unfinished business
- **Psychological Safety**: You feel safer in the world when you trust your own capabilities

Enhanced Self-Esteem and Identity

Identity Transformation. Perhaps the most profound change is the shift in how you see yourself:

- **Capability Belief**: You genuinely believe in your ability to handle challenges
- **Reliability Identity**: You see yourself as someone others can count on
- **Achievement Orientation**: You identify as someone who accomplishes goals
- **Growth Mindset**: You believe in your capacity for continued learning and development
- **Leadership Potential**: You see yourself as capable of leading and influencing others

Self-Respect Development. Consistent action builds genuine self-respect:

- **Integrity Alignment**: Your actions align with your values and commitments
- **Promise Keeping**: You keep promises to yourself as well as others
- **Standard Maintenance**: You maintain high standards for yourself
- **Boundary Setting**: You respect yourself enough to set and maintain healthy boundaries
- **Self-Advocacy**: You advocate for your needs and interests appropriately

Confidence Expansion. Success in overcoming procrastination creates expanding confidence:

- **Challenge Acceptance**: You're willing to take on increasingly difficult challenges
- **Risk Tolerance**: You can take calculated risks because you trust your ability to handle outcomes
- **Leadership Comfort**: You're comfortable in leadership roles and situations
- **Public Speaking**: Many people find their fear of public speaking diminishes
- **Social Confidence**: You feel more confident in social and professional situations

Paying It Forward: Helping Others Overcome Procrastination

One of the most fulfilling aspects of overcoming procrastination is the opportunity to help others who are struggling with the same challenges. This giving back not only helps others but also reinforces your own transformation and continued growth.

The Natural Desire to Help

Empathy and Understanding. Your experience with procrastination creates deep empathy for others facing similar struggles:

- **Recognition**: You can recognize the signs of procrastination in others
- **Compassion**: You understand the internal struggle and shame that often accompany procrastination
- **Hope Offering**: You can offer genuine hope because you've experienced transformation yourself

- **Practical Insight**: You understand what actually works versus what sounds good in theory
- **Patience**: You have patience for the change process because you remember your own journey

Credibility and Influence. Your transformation gives you unique credibility:

- **Living Proof**: You are living evidence that change is possible
- **Practical Experience**: You have real-world experience with what works and what doesn't
- **Relatable Story**: Others can relate to your struggle and be inspired by your success
- **Ongoing Journey**: You can share both successes and ongoing challenges honestly
- **Authentic Voice**: Your advice comes from experience rather than theory alone

Ways to Help Others

Informal Mentoring. Many opportunities exist for informal mentoring and support:

- **Workplace Guidance**: Help colleagues who struggle with deadlines and follow-through
- **Family Support**: Guide family members, especially children, in developing good habits
- **Friend Assistance**: Offer support and accountability to friends facing similar challenges
- **Community Involvement**: Participate in community groups focused on personal development
- **Online Sharing**: Share your experience and insights through social media or blogs

Formal Teaching and Training. Your experience may lead to formal teaching opportunities:

- **Workshop Leadership**: Lead workshops on productivity and procrastination for organizations
- **Speaking Engagements**: Share your story and strategies at conferences and events
- **Writing and Content Creation**: Write articles, books, or create content about overcoming procrastination
- **Coaching and Consulting**: Provide one-on-one coaching for individuals struggling with procrastination
- **Training Development**: Develop training programs for organizations dealing with productivity challenges

Peer Support and Community Building. Help create communities of support and growth:

- **Support Group Formation**: Start or participate in support groups for people overcoming procrastination

- **Accountability Partnerships**: Serve as an accountability partner for others
- **Study Groups**: Organize groups focused on productivity and personal development
- **Online Communities**: Participate in or moderate online communities focused on overcoming procrastination
- **Mastermind Groups**: Form or join mastermind groups focused on achievement and growth

The Benefits of Helping Others

Reinforcement of Your Own Learning. Teaching others reinforces your own transformation:

- **Knowledge Deepening**: Explaining concepts to others deepens your own understanding
- **Skill Reinforcement**: Helping others practice skills reinforces your own abilities
- **Commitment Strengthening**: Being a role model strengthens your own commitment to growth
- **Perspective Gaining**: Seeing others' challenges helps you appreciate your own progress
- **Continuous Learning**: Others' questions and challenges help you continue learning

Meaning and Purpose. Helping others adds deep meaning to your transformation:

- **Purpose Fulfillment**: Using your experience to help others creates a sense of purpose
- **Legacy Building**: You create a positive legacy through the people you help
- **Impact Multiplication**: Your transformation impacts not just you but everyone you help
- **Community Contribution**: You contribute to building a more productive and fulfilled community
- **Spiritual Growth**: Many people find deep spiritual satisfaction in helping others grow

Life-Long Learning: Staying Curious and Growing Beyond Procrastination

The journey of overcoming procrastination often awakens a broader appetite for growth and learning that extends far beyond productivity. This expanded curiosity and commitment to growth becomes a defining characteristic of the procrastination-free life.

Expanded Learning Appetite

Curiosity Renaissance. Many people experience a renaissance of curiosity after overcoming procrastination:

- **Intellectual Exploration**: You have mental energy available for exploring new ideas and concepts
- **Skill Development**: You're motivated to develop new skills because you trust your ability to follow through
- **Creative Pursuits**: You explore creative interests that were previously neglected
- **Cultural Exploration**: You have time and energy to explore different cultures and perspectives
- **Scientific Interest**: Many people develop new interest in understanding how things work

Learning Confidence. Success in overcoming procrastination builds confidence in your ability to learn:

- **Challenge Embrace**: You're willing to tackle challenging learning projects
- **Failure Tolerance**: You can handle the frustration and setbacks that come with learning
- **Persistence Development**: You've developed the persistence needed for deep learning
- **Growth Mindset**: You believe in your capacity for continued growth and development
- **Mastery Orientation**: You're motivated by the intrinsic satisfaction of mastery rather than just external rewards

Areas of Continued Growth

Professional Development. Your career growth often accelerates after overcoming procrastination:

- **Industry Expertise**: You develop deep expertise in your field through consistent learning
- **Leadership Skills**: You develop increasingly sophisticated leadership capabilities
- **Strategic Thinking**: You develop the ability to think strategically about complex challenges
- **Innovation Capability**: You become known for your ability to innovate and solve problems
- **Cross-Functional Knowledge**: You develop knowledge in areas beyond your primary expertise

Personal Development. Personal growth becomes a lifelong pursuit:

- **Emotional Intelligence**: You continue developing your emotional and social intelligence
- **Relationship Skills**: You work on becoming better at building and maintaining relationships

- **Communication Mastery**: You develop increasingly sophisticated communication skills
- **Self-Awareness**: You continue deepening your understanding of yourself
- **Wisdom Development**: You work on developing practical wisdom and good judgment

Contribution and Service. Many people develop a strong orientation toward service and contribution:

- **Community Leadership**: You take on leadership roles in your community
- **Mentoring and Teaching**: You become committed to helping others grow and develop
- **Social Impact**: You look for ways to make a positive impact on society
- **Legacy Building**: You think about the legacy you want to leave
- **Generational Impact**: You consider how your growth impacts future generations

The Continuous Growth Mindset

Learning as Lifestyle. Learning becomes a way of life rather than something you do occasionally:

- **Daily Learning**: You incorporate learning into your daily routine
- **Experiential Learning**: You see every experience as an opportunity to learn
- **Reflective Practice**: You regularly reflect on your experiences to extract learning
- **Teaching Others**: You use teaching as a way to deepen your own learning
- **Curiosity Cultivation**: You actively cultivate and maintain your curiosity

Growth Through Challenge. You actively seek out challenges as opportunities for growth:

- **Comfort Zone Expansion**: You regularly step outside your comfort zone
- **Skill Stretching**: You take on projects that require you to develop new capabilities
- **Leadership Opportunities**: You seek opportunities to lead and influence others
- **Creative Challenges**: You pursue creative challenges that stretch your abilities
- **Service Opportunities**: You look for ways to serve others and contribute to causes you care about

Your New Identity: Living as Someone Who Takes Consistent Action

The ultimate transformation in overcoming procrastination is the development of a new identity—seeing yourself as someone who takes consistent action toward meaningful goals. This identity shift is perhaps the most important and lasting change of all.

Identity Evolution

From Procrastinator to Action-Taker. The shift in identity is profound and multifaceted:

- **Self-Concept**: You see yourself as someone who follows through on commitments

- **Capability Belief**: You believe in your ability to handle whatever challenges arise
- **Reliability Identity**: Others see you as reliable, and you see yourself that way too
- **Achievement Orientation**: You identify as someone who accomplishes meaningful goals
- **Growth Mindset**: You see yourself as someone who is continuously growing and developing

Values Alignment. Your actions become aligned with your deepest values:
- **Integrity**: Your actions consistently match your stated values and commitments
- **Excellence**: You pursue excellence in the things that matter most to you
- **Service**: You look for ways to serve others and contribute to something larger than yourself
- **Growth**: You value continuous learning and development
- **Impact**: You focus on making a positive impact in the world

Living with Intention

Purposeful Action. Every action becomes more intentional and purposeful:
- **Goal Alignment**: Your daily actions align with your long-term goals
- **Value Expression**: Your actions express your deepest values and beliefs
- **Impact Consideration**: You consider the impact of your actions on others and the world
- **Legacy Thinking**: You think about how your actions contribute to the legacy you want to leave
- **Present Moment Awareness**: You're fully present in your actions rather than going through the motions

Authentic Living. You live more authentically because your actions match your intentions:
- **Genuine Expression**: You can be genuine because you're not hiding behind excuses
- **Confident Communication**: You communicate with confidence because you trust your follow-through
- **Relationship Authenticity**: Your relationships are more authentic because others can count on you
- **Self-Respect**: You respect yourself because you keep your commitments to yourself
- **Inner Peace**: You experience inner peace because your life is aligned with your values

The Ripple Effect

Personal Impact. Your transformation creates ripple effects throughout your personal life:
- **Family Influence**: Your family benefits from your reliability and achievement

- **Friend Inspiration**: Your friends are inspired by your transformation
- **Community Contribution**: Your community benefits from your increased involvement and leadership
- **Professional Impact**: Your workplace benefits from your enhanced productivity and reliability
- **Social Influence**: You influence others toward positive change through your example

Generational Impact. Your transformation can impact future generations:

- **Children's Learning**: Your children learn the value of commitment and follow-through
- **Modeling Behavior**: You model what's possible when someone commits to growth
- **Legacy Creation**: You create a legacy of achievement and contribution
- **Cultural Influence**: You contribute to a culture that values action and achievement
- **Future Inspiration**: Your story can inspire others for generations to come

The procrastination-free life is not about perfection—it's about progress, growth, and the deep satisfaction that comes from living with intention and purpose. It's about becoming the person you were meant to be and making the contribution you were meant to make. The journey of overcoming procrastination is ultimately a journey toward your best self and your most meaningful life.

As you continue on this path, remember that every day offers new opportunities to take action, to grow, and to contribute. The skills you've developed in overcoming procrastination will serve you well in every area of life, creating a foundation for continued success and fulfillment. Your procrastination-free life is not just about what you accomplish—it's about who you become in the process.

Appendices

Appendix A: Quick Reference Tools

This appendix provides you with essential tools and templates that you can use immediately to implement the strategies discussed throughout this book. These resources are designed to be practical, actionable, and easily adaptable to your specific situation.

Emergency Anti-Procrastination Checklist

Use this checklist when you find yourself procrastinating and need immediate intervention:

Immediate Response (First 5 Minutes)

☐ Stop and take three deep breaths

☐ Acknowledge that procrastination is happening without judgment

☐ Identify what triggered the procrastination

☐ Assess your current emotional and physical state

☐ Choose one emergency technique to try for 10 minutes

Emergency Techniques Menu

☐ **For Overwhelm**: Brain dump everything on paper, then choose one small item

☐ **For Perfectionism**: Define "good enough" standard and set a timer

☐ **For Lack of Motivation**: Commit to just 2 minutes of work

☐ **For Fear/Anxiety**: Write down worst-case scenario and assess its likelihood

☐ **For Boredom**: Add music, change location, or promise yourself a reward

Recovery Actions (Next 24 Hours)

☐ Complete the chosen emergency technique

☐ Identify what led to the procrastination episode

☐ Adjust your systems to prevent similar episodes

☐ Reach out to accountability partner if needed

☐ Plan your next action step

☐ Celebrate any progress made, however small

Daily and Weekly Planning Templates

Daily Priority Planning Template

Date: _____

Three Daily Priorities:

   1. **Big Priority** (Most important goal-related task):

Time allocated: _____ Energy level needed: _____

   2. **Relationship Priority** (Action to strengthen important relationship):

Time allocated: _____ Energy level needed: _____

   3. **Personal Priority** (Self-care or personal development):

Time allocated: _____ Energy level needed: _____

Time Blocks:

- **Morning (High Energy):** _____
- **Mid-Morning:** _____
- Afternoon (Medium Energy): _____
- **Late Afternoon:** _____
- **Evening (Low Energy):** _____

Potential Obstacles: _____

Contingency Plans: _____

End-of-Day Reflection:

☐ What did I accomplish today?

☐ What challenges did I face?

☐ What did I learn about myself?

☐ How can I improve tomorrow?

Weekly Review Template

Week of: _____

Weekly Accomplishments:

Challenges Faced:

- **Procrastination triggers:** _____
- **Time management issues:** _____
- Energy management problems: _____
- **External obstacles:** _____

Lessons Learned:

- **About myself:** _____
- **About my systems:** _____
- **About my environment:** _____

Next Week's Focus:
1. **Primary Goal**: _____
2. **System Improvement**: _____
3. **Skill Development**: _____

Adjustments to Make:

☐ Schedule changes needed

☐ Environment modifications

☐ Tool or system updates

☐ Support system changes

Goal-Setting Worksheets
BRILLIANT Goal Setting Worksheet

Goal Statement: _____

BRILLIANT Criteria Check:

☐ **Bull's-eye Specific**: Can a stranger understand exactly what I want to achieve?

Details: _____

☐ **Realistic**: Is this achievable given my current resources and constraints?

Assessment: _____

☐ **Inherently Measurable**: How will I know when I've achieved this goal?

Metrics: _____

☐ **Legitimate**: Does this align with my values and authentic desires?

Values connection: _____

☐ **Logical**: Does this make sense given my current situation?

Logic check: _____

☐ **Impeccably Clear**: Is there any ambiguity about what success looks like?

Clarity verification: _____

☐ **Action-Oriented**: What specific actions will I take?

Key actions: _____

☐ **Noteworthy**: Is this goal significant enough to justify the effort?

Significance: _____

☐ **Time-Based**: What is the specific deadline?

Deadline: _____

Goal Breakdown Worksheet

Major Goal: _____

Phase 1: _____

- Task 1.1: _____
- Task 1.2: _____
- Task 1.3: _____
- Deadline: _____

Phase 2: _____

- Task 2.1: _____
- Task 2.2: _____
- Task 2.3: _____
- Deadline: _____

Phase 3: _____

- Task 3.1: _____
- Task 3.2: _____
- Task 3.3: _____
- Deadline: _____

Milestones and Celebrations:

- 25% Complete: _____
- 50% Complete: _____
- 75% Complete: _____
- 100% Complete: _____

Time Audit Forms

Weekly Time Audit Log

Instructions: Track your time in 30-minute blocks for one week. Be honest and specific.

Day: _____

Time	Activity	Energy Level (1-10)	Productivity (1-10)	Notes
6:00-6:30				
6:30-7:00				
7:00-7:30				
7:30-8:00				
8:00-8:30				
8:30-9:00				
9:00-9:30				
9:30-10:00				
10:00-10:30				
10:30-11:00				
11:00-11:30				
11:30-12:00				
12:00-12:30				
12:30-1:00				
1:00-1:30				

1:30-2:00				
2:00-2:30				
2:30-3:00				
3:00-3:30				
3:30-4:00				
4:00-4:30				
4:30-5:00				
5:00-5:30				
5:30-6:00				
6:00-6:30				
6:30-7:00				
7:00-7:30				
7:30-8:00				
8:00-8:30				
8:30-9:00				
9:00-9:30				
9:30-10:00				

Time Audit Analysis Worksheet

Time Allocation Summary:

- Work/Career: _____ hours (____%)
- Personal/Family: _____ hours (____%)
- Health/Self-care: _____ hours (____%)
- Learning/Development: _____ hours (____%)
- Entertainment/Leisure: _____ hours (____%)
- Administrative: _____ hours (____%)
- Sleep: _____ hours (____%)

Energy Patterns:

- Highest energy time: _____
- Lowest energy time: _____
- Most productive hours: _____
- Least productive hours: _____

Time Leaks Identified:

1. Daily impact: _____ minutes
   Weekly total: _____ hours
   Annual projection: _____ hours
2. Daily impact: _____ minutes
   Weekly total: _____ hours
   Annual projection: _____ hours
3. Daily impact: _____ minutes
   Weekly total: _____ hours
   Annual projection: _____ hours

Priority Alignment Assessment:

☐ My time allocation matches my stated priorities

☐ I spend adequate time on my most important goals

☐ I have identified areas where I need to reallocate time

☐ I have a plan for addressing major time leaks

Appendix B: Recommended Resources

This appendix provides a curated list of additional resources to support your continued growth in overcoming procrastination and enhancing productivity. These recommendations are organized by category and include both classic and contemporary resources.

Books for Further Reading

Foundational Productivity and Time Management

- *Getting Things Done* by David Allen - The comprehensive system for stress-free productivity
- *The 7 Habits of Highly Effective People* by Stephen Covey - Timeless principles for personal effectiveness
- *First Things First* by Stephen Covey - Deep dive into priority management and life balance
- *The Time Trap* by Alec Mackenzie - Classic analysis of time management challenges and solutions

Habit Formation and Behavior Change

- *Atomic Habits* by James Clear - The definitive guide to building good habits and breaking bad ones
- *The Power of Habit* by Charles Duhigg - Understanding the science behind habit formation
- *Tiny Habits* by BJ Fogg - How to create lasting change through small actions
- *Switch* by Chip Heath and Dan Heath - How to change when change is hard

Psychology and Motivation

- *Mindset* by Carol Dweck - The psychology of success and the power of growth mindset
- *Drive* by Daniel Pink - What really motivates us and how to harness it
- *Flow* by Mihaly Csikszentmihalyi - The psychology of optimal experience
- *Self-Compassion* by Kristin Neff - How to be kind to yourself during the change process

Procrastination-Specific Resources

- *The Procrastination Equation* by Piers Steel - Scientific analysis of procrastination and evidence-based solutions
- *Solving the Procrastination Puzzle* by Timothy Pychyl - Practical strategies based on psychological research

- *The Now Habit* by Neil Fiore - Overcoming procrastination and enjoying guilt-free play
- *Eat That Frog!* by Brian Tracy - Practical techniques for overcoming procrastination

Goal Setting and Achievement

- *Your Best Year Ever* by Michael Hyatt - A proven system for achieving your most important goals
- *The One Thing* by Gary Keller - The surprisingly simple truth behind extraordinary results
- *Essentialism* by Greg McKeown - The disciplined pursuit of less but better
- *Deep Work* by Cal Newport - Rules for focused success in a distracted world

Personal Development and Growth

- *The Compound Effect* by Darren Hardy - How small changes create remarkable results
- *High Performance Habits* by Brendon Burchard - Six habits of high performers
- *The Slight Edge* by Jeff Olson - Simple disciplines for massive success
- *Man's Search for Meaning* by Viktor Frankl - Finding purpose and meaning in life

Apps and Digital Tools

Task Management and Organization

- **Todoist** - Comprehensive task management with natural language processing
- **Things 3** (Mac/iOS) - Elegant, award-winning task management
- **Asana** - Team and personal project management
- **Notion** - All-in-one workspace for notes, tasks, and databases
- **Omnifocus** (Mac/iOS) - Powerful GTD-based task management

Time Tracking and Management

- **RescueTime** - Automatic time tracking and productivity analysis
- **Toggl** - Simple, powerful time tracking for individuals and teams
- **Forest** - Gamified focus app that plants trees when you stay focused
- **Freedom** - Block distracting websites and apps across all devices
- **Cold Turkey** - Comprehensive website and application blocker

Habit Tracking

- **Habitica** - Gamified habit tracking that turns your life into an RPG
- **Streaks** (iOS) - Simple, elegant habit tracking
- **Way of Life** - Color-coded habit tracking for quick visual feedback
- **Loop Habit Tracker** (Android) - Open-source, detailed habit tracking
- **Productive** (iOS) - Beautiful, motivating habit tracker

Focus and Concentration

- **Brain.fm** - Scientifically designed music for focus and productivity
- **Noisli** - Background noise and color generator for focus
- **Focus Keeper** - Pomodoro timer with customizable work/break intervals
- **Be Focused** (Mac/iOS) - Simple, elegant Pomodoro timer
- **Tide** - Focus timer with natural sounds and mindfulness features

Note-Taking and Knowledge Management

- **Obsidian** - Powerful knowledge management with linked thinking
- **Roam Research** - Networked thought and bi-directional linking
- **Evernote** - Comprehensive note-taking and document management
- **OneNote** - Microsoft's versatile note-taking application
- **Bear** (Mac/iOS) - Beautiful, flexible writing app for notes

Calendar and Scheduling

- **Calendly** - Automated scheduling and meeting coordination
- **Google Calendar** - Comprehensive calendar with smart scheduling features
- **Fantastical** (Mac/iOS) - Natural language calendar with excellent design
- **TimeTree** - Shared calendar for families and teams
- **Acuity Scheduling** - Professional appointment scheduling

Professional Help Options

Types of Professional Support

Productivity Coaches. Professional coaches who specialize in helping people overcome procrastination and improve productivity:

- Certified productivity consultants
- Time management specialists
- Executive coaches with productivity focus
- ADHD coaches (for those with attention challenges)

Therapists and Counselors. Mental health professionals who can address underlying issues:

- Cognitive Behavioral Therapists (CBT) - for changing thought patterns
- Acceptance and Commitment Therapy (ACT) practitioners
- Psychologists specializing in procrastination research
- Licensed clinical social workers with productivity focus

Specialized Services

- Professional organizers for physical and digital spaces
- ADHD specialists for attention-related procrastination

- Career counselors for work-related procrastination
- Life coaches for general life management

Finding Professional Help

Questions to Ask Potential Helpers

- What is your experience with procrastination specifically?
- What approaches or methodologies do you use?
- How do you measure progress and success?
- What is your availability and preferred communication style?
- What are your rates and payment policies?

Professional Directories

- Psychology Today (therapists and coaches)
- International Coach Federation (certified coaches)
- National Association of Professional Organizers
- ADHD Coaches Organization

Online Communities and Support Groups

Reddit Communities

- r/getmotivated - Motivation and inspiration
- r/productivity - Tips, tools, and discussions about productivity
- r/getdisciplined - Building discipline and overcoming procrastination
- r/ADHD - Support for attention-related challenges
- r/studytips - Academic productivity and study strategies

Facebook Groups

- Productivity and Time Management groups
- Procrastination support communities
- Goal-setting and achievement groups
- Professional development communities

Specialized Platforms

- **Focusmate** - Virtual co-working sessions with accountability partners
- **Beeminder** - Quantified self and goal tracking with financial stakes
- **Stickk** - Commitment contracts with financial consequences
- Coach.me - Habit coaching and community support

Professional Networks

- LinkedIn productivity and professional development groups
- Industry-specific productivity communities

- Local meetup groups focused on personal development
- Toastmasters (for communication and leadership skills)

Academic and Research Resources

- Procrastination Research Group (University of Calgary)
- Centre for Mindfulness (University of Massachusetts)
- Positive Psychology Center (University of Pennsylvania)
- Behavioral Economics research publications

Appendix C: Troubleshooting Guide

This troubleshooting guide addresses the most common challenges people face when implementing anti-procrastination strategies. Use this as a quick reference when you encounter obstacles or setbacks in your journey.

Common Setbacks and Solutions

"I Started Strong But Lost Momentum"

Symptoms:

- Initial enthusiasm that faded after a few weeks
- Gradual return to old procrastination patterns
- Feeling like you've "failed" at change

Likely Causes:

- Tried to change too much too quickly
- Set unrealistic expectations for immediate transformation
- Didn't build adequate support systems
- Focused on motivation rather than systems

Solutions:

- Return to basics: Choose one simple habit to restart with
- Lower your standards temporarily to rebuild momentum
- Implement the "never miss twice" rule
- Create external accountability through partners or public commitment
- Review and simplify your systems
- Celebrate small wins to rebuild positive associations

Prevention:

- Start with minimum viable habits
- Build systems that don't rely on motivation
- Plan for motivation fluctuations
- Create multiple layers of accountability

"I Keep Making the Same Mistakes"

Symptoms:

- Repeating the same procrastination patterns despite awareness
- Feeling frustrated with lack of progress
- Knowing what to do but not doing it

Likely Causes:

- Insufficient analysis of triggers and patterns
- Trying to use willpower instead of changing environment
- Not addressing underlying emotional issues
- Lack of specific implementation plans

Solutions:

- Conduct detailed trigger analysis using a procrastination journal
- Modify your environment to make procrastination harder
- Create specific if-then implementation intentions
- Address underlying fears or perfectionism
- Seek professional help if patterns persist
- Use the Swiss Cheese method to make progress despite resistance

Prevention:

- Regular pattern analysis and system adjustment
- Environmental design that supports good choices
- Addressing root causes rather than just symptoms

"My System Works Sometimes But Not Others"

Symptoms:

- Inconsistent results with the same strategies
- Good days and bad days with no clear pattern
- Confusion about what actually works

Likely Causes:

- Not accounting for energy and mood fluctuations
- One-size-fits-all approach to different situations
- Insufficient tracking and analysis
- External factors not being considered

Solutions:

- Track energy levels, mood, and external factors along with productivity
- Develop different strategies for different energy levels
- Create context-specific approaches (work vs. home vs. travel)
- Build flexibility into your systems
- Identify your personal productivity patterns

Prevention:

- Design adaptive systems from the start

- Regular tracking and pattern analysis
- Multiple strategies for different situations

"I Feel Overwhelmed by All the Techniques"

Symptoms:

- Paralysis from too many options
- Constantly switching between different approaches
- Feeling like you need to implement everything at once

Likely Causes:

- Information overload
- Perfectionist approach to implementing systems
- Lack of clear prioritization
- Trying to optimize before establishing basics

Solutions:

- Choose one technique and master it before adding others
- Focus on the 80/20 of techniques that provide most benefit
- Create a simple implementation timeline
- Ignore new techniques until current ones are habitual
- Seek guidance from a coach or mentor

Prevention:

- Systematic, gradual implementation
- Focus on mastery over variety
- Clear implementation priorities

Frequently Asked Questions

Q: How long does it take to overcome procrastination?

A: The timeline varies significantly based on several factors:

- Severity of procrastination patterns (weeks to months for mild cases, months to years for severe cases)
- Consistency of implementation (daily practice accelerates progress)
- Underlying causes (simple habit change vs. addressing deep psychological issues)
- Support systems and accountability (external support accelerates change)
- Life circumstances (stable periods allow faster progress than chaotic ones)

Most people see initial improvements within 2-4 weeks of consistent implementation, with significant transformation typically occurring over 3-6 months.

Q: What if I have ADHD or other attention challenges?

A: Attention challenges require specialized approaches:

- Work with ADHD-trained coaches or therapists
- Use external structure and accountability more heavily
- Break tasks into smaller pieces than typically recommended
- Use timers and external cues more extensively
- Consider medication consultation with a psychiatrist
- Join ADHD-specific support communities
- Focus on environmental design and systems over willpower

Q: Is it normal to have setbacks?

A: Yes, setbacks are completely normal and expected:

- Change is rarely linear; expect ups and downs
- Setbacks provide valuable learning opportunities
- The key is getting back on track quickly rather than perfect consistency
- Most successful people experience multiple setbacks during their transformation
- Focus on overall trend rather than day-to-day fluctuations

Q: What if my family/friends don't support my changes?

A: Resistance from others is common:

- Some people may feel threatened by your positive changes
- Others may prefer the predictable "old you"
- Focus on your own growth rather than trying to change others
- Find support from people who encourage your growth
- Be patient; others often come around as they see positive results
- Set boundaries if necessary to protect your progress
- Consider that some relationships may need to evolve

Q: Should I tell others about my goals to overcome procrastination?

A: It depends on your personality and the people involved:

- Public commitment can create helpful accountability
- However, some research suggests that talking about goals can reduce motivation to achieve them
- Share with supportive people who will encourage your progress
- Avoid sharing with people who might sabotage or discourage you
- Focus on sharing your process and progress rather than just intentions

Q: What if I procrastinate on implementing anti-procrastination strategies?

A: This is ironically common:

- Start with the smallest possible step (even 2 minutes)
- Use implementation intentions: "If it's 9 AM, then I will..."
- Create external accountability for implementing strategies
- Begin with the easiest, most appealing techniques
- Remember that imperfect implementation is better than perfect planning

Q: How do I handle perfectionism that leads to procrastination?

A: Perfectionism requires specific approaches:

- Set "good enough" standards explicitly before starting tasks
- Use time limits to force completion rather than endless refinement
- Practice the "shitty first draft" approach
- Focus on progress over perfection
- Celebrate completion regardless of quality
- Understand that done is better than perfect
- Consider therapy if perfectionism is severe

When to Seek Professional Help

Signs You May Need Professional Support

Severe Impact on Life Functioning

- Procrastination is affecting your job security or career advancement
- Relationships are being damaged by your unreliability
- Financial problems due to missed deadlines or avoided tasks
- Health issues from stress or neglected self-care
- Academic performance is suffering significantly

Underlying Mental Health Issues

- Depression or anxiety that may be contributing to procrastination
- ADHD or other attention disorders
- Perfectionism that causes significant distress
- Trauma or past experiences that affect your ability to take action
- Substance use as a way to cope with procrastination stress

Persistent Patterns Despite Effort

- You've tried multiple approaches consistently without success
- Procrastination patterns have persisted for years despite awareness
- You feel stuck and unable to make progress on your own
- Self-help approaches haven't created lasting change

Types of Professional Help

Cognitive Behavioral Therapy (CBT)

Best for:

- Changing thought patterns that lead to procrastination
- Addressing perfectionism and fear-based procrastination
- Learning practical coping strategies
- Developing better problem-solving skills

Acceptance and Commitment Therapy (ACT)

Best for:

- Learning to accept difficult emotions without avoiding tasks
- Clarifying values and connecting actions to meaning
- Developing psychological flexibility
- Mindfulness-based approaches to procrastination

ADHD Coaching

Best for:

- Attention-related procrastination challenges
- Developing external structure and accountability
- Learning ADHD-specific productivity strategies
- Managing time and organization challenges

Life/Productivity Coaching

Best for:

- Goal setting and achievement
- Developing personalized productivity systems
- Accountability and motivation support
- Career and life transitions

How to Find the Right Professional

Research and Referrals

- Ask your primary care physician for referrals
- Check with your insurance for covered providers
- Use professional directories (Psychology Today, ICF)
- Ask friends or colleagues for recommendations
- Research providers' specialties and approaches

Questions to Ask Potential Providers

- What experience do you have with procrastination specifically?
- What approach or methodology do you use?

- How do you measure progress?
- What is your availability and communication style?
- What are your fees and payment policies?
- Do you offer any guarantees or trial periods?

Red Flags to Avoid

- Promises of quick fixes or guaranteed results
- Lack of specific experience with procrastination
- Unwillingness to discuss their approach or methods
- Pressure to commit to long-term contracts immediately
- Lack of professional credentials or training
- Poor communication or unprofessional behavior

Remember, seeking professional help is a sign of strength and self-awareness, not weakness. Many successful people have worked with coaches, therapists, or other professionals to overcome procrastination and achieve their goals. The investment in professional support often pays for itself many times over through improved productivity, reduced stress, and better life outcomes.

Bibliography

Major Research Foundations Referenced

- Harvard's Grant Study – 80-year longitudinal study on human flourishing.
- Stanford University research – Growth mindset and achievement, notably work by Dr. Carol Dweck.
- MIT – Studies on habit formation and behavioral change.
- Organizational psychology research – high-performance teamwork and support.

PART 3 – SELF-ESTEEM THAT MATTERS

For the leaders, parents, and changemakers who understand that true confidence creates ripples that transform communities.

And for everyone ready to discover that self-esteem is not selfish, but the foundation for serving others at your highest level.

"Confidence is not 'they will like me.' Confidence is 'I'll be fine if they don't."**—Christina Grimmie**

Self-Esteem That Matters
BUILDING UNSHAKABLE CONFIDENCE FROM THE INSIDE OUT

About Things That Matter
A SELF-IMPROVEMENT SERIES FOR SUCCESS

Book 11

JC Ryan

About This Book

CONFIDENCE ISN'T SELFISH. IT'S THE GIFT THAT KEEPS ON GIVING

What if the secret to transforming your career, relationships, and impact lies not in learning new techniques but in unleashing the confidence you already possess? Self-Esteem That Matters isn't another feel-good self-help book filled with empty affirmations. This is a leadership development guide disguised as a confidence book, grounded in cutting-edge neuroscience and proven in high-pressure professional environments. You'll discover how to rewire your brain for unshakable self-assurance, transform impostor syndrome into authentic authority, and master the four pillars that create lasting confidence. More importantly, you'll learn the revolutionary "ripple effect" principle that shows how your confidence doesn't just change your life; it transforms everyone around you.

This book is designed for leaders, professionals, and changemakers who understand that confidence is not a luxury but a leadership responsibility. Through systematic assessments, evidence-based techniques, and a comprehensive 30-day program, you'll build the kind of self-esteem that creates psychological safety for your team, multiplies others' confidence, and generates the authentic authority that inspires trust and drives results. Whether you're leading a Fortune 500 company or a family dinner table, the principles in this book will help you become the confident catalyst that others need to unlock their own potential. Your confidence journey doesn't end with you; it's just the beginning of the positive change you'll create in the world.

Prologue

THE REAL MEANING OF SELF-ESTEEM

Self-esteem is not what you think it is.

It is not positive thinking, daily affirmations, or telling yourself you are amazing when the evidence suggests otherwise. It is not fake-it-till-you-make-it confidence or the shallow bravado that crumbles under pressure.

Real self-esteem is the quiet, unshakable knowledge that you have value regardless of your performance, achievements, or the opinions of others. It is the foundation that allows you to take risks because your worth is not on the line. It is the inner strength that helps you bounce back from failure because setbacks do not define you. It is the authentic authority that lets you lead without needing to dominate, influence without manipulating, and succeed without stepping on others.

This book will teach you to build that kind of confidence. Not the superficial version that depends on external circumstances, but the deep, lasting self-esteem that becomes your superpower in every area of life.

Self-esteem is the multiplier. It amplifies your ability to handle change, achieve goals, manage time effectively, and build meaningful relationships. Without it, you might learn the techniques but lack the inner strength to apply them when it counts.

This is not another generic self-help book filled with feel-good platitudes. This is a leadership development guide disguised as a confidence book. You will learn evidence-based strategies grounded in neuroscience research and proven in high-pressure professional environments.

You will discover:
- How to rewire your brain for confidence using neuroplasticity principles

- The four pillars that create unshakable self-esteem

- A systematic method for transforming negative self-talk into an inner voice that builds you up

- How to turn impostor syndrome into authentic authority

- Strategies for building a confidence culture in your workplace or community

- The ripple effect model shows how your confidence transforms others

- A 30-day program that creates measurable confidence improvement

Your Confidence Promise

By the time you finish this book and complete the 30-day program, you will not just *feel* more confident. You *will* be more confident. You will have evidence, systems, and habits that create lasting change. More importantly, you will understand how to use your confidence to lift others and create positive change in every environment you enter.

This is your invitation to step into the leader, parent, professional, and human being you are meant to be. The world is waiting for what you have to offer. Your confidence is the key that unlocks it all.

Introduction

In a world obsessed with external validation, likes, and approval ratings, genuine confidence has become both rare and revolutionary. Most people mistake confidence for arrogance, self-esteem for selfishness, and authentic authority for aggressive dominance. They could not be more wrong.

True confidence is quiet power. It is the ability to stand in your worth without diminishing others. It is the foundation that allows you to take risks, embrace change, pursue meaningful goals, and build relationships based on mutual respect rather than a desperate need for approval.

This book is the third pillar in the About Things That Matter series because self-esteem amplifies everything else. When you master the change principles in Book 1, confidence gives you the courage to navigate uncertainty. When you apply the goal strategies in Book 2, self-worth provides the persistence to push through obstacles. When you eventually read about time management and relationships in Books 4 and 5, confidence will be the bedrock that makes those principles sustainable.

But here is what makes this book different from the hundreds of other confidence guides filling bookstore shelves: this is not about you alone. This is about understanding that your confidence creates ripples that transform everyone around you. When you walk into a room with genuine self-assurance, you give others permission to do the same. When you speak up with authentic authority, you inspire others to find their voice. When you recover from setbacks with resilience, you model what is possible for your team, your family, and your community.

The strategies in this book are not theoretical. They are field-tested by leaders who have built confidence cultures in Fortune 500 companies, parents who have raised resilient children, and individuals who have transformed their lives from the inside out. Every technique is grounded in neuroscience research and proven in real-world applications.

You are not reading this book by accident. You picked it up because something inside you knows that you are capable of more. You sense that your confidence could be the key that unlocks not just your potential, but your ability to unlock potential in others.

You are right.

The world needs confident leaders, parents, teachers, and changemakers who understand that self-esteem is not selfish but essential. Those who recognize that building your confidence is not about getting ahead of others but about lifting others up with you.

Your journey to unshakable confidence starts now. But remember, it is not just about you. It is about everyone whose life you will touch when you finally step into the fullness of who you are meant to be.

Chapter 1: The Science Of Self-Worth

"The brain is not designed to make you happy. It's designed to make you survive." — Rick Hanson.

Sarah stared at her laptop screen, cursor blinking in the empty email draft. The promotion opportunity required her to present to the executive team next week, but every time she tried to write her proposal, the same voice echoed in her head: "Who are you to think you deserve this? They'll see right through you."

Meanwhile, across town, her colleague Marcus was crafting his own proposal with excitement. He had the same qualifications, similar experience, and comparable results. The difference? Marcus believed he belonged in that room. Sarah believed she would be exposed as a fraud.

Same opportunity. Same capabilities. Radically different outcomes. The difference was not talent, experience, or even preparation. The difference was self-esteem.

For too long, we have treated confidence as a soft skill, a nice-to-have trait that some people are born with and others are not. Recent advances in neuroscience reveal a different truth: self-esteem is a learnable skill based on how your brain processes information about yourself and your capabilities. More importantly, it is a skill that can be developed, strengthened, and mastered at any age.

This chapter will show you exactly how.

What Neuroscience Reveals About Confidence

Your brain is not neutral about you. Every day, it processes thousands of pieces of information about your performance, interactions, and experiences, then creates a running narrative about your worth and capabilities. For most people, this narrative skews negative, not because they are failures, but because the brain is wired for survival, not confidence.

The human brain evolved to keep you alive in dangerous environments where overconfidence could get you killed. Your ancestors who assumed that rustling bush contained a predator (even when it was just wind) survived longer than those who assumed it was harmless. This survival mechanism, called the negativity bias, means your brain naturally focuses on threats, problems, and potential failures.

In modern life, this ancient wiring works against you. Your brain treats professional challenges, social situations, and personal goals as potential threats to your survival. The same mechanism that kept your ancestors alive now keeps you awake at night worrying about tomorrow's presentation.

But here is the breakthrough: neuroscience has revealed that your brain is not fixed. It is neuroplastic, meaning it can form new neural pathways throughout your entire life. The confidence pathways in your brain can be strengthened just like muscles through targeted exercise.

The Confidence Neural Network

Advanced brain imaging studies have identified three key regions that activate when you experience genuine confidence:

The Prefrontal Cortex serves as your brain's CEO, responsible for executive functions like decision-making, planning, and self-reflection. When this region is strong and well-connected, you make decisions with clarity rather than getting stuck in analysis paralysis.

The Anterior Cingulate Cortex acts as your emotional regulation center, helping you manage stress, recover from setbacks, and maintain emotional balance under pressure. A well-developed anterior cingulate cortex means you can stay calm and focused when the stakes are high.

The Default Mode Network influences your internal dialogue and self-referential thinking. When this network operates optimally, your inner voice becomes supportive rather than critical, helping you maintain confidence even when facing challenges.

Research from Stanford University shows that people with higher self-esteem have stronger connections between these three regions. More importantly, studies demonstrate that targeted interventions can strengthen these connections within 30 to 60 days of consistent practice.

The Neuroplasticity of Self-Worth

Dr. Carol Dweck's groundbreaking research on neuroplasticity reveals that your brain literally rewires itself based on what you repeatedly think, feel, and do. When you consistently practice confidence-building behaviors, you strengthen the neural pathways associated with self-assurance. When you repeatedly engage in self-criticism and doubt, you reinforce those pathways instead.

This means that every thought you think about yourself is either building confidence or eroding it. There is no neutral. Your brain is constantly adapting based on the mental habits you feed it.

Consider the difference between Sarah and Marcus. Sarah's brain had been trained through years of self-doubt to automatically scan for evidence of inadequacy. Marcus's brain had been trained to look for evidence of capability. Neither was born with these patterns; they developed them through repetition.

The exciting news is that Sarah can retrain her brain. With the right techniques and consistent practice, she can literally rewire her confidence pathways. The same is true for you.

The Self-Esteem Assessment Matrix

Traditional confidence assessments often provide generic, one-size-fits-all results that do not account for the complexity of self-esteem in different contexts. You might feel confident presenting to your team, but anxious at networking events. You might be comfortable advocating for others but struggle to advocate for yourself.

The Self-Esteem Assessment Matrix evaluates your confidence across four critical dimensions, giving you a detailed map of your current confidence landscape and a clear path for development.

Professional Confidence

This dimension measures your self-assurance in work-related contexts:

Decision-Making Authority: How confident are you in making important decisions under pressure? Do you trust your judgment, or do you second-guess yourself constantly?

Communication and Influence: Can you express your ideas clearly and persuasively? Do you speak up in meetings, or do you hold back valuable contributions?

Leadership Presence: When you enter a room, do people naturally look to you for guidance? Do you feel comfortable taking charge when situations require leadership?

Conflict Resolution: Can you navigate difficult conversations and disagreements with confidence? Do you address problems directly, or do you avoid confrontation?

Rate yourself on each element using a scale of 1 to 10, where 1 means you feel completely insecure and 10 means you feel completely confident.

Personal Confidence

This dimension evaluates your self-assurance in individual and private contexts:

Boundary Setting: Can you say no when necessary without feeling guilty? Do you protect your time, energy, and values, or do you constantly overcommit?

Authentic Self-Expression: Do you feel comfortable being yourself in various situations? Can you share your true thoughts and feelings, or do you constantly monitor and adjust yourself based on others' reactions?

Self-Advocacy: Can you ask for what you need and deserve? Do you pursue opportunities that align with your goals, or do you wait for permission or invitation?

Personal Growth: Do you embrace challenges as opportunities to learn and improve? When you make mistakes, do you learn from them, or do you interpret them as evidence of your inadequacy?

Again, rate yourself on each element from 1 to 10.

Social Confidence

This dimension measures your comfort and effectiveness in interpersonal situations:

Relationship Initiation: Can you start conversations with new people and build connections? Do you feel comfortable at social events, or do you avoid them whenever possible?

Group Dynamics: Do you contribute meaningfully to group discussions and activities? Can you hold your own in social situations without feeling like an outsider?

Influence and Persuasion: Can you influence others' thinking and decisions in positive ways? Do people seek your input and value your opinions?

Community Leadership: Do you feel comfortable taking leadership roles in your community, volunteer organizations, or social groups?

Rate each element from 1 to 10.

Resilience Confidence

This dimension assesses your ability to maintain confidence through challenges and setbacks:

Setback Recovery: How quickly do you bounce back from failures, rejections, or disappointments? Do setbacks motivate you to try harder, or do they cause you to give up?

Learning from Failure: Can you extract valuable lessons from your mistakes and use them to improve? Do you see failure as feedback or as a reflection of your worth?

Stress Management: Do you maintain your confidence under pressure? Can you perform well when stakes are high, or does stress cause your confidence to crumble?

Adaptation to Change: How well do you handle unexpected changes and new challenges? Do you see change as an opportunity for growth or as a threat to your security?

Rate each element from 1 to 10.

Interpreting Your Results

Add up your scores in each dimension:

32-40 points in any dimension: You have strong confidence in this area. Focus on maintaining these strengths while developing other dimensions.

24-31 points: You have moderate confidence with room for improvement. This is often the best starting point for development because you have a foundation to build upon.

16-23 points: You have a significant opportunity for growth in this area. Focused attention here could yield substantial improvements in your overall confidence.

Below 16 points: This dimension requires immediate attention and may be undermining your confidence in other areas.

Most people discover they are strong in some dimensions and weaker in others. This is normal and actually helpful because it allows you to focus your development efforts where they will have the most impact.

Your Confidence Blueprint

Based on your assessment results, you will now create a personalized confidence development plan that integrates with the principles you learned in Change That Matters and Goals That Matter.

Step 1: Identify Your Confidence Strengths

Look at your highest-scoring dimension. This represents your confidence strength, the area where you already demonstrate self-assurance and capability. Understanding your strengths is crucial because:

1. **They provide evidence** that you are capable of confidence in at least some contexts
2. **They serve as a foundation** for building confidence in other areas
3. **They can be leveraged** to support your development in weaker dimensions

Write down your strongest dimension and reflect on what contributes to your confidence in this area. What thoughts, behaviors, or experiences support your self-assurance here? How can you apply these same principles to other dimensions?

Step 2: Choose Your Development Priority

Rather than trying to improve everything at once, choose one dimension for focused development over the next 30 days. Consider these factors when making your choice:
Impact Potential: Which dimension, if improved, would have the biggest positive impact on your life and career?

Foundation Building: Which dimension might support improvement in other areas? For example, improving personal confidence often makes professional confidence easier to develop.

Current Opportunities: Which dimension aligns with opportunities or challenges you are currently facing?

Motivation Level: Which dimension are you most motivated to work on right now?

Step 3: Set Your 30-Day Confidence Goal

Using the SMART goal framework from Goals That Matter, create a specific, measurable confidence goal for your chosen dimension. Your goal should be:

Specific: Clearly define what confidence improvement looks like in behavioral terms.

Measurable: Include numeric targets or observable outcomes.

Achievable: Set a goal that stretches you but remains realistic for 30 days.

Relevant: Ensure the goal aligns with your broader life and career objectives.

Time-bound: Commit to a 30-day timeline with weekly check-ins

Example goals:

"Increase my Professional Confidence score from 22 to 28 by speaking up at least once in every team meeting, volunteering for one stretch assignment, and having one difficult conversation I have been avoiding."

"Improve my Personal Confidence score from 18 to 25 by setting and maintaining two clear boundaries, saying no to three requests that do not align with my priorities, and expressing my authentic opinion in five situations where I would normally stay quiet."

Step 4: Create Your Integration Plan

Your confidence development does not happen in isolation. Plan how you will integrate confidence-building with the Change That Matters and Goals That Matter principles you have already learned:

Change Integration: How will you use change management strategies to support your confidence development? What old patterns do you need to release? What new habits do you need to adopt?

Goal Integration: How does your confidence goal support your broader life and career objectives? How will increased confidence help you achieve the goals you set using Goals That Matter principles?

Habit Integration: What daily practices will you implement to support your confidence development? How will you track progress and maintain accountability?

Step 5: Prepare for Challenges

Confidence development is not a smooth, linear process. Prepare for the inevitable ups and downs by planning how you will handle common challenges:

Setbacks: When you have a confidence failure, how will you respond? What will you tell yourself? What actions will you take to get back on track?

Resistance: Your brain will resist changing established patterns. How will you push through internal resistance when confidence-building feels uncomfortable or unnatural?

Impatience: Confidence development takes time. How will you stay motivated when progress feels slow?

External Pressure: Some people in your life may not support your confidence growth. How will you maintain your development despite potential negativity or resistance from others?

Reflection Questions

Take time to thoughtfully consider these questions. Your honest answers will guide your confidence development journey:

1. **Which dimension of confidence feels most natural to you?** What makes this area easier for you than others?

2. **Which dimension of confidence feels most challenging?** What specific situations or triggers undermine your confidence in this area?

3. **How has low confidence cost you in the past?** What opportunities have you missed or avoided because you doubted yourself?

4. **What would change in your life if you had unshakable confidence in all four dimensions?** How would your relationships, career, and personal fulfillment improve?

5. **Who in your life models the kind of confidence you want to develop?** What specific behaviors or attitudes do they demonstrate that you could adopt?

6. **What stories do you tell yourself about why you lack confidence?** Are these stories based on evidence, or are they assumptions you have never questioned?

Action Steps

Complete these steps before moving to Chapter 2:

1. **Complete the Self-Esteem Assessment Matrix** for all four dimensions. Be honest in your ratings, as this baseline will guide your entire development plan.

2. **Identify your confidence blueprint** by determining your strongest dimension and choosing your development priority for the next 30 days.

3. **Set your 30-day confidence goal** using the SMART framework. Write it down and put it somewhere you will see it daily.

4. **Create your integration plan** connecting confidence development with Change That Matters and Goals That Matter principles.

5. **Schedule your weekly check-ins** to track progress and adjust your approach as needed.

Your confidence journey begins with understanding where you are now and where you want to go. The assessment matrix provides the map. Your 30-day goal provides the destination. The remaining chapters will provide the vehicle to get you there.

Remember, confidence is not a personality trait you either have or lack. It is a skill set you can develop through understanding, practice, and persistence. The science is clear: your brain can learn confidence just as it learned doubt. The choice of what to teach next is entirely yours.

Chapter 2: The Four Pillars Of Lasting Self-Esteem

"The curious paradox is that when I accept myself just as I am, then I can change." — Carl Rogers.

When David took over as department head, he inherited a team that had been through three leadership changes in two years. Morale was low, trust was broken, and productivity had plummeted. Previous leaders had tried motivational speeches, team-building exercises, and performance improvement plans. Nothing worked.

David tried something different. Instead of focusing on what was wrong with the team, he focused on building four foundational elements within himself: deep self-awareness of his leadership strengths and blind spots, complete acceptance of the current reality without judgment, unwavering belief in his ability to create positive change, and clear advocacy for both his needs and his team's needs.

Within six months, his team had the highest engagement scores in the company. The transformation was not the result of charismatic leadership or innovative management techniques. It was the natural outcome of a leader who had built unshakable confidence on four solid pillars.

Lasting self-esteem is not built on wishful thinking or positive affirmations. It is constructed on four foundational pillars that support each other and create a stable platform for confidence in any situation. When all four pillars are strong, you develop what researchers call "stable self-esteem" that persists through challenges, setbacks, and changing circumstances.

This chapter will show you how to build each pillar systematically.

Pillar 1: Self-Awareness

Self-awareness is the foundation of all lasting confidence. You cannot build upon strengths you do not recognize, address weaknesses you do not acknowledge, or change patterns you do not see. Self-awareness means developing a clear, accurate, and non-judgmental understanding of your thoughts, emotions, behaviors, strengths, and areas for growth.

The Awareness-Confidence Connection

Harvard Business School research led by Dr. Tasha Eurich reveals that people with high self-awareness are 79% more likely to demonstrate consistent confidence across various situations. This correlation exists because self-aware people make decisions based on accurate self-knowledge rather than assumptions, fears, or other people's expectations.

Self-aware individuals know their capabilities and limitations, which allows them to take on appropriate challenges with confidence while seeking support in areas where they need development. They understand their emotional patterns, which helps them manage stress and recover from setbacks more quickly. They recognize their values and motivations, which enables them to make decisions aligned with their authentic selves.

Developing Meta-Awareness

Drawing from the techniques you learned in Change That Matters, meta-awareness means observing your confidence patterns without immediately trying to fix or judge them. This objective observation creates the space necessary for conscious choice and intentional change.

Confidence Trigger Identification: Systematically identify the situations, people, or circumstances that consistently challenge your confidence. Common triggers include:

- Performance evaluations or feedback sessions

- Public speaking or presentation opportunities

- Networking events or meeting new people

- Conflict or difficult conversations

- Taking on new responsibilities or challenges

- Receiving criticism or correction

- Comparison situations (social media, professional gatherings)

For each trigger, note not just what happens externally, but what happens internally: What thoughts arise? What emotions do you experience? How does your body respond? What behaviors do you engage in?

Response Pattern Recognition: Once you identify your triggers, examine your typical response patterns. Do you avoid the situation entirely? Do you over-prepare to the point of exhaustion? Do you seek excessive reassurance from others? Do you diminish your accomplishments or deflect compliments?

Understanding your patterns without judgment creates the foundation for conscious choice. When you can see your automatic responses clearly, you can begin to choose different responses that better serve your confidence development.

Recovery Strategy Assessment: Examine how you typically recover from confidence challenges. What helps you bounce back from setbacks? What thoughts, activities, or people restore your sense of capability? What makes recovery faster or slower?

This analysis helps you develop a personalized confidence recovery toolkit that you can deploy intentionally when challenges arise.

Practical Self-Awareness Exercises

The Confidence Journal Method: For one week, track your confidence levels three times daily (morning, afternoon, evening) using a 1-10 scale. Note what situations, interactions, or thoughts influenced your confidence in each direction. Look for patterns in your triggers, responses, and recovery strategies.

The Strength Inventory Process: List 20 of your genuine strengths, capabilities, and positive qualities. If this feels difficult, ask trusted colleagues, friends, or family members to contribute. Include technical skills, personality traits, character qualities, and unique talents. This inventory becomes evidence you can reference when self-doubt arises.

The Values Alignment Audit: Identify your core values and assess how well your current life and work align with these values. Low confidence often results from living in ways that contradict your authentic values. When your actions align with your values, confidence flows naturally.

Pillar 2: Self-Acceptance

Self-acceptance is perhaps the most misunderstood aspect of confidence development. Many people fear that accepting their current reality means resigning themselves to mediocrity or giving up on growth. The opposite is true. Self-acceptance is the strategic acknowledgment of your current reality as the starting point for intentional development.

The Acceptance Paradox

Research from Stanford's Center for Compassion and Altruism demonstrates that people who fully accept their current limitations achieve 40% faster improvement in those areas compared to those who fight against their reality. This happens because acceptance eliminates the mental and emotional energy wasted on denial, self-criticism, and resistance, freeing that energy for productive change efforts.

Self-acceptance does not mean complacency. It means approaching your development from a place of self-compassion rather than self-criticism. It means seeing your current confidence level as information rather than judgment. It means recognizing that everyone, including the most confident people you know, has areas where they feel uncertain or inadequate.

Components of Authentic Self-Acceptance

Reality Acknowledgment: Honestly assess your current confidence strengths and challenges without minimizing your capabilities or catastrophizing your limitations. This means accepting feedback about areas where you need development without interpreting that feedback as evidence that you are fundamentally flawed.

Humanity Recognition: Accept that imperfection, uncertainty, and ongoing growth are universal human experiences. The most confident people are not those who never feel doubt, but those who feel doubt and act with courage anyway.

Temporal Perspective: Understand that your current confidence level represents where you are now, not where you will always be. Self-acceptance includes accepting your capacity for growth and change.

Comparison Rejection: Accept that your confidence journey is unique to you. Comparing your internal experience to others' external presentations is both inaccurate and counterproductive.

Practical Self-Acceptance Strategies

The Reality Audit Exercise: Write an honest assessment of your current confidence situation without self-judgment. Include both strengths and areas for development. Use neutral, descriptive language rather than evaluative or emotional language. For example, write "I feel nervous speaking in large group meetings" rather than "I'm terrible at public speaking."

The Self-Compassion Letter Practice: When you notice self-criticism arising, write yourself a letter from the perspective of a wise, compassionate friend. What would this friend say about your struggles? How would they encourage you while acknowledging the reality of your challenges?

The Growth Timeline Review: Reflect on areas where you have grown and developed confidence over time. What were you like five years ago compared to now? This exercise helps you accept that growth is ongoing and that current limitations are temporary.

Pillar 3: Self-Efficacy

Self-efficacy is your belief in your ability to achieve specific outcomes through your actions. It is confidence in action. While self-esteem is your general sense of worth, self-efficacy is your specific belief that you can learn new skills, overcome challenges, and achieve meaningful goals.

The Efficacy-Achievement Cycle

Psychologist Albert Bandura's research demonstrates that self-efficacy and achievement create a reinforcing cycle. When you believe you can achieve something, you are more likely to take the actions necessary for success. When you achieve that goal, your belief in your capability increases, making you more likely to attempt and achieve even more challenging goals.

Using the goal-setting principles from Goals That Matter, you can systematically build self-efficacy through what we call "confidence wins" that create momentum and evidence of your capability.

Building Self-Efficacy Through Strategic Goal Setting

Micro-Wins Strategy: Begin with small, virtually guaranteed successes that build momentum and evidence of your capability. These wins should be:

- Specific and measurable

- Achievable within 1-7 days

- Related to your confidence development goals

- Meaningful enough to feel satisfying

Examples: "I will speak up once in tomorrow's team meeting," "I will introduce myself to one new person at Thursday's networking event," "I will ask my manager for feedback on my recent project by Friday."

Skill Stacking Method: Combine existing strengths in new ways rather than starting from zero. This approach builds confidence because you are expanding capabilities you already possess rather than developing entirely new ones.

For example, if you are confident in one-on-one conversations but nervous about group presentations, you might start by facilitating small group discussions before moving to larger presentations.

Progressive Challenge System: Once you have built momentum through micro-wins and skill stacking, gradually increase the difficulty of your confidence challenges. Each level should stretch you without overwhelming you.

Level 1: Low-risk situations with high probability of success

Level 2: Moderate-risk situations where success requires some effort

Level 3: Higher-risk situations that represent meaningful growth

Level 4: Stretch challenges that would have seemed impossible at Level 1

Mastery Documentation Process

Keep detailed records of your growing competence and confidence. This documentation serves multiple purposes:

Evidence Collection: Build an objective record of your capabilities that you can reference when self-doubt arises.

Pattern Recognition: Identify what strategies and approaches work best for your confidence development.

Progress Tracking: Measure your development over time to maintain motivation and adjust your approach.

Success Story Development: Create narratives about your growth that reinforce your belief in your ability to continue developing.

Pillar 4: Self-Advocacy

Self-advocacy is the external expression of internal self-worth. It is how you communicate your value to the world, set and maintain boundaries, and pursue opportunities that align with your goals and values. Without self-advocacy, even strong self-awareness, self-acceptance, and self-efficacy remain internal and cannot create the external results that reinforce confidence.

The Four Dimensions of Self-Advocacy

Value Articulation: Clearly knowing and expressing your unique contributions, strengths, and perspectives. This does not mean bragging or self-promotion, but rather honest, accurate communication about what you bring to situations and relationships.

Boundary Communication: Expressing your limits, needs, and non-negotiables with clarity and confidence. Healthy boundaries protect your time, energy, and values while communicating self-respect to others.

Opportunity Creation: Proactively seeking growth, advancement, and experiences that align with your goals. Rather than waiting for permission or invitation, self-advocacy means creating and pursuing opportunities.

Feedback Integration: Actively seeking input about your performance and impact, then using that feedback to strengthen rather than diminish your confidence. This includes both soliciting feedback and responding to unsolicited feedback in ways that support your development.

Developing Your Self-Advocacy Skills

The Value Proposition Exercise: Write a clear, concise description of the unique value you bring to your work, relationships, and community. Include specific examples and measurable contributions. Practice articulating this value in various contexts and situations.

Boundary Setting Practice: Identify three areas where you need stronger boundaries. Practice expressing these boundaries using clear, direct language that communicates your limits without over-explaining or apologizing.

Opportunity Mapping: List five opportunities you would like to pursue in the next six months. For each opportunity, identify specific actions you can take to create or access these opportunities rather than waiting for them to come to you.

Feedback Systems Development: Create systematic ways to gather feedback about your performance, impact, and development. This might include regular check-ins with your manager, 360-degree feedback from colleagues, or structured conversations with mentors and peers.

Integrating The Four Pillars

The four pillars of lasting self-esteem work together synergistically. Self-awareness provides the foundation of accurate self-knowledge. Self-acceptance creates the emotional stability necessary for growth. Self-efficacy builds belief in your ability to achieve your goals. Self-advocacy ensures that your internal confidence translates into external results that reinforce your belief in yourself.

When all four pillars are strong, you develop what researchers call "optimal self-esteem," characterized by:

- Stability under pressure and criticism

- Resilience in the face of setbacks and failures

- Authenticity in your self-expression and relationships

- Courage to pursue meaningful challenges and opportunities

- Generosity in supporting others' confidence and growth

Your Four-Pillar Development Plan

Based on your assessment from Chapter 1, identify which pillar needs the most attention over the next 30 days. While you will develop all four pillars over time, focusing on one allows for deeper, more sustainable change.

Pillar Assessment: Rate yourself 1-10 on each pillar:

- Self-Awareness: How well do you understand your confidence patterns, triggers, and responses?

- Self-Acceptance: How completely do you accept your current reality without self-judgment?

- Self-Efficacy: How strongly do you believe in your ability to achieve your confidence goals?

- Self-Advocacy: How effectively do you communicate your value and pursue opportunities?

Priority Selection: Choose the pillar with the lowest score for focused development, unless another pillar would better support your current confidence goals or life circumstances.

Development Strategy: Create a specific 30-day plan for strengthening your chosen pillar using the exercises and strategies outlined in this chapter.

Reflection Questions

1. **Which of the four pillars feels most natural and developed for you?** How has this pillar supported your confidence in the past?

2. **Which pillar represents your biggest opportunity for growth?** What specific situations or challenges highlight the need for development in this area?

3. **How do you currently handle self-criticism and negative self-judgment?** What would change if you approached yourself with the same compassion you show to good friends?

4. **What opportunities have you avoided or delayed because you felt you needed permission or an invitation?** How could stronger self-advocacy change these patterns?

5. **What evidence do you have of your growing competence and confidence over time?** How can you use this evidence to support continued development?

Action Steps

1. **Complete the Four-Pillar Assessment** by rating yourself 1-10 on each pillar and identifying your development priority.

2. **Choose one practical exercise** from your priority pillar and implement it for the next seven days.

3. **Create your integration plan** by identifying how your pillar development connects with the confidence goal you set in Chapter 1.

4. **Establish your support system** by identifying people who can provide feedback, encouragement, and accountability for your pillar development.

5. **Schedule weekly pillar reviews** to track your progress and adjust your development strategy as needed.

The four pillars provide the stable foundation for unshakable confidence. In Chapter 3, you will learn how to transform the voice in your head from your biggest critic into your strongest supporter.

Chapter 3: The Inner Voice Revolution

"You have been critical of yourself for years, and it hasn't worked. Try approving of yourself and see what happens." — **Louise Hay**

Maria was brilliant. Her colleagues knew it, her clients knew it, even her competitors knew it. But Maria did not know it. Despite a track record of success that would make most professionals envious, she lived with a constant soundtrack of self-criticism: "That presentation could have been better. You're behind on that project. You don't deserve this promotion. You're going to be found out."

Meanwhile, her colleague James, with similar credentials and performance, approached each day with an entirely different internal dialogue: "I handled that challenge well. I'm learning from this setback. I have valuable ideas to contribute. I can figure this out."

Same workplace, similar capabilities, radically different internal experiences. The difference was not talent, training, or natural ability. The difference was the quality of their self-talk.

Your inner voice runs constantly, generating approximately 50,000 thoughts per day. For many people, up to 80% of these thoughts skew negative, creating a mental environment that undermines confidence and achievement. But neuroscience research reveals something remarkable: you can train your brain to become your biggest supporter instead of your harshest critic.

This chapter will show you exactly how to engineer that transformation.

The Neuroscience Of Self-Talk

Your brain does not distinguish between thoughts you think about yourself and comments other people make about you. When you think "I'm not good enough," your brain processes this the same way it would process someone else saying "You're not good enough." This means that negative self-talk triggers the same stress response, emotional pain, and confidence damage as external criticism.

Conversely, positive self-talk activates the same neural pathways as receiving genuine compliments from others. fMRI studies show that self-affirmation and external validation light up identical brain regions, suggesting that learning to speak kindly to yourself is not just psychological comfort but neurological reality.

The Self-Talk Brain Network

When you engage in self-talk, several brain networks activate simultaneously:

The Medial Prefrontal Cortex processes self-referential information and determines how personally you take various thoughts and experiences. When this region operates optimally, you can maintain perspective during challenges rather than interpreting every setback as a personal indictment.

The Amygdala serves as your brain's alarm system, triggering fight-or-flight responses when it perceives threats. Negative self-talk consistently activates the amygdala, creating chronic stress that undermines both confidence and performance.

The Default Mode Network generates the ongoing stream of thoughts that comprise your internal dialogue. This network can be trained to default toward supportive rather than critical patterns.

The Anterior Cingulate Cortex helps regulate emotional responses and recovery from setbacks. Strong self-talk skills strengthen this region, improving your resilience and emotional regulation.

The Confidence Language Patterns

Research has identified specific language patterns that either build or erode confidence over time:

Confidence-Building Language Patterns:

- Process focus: "I am learning" versus "I am failing"

- Growth orientation: "This is challenging" versus "This is impossible"

- Self-compassion: "I made a mistake" versus "I am a mistake"

- Agency emphasis: "I choose to" versus "I have to"

- Evidence-based: "Based on my experience" versus "I always"

- Solution-focused: "How can I improve this?" versus "Why does this always happen to me?"

Confidence-Eroding Language Patterns:

- Absolute thinking: "I never" or "I always"

- Catastrophizing: "This is terrible," or "Everything is ruined."

- Personalization: "It's all my fault," or "I'm responsible for everything."

- Mind reading: "They think I'm incompetent," or "Everyone can see I'm a fraud."
- Fortune telling: "This will never work," or "I'll definitely fail."
- Comparison: "Everyone else is better," or "I'm the only one struggling."

The goal is not to eliminate all negative thoughts, which is neither possible nor healthy, but to shift the overall balance toward patterns that support your confidence and growth.

The Reframe Method For Cognitive Restructuring

The REFRAME method provides a systematic approach to transforming negative self-talk into confidence-building internal dialogue. Each step builds upon the previous one, creating a comprehensive process for cognitive restructuring.

R - Recognize the Negative Pattern

The first step is developing awareness of your specific self-talk patterns without immediately trying to change them. Most negative self-talk happens automatically, below the threshold of conscious awareness. Recognition brings these patterns into conscious focus, where you can work with them intentionally.

Thought Catching Practice: For 48 hours, carry a small notebook or use your phone to record instances of negative self-talk as they occur. Note the trigger situation, the specific thought, and the emotional impact. Do not try to change the thoughts yet; simply notice them.

Pattern Identification: After your observation period, review your notes and identify the most common negative thought patterns. You might notice themes like perfectionism ("This has to be perfect or it's worthless"), comparison ("Everyone else is more qualified than I am"), or catastrophizing ("One mistake will ruin everything").

Trigger Mapping: Identify the situations, people, or circumstances that most consistently trigger negative self-talk. Common triggers include performance evaluations, social situations, new challenges, or interactions with specific individuals.

E - Examine the Evidence

Once you recognize a negative thought pattern, examine it objectively like a scientist evaluating a hypothesis. Most negative self-talk is based on assumptions, fears, or distorted thinking rather than actual evidence.

Evidence For and Against: When you catch a negative thought, ask yourself: "What evidence supports this thought? What evidence contradicts it?" Write down both sides objectively.

Reality Testing Questions:

- Is this thought 100% true, 100% of the time?
- What would I tell a good friend who had this thought about themselves?
- Am I confusing a feeling with a fact?
- What would someone who cares about me say about this thought?
- How will this matter in five years?

Perspective Shifting: Consider alternative explanations for the situation that triggered the negative thought. What other factors might be involved? What context might you be missing?

F - Find Alternative Perspectives

Rather than jumping immediately to positive thinking, explore multiple ways of interpreting the same situation. This step develops cognitive flexibility and reduces the tendency toward black-and-white thinking.

Multiple Interpretation Exercise: For any situation that triggered negative self-talk, generate at least three different interpretations:

1. The negative interpretation (what you thought initially)
2. A neutral interpretation (factual, without emotional coloring)
3. A growth-oriented interpretation (focusing on learning and opportunity)

Balanced Thinking: Create thoughts that acknowledge challenges while maintaining self-compassion and possibility for growth. For example, instead of "I'm terrible at presentations" or "I'm amazing at presentations," try "I'm developing my presentation skills and improving with practice."

R - Rewrite the Narrative

Based on your evidence examination and alternative perspectives, create a new, more accurate and supportive narrative about yourself and the situation.

The Compassionate Rewrite: Take your original negative thought and rewrite it as if you were speaking to a beloved friend facing the same situation. Use kind, encouraging language while acknowledging real challenges.

The Growth Rewrite: Focus on learning, development, and possibility rather than fixed judgments about your abilities or worth.

The Evidence-Based Rewrite: Ground your new narrative in actual facts and experiences rather than assumptions or fears.

A - Affirm the New Pattern

Consciously reinforce the new thought pattern through repetition and action. This step helps encode the new neural pathway and makes the supportive self-talk more automatic over time.

Repetition Practice: When you catch yourself returning to the old negative pattern, consciously repeat the new narrative. This may feel forced initially, but repetition strengthens the new neural pathway.

Action Alignment: Take actions that support your new narrative. If your new thought is "I'm learning and improving," seek learning opportunities. If it is "I have valuable contributions to make," look for ways to contribute.

M - Monitor and Maintain

Track your progress in shifting self-talk patterns and adjust your approach based on what works best for your specific patterns and triggers.

Progress Tracking: Keep a weekly log of your most common self-talk patterns and note improvements over time. Focus on trending in a positive direction rather than perfection.

Adjustment Strategy: If certain thoughts or triggers prove particularly resistant to change, try different reframing approaches or seek additional support.

E - Evolve the Practice

Continuously refine your self-talk skills as you grow and face new challenges. Advanced practitioners learn to catch and reframe negative thoughts in real-time, often within seconds of their arising.

Advanced Techniques: As basic reframing becomes more natural, experiment with advanced approaches like humor, metaphor, or visualization to make your internal dialogue even more supportive.

Teaching Others: One of the best ways to solidify your own self-talk skills is to help others develop theirs. Consider mentoring colleagues or family members in positive self-talk techniques.

Building Your Evidence-Based Affirmation System

Traditional affirmations often fail because they lack personal relevance and credibility. Telling yourself "I am successful" when you feel like a failure creates cognitive dissonance rather than confidence. Evidence-based affirmations are grounded in your actual strengths, experiences, and capabilities, making them both believable and powerful.

The Evidence-Based Affirmation Formula

Structure: "I am [quality] because [specific evidence], which enables me to [specific capability]."

This three-part structure creates affirmations that are:

- **Believable** because they are based on real evidence
- **Specific** rather than vague or generic
- **Forward-looking** by connecting past evidence to future capability

Examples:

- "I am a skilled problem-solver because I successfully navigated three major project challenges last quarter, which enables me to handle complex situations with confidence."
- "I am a trusted team member because colleagues regularly seek my input on important decisions, which enables me to contribute meaningfully to our success."
- "I am resilient because I have bounced back from every setback I have faced, which enables me to approach new challenges with courage."

Creating Your Personal Affirmation Categories

Develop evidence-based affirmations across four key categories that support comprehensive confidence development:

Professional Competence Affirmations: Based on actual skills, achievements, and recognition in your work life. Include specific projects, results, feedback, and growth over time.

Personal Growth Affirmations: Acknowledging progress, learning, and development in various areas of your life. Focus on how you have changed, adapted, and improved over time.

Relationship Value Affirmations: Recognition of the positive impact you have on others and the value you bring to relationships. Include feedback from friends, family, colleagues, and community members.

Resilience Capacity Affirmations: Evidence of your ability to overcome challenges, learn from setbacks, and persist through difficulties. Include specific examples of challenges you have faced and overcome.

Implementation Guidelines

Quality Over Quantity: Develop 5-10 powerful, evidence-based affirmations rather than dozens of generic ones. Focus on affirmations that address your specific confidence challenges and goals.

Regular Review and Update: As you grow and achieve new things, update your affirmations to reflect your expanding capabilities and evidence base.

Strategic Timing: Use affirmations preventively before challenging situations and reactively when negative self-talk arises. Morning affirmation practice sets a positive tone for the day.

Emotional Connection: Choose affirmations that resonate emotionally as well as logically. The most powerful affirmations combine factual evidence with emotional significance.

Advanced Self-Talk Strategies For Leaders

Leaders face unique self-talk challenges because their confidence directly impacts others. Developing advanced self-talk skills is not just personal development but leadership development.

The Leadership Voice Technique

Develop a distinct internal voice that reflects your leadership role and responsibilities. This voice should emphasize:

Team and Organizational Impact: "My confidence and decision-making capability support my team's success and the organization's mission."

Influence and Inspiration: "My authentic leadership helps others develop their confidence and capabilities."

Responsibility and Accountability: "I take ownership of results while maintaining self-compassion during challenges."

Vision and Possibility: "I can see opportunities and solutions that others might miss."

Pressure Performance Self-Talk

Develop specific self-talk scripts for high-pressure leadership situations:

Pre-Meeting Confidence Builders:
- "I am prepared and have valuable insights to contribute."
- "My perspective matters and adds value to this discussion."
- "I can listen actively and respond thoughtfully."

Crisis Leadership Mantras:
- "I can stay calm and think clearly under pressure."
- "My team looks to me for stability and direction."
- "I have successfully navigated challenges before."

Difficult Conversation Preparation:
- "I can have this conversation with both honesty and compassion."
- "Addressing this issue serves everyone's best interests."
- "I am capable of finding solutions that work for all parties."

Public Speaking Confidence Phrases:
- "I have important information to share with this audience."
- "My message can make a positive difference."
- "I am prepared and capable of handling questions or challenges."

Reflection Questions

1. **What are your three most common negative self-talk patterns?** When and where do these patterns typically arise?
2. **How does your inner voice change under stress or pressure?** What happens to your self-talk during challenging situations?
3. **What evidence do you have of your capabilities and growth that you rarely acknowledge?** How could this evidence support more positive self-talk?
4. **How does your self-talk impact others around you?** Do you model confidence or self-doubt in your interactions?
5. **What would change in your life if your inner voice became your biggest supporter rather than your biggest critic?**

Action Steps

1. **Complete the 48-hour thought tracking exercise** to identify your specific negative self-talk patterns and triggers.
2. **Apply the REFRAME method** to your most common negative thought pattern for one week, working through each step systematically.
3. **Create five evidence-based affirmations** using the three-part formula, ensuring each is grounded in actual experiences and achievements.
4. **Establish a daily affirmation practice** by choosing a consistent time and method for reinforcing your positive self-talk.
5. **Practice the leadership voice technique** if you are in any leadership role, developing specific scripts for common challenging situations.

Your inner voice will either be your greatest asset or your biggest obstacle in building confidence. Chapter 4 will show you how to transform one of the most common confidence challenges into authentic authority.

Chapter 4: Conquering Impostor Syndrome

*"The expert in anything was once a beginner who refused to give up." — **Helen Hayes.***

Tom had been promoted to senior director after leading three consecutive successful product launches. His team respected him, his peers sought his input, and his leadership had delivered measurable results. Yet as he prepared for his first executive presentation, one thought dominated his mind: "They're going to realize I don't belong here."

Across the company, his colleague Sarah was experiencing the opposite. Despite being new to her management role and facing steep learning curves, she approached each challenge with curiosity rather than fear. When she did not know something, she said so. When she made mistakes, she learned from them. When others questioned her decisions, she listened thoughtfully and adjusted when appropriate.

Both Tom and Sarah were dealing with the gap between their current capabilities and their role requirements. Tom experienced this gap as evidence of fraud. Sarah experienced it as an opportunity for growth. The difference was not competence but perspective.

Impostor syndrome affects 70% of professionals at some point in their careers, making it one of the most common barriers to confident leadership. But impostor syndrome is not a character flaw or permanent condition. It is a thinking pattern that can be understood, managed, and ultimately transformed into authentic authority.

This chapter will show you how.

The Impostor Syndrome Spectrum

Rather than viewing impostor syndrome as a binary condition, you either have or do not have, it is more helpful to understand it as a spectrum with different levels requiring different intervention strategies.

Level 1: Situational Uncertainty

This is the mildest form, characterized by occasional self-doubt in new or challenging situations. Almost everyone experiences this level when stepping into unfamiliar territory.

Characteristics:
- Self-doubt arises only in specific, new situations
- Quick recovery with minimal impact on performance

- Generally positive self-concept with isolated concerns
- Responds well to preparation and support

Common Triggers:
- Starting a new job or taking on new responsibilities
- Speaking to unfamiliar audiences
- Working with senior-level stakeholders
- Entering new industries or functional areas

Intervention Approach: Focus on preparation, skill building, and perspective. This level often resolves naturally as competence develops.

Level 2: Pattern-Based Doubt

This represents moderate impostor syndrome with recurring doubts in specific contexts or situations.

Characteristics:
- Predictable patterns of self-doubt in certain contexts
- Moderate impact on performance and opportunity pursuit
- Tends to ruminate on mistakes or negative feedback
- May avoid stretch opportunities due to confidence concerns

Common Patterns:
- Doubting technical competence despite strong performance
- Feeling fraudulent in leadership roles
- Minimizing achievements and attributing success to luck
- Comparing internal experience to others' external confidence

Intervention Approach: Requires systematic intervention including evidence collection, cognitive restructuring, and gradual exposure to challenging situations.

Level 3: Pervasive Impostor Beliefs

This represents severe impostor syndrome that significantly impacts multiple areas of life and work.

Characteristics:
- Persistent feelings of inadequacy across various contexts
- Significant impact on career advancement and personal growth

- Chronic stress and anxiety about being "found out"
- May engage in overwork or perfectionism to compensate

Deep-Seated Beliefs:
- "I don't deserve my successes."
- "I'm fooling everyone about my capabilities."
- "It's only a matter of time before I'm exposed."
- "Everyone else belongs here more than I do."

Intervention Approach: Needs comprehensive restructuring of self-concept, often benefiting from professional support in addition to self-directed techniques.

The Competence Inventory Method

One of the most effective ways to combat impostor syndrome is to systematically document your actual competence and contributions. The Competence Inventory creates an objective record of your capabilities that you can reference when self-doubt arises.

Skills Audit

Create a comprehensive list of your technical and soft skills, organized by category and proficiency level.

Technical Skills Inventory:
- Software, systems, and tools you can use effectively
- Methodologies and frameworks you understand and apply
- Industry knowledge and subject matter expertise
- Certifications, training, and formal education

Soft Skills Inventory:
- Communication and presentation abilities
- Leadership and influence capabilities
- Problem-solving and analytical skills
- Relationship building and collaboration strengths

Proficiency Levels:
- **Novice**: Basic understanding with limited application
- **Developing**: Can apply with guidance and support

- **Proficient**: Can apply independently with good results
- **Advanced**: Can teach others and innovate within the skill area
- **Expert**: Recognized authority with the ability to influence field standards

Achievement Archive

Document specific accomplishments, contributions, and positive impacts you have made throughout your career.

Project Successes: List major projects you have led or contributed to significantly, including specific outcomes and your role in achieving them.

Problem-Solving Examples: Document times you identified important problems and developed effective solutions.

Leadership Instances: Record occasions when you provided direction, influence, or inspiration to others.

Innovation Contributions: Note ideas, improvements, or innovations you have introduced.

Recognition and Feedback: Compile positive feedback, awards, promotions, and other forms of recognition you have received.

For each achievement, record:
- The situation and challenge faced
- Your specific actions and contributions
- The measurable outcomes and impact
- Skills and capabilities demonstrated

Impact Documentation

Track the positive effects your work and presence have on others and the organization.

Individual Impact: How have you helped specific colleagues, team members, or stakeholders grow, succeed, or overcome challenges?

Team Impact: What contributions have you made to team performance, culture, or capability?

Organizational Impact: How has your work contributed to business results, process improvements, or strategic objectives?

Industry Impact: Have you contributed to industry knowledge, standards, or best practices through speaking, writing, or innovation?

Quantifiable Metrics: Include specific numbers, percentages, or measurable outcomes wherever possible.

Growth Timeline

Document your professional and personal development over time to recognize patterns of continuous learning and improvement.

Skill Development Progression: Chart how your capabilities have expanded over months and years.

Responsibility Evolution: Track how your roles and responsibilities have grown.

Challenge Mastery: Note challenges that once seemed impossible but now feel manageable.

Learning Acceleration: Identify areas where you learn and develop quickly.

This timeline helps you see that feeling uncertain about new challenges is normal and temporary, not evidence of inadequacy.

The Confidence Banking System

The Confidence Banking System helps you build and maintain a "savings account" of evidence and experiences that you can draw upon during periods of self-doubt. Like a financial savings account, regular deposits ensure you have resources available when you need them.

Making Regular Deposits

Daily Accomplishment Deposits: Each day, record at least one thing you did well, learned, or contributed. These do not need to be major achievements; small wins accumulate into significant confidence over time.

Weekly Reflection Deposits: Each week, review your accomplishments and note patterns of competence and growth.

Monthly Achievement Deposits: Each month, document significant accomplishments, positive feedback received, or challenges overcome.

Quarterly Growth Deposits: Every quarter, assess your development across various skill and confidence areas.

Types of Confidence Currency

Competence Currency: Evidence of your skills, knowledge, and capabilities in action.

Character Currency: Examples of your integrity, reliability, and positive impact on others.

Courage Currency: Times you have taken appropriate risks, faced fears, or persevered through challenges.

Contribution Currency: Documentation of the value you have added to teams, organizations, or communities.

Making Emergency Withdrawals

When impostor syndrome strikes, you can make withdrawals from your confidence bank by:

Reviewing Recent Deposits: Look at evidence from the past week or month that demonstrates your competence.

Consulting Your Achievement Archive: Reference specific examples of past successes in similar situations.

Reading Positive Feedback: Review compliments, recognition, or positive feedback you have received.

Connecting with Supporters: Reach out to people who know your capabilities and can provide perspective.

Building Compound Interest

Your confidence bank gains compound interest when you:

Share Your Experiences: Help others by sharing what you have learned from your challenges and successes.

Mentor Others: Teaching and supporting others reinforces your own competence and value.

Seek New Challenges: Taking on appropriate stretch assignments adds high-value deposits to your account.

Reflect on Growth: Regularly acknowledge how far you have come and how much you have learned.

Transforming Setbacks Into Stepping Stones

One of the key differences between people who overcome impostor syndrome and those who remain stuck is how they interpret and respond to setbacks. Confident individuals do not avoid failure; they extract maximum learning value from it.

The Resilience Reframe Protocol

When you experience a setback, mistake, or failure, follow this systematic approach to maintain and even build confidence:

Step 1: Rapid Stabilization Response. Immediately after a setback, focus on emotional regulation and perspective rather than analysis:

- Take deep breaths and remind yourself that one setback does not define you
- Remember that everyone experiences failures and mistakes
- Acknowledge your emotions without judgment
- Seek support from trusted colleagues, friends, or mentors if needed

Step 2: Objective Learning Extraction. Once emotions have stabilized, analyze the situation objectively:

- What specific factors contributed to the setback?
- Which factors were within your control and which were not?
- What worked well, even though the overall outcome was disappointing?
- What would you do differently if facing a similar situation?

- What new knowledge or skills would help you handle this better?

Step 3: Strength Integration Identify how this experience can actually strengthen your confidence:

- What did you learn about your resilience and recovery capability?
- How did you demonstrate character or courage during the challenge?
- What skills did you use or develop while dealing with the situation?
- How can this experience help you support others facing similar challenges?

Step 4: Forward Momentum Generation Convert the setback into energy for future success:

- Set specific learning goals based on your analysis
- Take concrete actions to develop identified skill gaps
- Apply lessons learned to current projects and challenges
- Share your learning with others who might benefit

Failure Immunization Training

Just as vaccines expose you to small amounts of a virus to build immunity, you can build confidence and resilience by deliberately exposing yourself to controlled, low-stakes failures.

Level 1: Low-Stakes Practice Failures. Intentionally put yourself in situations where small failures are likely and safe:

- Try a new hobby where you will obviously be a beginner
- Attempt a challenging recipe, and you might not execute it perfectly
- Play a sport or game where you are clearly outmatched
- Take on a creative project outside your expertise area

Level 2: Professional Learning Failures Seek work situations that stretch your capabilities with limited downside risk:

- Volunteer for challenging assignments with good support systems
- Present ideas that might be rejected but could add value if accepted
- Ask questions that reveal knowledge gaps but demonstrate learning interest
- Propose solutions that might not work, but show creative thinking

Level 3: Strategic Growth Failures Take calculated risks in areas important to your development:

- Apply for stretch roles that might be beyond your current capabilities
- Speak at conferences on topics where you are still developing expertise
- Lead initiatives that challenge your current skill level
- Start projects that have uncertain outcomes but high learning potential

The goal is not to fail but to desensitize yourself to the fear of failure and build evidence that you can recover and learn from setbacks.

The Post-Failure Confidence Protocol

After any failure or significant mistake:

- **Acknowledge reality without catastrophizing**: "This did not go as planned," rather than "I am a total failure."
- **Identify specific learning**: What concrete lessons can you extract from this experience?
- **Recognize effort and growth**: What did you do well, even if the outcome was disappointing?
- **Plan improvement actions**: What specific steps will you take to improve based on this experience?
- **Maintain forward focus**: How will this experience help you succeed in future situations?

Reflection Questions

1. **Where do you fall on the impostor syndrome spectrum?** What specific situations or contexts trigger the strongest impostor feelings?
2. **What evidence do you have of your competence that you rarely acknowledge or celebrate?** How could you systematically document this evidence?
3. **How do you currently respond to setbacks and failures?** What would change if you viewed these as learning opportunities rather than evidence of inadequacy?
4. **What "failure immunization" experiences could you pursue to build your resilience and confidence?** What low-stakes failures could you practice with?

5. **Who could serve as objective observers of your competence and growth?** How could you better utilize an external perspective to counter internal doubt?

Action Steps

1. **Assess your impostor syndrome level** using the spectrum framework and identify which intervention strategies are most appropriate for your situation.

2. **Complete your Competence Inventory** by systematically documenting your skills, achievements, impact, and growth over time.

3. **Establish your Confidence Banking System** by setting up daily, weekly, and monthly practices for documenting accomplishments and building evidence.

4. **Practice the Resilience Reframe Protocol** on a recent setback or challenge, working through each step systematically.

5. **Design one "failure immunization" experience** appropriate to your Level 1, 2, or 3 development needs and commit to pursuing it within the next two weeks.

Impostor syndrome is not a permanent condition but a thinking pattern that can be changed through systematic intervention and practice. In Chapter 5, you will learn how to apply your growing confidence specifically in professional contexts where it can have maximum impact on your career and leadership effectiveness.

Chapter 5: Professional Confidence Mastery

"Leadership is not about being in charge. It is about taking care of those in your charge." — Simon Sinek.

When Jennifer was promoted to VP of Operations, she inherited a demoralized team, declining metrics, and a reputation for being the "problem department." Previous leaders had tried restructuring, new processes, and performance improvement plans. Nothing worked.

Jennifer tried something different. Instead of immediately implementing changes, she spent her first 30 days building what she called "confidence infrastructure." She created systems for recognizing individual contributions, established clear communication channels, and most importantly, she modeled the kind of authentic authority she wanted to see throughout the organization.

Within six months, her department had the highest employee engagement scores in the company and exceeded all performance targets. The transformation was not the result of new processes or procedures but of a leader who understood that professional confidence is both individual capability and organizational culture.

Your workplace confidence does not just impact your own career trajectory. It shapes team dynamics, influences organizational culture, and creates ripple effects that can transform entire departments or companies. This chapter will show you how to master professional confidence in ways that elevate both your leadership effectiveness and your team's performance.

Workplace Confidence Strategies

Professional environments present unique confidence challenges because your self-assurance directly impacts business results, team morale, and organizational success. Workplace confidence requires a sophisticated understanding of how to navigate complex relationships, handle pressure, and demonstrate authority without undermining others.

The Professional Confidence Assessment

Evaluate your confidence across key workplace dimensions using this detailed framework:

Decision-Making Confidence Rate yourself 1-10 on each element:
- Making important decisions under time pressure

- Standing behind your decisions when questioned
- Adjusting decisions based on new information without defensiveness
- Communicating decision rationale clearly to stakeholders
- Taking responsibility for decision outcomes, both positive and negative

Communication Confidence Rate yourself 1-10 on each element:
- Contributing meaningfully in meetings with senior stakeholders
- Presenting complex information clearly and persuasively
- Asking clarifying questions without feeling ignorant
- Providing constructive feedback to colleagues and direct reports
- Handling disagreement and pushback professionally

Leadership Presence Confidence Rate yourself 1-10 on each element:
- Commanding attention and respect when you enter a room
- Inspiring others to follow your vision and direction
- Maintaining composure and effectiveness under stress
- Delegating responsibilities without micromanaging
- Taking charge when situations require decisive leadership

Influence and Persuasion Confidence Rate yourself 1-10 on each element:
- Changing others' minds through logical argument and emotional connection
- Building coalitions and support for your initiatives
- Negotiating favorable outcomes while maintaining relationships
- Managing up effectively with senior leadership
- Creating buy-in for changes and new approaches

Confidence Calibration for Professional Growth

One of the most sophisticated aspects of workplace confidence is calibrating your self-assurance to match the situation. Underconfidence causes you to miss opportunities and underperform. Overconfidence leads to poor decisions and damaged relationships.

Under-Confidence Indicators:
- Consistently deferring to others even when you have relevant expertise
- Avoiding stretch assignments or leadership opportunities
- Over-preparing to the point of analysis paralysis

- Seeking excessive validation before making decisions

- Minimizing your contributions in team settings

Appropriate Confidence Indicators:

- Taking on challenges that stretch your capabilities with adequate preparation

- Speaking up when you have valuable insights to contribute

- Making decisions efficiently with available information

- Seeking input without requiring consensus for every choice

- Advocating for your ideas while remaining open to feedback

Over-Confidence Indicators:

- Making important decisions without gathering sufficient input

- Dismissing others' concerns or alternative perspectives

- Taking on responsibilities beyond your current capabilities

- Communicating with arrogance rather than authentic authority

- Failing to acknowledge mistakes or adjust course when needed

The goal is to develop sophisticated judgment about when to demonstrate high confidence, when to show appropriate humility, and when to seek support or guidance.

Leading With Authentic Authority

Authentic authority is the integration of competence, character, and confidence in service of others. It is the kind of leadership that inspires trust, motivates performance, and creates environments where others can do their best work.

The Authentic Authority Model

True leadership authority emerges from the alignment of three foundational elements:

Competence Authority stems from demonstrated expertise, consistent results, and continuous learning:

- Deep knowledge in your areas of responsibility

- Track record of successful project delivery and problem-solving

- Commitment to staying current with industry trends and best practices

- Ability to make sound decisions based on experience and analysis

- Willingness to acknowledge the limits of your expertise

Character Authority flows from integrity, reliability, and values-based leadership:

- Consistency between your stated values and daily actions

- Trustworthiness in handling confidential information and difficult situations

- Reliability in following through on commitments and promises

- Fairness in dealing with team members and stakeholders

- Courage to make difficult decisions and have hard conversations

Confidence Authority manifests through self-assurance, vulnerability, and inspirational presence:

- Belief in your ability to lead and make a positive impact

- Willingness to be vulnerable and admit when you do not know something

- Calm presence under pressure that reassures others

- Ability to inspire others to achieve beyond what they thought possible

- Resilience that models how to handle setbacks and challenges

Building Authority Without Arrogance

One of the most common fears about developing confidence is becoming arrogant or alienating others. Understanding the distinction between confident leadership and problematic ego helps you build authentic authority while maintaining strong relationships.

Confident Leadership Characteristics:

- Admits mistakes quickly and focuses on learning rather than blaming

- Shares credit generously while taking responsibility for failures

- Seeks feedback actively and integrates input thoughtfully

- Focuses conversations on team success and organizational goals

- Demonstrates curiosity about others' perspectives and ideas

- Shows appreciation for team members' contributions and growth

Arrogant Leadership Warning Signs:

- Becomes defensive when receiving criticism or challenging feedback

- Takes credit for successes while deflecting responsibility for failures

- Dismisses others' ideas without serious consideration

- Dominates conversations and meetings without encouraging input

- Makes decisions without consulting relevant stakeholders

- Treats disagreement as personal attacks rather than professional discourse

The key difference is whether your confidence serves yourself or serves others. Authentic authority uses confidence to create environments where everyone can succeed.

Developing Your Leadership Voice

Your leadership voice is the consistent way you communicate authority, make decisions, and influence others. Developing this voice requires intentional practice and continuous refinement.

Clarity and Directness: Communicate expectations, decisions, and feedback clearly without ambiguity. Avoid softening important messages to the point where they lose impact.

Thoughtful Listening: Demonstrate that you value others' input by listening actively and asking clarifying questions before responding.

Strategic Questioning: Use questions to guide thinking and encourage ownership rather than simply providing answers.

Confident Vulnerability: Share appropriate challenges and uncertainties to model authenticity while maintaining overall confidence in your leadership capability.

Inspirational Framing: Help others see how their work contributes to larger purposes and meaningful outcomes.

The Feedback Integration Framework

Professional confidence requires the ability to receive, process, and integrate feedback without having your self-worth destabilized by criticism or inflated by praise. This sophisticated skill distinguishes confident professionals from those whose performance fluctuates based on external validation.

The Five-Phase Feedback Integration Process

Phase 1: Reception Without Reaction When receiving feedback, focus entirely on understanding the message rather than formulating responses or defenses:
- Listen actively without interrupting or preparing counterarguments
- Ask clarifying questions to ensure you understand the feedback accurately
- Thank the person for their input, regardless of whether you agree with it

- Avoid immediate emotional reactions or defensive responses
- Take notes if the feedback is complex or detailed

Phase 2: Objective Analysis and Evaluation. After receiving feedback, analyze it systematically to determine its accuracy and usefulness:
- Separate the factual content from the emotional delivery
- Consider the credibility and perspective of the feedback provider
- Look for patterns if similar feedback has come from multiple sources
- Identify specific behaviors or outcomes that the feedback addresses
- Distinguish between feedback about performance and feedback about character

Phase 3: Integration Planning and Implementation. For feedback that proves accurate and useful, create specific plans for improvement:
- Set specific, measurable goals for addressing the feedback
- Identify resources, training, or support needed for improvement
- Create accountability systems to track progress
- Communicate your improvement plan to relevant stakeholders
- Schedule follow-up conversations to assess progress

Phase 4: Application and Practice. Implement changes systematically while monitoring their effectiveness:
- Practice new behaviors in low-stakes situations before applying them in critical contexts
- Seek coaching or mentoring to accelerate improvement
- Document progress and challenges in your development journal
- Adjust your approach based on results and additional feedback
- Celebrate incremental improvements while maintaining focus on continued growth

Phase 5: Follow-Up and Relationship Maintenance. Circle back with feedback providers to demonstrate your commitment to growth and maintain professional relationships:
- Update them on specific actions you have taken based on their input
- Ask for additional feedback on your improvement efforts
- Thank them again for their willingness to provide honest input
- Offer to provide feedback for them if appropriate
- Model the feedback integration process for others in your organization

Developing Criticism Resilience

Building immunity to destructive criticism while remaining open to constructive input requires sophisticated discernment skills.

Destructive Criticism Characteristics:
- Focuses on personal character rather than specific behaviors
- Provides vague complaints without specific examples or suggestions
- Delivered with the intent to hurt rather than help
- Represents a pattern of negativity without a balanced perspective
- Comes from sources with questionable credibility or obvious bias

Constructive Criticism Characteristics:
- Addresses specific behaviors, decisions, or outcomes
- Provides clear examples and actionable suggestions for improvement
- Delivered with the intent to support your growth and success
- Represents a balanced perspective that acknowledges both strengths and areas for development
- Comes from credible sources who have your best interests in mind

Resilience Building Strategies:
- Develop a strong sense of your core values and identity that cannot be shaken by external opinions
- Build a network of trusted advisors who can provide perspective during challenging feedback situations
- Practice separating your worth as a person from your performance in specific situations
- Create systems for processing difficult feedback with time and space rather than immediate reaction
- Focus on learning and growth rather than being right or avoiding discomfort

Building Team Confidence Culture

Your confidence as a leader does not just impact your own effectiveness; it creates the environment that either supports or undermines your team's confidence development.

Building a confidence culture requires intentional systems and practices that make self-assurance contagious throughout your organization.

Direct Influence Methods

Confidence Modeling: Demonstrate the behaviors and attitudes you want to see in your team:
- Make decisions with appropriate confidence while acknowledging uncertainty
- Admit mistakes quickly and focus on learning rather than blaming
- Take calculated risks and view failures as learning opportunities
- Communicate with clarity and conviction while remaining open to input
- Show vulnerability appropriately while maintaining overall leadership presence

Specific Recognition and Encouragement: Provide feedback that builds confidence rather than simply evaluating performance:
- Acknowledge specific behaviors and contributions rather than giving generic praise
- Connect individual contributions to team and organizational success
- Recognize growth and improvement, not just final results
- Celebrate intelligent failures and learning from setbacks
- Provide specific suggestions for continued development

Stretch Opportunity Creation: Design assignments that build team members' confidence through progressive challenges:
- Match opportunities to individuals' development needs and readiness levels
- Provide appropriate support and resources for success
- Allow team members to lead initiatives in their areas of strength
- Create safe opportunities for practicing new skills
- Debrief experiences to maximize learning and confidence-building

Protective Leadership: Shield your team from organizational politics and external pressures that could undermine their confidence:
- Handle organizational criticism or pressure without passing stress to team members
- Advocate upward for your team's needs and recognition
- Create psychological safety by addressing conflicts and tensions directly

- Maintain consistent expectations and communication during organizational changes
- Take responsibility for team failures while sharing credit for successes

Indirect Influence Methods

Psychological Safety Establishment: Create an environment where team members feel safe to take risks, make mistakes, and express different perspectives:
- Encourage questions and idea sharing without judgment
- Respond to mistakes with curiosity about learning rather than blame
- Model vulnerability by sharing your own challenges and uncertainties
- Address conflicts directly and fairly rather than avoiding difficult conversations
- Establish clear expectations while allowing flexibility in how results are achieved

Collaborative Decision-Making: Include team members in decision-making processes to build their confidence in their judgment and influence:
- Seek input on decisions that affect team members' work
- Explain your decision-making rationale to help others develop judgment
- Allow team members to make decisions in their areas of responsibility
- Provide coaching and feedback on decision-making processes
- Create opportunities for team members to present recommendations to senior leadership

Professional Development Investment: Demonstrate commitment to team members' growth through systematic development planning:
- Have regular career development conversations with each team member
- Provide access to training, conferences, and learning opportunities
- Create internal mentoring and coaching relationships
- Support team members' pursuit of stretch assignments and new responsibilities
- Help team members build networks and relationships outside your immediate team

Confidence Culture Measurement

Track the confidence health of your team through both quantitative and qualitative indicators:

Quantitative Indicators:

- Employee engagement survey scores, particularly questions about empowerment and growth
- Performance improvement rates across team members
- Innovation metrics such as ideas generated and implemented
- Internal promotion and advancement rates
- Retention rates and exit interview feedback

Qualitative Indicators:

- Quality of communication in team meetings and one-on-one conversations
- Willingness of team members to take on challenging assignments
- Speed of recovery from setbacks and ability to learn from failures
- Level of initiative and proactive problem-solving
- Degree of collaboration and mutual support among team members

Regular assessment helps you adjust your leadership approach to maximize confidence-building impact.

Reflection Questions

1. **How does your confidence level vary across different professional situations?** What patterns do you notice in your workplace confidence?
2. **What feedback have you received about your leadership presence and authority?** How do others experience your confidence?
3. **In what ways does your confidence impact your team's performance and morale?** What evidence do you see of confidence contagion in your workplace?
4. **How do you currently handle criticism and challenging feedback?** What would change if you viewed all feedback as data for improvement?
5. **What systems could you create to build a confidence culture in your team or organization?** How could you measure the effectiveness of these systems?

Action Steps

1. **Complete the Professional Confidence Assessment** across all four dimensions and identify your strongest area and biggest opportunity for growth.

2. **Evaluate your current leadership authority** using the Competence-Character-Confidence model and create a development plan for your weakest area.

3. **Practice the Feedback Integration Framework** on recent feedback you have received, working through all five phases systematically.

4. **Implement one confidence culture initiative** with your team, whether through recognition systems, stretch opportunities, or psychological safety improvements.

5. **Establish measurement systems** for tracking your team's confidence development through both quantitative and qualitative indicators.

Professional confidence is not just personal development; it is leadership development that impacts everyone around you. In Chapter 6, you will learn how to systematically multiply your confidence impact to create positive change far beyond your immediate sphere of influence.

Chapter 6: The Ripple Effect Leadership Model

"A candle loses nothing by lighting another candle." — **James Keller**

Rebecca had always been a high performer, but she kept her head down and focused on her own work. When she was promoted to team lead, she continued this approach, assuming that individual excellence would naturally translate to team success. It did not.

After six months of mediocre team results despite her personal achievements, Rebecca received feedback that changed her perspective entirely: "You're incredibly capable, but your team doesn't know it. They can't catch confidence from someone who hides her light."

This feedback sparked what Rebecca later called her "confidence multiplication transformation." She began intentionally modeling authentic authority, celebrating team members' wins, and creating opportunities for others to shine. Within a year, her team had the highest performance ratings in the division, and three team members had been promoted to leadership roles themselves.

Rebecca discovered what confident leaders understand intuitively: your confidence is not just personal capital but social currency that can be invested to create exponential returns through others.

This chapter will show you how to systematically multiply your confidence impact to transform not just your own effectiveness but the capability and self-assurance of everyone around you.

How Your Confidence Transforms Others

Confidence is contagious through multiple channels that operate below conscious awareness. When you understand these transmission mechanisms, you can use them intentionally to create positive change in your family, team, and community.

The Confidence Transmission Theory

Social psychology research demonstrates that confidence transfers through three primary channels, each operating simultaneously to influence others' self-assurance and performance.

Verbal Transmission. Your words carry confidence signals that others absorb unconsciously:

Tone and Certainty: The vocal qualities you use when speaking convey confidence independent of content. Research shows that people form judgments about speaker confidence within the first seven words of any statement.

Language Choices: Confident language patterns include specific rather than vague statements, solution-focused rather than problem-focused framing, and inclusive rather than divisive phrasing.

Encouragement Quality: The specificity and timing of your encouragement impact others' confidence development. Generic praise ("Good job") has minimal impact compared to specific recognition ("Your analysis of the market data helped us identify the key risk factors we needed to address").

Question Patterns: Confident leaders ask questions that assume capability ("How will you approach this challenge?") rather than questions that assume incapability ("Do you think you can handle this?").

Non-Verbal Transmission. Your physical presence communicates confidence through multiple channels:

Posture and Movement: Confident posture (shoulders back, head up, grounded stance) triggers confidence responses in others through mirror neuron activation.

Eye Contact Quality: Appropriate eye contact conveys attention, respect, and confidence simultaneously. It signals that you are comfortable with yourself and genuinely interested in others.

Energy and Presence: Confident people bring positive energy to interactions that others find attractive and energizing. This energy is not forced enthusiasm but authentic engagement and optimism.

Spatial Awareness: How you use physical space, enter rooms, and position yourself in groups communicates confidence levels that others unconsciously mirror.

Behavioral Transmission. Your actions model confidence in ways that give others permission to act similarly:

Decision-Making Speed and Quality: When you make decisions efficiently with available information, others learn that perfect information is not required for effective action.

Risk-Taking and Innovation: Your willingness to try new approaches and learn from failures shows others that taking intelligent risks is not only acceptable but necessary for growth.

Resilience and Recovery: How you handle setbacks and bounce back from challenges teaches others that failure is temporary and learning is permanent.

Initiative and Ownership: When you take responsibility for results and proactively address challenges, you model the kind of ownership that builds confidence in others.

Measuring Your Confidence Impact

To maximize your confidence multiplication effect, you need systematic ways to assess your current impact and track improvements over time.

Individual Impact Indicators:
- Increased participation in meetings and discussions among your team members
- Higher quality and frequency of ideas and suggestions from others
- Greater willingness of others to take on challenging assignments
- Improved performance and results delivery across your team
- More proactive problem-solving and initiative from team members

Team Impact Indicators:
- Enhanced collaboration and mutual support among team members
- Increased innovation and creative solution development
- Faster recovery from setbacks and the ability to learn from failures
- Higher levels of engagement and energy in team interactions
- Improved communication quality and frequency

Organizational Impact Indicators:
- Enhanced reputation and external perception of your department or team
- Increased employee satisfaction and retention in your area of influence
- Better cross-functional collaboration and relationship quality
- Higher customer satisfaction scores and stakeholder feedback
- Improved financial performance and business results

Community Impact Indicators:
- Greater participation in voluntary initiatives and improvement projects
- Increased leadership development and advancement among your network

- Enhanced culture and morale in organizations where you have influence

- More mentoring and coaching relationships initiated by others

- Positive feedback about your influence from external stakeholders

Creating Psychological Safety Through Self-Esteem

Psychological safety is the foundation for team confidence because it creates an environment where people feel safe to take risks, make mistakes, and express authentic perspectives. Your confidence as a leader is the primary driver of psychological safety in your team.

The Safety-Confidence Connection

Research from Harvard Business School shows that psychological safety and team performance have a direct correlation, with confidence serving as the critical mediating factor. When people feel psychologically safe, they are more likely to:

- Share ideas and perspectives without fear of ridicule or punishment

- Admit mistakes and ask for help when needed

- Take calculated risks and try innovative approaches

- Provide honest feedback and engage in constructive conflict

- Support team members' development and success

Your confidence creates this safety through several mechanisms:

Confidence Provides Stability: When team members know you will not overreact to problems or mistakes, they feel safe bringing issues to your attention early when they can still be addressed effectively.

Confidence Enables Vulnerability: Your willingness to admit uncertainty, ask for help, and acknowledge mistakes gives others permission to be equally authentic.

Confidence Supports Growth: Your belief in others' capacity to learn and improve creates an environment where people are willing to stretch beyond their comfort zones.

Confidence Manages Pressure: Your ability to stay calm under stress helps others maintain their composure and effectiveness during challenging periods.

The Five-Phase Psychological Safety Implementation Plan

Phase 1: Assessment of Current Safety Levels. Evaluate the current psychological safety in your team through surveys, observation, and direct conversation:

Anonymous Team Assessment: Use tools like Google's Project Aristotle psychological safety survey to get baseline measurements.

Behavioral Observation: Track indicators like meeting participation rates, frequency of questions and ideas, and willingness to disagree or debate.

Individual Conversations: Have one-on-one discussions with team members about their comfort level with risk-taking, mistake-making, and honest communication.

External Feedback: Gather input from other leaders and stakeholders about your team's openness and collaboration.

Phase 2: Personal Vulnerability Modeling. Demonstrate the behaviors you want to see by being appropriately vulnerable yourself:

Mistake Acknowledgment: Share your own mistakes and learning experiences without over-sharing or undermining your authority.

Uncertainty Admission: Acknowledge when you do not know something and need to gather more information or seek expert input.

Help Seeking: Ask for assistance, input, and feedback in ways that model collaborative problem-solving.

Growth Mindset Demonstration: Show how you approach challenges as learning opportunities rather than threats.

Phase 3: Active Encouragement and Support. Systematically encourage risk-taking, innovation, and authentic communication:

Idea Solicitation: Actively seek input and ideas from all team members, especially those who tend to be quieter.

Intelligent Failure Celebration: Publicly recognize and learn from failures that were well-intentioned and generated valuable learning.

Diverse Perspective Integration: Show that you value different viewpoints and approaches rather than seeking conformity.

Development Investment: Provide resources, training, and opportunities that demonstrate your commitment to team members' growth.

Phase 4: Protection and Advocacy. Shield your team from external pressures and politics that could undermine psychological safety:

Buffer External Criticism: Handle organizational pressure and criticism without passing stress to team members unnecessarily.

Upward Advocacy: Represent your team's interests and needs in senior leadership discussions and decisions.

Conflict Resolution: Address interpersonal conflicts and tensions directly rather than allowing them to fester.

Consistent Communication: Maintain transparent, regular communication about organizational changes and their implications.

Phase 5: Systematic Reinforcement and Evolution. Embed psychological safety practices into your team's regular operations:

Regular Check-ins: Schedule systematic assessment of psychological safety levels and team feedback.

Process Integration: Build safety practices into meeting structures, decision-making processes, and project management approaches.

Leadership Development: Train other leaders in your organization to create psychological safety in their teams.

Continuous Improvement: Evolve your approach based on feedback and changing team needs.

The Confidence Multiplication Strategy

Confidence multiplication means systematically identifying and developing the confidence of specific individuals who can create additional ripple effects throughout your organization and community.

Identifying Confidence Multiplier Opportunities

Look for people who have high potential but low confidence, as these individuals often represent the greatest opportunities for confidence multiplication:

High-Potential, Low-Confidence Characteristics:

- Strong technical skills with limited self-promotion or visibility
- Excellent ideas that they rarely share in group settings
- High-quality work performance with minimal recognition seeking
- Natural leadership capabilities that they do not exercise
- Deep expertise that they hesitate to leverage for influence

Assessment Questions for Potential Confidence Multipliers:

- Who in your organization has capabilities that exceed their current confidence level?
- Which team members avoid stretch opportunities despite being well-qualified?
- Who provides valuable input in private but rarely speaks up in groups?
- Which individuals have leadership potential but lack belief in their authority?
- Who could have a significantly greater impact with increased confidence?

Targeted Confidence Development Interventions

Once you identify confidence multiplication targets, create systematic development approaches tailored to their specific needs and situations:

Mentoring and Coaching Relationships:

- Establish regular one-on-one meetings focused on confidence development
- Provide specific feedback about observed capabilities and potential
- Share your own confidence development experiences and challenges
- Create accountability for confidence-building actions and goals

Stretch Assignment Design:

- Offer challenges that match their capability level but exceed their confidence level
- Provide appropriate support and resources for success
- Debrief experiences to maximize learning and confidence-building
- Gradually increase responsibility and visibility over time

Public Recognition and Visibility:

- Highlight their contributions in team meetings and organizational communications
- Create opportunities for them to present their work to senior leadership
- Nominate them for awards, recognition programs, and speaking opportunities

- Connect them with senior leaders who can provide additional support and advocacy

Skill Development Investment:
- Provide training and development opportunities that build both competence and confidence
- Send them to conferences, workshops, and professional development programs
- Support their pursuit of certifications, advanced education, or specialized training
- Create internal learning opportunities, like project leadership or cross-functional assignments

The Systematic Confidence Coaching Methodology

Develop a repeatable process for building others' confidence that you can apply consistently across different individuals and situations:

Step 1: Confidence Assessment and Goal Setting
- Evaluate their current confidence levels across different dimensions
- Identify specific areas where increased confidence would have the most impact
- Set measurable confidence development goals with clear timelines
- Create accountability systems for tracking progress

Step 2: Strength Recognition and Evidence Building
- Help them identify and acknowledge their existing capabilities and achievements
- Create systematic documentation of their contributions and successes
- Provide objective feedback about their performance and potential
- Connect them with others who can validate their capabilities

Step 3: Skill Building and Competence Development
- Provide training and development opportunities that build both skills and confidence
- Create progressively challenging assignments that stretch their capabilities
- Offer coaching and feedback to accelerate their learning and development
- Connect them with experts and mentors in their areas of interest

Step 4: Practice Opportunities and Safe Challenges
- Design low-risk opportunities to practice new confidence behaviors

- Create supportive environments for experimenting with leadership and influence
- Provide feedback and coaching during practice opportunities
- Gradually increase the stakes and visibility of their challenges

Step 5: Recognition and Reinforcement
- Acknowledge their progress and growth publicly and privately
- Connect their increased confidence to improved results and impact
- Share their success stories with others to reinforce positive changes
- Create opportunities for them to mentor and coach others

Step 6: Independence and Leadership Development
- Gradually reduce your direct support as their confidence increases
- Encourage them to take on confidence-building initiatives with others
- Support their transition into formal and informal leadership roles
- Create systems for them to continue developing without your direct involvement

Legacy Leadership Through Confidence

The highest level of confidence multiplication is creating a lasting impact that continues long after your direct involvement ends. Legacy leadership means building systems, cultures, and people that perpetuate confidence development independently.

The Confidence Legacy Framework

Personal Legacy Elements:
- Individuals whose confidence you have directly influenced who then influence others
- Systems and processes you have created that continue to build confidence
- Cultural changes you have initiated that outlast your direct involvement
- Next-generation leaders who carry forward your confidence-building approach

Organizational Legacy Elements:
- Confidence-building practices embedded in organizational policies and procedures
- Leadership development programs that emphasize confidence multiplication
- Performance management systems that recognize and reward confidence-building leadership
- Recruitment and promotion criteria that value confidence development capabilities

Community Legacy Elements:
- Networks of confident leaders who support each other's continued growth
- Mentoring and coaching programs that systematically develop confidence
- Community organizations and initiatives that promote confidence development
- Educational programs that teach confidence-building skills to broader audiences

Scaling Your Confidence Impact

Direct Scaling Methods:
- Develop training programs and workshops that teach confidence-building skills
- Create mentoring and coaching programs that multiply your influence
- Document and share best practices for confidence development
- Speak at conferences and events about confidence leadership approaches

Indirect Scaling Methods:
- Train other leaders to become confidence builders in their organizations
- Influence organizational policies and practices that support confidence development
- Build communities of practice around confidence-building leadership
- Support research and thought leadership in confidence development

Systematic Scaling Methods:
- Create certification programs for confidence coaching and leadership
- Develop assessment tools and methodologies that others can use
- Build technology platforms that support confidence development
- Establish foundations or organizations dedicated to confidence-building

Documentation and Measurement of Legacy Impact

Story Collection and Documentation:
- Gather testimonials and case studies from individuals you have influenced
- Document the ripple effects of confidence-building through multiple generations
- Track quantitative outcomes of your confidence multiplication efforts
- Create narratives that inspire others to become confidence multipliers

Impact Measurement Systems:
- Develop metrics for assessing confidence culture in organizations

- Track the advancement and leadership development of people you have influenced
- Measure organizational performance improvements linked to confidence-building
- Assess community and industry changes resulting from your influence

Succession Planning and Continuity:
- Identify and develop others who can carry forward your confidence-building work
- Create systems that continue operating without your direct involvement
- Establish governance and leadership structures for ongoing programs
- Build financial sustainability for confidence development initiatives

Reflection Questions

1. **Who has been most influenced by your confidence example, and how do you know?** What evidence do you see of your ripple effect impact?

2. **What systems could you create to multiply your confidence impact beyond your direct relationships?** How could you scale your influence systematically?

3. **How do you currently create psychological safety for others?** What could you do to make people feel safer to take risks and be authentic?

4. **Who in your sphere of influence has high potential but low confidence?** What specific interventions could help them develop greater self-assurance?

5. **What legacy do you want to create through your confident leadership?** How will you measure and track your long-term impact?

Action Steps

1. **Assess your current ripple effect impact** using the measurement frameworks provided, gathering feedback from others about how your confidence affects them.

2. **Implement one psychological safety initiative** with your team, focusing on creating an environment where others feel safe to take risks and be authentic.

3. **Identify three high-potential, low-confidence individuals** in your network and design specific confidence development interventions for each.

4. **Create one systematic confidence multiplication system,** such as a mentoring program, recognition system, or development initiative.

5. **Begin documenting your confidence legacy** by collecting stories, testimonials, and evidence of your positive impact on others' confidence and leadership development.

Your confidence is not just personal capability but social responsibility. In Chapter 7, you will learn how to implement a systematic 30-day program that integrates all the strategies you have learned into a practical, measurable confidence transformation plan.

Chapter 7: The 30-Day Confidence Amplifier

"You are never too old to set another goal or to dream a new dream." — **C.S. Lewis.**

Mark had read dozens of personal development books, attended leadership seminars, and even worked with an executive coach. He understood confidence concepts intellectually but struggled to translate knowledge into lasting behavioral change. Like many high achievers, he suffered from what psychologists call the "implementation gap" – knowing what to do but not systematically doing it.

When Mark committed to the 30-Day Confidence Amplifier Program, he approached it like a business project with clear objectives, daily metrics, and weekly reviews. The structure and accountability transformed his relationship with confidence development from sporadic effort to systematic practice.

By day 30, Mark had not only measurably increased his confidence across all four dimensions but had created sustainable systems for continued growth. More importantly, his colleagues noticed the change. His team's engagement scores improved, he was selected for a high-visibility project, and two team members asked him to mentor them in confidence development.

The 30-Day Confidence Amplifier Program integrates all the strategies, tools, and techniques from this book into a systematic, progressive development experience that creates measurable confidence improvement and sustainable confidence-building habits.

Program Structure And Methodology

The 30-Day Program is designed around proven behavior change principles that maximize the likelihood of lasting transformation rather than temporary improvement.

Scientific Foundation

Neuroplasticity Optimization: Research shows that focused practice for 30 consecutive days creates measurable changes in brain structure and function. The program timing aligns with neuroplasticity windows for maximum impact.

Habit Formation Timeline: Studies indicate that simple habits take 21 days to form, while complex behavioral changes require 30-66 days. The 30-day timeframe provides sufficient repetition for basic habit formation while setting the foundation for continued development.

Progressive Complexity: Each week builds systematically on the previous week, moving from foundation building through skill development, integration, and advanced application.

Measurement and Accountability: Daily tracking and weekly reviews provide the feedback loops necessary for sustained motivation and course correction.

Weekly Progression Framework

Week 1: Foundation Building

- Establish baseline confidence measurements across all four dimensions
- Implement core daily practices and tracking systems
- Begin basic self-talk monitoring and reframing techniques
- Create a personal confidence tracking dashboard

Week 2: Skill Development

- Practice intermediate confidence techniques in controlled situations
- Apply the REFRAME method systematically to persistent negative patterns
- Build an evidence-based affirmation system and daily practice routine
- Begin confidence challenges in low-risk professional and personal contexts

Week 3: Integration and Application

- Apply confidence strategies in higher-stakes professional situations
- Practice leadership confidence and authentic authority techniques
- Implement feedback integration frameworks with real-world feedback
- Focus on psychological safety creation and confidence multiplication with others

Week 4: Leadership and Influence

- Demonstrate mastery-level confidence application in challenging situations
- Lead confidence development initiatives for team members or colleagues
- Measure and document confidence impact on others and organizational culture
- Plan long-term confidence maintenance and continued growth strategies

Implementation Guidelines

Daily Commitment: 15-20 minutes of focused confidence development activity each day, including tracking, reflection, and specific skill practice.

Weekly Reviews: 30-60 minutes each week for comprehensive progress assessment, pattern analysis, and strategy adjustment.

Accountability Systems: Partner with a colleague, friend, or coach for regular check-ins and external perspective on progress.

Flexibility Within Structure: While the overall framework is fixed, specific daily activities can be adapted to your schedule, preferences, and development needs.

Week 1: Foundation Building

The first week focuses on establishing the measurement systems, daily practices, and basic techniques that will support your confidence development throughout the program.

Day 1: Comprehensive Assessment and Goal Setting

Morning Activity (10 minutes):
- Complete the full Self-Esteem Assessment Matrix from Chapter 1
- Review your scores and identify your strongest and weakest confidence dimensions
- Set your primary 30-day confidence development goal using the SMART framework

Evening Activity (10 minutes):
- Establish your daily confidence tracking system using the provided dashboard
- Record your first day's confidence level (1-10) across all four dimensions
- Identify three specific situations where you want to demonstrate increased confidence

Reflection Questions:
- What surprised you about your assessment results?
- Which confidence dimension, if improved, would have the biggest impact on your life and career?
- What specific evidence will demonstrate that you have achieved your 30-day goal?

Day 2: Daily Practice Implementation

Morning Activity (10 minutes):

- Implement your morning confidence micro-routine: posture, power pose, success statement review, and daily intention setting
- Begin self-talk monitoring using the thought tracking worksheet
- Practice one evidence-based affirmation related to your development goal

Evening Activity (10 minutes):

- Complete your first daily confidence reflection: What went well? What challenged your confidence? What did you learn?
- Review your self-talk notes and identify patterns or triggers
- Plan tomorrow's confidence challenge: one small action outside your comfort zone

Action Focus: Begin noticing your automatic confidence responses without trying to change them yet.

Day 3: REFRAME Method Introduction

Morning Activity (10 minutes):

- Identify one recurring negative thought pattern from your monitoring
- Apply the first three steps of the REFRAME method: Recognize, Examine evidence, Find alternatives
- Practice your morning confidence routine and affirmation

Evening Activity (10 minutes):

- Complete the REFRAME process for your chosen negative thought: Rewrite, Affirm, Monitor
- Document the experience: Was the reframed thought more accurate and helpful?
- Update your confidence tracking dashboard

Action Focus: Take one small professional risk, such as speaking up in a meeting or volunteering for a task.

Day 4: Evidence Building and Competence Documentation

Morning Activity (10 minutes):

- Begin your Competence Inventory by listing 10 professional strengths and capabilities

- Review recent achievements and positive feedback you have received
- Practice your confidence routine and affirmation

Evening Activity (10 minutes):
- Add 5 personal strengths and 5 relationship/social capabilities to your inventory
- Seek one piece of positive feedback from a colleague, friend, or family member
- Reflect on how evidence-gathering affects your self-perception

Action Focus: Set and honor one personal boundary, practicing self-advocacy in a low-stakes situation.

Day 5: Routine Optimization and Challenge Preparation

Morning Activity (10 minutes):
- Evaluate your morning routine effectiveness and make adjustments
- Complete your evolving Competence Inventory with specific examples and evidence
- Set your intention for today's confidence challenge

Evening Activity (10 minutes):
- Conduct your first weekly review: What patterns do you notice in your confidence levels?
- Assess which techniques are most effective for your specific challenges
- Plan Week 2 goals and challenges

Action Focus: Take on a slightly bigger challenge, such as initiating a difficult conversation or proposing a new idea.

Days 6-7: Integration and Momentum Building

Weekend Focus: Practice confidence techniques in personal and social contexts outside of work. Apply your developing skills in family relationships, social situations, or community activities.

Reflection Activity: Complete a comprehensive review of Week 1: What changes do you notice in your thoughts, feelings, or behaviors? Which techniques feel most natural and effective? What adjustments will you make for Week 2?

Week 2: Skill Development

Week 2 focuses on building proficiency with confidence techniques and applying them in progressively challenging situations.

Days 8-10: Professional Confidence Application

Daily Structure:

- **Morning**: Advanced confidence routine + specific preparation for professional confidence challenges
- **Midday**: Apply confidence techniques in professional contexts (meetings, presentations, difficult conversations)
- **Evening**: Detailed reflection on professional confidence application + evidence documentation

Progressive Challenges:

- Day 8: Contribute meaningfully in a challenging meeting
- Day 9: Volunteer for a stretch assignment or responsibility
- Day 10: Provide constructive feedback to a colleague or direct report

Skill Focus: Practice the Professional Confidence strategies from Chapter 5, particularly decision-making confidence and authentic authority.

Days 11-14: Personal and Social Confidence Development

Daily Structure:

- **Morning**: Confidence routine + personal/social challenge preparation
- **Afternoon/Evening**: Apply confidence in personal relationships and social situations
- **Evening**: Reflection on personal confidence growth + relationship impact assessment

Progressive Challenges:

- Day 11: Practice vulnerability and authenticity in a safe relationship
- Day 12: Set a challenging but necessary boundary with someone
- Day 13: Take social initiative (networking, community involvement, new relationship building)

- Day 14: Help someone else build their confidence through encouragement or support

Skill Focus: Develop Personal Confidence dimensions, including self-advocacy, authenticity, and boundary setting.

Week 3: Integration And Application

Week 3 emphasizes integrating confidence skills into complex, high-stakes situations and beginning to impact others' confidence development.

Days 15-17: Advanced Professional Application
Advanced Challenges:
- Lead a high-visibility initiative or project
- Practice influence and persuasion in challenging stakeholder situations
- Apply confidence skills in crisis or high-pressure contexts
- Demonstrate authentic authority with senior leadership

Integration Focus: Combine multiple confidence techniques simultaneously while maintaining authenticity and effectiveness.

Days 18-21: Confidence Multiplication and Ripple Effect

Focus Areas:
- Systematically assess your confidence impact on others
- Implement confidence coaching with a team member or colleague
- Create psychological safety initiatives in your work environment
- Practice confidence transmission through verbal, non-verbal, and behavioral channels

Measurement Activity: Gather feedback from others about changes they have noticed in your confidence and leadership presence.

Week 4: Leadership And Influence

The final week focuses on confidence mastery, leadership application, and creating sustainable systems for continued growth.

Days 22-24: Confidence Leadership Mastery

Mastery Demonstrations:

- Lead confidence culture initiatives in your team or organization

- Apply complete confidence methodology in complex, multi-stakeholder situations

- Coach multiple individuals simultaneously in confidence development

- Create systematic confidence development processes for others

Documentation Focus: Record detailed examples of confidence leadership for future reference and teaching.

Days 25-27: Impact Assessment and Future Planning

Assessment Activities:

- Complete a comprehensive 30-day confidence assessment and compare to baseline

- Gather quantitative and qualitative feedback about your confidence development

- Document specific behavioral changes and capability improvements

- Evaluate the program's methodology effectiveness

Planning Activities:

- Design personal confidence maintenance and growth plan for months 2-6

- Create accountability systems for continued development

- Plan integration with Time That Matters and Relationships That Matter principles

- Establish confidence leadership and mentoring opportunities

Days 28-30: Integration and Commitment

Final Activities:

- Complete program documentation and reflection

- Celebrate achievements and acknowledge growth

- Commit to continued confidence development and leadership

- Plan next-level confidence challenges and development goals

Tracking And Measurement Systems

Effective confidence development requires systematic measurement and tracking to maintain motivation and guide adjustments.

Daily Confidence Dashboard

Track these metrics daily using a 1-10 scale:

Confidence Levels:

- Overall confidence level
- Professional confidence in specific situations
- Personal confidence in relationships and self-advocacy
- Social confidence in group and networking contexts
- Resilience confidence when facing challenges

Behavior Tracking:

- Number of confidence challenges attempted
- Quality of self-talk and affirmation practice
- Boundary setting and self-advocacy instances
- Confidence support provided to others
- Recovery time from confidence setbacks

Evidence Collection:

- Specific accomplishments and contributions
- Positive feedback received
- Challenges overcome
- Growth and learning instances
- Impact on others' confidence

Weekly Review Process

Pattern Analysis: Identify trends in confidence levels, challenging situations, and effective techniques.

Growth Measurement: Quantify improvement across confidence dimensions and specific behaviors.

Challenge Assessment: Evaluate progress on current challenges and set new stretch goals.

Strategy Adjustment: Refine techniques and approaches based on effectiveness and feedback.

Social Impact Review: Assess confidence impact on others and relationship quality.

30-Day Comprehensive Assessment

Quantitative Measures:

- Before/after scores on Self-Esteem Assessment Matrix
- Frequency of confidence challenges attempted and successfully completed
- Number of confidence-building interactions with others
- Measurable professional and personal outcomes linked to increased confidence

Qualitative Measures:

- Detailed behavioral change examples and stories
- Feedback from colleagues, friends, and family about observed changes
- Quality of internal dialogue and self-talk improvements
- Confidence impact on team culture and organizational effectiveness

Integration Measures:

- Sustainability of new confidence habits and practices
- Integration with Change That Matters and Goals That Matter principles
- Preparation for the Time That Matters and Relationships That Matter application
- Leadership development and confidence multiplication capability

Reflection Questions

1. **What aspects of the 30-day program structure appeal most to you, and what concerns do you have?** How will you address potential obstacles to completion?

2. **Which week do you anticipate being most challenging, and how will you prepare for it?** What support systems will you need?

3. **How will you measure success beyond the formal assessment tools?** What changes would indicate meaningful confidence development?

4. **Who could serve as accountability partners or supporters during your 30-day program?** How will you engage them in your development?

5. **How will you maintain momentum after the 30-day program ends?** What systems will support continued confidence growth?

Action Steps

1. **Schedule your 30-day program start date** and block time in your calendar for daily practice and weekly reviews.

2. **Set up your tracking and measurement systems** using the provided templates or create your own based on the framework.

3. **Identify your accountability partner** and schedule regular check-ins throughout the program.

4. **Complete your baseline assessment** using all the tools from previous chapters to establish your starting point.

5. **Prepare your support materials,** including worksheets, tracking tools, and reference guides for easy daily access.

The 30-Day Confidence Amplifier Program transforms confidence knowledge into confidence capability through systematic practice and measurement. In the final section, you will learn how to integrate your confidence development with the broader About Things That Matter system for comprehensive life transformation.

Chapter 8: Integration - Your Self-Esteem Action Plan

"The best time to plant a tree was 20 years ago. The second best time is now." — Chinese Proverb.

Lisa completed the 30-Day Confidence Amplifier Program with impressive results. Her assessment scores had improved across all dimensions, her team gave her higher leadership ratings, and she had successfully tackled several challenges that would have paralyzed her with anxiety just months before.

But Lisa's transformation really began when she realized that confidence was not a destination but a foundation. Her newfound self-assurance amplified everything else she had learned about change management from Book 1 and goal achievement from Book 2. More importantly, it prepared her to master time management and relationship building in the upcoming books of the series.

Lisa discovered what confident people understand intuitively: self-esteem is not a standalone skill but the multiplier that makes every other area of personal and professional development more effective and sustainable.

This chapter will show you how to integrate your confidence development with the complete About Things That Matter system to create comprehensive life transformation that lasts.

Connecting With The About Things That Matter System

Your confidence development exists within the broader framework of the five foundational elements that create a meaningful, successful, and fulfilling life. Understanding these connections helps you leverage your growing confidence to accelerate progress in every other area.

Self-Esteem as the Series Foundation

The Multiplier Effect Principle: Self-esteem amplifies your capability in every other domain because confidence affects your willingness to take risks, persist through challenges, and maintain effort when results are not immediately visible.

Integration with Change That Matters: Your confidence transforms how you navigate change from something that happens to you into something you can influence and direct:

- **Change Resilience**: Strong self-esteem helps you view change as an opportunity rather than a threat, maintaining stability while adapting to new circumstances.

- **Change Leadership**: Confident individuals are more likely to initiate necessary changes and influence others through transitions.

- **Change Recovery**: When changes do not go as planned, confidence helps you adjust course quickly rather than abandoning important transformations.

- **Change Influence**: Your self-assurance enables you to help others navigate change more effectively, creating positive ripple effects through organizations and communities.

Integration with Goals That Matter: Confidence fuels goal achievement through enhanced motivation, persistence, and strategic thinking:

- **Goal Ambition**: Higher self-esteem enables you to set bigger, more meaningful goals aligned with your deepest values rather than playing it safe.

- **Goal Persistence**: Confident individuals continue pursuing important objectives even when progress is slow or obstacles arise.

- **Goal Adjustment**: Strong self-worth allows you to modify goals based on new information without interpreting changes as personal failure.

- **Goal Communication**: Confidence helps you articulate your objectives clearly and gain support from others for your initiatives.

Integration with Time That Matters (Future Book): Self-esteem transforms time management from an external technique into authentic priority alignment:

- **Priority Clarity**: Confident people are more likely to align their time with their values rather than others' expectations or urgent but unimportant demands.

- **Boundary Setting**: Strong self-worth enables you to protect your time from activities and relationships that do not serve your growth and goals.

- **Delegation Capability**: Confidence allows you to delegate effectively because you are not threatened by others' competence or success.

- **Present Moment Engagement**: Self-assured individuals spend less mental energy on worry and self-doubt, allowing greater focus on current priorities.

Integration with Relationships That Matter: Confidence is the foundation for authentic, mutually supportive relationships:

- **Authentic Connection**: Self-esteem enables vulnerability and genuineness that create deeper, more meaningful relationships.

- **Boundary Maintenance**: Confident people can set and maintain healthy boundaries while remaining open and caring.

- **Conflict Navigation**: Strong self-worth helps you address disagreements and difficulties directly rather than avoiding or escalating conflicts.

- **Influence and Support**: Confidence allows you to both seek support when needed and provide meaningful help to others without keeping score.

Creating Your Integrated Development Plan

Rather than treating confidence as a separate project, integrate it with your ongoing development in other areas using this systematic approach:

Phase 1: Foundation Integration (Months 1-2)
- Complete the 30-Day Confidence Amplifier Program
- Apply confidence skills to any current change initiatives from Change That Matters
- Use growing self-assurance to pursue more ambitious goals from Goals That Matter
- Document evidence of how confidence amplifies other areas of development

Phase 2: Skill Combination (Months 3-4)
- Practice advanced confidence techniques in complex change and goal situations
- Lead change initiatives using authentic authority and psychological safety creation
- Achieve significant objectives through confident persistence and influence
- Begin preparing for Time That Matters integration by examining how confidence affects priority setting

Phase 3: Mastery Integration (Months 5-6)
- Demonstrate confident leadership in organizational or community change efforts
- Mentor others in the integrated About Things That Matter approach
- Achieve breakthrough results through combined application of series principles
- Begin preparing for Relationships That Matter integration by examining how confidence transforms relationship quality

Phase 4: Teaching and Multiplication (Months 7-12)
- Become a resource for others by implementing the About Things That Matter system
- Create confidence culture initiatives that support comprehensive development
- Achieve significant life and career goals through an integrated series application
- Build legacy impact through sustained confidence multiplication and leadership

Immediate Action Plan (Next 30 Days)

Your confidence journey begins with concrete actions that create immediate momentum while building the foundation for long-term transformation.

Week 1: Program Launch and Foundation

Days 1-2: Assessment and Goal Setting
- Complete comprehensive confidence assessment across all four dimensions
- Set specific, measurable confidence goals for the next 30 days
- Identify current Change That Matters and Goals That Matter initiatives that could benefit from increased confidence
- Establish daily tracking and accountability systems

Days 3-4: Routine Implementation
- Implement daily confidence micro-habits and tracking routine
- Begin self-talk monitoring and the REFRAME method practice
- Apply confidence skills to support one current change or goal initiative
- Practice evidence-based affirmations related to your development priorities

Days 5-7: Challenge Introduction
- Take on first confidence challenges in low-risk professional and personal situations
- Document evidence of growing competence and capability
- Apply confidence techniques to current Goals That Matter objectives
- Complete the first weekly review and plan Week 2 development focus

Week 2: Skill Development and Application

Professional Confidence Application:
- Practice decision-making confidence in work contexts
- Apply authentic authority techniques in leadership situations
- Use confidence skills to advance current goal achievement
- Implement feedback integration framework with recent input

Personal Confidence Development:
- Practice boundary setting and self-advocacy in personal relationships
- Apply confidence to any current change initiatives in personal life
- Use growing self-assurance to pursue stretch goals or new opportunities
- Document confidence impact on relationship quality and personal effectiveness

Week 3: Integration and Multiplication

Advanced Application Focus:
- Combine confidence techniques with change leadership and goal achievement
- Practice confidence multiplication by helping others build self-assurance
- Apply psychological safety creation in team or family contexts
- Use confidence to accelerate progress on important long-term objectives

Evidence Documentation:
- Gather feedback about observed changes in your confidence and leadership
- Measure the impact of confidence development on goal achievement and change navigation
- Document specific examples of confidence multiplication and ripple effects
- Assess integration effectiveness and plan adjustments

Week 4: Leadership and Commitment

Mastery Demonstration:
- Lead confidence culture initiatives in appropriate contexts
- Apply integrated confidence, change, and goal principles to significant challenges
- Mentor others in confidence development and series integration
- Plan long-term confidence development and maintenance strategies

Future Planning:
- Design 3-6 month confidence and integration development plan
- Establish accountability systems for continued growth
- Plan for Time That Matters and Relationships That Matter integration
- Commit to confidence leadership and multiplication in your sphere of influence

Medium-Term Development Plan (3-6 Months)

Sustainable confidence development requires systematic attention over months and years, not just days and weeks.

Month 2: Advanced Application and Integration

Advanced Confidence Techniques:
- Master complex confidence challenges in high-stakes professional situations
- Develop sophisticated judgment about when to demonstrate confidence versus when to show appropriate humility
- Practice confidence calibration across different relationships and contexts
- Build expertise in confidence coaching and multiplication with others

Series Integration Deepening:
- Apply confidence skills to accelerate Change That Matters initiatives
- Use growing self-assurance to pursue more ambitious Goals That Matter objectives
- Document evidence of how confidence amplifies other areas of development
- Begin examining how confidence will enhance time management and relationship effectiveness

Month 3: Confidence Leadership Development

Leadership Focus Areas:

- Lead confidence development initiatives for team, organization, or community
- Create psychological safety and confidence culture in appropriate contexts
- Mentor multiple individuals in confidence-building and series integration
- Measure and document confidence multiplication impact and effectiveness

Integration Mastery:

- Achieve significant change or goal objectives through confident leadership
- Demonstrate sustained confidence across various challenging situations
- Build reputation as an effective confidence leader and series practitioner
- Prepare for advanced integration with Time and Relationships books

Months 4-6: Mastery and Legacy Building

Mastery Indicators:

- Consistent confidence across all personal and professional contexts
- Successful integration of confidence with change management and goal achievement
- Recognized leadership in confidence development and series application
- Sustainable systems for continued growth and development

Legacy Development:

- Build lasting confidence culture in your sphere of influence
- Develop expertise in teaching and coaching comprehensive series integration
- Create systematic approaches for confidence multiplication and leadership development
- Prepare for combining all five About Things That Matter elements

Long-Term Growth Vision (6-12 Months)

True confidence mastery means building capability that continues expanding throughout your life while creating positive impact that extends far beyond your immediate circle.

Advanced Leadership Development (Months 6-9)

Confidence Leadership Mastery:

- Become a recognized expert in confidence development and application
- Lead organizational or community transformation through confidence culture initiatives
- Develop sophisticated expertise in confidence multiplication and ripple effect creation
- Build a reputation for integrated About Things That Matter leadership

Series Integration Excellence:

- Master complex integration of confidence, change, and goal achievement
- Successfully incorporate time management and relationship principles as new books are released
- Achieve significant life and career objectives through comprehensive series application
- Become a resource and mentor for others pursuing series mastery

Legacy and Impact Creation (Months 9-12)

Legacy Building Focus:

- Create lasting confidence culture in organization, community, or industry
- Develop next generation of confidence leaders through mentoring and teaching
- Build systematic processes and programs for confidence development that operate independently
- Contribute to broader conversation about confidence leadership and personal development

Comprehensive Life Transformation:

- Achieve integration mastery across all About Things That Matter elements

- Demonstrate sustained excellence in confidence, change, goals, time, and relationships

- Create a life of meaning, impact, and fulfillment through series application

- Serve as model and resource for others pursuing comprehensive personal development

Accountability And Support Systems

Sustainable confidence development requires robust support systems that provide encouragement, feedback, and accountability throughout your journey.

Building Your Confidence Development Network

Accountability Partnership Structure:

- Choose an accountability partner committed to personal growth and development

- Establish a regular check-in schedule with a specific agenda and focus areas

- Create mutual benefit and support rather than one-way accountability

- Include both encouragement and honest feedback about progress and challenges

Professional Support Integration:

- Identify colleagues and mentors who model strong confidence and integrated development

- Create reciprocal coaching relationships focused on confidence and series application

- Join or create professional development groups emphasizing confidence leadership

- Seek mentoring relationships with leaders who demonstrate mastery in multiple skill areas

Personal Support Network Expansion:

- Include family and friends who support your growth and celebrate your progress

- Find community groups or organizations that encourage personal development

- Consider professional coaching or therapy for deeper confidence work if needed

- Build relationships with others pursuing About Things That Matter mastery

Continuing Education and Development Resources

Ongoing Learning Priorities:

- Advanced confidence and leadership development programs

- Integration training for comprehensive personal development systems

- Teaching and coaching skills to enhance your confidence multiplication capability

- Industry or professional development that leverages your growing confidence

Knowledge and Skill Expansion:

- Regular reading and study in confidence, leadership, and personal development

- Conference attendance and networking with other series practitioners

- Workshop and seminar participation focused on advanced confidence application

- Peer learning groups and discussion forums for series integration

Practice and Application Opportunities:

- Volunteer leadership roles that provide confidence development opportunities

- Speaking and presentation opportunities to build communication confidence

- Mentoring and coaching opportunities to develop confidence multiplication skills

- Community service and contribution that leverages your confidence for positive impact

Reflection Questions

1. **How will you integrate confidence development with your other growth priorities and life goals?** What specific connections do you see between confidence and other areas?

2. **What accountability and support systems will best serve your long-term confidence development?** Who can provide both encouragement and honest feedback?

3. **What does confidence mastery look like for you personally and professionally?** How will you know when you have achieved sustainable, integrated confidence?

4. **How will you use your growing confidence to create positive impact for others?** What legacy do you want to build through confidence leadership?

5. **What challenges do you anticipate in maintaining momentum over 6-12 months?** How will you prepare for and overcome these obstacles?

Action Steps

1. **Create your comprehensive integration plan** connecting confidence development with Change That Matters and Goals That Matter principles you have already learned.

2. **Establish your accountability and support network** by identifying specific people who can provide encouragement, feedback, and partnership in your development.

3. **Begin your immediate 30-day action plan** with daily confidence practice and weekly review systems for tracking progress and adjusting strategy.

4. **Schedule your medium and long-term development planning sessions** to maintain focus on continued growth beyond the initial 30-day program.

5. **Commit to confidence leadership and multiplication** by identifying specific opportunities to help others develop confidence while building your own mastery.

Your confidence journey is not about becoming perfect or never experiencing doubt. It is about developing unshakable belief in your worth, capability, and potential to create positive change in your life and the lives of others. When you combine this confidence with the change mastery and goal achievement you have already learned, you create a foundation for success that can weather any storm and achieve any meaningful objective.

The world needs confident leaders who understand that self-esteem is not selfish but essential, not individual but social, not an end in itself but a means to serving others at your highest level. Your confidence is your gift to the world. The only question is how you will choose to share it.

Appendix A: Assessment Tools And Worksheets

Self-Esteem Assessment Matrix

Rate yourself on a scale of 1-10 for each element, where 1 = completely insecure and 10 = completely confident.

Professional Confidence Dimension

Decision-Making Authority

- Making important decisions under pressure: ___
- Standing behind decisions when questioned: ___
- Adjusting decisions based on new information: ___
- Communicating decision rationale clearly: ___
- Taking responsibility for decision outcomes: ___

Communication and Influence

- Contributing meaningfully in senior meetings: ___
- Presenting complex information persuasively: ___
- Asking clarifying questions without feeling ignorant: ___
- Providing constructive feedback to others: ___
- Handling disagreement professionally: ___

Leadership Presence

- Commanding attention and respect in groups: ___
- Inspiring others to follow your direction: ___
- Maintaining composure under stress: ___
- Delegating without micromanaging: ___
- Taking charge when leadership is needed: ___

Conflict Resolution

- Navigating difficult conversations: ___
- Addressing problems directly: ___
- Managing disagreements constructively: ___

- Mediating conflicts between others: ___
- Maintaining relationships during disputes: ___

Professional Confidence Total: ___/200

Personal Confidence Dimension

Boundary Setting and Maintenance
- Saying no without feeling guilty: ___
- Protecting time and energy: ___
- Maintaining values under pressure: ___
- Expressing limits clearly: ___
- Following through on boundaries: ___

Authentic Self-Expression
- Being yourself in various situations: ___
- Sharing true thoughts and feelings: ___
- Acting according to your values: ___
- Expressing creativity and uniqueness: ___
- Resisting pressure to conform: ___

Self-Advocacy
- Asking for what you need: ___
- Pursuing deserved opportunities: ___
- Promoting your accomplishments appropriately: ___
- Seeking fair treatment: ___
- Standing up for your rights: ___

Personal Growth Orientation
- Embracing challenges as learning opportunities: ___
- Learning from mistakes without harsh self-judgment: ___
- Seeking feedback for improvement: ___
- Taking on stretch assignments: ___
- Viewing setbacks as temporary: ___

Personal Confidence Total: ___/200

Social Confidence Dimension

Relationship Initiation and Building

- Starting conversations with new people: ___

- Building connections at networking events: ___

- Joining new groups or communities: ___

- Maintaining friendships and professional relationships: ___

- Reaching out for support when needed: ___

Group Dynamics Navigation

- Contributing meaningfully in group discussions: ___

- Feeling comfortable in social situations: ___

- Handling group conflict or tension: ___

- Taking on group leadership when appropriate: ___

- Balancing individual needs with group harmony: ___

Influence and Persuasion

- Changing others' minds through logical argument: ___

- Building coalitions and support: ___

- Negotiating favorable outcomes: ___

- Inspiring others to action: ___

- Creating buy-in for new ideas: ___

Community Leadership

- Taking leadership roles in organizations: ___

- Volunteering for community initiatives: ___

- Speaking up for causes you believe in: ___

- Organizing others around shared goals: ___

- Representing groups or causes publicly: ___

Social Confidence Total: ___/200

Resilience Confidence Dimension

Setback Recovery

- Bouncing back quickly from failures: ___

- Maintaining motivation after disappointments: ___

- Learning from rejection without personalizing: ___

- Adjusting course without abandoning goals: ___

- Supporting others through their setbacks: ___

Learning from Failure

- Extracting lessons from mistakes: ___

- Using failure as improvement data: ___

- Sharing failure stories to help others: ___

- Maintaining self-worth despite poor outcomes: ___

- Taking appropriate risks despite the possibility of failure: ___

Stress Management Under Pressure

- Performing well when stakes are high: ___

- Maintaining confidence during crises: ___

- Making clear decisions under time pressure: ___

- Supporting others during stressful times: ___

- Recovering quickly from high-stress periods: ___

Adaptation to Change

- Embracing new challenges and opportunities: ___

- Adjusting strategies based on changing circumstances: ___

- Learning new skills as required: ___

- Helping others navigate change: ___

- Viewing change as a growth opportunity: ___

Resilience Confidence Total: ___/200
Overall Confidence Score: ___/800

Confidence Development Priority Matrix

Based on your assessment scores, use this matrix to prioritize your development focus:

Scoring Guide:

- 160-200 points: Strong confidence area - maintain and leverage

- 120-159 points: Moderate confidence - good foundation for building

- 80-119 points: Significant opportunity - focus development here

- Below 80 points: Critical development need - requires immediate attention

Development Priority (choose one for 30-day focus):

☐ Professional Confidence

☐ Personal Confidence

☐ Social Confidence

☐ Resilience Confidence

Rationale for choice: _____

30-Day Confidence Tracking Dashboard

Use this daily tracking system throughout your Confidence Amplifier Program.

Daily Confidence Levels (Rate 1-10)

Day	Overall	Professional	Personal	Social	Resilience	Notes
1						
2						
3						
...						
30						

<u>Weekly Confidence Review Template</u>
Week ___:
Focus Area: _____
Patterns Observed:

- Situations that boosted confidence: _____

- Situations that challenged confidence: _____

- Most effective techniques: _____

- Areas needing attention: _____

Evidence of Growth:

- Specific accomplishments: _____

- Positive feedback received: _____

- Challenges overcome: _____
- Impact on others: _____

Next Week's Goals:

1. _____
2. _____
3. _____

Appendix B: Quick Reference Guides

The REFRAME Method Worksheet

Use this worksheet to transform negative self-talk systematically.

R - Recognize the Negative Pattern
Write the specific negative thought: _____

E - Examine the Evidence
Evidence supporting this thought: _____

Evidence contradicting this thought: _____

F - Find Alternative Perspectives
Alternative interpretation #1: _____

Alternative interpretation #2: _____

Alternative interpretation #3: _____

R - Rewrite the Narrative
New, more accurate thought: _____

A - Affirm the New Pattern
Positive affirmation based on evidence: _____

M - Monitor and Maintain
How will you remember this reframe? _____

E - Evolve the Practice
How can you apply this learning to similar situations? _____

Evidence-Based Affirmation Templates

Professional Competence Formula:
"I am a _____ [quality] because _____ [specific evidence], which enables me to _____ [capability]."

Example: "I am a skilled problem-solver because I successfully resolved three major project crises last quarter, which enables me to handle complex challenges with confidence."

Personal Growth Formula:

"I am growing in _____ [area] as evidenced by _____ [specific progress], which shows I can _____ [future capability]."

Example: "I am growing in assertiveness as evidenced by successfully setting boundaries with my manager last month, which shows I can advocate for my needs professionally."

Relationship Value Formula:

"I contribute _____ [value] to others as shown by _____ [specific feedback/examples], which means _____ [impact statement]."

Example: "I contribute stability and perspective to my team as shown by colleagues regularly seeking my input during stressful situations, which means I have a positive influence on group effectiveness."

Resilience Capacity Formula:

"I have demonstrated _____ [resilience quality] by _____ [specific example], which proves I can _____ [handle future challenges]."

Example: "I have demonstrated adaptability by successfully transitioning to remote work and maintaining productivity, which proves I can handle unexpected changes effectively."

Confidence Emergency Response Protocols

When Experiencing Sudden Confidence Drop:

Immediate Response (First 5 minutes):

1. Take 5 deep breaths and remind yourself that this feeling is temporary
2. Recall one recent specific accomplishment or success
3. Use your prepared confidence affirmation
4. Adjust your posture to a confident position

Short-term Stabilization (Next 15 minutes):

1. Review your evidence file for objective capability reminders
2. Contact your accountability partner or trusted supporter
3. Apply the REFRAME method to any negative thoughts
4. Focus on the next small action you can take successfully

Recovery Planning (Next 30 minutes):

1. Analyze what triggered the confidence drop

2. Plan specific actions to address the underlying issue

3. Schedule follow-up support or skill development if needed

4. Document the experience for future learning

Before High-Stakes Situations:

24 Hours Before:

- Review relevant accomplishments and capabilities

- Prepare thoroughly while avoiding over-preparation

- Visualize successful outcomes and your confident response

- Connect with supporters who believe in your abilities

1 Hour Before:

- Use power posing for 2 minutes to boost confidence hormones

- Review your key affirmations and evidence statements

- Practice deep breathing and relaxation techniques

- Set the intention to learn and contribute rather than to be perfect

Immediately Before:

- Remind yourself of your preparation and capability

- Focus on serving others rather than protecting your ego

- Use confident body language and vocal tone

- Remember that nervousness is normal and often helpful

Professional Confidence Checklists

Before Important Meetings:

☐ Review the agenda and prepare key talking points

☐ Identify opportunities to contribute valuable insights

☐ Prepare questions that demonstrate engagement

☐ Practice confident body language and vocal tone

☐ Set the intention to add value to the discussion

When Receiving Feedback:

☐ Listen actively without preparing defensive responses

☐ Ask clarifying questions to ensure understanding

☐ Thank the person for their input, regardless of content

☐ Separate feedback about performance from personal worth

☐ Plan specific actions based on useful feedback

When Making Difficult Decisions:

☐ Gather sufficient information without seeking perfection

☐ Consult relevant stakeholders and experts

☐ Consider multiple options and potential outcomes

☐ Make the decision based on available information

☐ Communicate rationale clearly to affected parties

☐ Take responsibility for outcomes and adjust as needed

When Leading Others:

☐ Model the confidence and behavior you want to see

☐ Provide specific, actionable feedback to team members

☐ Create psychological safety for risk-taking and learning

☐ Acknowledge mistakes quickly and focus on solutions

☐ Recognize and celebrate team members' contributions

☐ Support others' confidence development through encouragement

Resources And Further Reading

Recommended Books

Confidence and Self-Esteem

- **The Confidence Code** by Kay and Shipman - Research-based approach to building confidence, particularly relevant for professional women
- **Presence** by Amy Cuddy - Body language and its impact on confidence and performance
- **The Gifts of Imperfection** by Brené Brown - Vulnerability, authenticity, and shame resilience
- **Self-Compassion** by Kristin Neff - Scientific approach to treating yourself with kindness
- **Mindset** by Carol Dweck - Growth mindset and its impact on confidence and achievement

Leadership and Influence

- **Dare to Lead** by Brené Brown - Courage, vulnerability, and authentic leadership
- **The Leadership Challenge** by Kouzes and Posner - Evidence-based leadership practices
- **Emotional Intelligence 2.0** by Bradberry and Greaves - EQ skills for leadership effectiveness
- **Multipliers** by Liz Wiseman - How leaders amplify intelligence and capability in others
- **The Power of Moments** by Heath and Heath - Creating memorable experiences that inspire others

Professional Development

- **Atomic Habits** by James Clear - Building systems and habits for sustained improvement
- **Peak Performance** by Stulberg and Magness - Sustained excellence in work and life

- **The 7 Habits of Highly Effective People** by Stephen Covey - Principle-based personal effectiveness

- **Getting to Yes** by Fisher and Ury - Principled negotiation and influence

- **Thanks for the Feedback** by Stone and Heen - Receiving and integrating feedback effectively

Neuroscience and Psychology

- **The Brain That Changes Itself** by Norman Doidge - Neuroplasticity and personal transformation

- **Thinking, Fast and Slow** by Daniel Kahneman - Cognitive biases and decision-making

- **The Happiness Hypothesis** by Jonathan Haidt - Psychology of well-being and flourishing

- **Flow** by Mihaly Csikszentmihalyi - Psychology of optimal experience and performance

Online Resources and Communities

Professional Development Platforms

- **LinkedIn Learning** - Courses on confidence, leadership, and professional development

- **Coursera** - University-level courses in psychology, leadership, and personal development

- **MasterClass** - Expert instruction in communication, leadership, and performance

- **Toastmasters International** - Public speaking and leadership skill development

Assessment and Measurement Tools

- **VIA Character Strengths Survey** - Identify your top character strengths and virtues

- **CliftonStrengths** - Discover and develop your natural talents

- **Enneagram Institute** - Personality assessment for self-awareness and growth

- **360-Degree Feedback Tools** - Multi-source feedback for leadership development

Podcasts and Audio Content

- **The Confidence Podcast** - Weekly episodes on building unshakable confidence
- **Unlocking Us** with Brené Brown - Conversations about courage, vulnerability, and leadership
- **The Tim Ferriss Show** - Interviews with high performers across various fields
- **WorkLife** with Adam Grant - Psychology of work and organizational behavior
- **The Learning Leader Show** - Leadership development and personal growth

Research and Academic Resources

- **Harvard Business Review** - Latest research on leadership, confidence, and organizational behavior
- **Greater Good Science Center** - UC Berkeley research on well-being and social connection
- **Center for Creative Leadership** - Research and tools for leadership development
- **Gallup Research** - Workplace engagement and strengths-based development

Professional Development Opportunities

Conferences and Events

- **Global Leadership Summit** - Annual event focused on leadership development
- **TEDx Events** - Local events featuring innovative ideas and presentations
- **Industry-Specific Conferences** - Professional development within your field
- **Regional Leadership Forums** - Local networking and development opportunities

Certification Programs

- **Certified Professional Coach (CPC)** - Training in coaching skills and methodologies
- **Leadership Development Programs** - University and corporate leadership training
- **Dale Carnegie Training** - Communication, leadership, and confidence building
- **Franklin Covey Leadership** - Principle-based leadership and effectiveness training

Volunteer and Practice Opportunities

- **Professional Association Leadership** - Board positions and committee leadership

- **Community Organization Involvement** - Nonprofit leadership and volunteer coordination
- **Mentoring Programs** - Formal and informal mentoring relationships
- **Speaking Opportunities** - Local groups, conferences, and professional events

Start with your biggest challenge - Choose the book addressing your most pressing development need

Build your foundation - Most readers benefit from establishing confidence through Self-Esteem That Matters

Create integration - Combine principles from multiple books for compound benefits

Join the community - Connect with others for accountability and support

Become a multiplier - Help others implement series principles in their lives and organizations

The journey of mastering things that matter is lifelong, but the benefits begin immediately. Every step you take toward mastering these foundational elements creates positive change that ripples through every area of your life and touches everyone around you.

Bibliography

Primary Research Sources

Neuroscience and Brain Research

Bandura, Albert. *Self-Efficacy: The Exercise of Control*. New York: W.H. Freeman, 1997.

Cuddy, Amy J.C., Caroline A. Wilmuth, Andy J. Yap, and Dana R. Carney. "Preparatory Power Posing Affects Nonverbal Presence and Job Interview Performance." *Journal of Applied Psychology* 100, no. 4 (2015): 1286-1295.

Doidge, Norman. *The Brain That Changes Itself: Stories of Personal Triumph from the Frontiers of Brain Science*. New York: Penguin Books, 2007.

Dweck, Carol S. *Mindset: The New Psychology of Success*. New York: Random House, 2006.

Hanson, Rick. *Buddha's Brain: The Practical Neuroscience of Happiness, Love, and Wisdom*. Oakland: New Harbinger Publications, 2009.

Lieberman, Matthew D. *Social: Why Our Brains Are Wired to Connect*. New York: Crown Publishers, 2013.

Neff, Kristin D. "The Development and Validation of a Scale to Measure Self-Compassion." *Self and Identity* 2, no. 3 (2003): 223-250.

Rock, David. *Your Brain at Work: Strategies for Overcoming Distraction, Regaining Focus, and Working Smarter All Day Long*. New York: HarperBusiness, 2009.

Confidence and Self-Esteem Research

Branden, Nathaniel. *The Six Pillars of Self-Esteem*. New York: Bantam Books, 1994.

Brown, Brené. *Daring Greatly: How the Courage to Be Vulnerable Transforms the Way We Live, Love, Parent, and Lead*. New York: Gotham Books, 2012.

Clance, Pauline Rose, and Suzanne Ament Imes. "The Impostor Phenomenon in High Achieving Women: Dynamics and Therapeutic Intervention." *Psychotherapy: Theory, Research & Practice* 15, no. 3 (1978): 241-247.

Kay, Katty, and Claire Shipman. *The Confidence Code: The Science and Art of Self-Assurance—What Women Should Know*. New York: HarperBusiness, 2014.

Mruk, Christopher J. *Self-Esteem and Positive Psychology: Research, Theory, and Practice*. 4th ed. New York: Springer Publishing, 2013.

Neff, Kristin. *Self-Compassion: The Proven Power of Being Kind to Yourself*. New York: William Morrow Paperbacks, 2011.

Rosenberg, Morris. *Society and the Adolescent Self-Image*. Princeton: Princeton University Press, 1965.

Sakulku, Jaruwan, and James Alexander. "The Impostor Phenomenon." *International Journal of Behavioral Science* 6, no. 1 (2011): 73-92.

Leadership and Organizational Psychology

Edmondson, Amy C. *The Fearless Organization: Creating Psychological Safety in the Workplace for Learning, Innovation, and Growth*. Hoboken: John Wiley & Sons, 2019.

Edmondson, Amy C. "Psychological Safety and Learning Behavior in Work Teams." *Administrative Science Quarterly* 44, no. 2 (1999): 350-383.

Eurich, Tasha. *Insight: Why We're Not as Self-Aware as We Think, and How Seeing Ourselves Clearly Helps Us Succeed at Work and in Life*. New York: Crown Business, 2017.

Goleman, Daniel. *Emotional Intelligence: Why It Matters More Than IQ*. New York: Bantam Books, 1995.

Kouzes, James M., and Barry Z. Posner. *The Leadership Challenge: How to Make Extraordinary Things Happen in Organizations*. 6th ed. San Francisco: Jossey-Bass, 2017.

Lencioni, Patrick. *The Five Dysfunctions of a Team: A Leadership Fable*. San Francisco: Jossey-Bass, 2002.

Sinek, Simon. *Leaders Eat Last: Why Some Teams Pull Together and Others Don't*. New York: Portfolio, 2014.

Wiseman, Liz. *Multipliers: How the Best Leaders Make Everyone Smarter*. New York: HarperBusiness, 2010.

Psychology and Behavior Change

Cialdini, Robert B. *Influence: The Psychology of Persuasion*. Revised ed. New York: Harper Business, 2006.

Clear, James. *Atomic Habits: An Easy & Proven Way to Build Good Habits & Break Bad Ones*. New York: Avery, 2018.

Csikszentmihalyi, Mihaly. *Flow: The Psychology of Optimal Experience*. New York: Harper & Row, 1990.

Duhigg, Charles. *The Power of Habit: Why We Do What We Do in Life and Business*. New York: Random House, 2012.

Kahneman, Daniel. *Thinking, Fast and Slow*. New York: Farrar, Straus and Giroux, 2011.

Prochaska, James O., John C. Norcross, and Carlo C. DiClemente. *Changing for Good: A Revolutionary Six-Stage Program for Overcoming Bad Habits and Moving Your Life Positively Forward*. New York: Avery, 1994.

Seligman, Martin E.P. *Learned Optimism: How to Change Your Mind and Your Life*. New York: Vintage Books, 2006.

Communication and Influence

Carnegie, Dale. *How to Win Friends and Influence People*. Revised ed. New York: Simon & Schuster, 1981.

Heath, Chip, and Dan Heath. *Made to Stick: Why Some Ideas Survive and Others Die*. New York: Random House, 2007.

Patterson, Kerry, Joseph Grenny, Ron McMillan, and Al Switzler. *Crucial Conversations: Tools for Talking When Stakes Are High*. 2nd ed. New York: McGraw-Hill Education, 2011.

Stone, Douglas, and Sheila Heen. *Thanks for the Feedback: The Science and Art of Receiving Feedback Well*. New York: Viking, 2014.

Journal Articles and Academic Papers

Baumeister, Roy F., Jennifer D. Campbell, Joachim I. Krueger, and Kathleen D. Vohs. "Does High Self-Esteem Cause Better Performance, Interpersonal Success, Happiness, or Healthier Lifestyles?" *Psychological Science in the Public Interest* 4, no. 1 (2003): 1-44.

Blascovich, Jim, and Joseph Tomaka. "Measures of Self-Esteem." In *Measures of Personality and Social Psychological Attitudes*, edited by John P. Robinson, Phillip R. Shaver, and Lawrence S. Wrightsman, 115-160. San Diego: Academic Press, 1991.

Brown, Jonathon D. "High Self-Esteem Buffers Negative Feedback: Once More with Feeling." *Cognition and Emotion* 24, no. 8 (2010): 1389-1404.

Coopersmith, Stanley. "A Method for Determining Types of Self-Esteem." *Journal of Abnormal and Social Psychology* 59, no. 1 (1959): 87-94.

Crocker, Jennifer, and Lora E. Park. "The Costly Pursuit of Self-Esteem." *Psychological Bulletin* 130, no. 3 (2004): 392-414.

Deci, Edward L., and Richard M. Ryan. "The 'What' and 'Why' of Goal Pursuits: Human Needs and the Self-Determination of Behavior." *Psychological Inquiry* 11, no. 4 (2000): 227-268.

Kark, Ronit, and Dina Van Dijk. "Motivation to Lead, Motivation to Follow: The Role of the Self-Regulatory Focus in Leadership Processes." *Academy of Management Review* 32, no. 2 (2007): 500-528.

Kernis, Michael H. "Toward a Conceptualization of Optimal Self-Esteem." *Psychological Inquiry* 14, no. 1 (2003): 1-26.

Locke, Edwin A., and Gary P. Latham. "Building a Practically Useful Theory of Goal Setting and Task Motivation: A 35-Year Odyssey." *American Psychologist* 57, no. 9 (2002): 705-717.

Research Reports and Studies

Deloitte. "The Social Enterprise at Work: Paradox as a Path Forward - 2020 Deloitte Global Human Capital Trends." Deloitte Insights, 2020.

Gallup. "State of the Global Workplace: 2021 Report." Gallup Press, 2021.

Google. "Project Aristotle: What Makes a Team Effective?" re: Work with Google, 2016.

Harvard Business Review. "The Future of Leadership Development." Harvard Business Review Press, 2019.

McKinsey & Company. "Leadership in a Crisis: Responding to the Coronavirus Outbreak and Future Challenges." McKinsey Global Institute, 2020.

PwC. "22nd Annual Global CEO Survey: CEOs' Curbed Confidence Spells Caution."
PricewaterhouseCoopers, 2019.

Secondary Sources and Popular Literature

Bradberry, Travis, and Jean Greaves. *Emotional Intelligence 2.0*. San Diego: TalentSmart, 2009.

Brown, Brené. *The Gifts of Imperfection: Let Go of Who You Think You're Supposed to Be and Embrace Who You Are*. Center City: Hazelden Publishing, 2010.

Covey, Stephen R. *The 7 Habits of Highly Effective People: Powerful Lessons in Personal Change*. 30th Anniversary ed. New York: Simon & Schuster, 2020.

Gilbert, Elizabeth. *Big Magic: Creative Living Beyond Fear*. New York: Riverhead Books, 2015.

Gladwell, Malcolm. *Outliers: The Story of Success*. New York: Little, Brown and Company, 2008.

Grant, Adam. *Think Again: The Power of Knowing What You Don't Know*. New York: Viking, 2021.

Haidt, Jonathan. *The Happiness Hypothesis: Finding Modern Truth in Ancient Wisdom*. New York: Basic Books, 2006.

Holiday, Ryan. *The Obstacle Is the Way: The Timeless Art of Turning Trials into Triumph*. New York: Portfolio, 2014.

Newport, Cal. *Deep Work: Rules for Focused Success in a Distracted World*. New York: Grand Central Publishing, 2016.

Pink, Daniel H. *Drive: The Surprising Truth About What Motivates Us*. New York: Riverhead Books, 2009.

PART 4 – THOUGHTS THAT MATTER

To those who dare to dream and to those who act on their dreams.

"We are products of our past, but we don't have to be prisoners of it."—**Rick Warren**.

Thoughts That Matter

A MODERN GUIDE TO AS A MAN THINKETH

A 21-Day Journey Based on James Allen's Timeless Classic

About Things That Matter

A SELF-IMPROVEMENT SERIES FOR SUCCESS

Book 2

JC Ryan

About This Book

In 1903, James Allen wrote 24 pages that changed millions of lives with a revolutionary insight: "A man is literally what he thinks."

Today, neuroscience proves Allen was remarkably ahead of his time—every thought you think physically reshapes your brain, influences your emotions, and creates your lived experience. But while Allen's **As A Man Thinketh** reveals profound truths about the power of conscious thinking, it tells you what to think without explaining how to think it. For over a century, readers have been inspired by Allen's wisdom, yet struggled to apply it consistently in their daily lives.

Thoughts That Matter bridges that gap with a practical 21-day journey that transforms Allen's timeless philosophy into daily practices you can master. Through three progressive weeks, Reclaim Your Mind, Master Your Emotions, Live Your Purpose—you'll develop the actual skills Allen described: conscious thought direction, emotional intelligence, and purposeful living. This isn't another positive thinking program or wishful manifestation guide. It's systematic training in the most important human capacity: the ability to choose your thoughts and shape your life from the inside out. By Day 21, you'll have experienced firsthand what Allen knew intellectually—that you are literally the master of your fate and the captain of your soul.

Introduction

In 1903, a British philosopher named James Allen sat down in his small cottage in Ilfracombe, England, and wrote 24 pages that would change millions of lives. His little book, "As A Man Thinketh," revealed a truth so profound it seemed almost too simple to believe:

"A man is literally what he thinks, his character being the complete sum of all his thoughts."

At the time, this was revolutionary philosophy. Today, it's proven neuroscience.

But here's what makes Allen's insight even more remarkable: he wrote these words without access to brain scans, without understanding neurons, without any of the sophisticated technology we use today to peer inside the human mind. He simply observed life with extraordinary clarity and intuited a fundamental law of human existence.

Allen saw that thoughts weren't just fleeting mental events; they were the actual building blocks of character, circumstances, and destiny. He understood that every external condition in a person's life was somehow connected to their internal thought patterns. He recognized that changing your thoughts was the key to changing everything else.

For over a century, "As A Man Thinketh" has inspired millions of readers. Presidents and prisoners, entrepreneurs and artists, teachers and students have found wisdom in Allen's elegant prose. His insights have been quoted, referenced, and built upon by virtually every major self-help author since.

Yet for all its profound truth, Allen's original work has one significant limitation: it tells you what to think, but not how to think it. **This book bridges that gap.**

Over the next 21 days, you'll take Allen's timeless insights and transform them into daily practices. You'll discover not just WHY his principles work, the modern science that validates his wisdom, but HOW to apply them in your real, messy, complicated 21st-century life.

What Allen Knew Then, Science Proves Now

When James Allen wrote that thoughts literally shape character and circumstances, he was working purely from observation and intuition. He had no way to see inside the brain, no understanding of neural pathways, no knowledge of the mechanisms that make his insights true.

Today, we do.

Modern neuroscience has revealed that Allen was remarkably prescient. Every thought you think, every mental pattern you repeat, every focus of attention you sustain literally reshapes your brain. Scientists call this neuroplasticity, the brain's ability to reorganize itself throughout your entire life.

Allen wrote: *"The mind is the master-weaver, both of the inner garment of character and the outer garment of circumstance."*

Science shows: Neuroplasticity research confirms that focused attention literally rewires your brain, changing both personality patterns and behavioral responses. Dr. Sara Lazar at Harvard proved that just eight weeks of meditation practice can measurably thicken the prefrontal cortex—the brain region responsible for focus, decision-making, and emotional regulation.

Allen wrote: *"Men do not attract that which they want, but that which they are."*

Science shows: Your Reticular Activating System (RAS), your brain's filtering mechanism, determines what you notice in your environment based on your dominant thoughts and beliefs. Change your internal focus, and you literally change what opportunities, resources, and possibilities you perceive in the world around you.

Allen wrote: *"Circumstance does not make the man; it reveals him to himself."*

Science shows: Decades of cognitive behavioral research prove that external situations don't determine your emotional and behavioral responses; your thought patterns do. Two people can face identical circumstances and have completely different experiences based solely on how they interpret and think about what's happening.

Allen wrote: *"As the plant springs from, and could not be without, the seed, so every act of a man springs from the hidden seeds of thought."*

Science shows: Brain imaging reveals that conscious intention activates motor cortex neurons before any physical action occurs. Your thoughts literally set the stage for every behavior, creating what neuroscientists call "action potentials" that make movement possible.

Allen intuited what we can now measure: thoughts aren't just mental events happening inside your head. They're physical forces that reshape your brain, influence your emotions, direct your attention, and ultimately create your lived experience.

The man was a genius who saw clearly what science would spend the next century proving.

Why Allen's Wisdom Feels Hard to Apply

If Allen's insights are so profound and scientifically validated, why do so many people struggle to apply them? Why do readers finish "As A Man Thinketh" feeling inspired but not necessarily transformed?

The answer is simple: Allen was a philosopher, not a practitioner. He was brilliant at identifying universal principles but less concerned with the nuts and bolts of implementation. His writing is beautifully contemplative but lacks specific, step-by-step guidance.

Consider some of Allen's most famous advice: *"A man should conceive of a legitimate purpose in his heart, and set out to accomplish it. He should make this purpose the centralizing point of his thoughts."*

This is profound wisdom. But how, exactly, do you make purpose "the centralizing point of your thoughts"? What does that look like on a Tuesday morning when you're stressed about work? How do you practically train your mind to stay focused on purpose when you're dealing with difficult relationships, financial pressure, or health challenges?

"Let a man radically alter his thoughts, and he will be astonished at the rapid transformation it will effect in the material conditions of his life."

Again, beautiful truth. But how do you "radically alter" thought patterns that have been running automatically for decades? What specific techniques allow you to change deep-seated mental habits? How do you know if you're doing it right?

"Thought and character are one, and as character can only manifest and discover itself through environment and circumstance, the outer conditions of a person's life will always be found to be harmoniously related to his inner state."

Intellectually compelling. But when you're stuck in circumstances you don't like, how do you identify which thoughts are creating them? How do you shift mental patterns you might not even be aware of? How do you maintain new thought habits when old ones feel so familiar and automatic?

Allen points you toward the promised land but doesn't provide a map for the journey.

This book is that map.

Your 21-Day Transformation Journey

What you're about to begin isn't just another self-improvement program. It's a systematic training in the most important skill of human existence: the ability to consciously direct your thoughts.

Allen wrote that this skill separates "the wise master" from "the foolish master" of one's life. The wise master directs mental energy with intelligence and purpose. The foolish master lets thoughts run wild, creating unwanted results while wondering why life feels so difficult.

Over the next 21 days, you'll become the wise master Allen described.

Week One: Reclaim Your Mind (Days 1-7)
Based on Allen's "Thought and Character" and "Effect of Thought on Circumstances"

You'll discover that you're not a victim of your thoughts, you're their creator. You'll learn to notice mental patterns that have been running unconsciously and begin directing them consciously. By the end of week one, you'll have practical tools for:

- Recognizing automatic thought patterns
- Interrupting mental loops that don't serve you
- Programming your brain's attention system
- Building new neural pathways through focused practice

Week Two: Master Your Emotions (Days 8-14)
Based on Allen's "Effect of Thought on Health and the Body," plus modern emotional intelligence

Allen understood that thoughts create emotions, and emotions shape your physical experience. You'll learn to work with your emotional system as Allen intended—not by suppressing feelings, but by understanding how thoughts generate emotions and how to consciously influence that process. You'll master:

- The thought-emotion-body connection
- How to interrupt emotional reactions before they overwhelm you
- Techniques for transforming difficult emotions into useful energy
- Building emotional resilience through thought training

Week Three: Live Your Purpose (Days 15-21)
Based on Allen's "Thought and Purpose," "Visions and Ideals," and "Serenity"

Allen wrote extensively about linking thought with purpose, cherishing ideals, and maintaining calm regardless of circumstances. In your final week, you'll discover how thought mastery and emotional intelligence naturally lead to purposeful living. You'll learn:

- How to identify your unique purpose through thought observation
- Techniques for aligning daily thoughts with meaningful goals
- How to maintain inner calm while pursuing ambitious visions
- Building a life that expresses Allen's highest ideals

What Makes This Different

This isn't about positive thinking or wishful manifestation. This is about practical mental training based on both Allen's timeless wisdom and modern neuroscience.

Every day includes:
- One core insight from Allen's original work
- The scientific explanation for why it works
- A specific practice you can complete in 5-15 minutes
- Real-world examples of people who've applied these principles
- Integration exercises that build on previous days

You won't need:
- Hours of daily practice
- Perfect conditions or circumstances
- Special equipment or apps
- A complete personality overhaul
- Isolation from your regular life

You will develop:
- Conscious control over your mental state
- Emotional resilience and stability
- Clear sense of purpose and direction
- Practical tools that work under pressure
- The deep satisfaction that comes from living by Allen's principles

Why 21 Days?

Twenty-one days isn't long enough to completely transform decades of mental conditioning, that's not a realistic promise, but it is long enough to:

- **Establish new neural pathways**: Neuroscience research shows that consistent practice for 21 days begins creating measurable brain changes.

- **Build practical skills**: You'll have enough repetition to make these techniques feel natural and accessible.
- **Experience real results**: Three weeks of applied practice will produce noticeable changes in how you think, feel, and respond to life.
- **Create sustainable habits**: Short enough to maintain motivation, long enough to establish lasting patterns.
- **Prove the principles work**: You'll have experiential evidence that Allen's insights are practical, not just philosophical.

The goal isn't perfection in 21 days; the goal is establishing a foundation of conscious thinking that you can build on for the rest of your life.

What to Expect

Days 1-3: You'll likely feel excited and motivated. New practices feel fresh, and possibility seems unlimited. Use this energy to establish your daily routine.

Days 4-7: Initial enthusiasm may wane as the work becomes more real. This is normal and expected. The key is showing up consistently, even when motivation dips.

Days 8-12: You'll begin noticing changes in how you respond to stress, conflict, and challenges. Others might comment that you seem different, calmer, more centered, and less reactive.

Days 13-17: The practices start feeling more natural. You'll catch yourself applying techniques automatically rather than having to remember to use them.

Days 18-21: Integration occurs. Instead of separate practices, these become part of how you naturally think and respond. You'll understand viscerally what Allen meant by becoming "master of your thoughts."

Throughout the journey, expect resistance, doubt, and moments when you want to quit. Expect days when the practices feel mechanical or forced. Expect your mind to generate creative reasons why this won't work for you specifically.

All of this is part of the process. Allen himself wrote about the necessity of persistence: *"The weakest soul, knowing its own weakness, and believing this truth that strength can only be developed by effort and practice, will, thus believing, at once begin to exert itself, and, adding effort to effort, patience to patience, and strength to strength, will never cease to develop, and will at last grow divinely strong."*

A Personal Note

Before we begin, I want to acknowledge something that Allen, writing in 1903, couldn't have anticipated: the unprecedented assault on human attention that defines modern life.

Allen lived in a world where a person might receive a few letters per week and read one newspaper daily. The biggest distraction was perhaps the sound of horses on cobblestone streets. His mind was free to contemplate, reflect, and develop the sustained attention necessary for deep thought.

You live in a world where the average person receives over 100 messages daily, checks their phone 96 times, and consumes five times more information than people did in the 1980s. Your attention is under constant siege by notifications, news cycles, social media, and entertainment designed by teams of neuroscientists to be irresistible.

This makes Allen's wisdom more relevant, not less. But it also means that developing mastery over your thoughts requires more intentional effort than it did in his era.

The practices in this book account for modern realities. They're designed to work not in a monastery or philosophical retreat, but in the middle of your actual life, with its deadlines, relationships, responsibilities, and digital distractions.

You don't need to become a monk to apply Allen's principles. You just need to become more conscious.

How to Use This Book

Read one chapter each day. Don't rush ahead, even if you're excited. Each day's practice builds on the previous day's foundation.

Do the daily practice. Reading about these principles without applying them is like reading about exercise without moving your body. The transformation happens in the doing.

Be patient with yourself. You're rewiring neural pathways that have been operating automatically for years or decades. Some days will feel easier than others.

Track your experience. Keep a simple journal of what you notice, what challenges arise, and what shifts occur. This documentation will become valuable evidence of your growth.

Return to Allen's original. Once you complete this 21-day journey, go back and read "As A Man Thinketh" again. You'll be amazed at how much deeper his insights feel when you have practical experience applying them.

The Promise

James Allen concluded his masterpiece with these words: *"Self-control is strength; Right Thought is mastery; Calmness is power. Say unto your heart, 'Peace, be still!'"*

This book will teach you exactly how to develop that self-control, achieve that mastery, and cultivate that power. Not through philosophical contemplation alone, but through daily practice that transforms Allen's timeless wisdom into lived experience.

By Day 21, you'll understand in your bones what Allen knew in his mind: you are literally what you think, and you have far more control over what you think than you've ever realized.

The master of your fate, the captain of your soul—as Allen's contemporary William Ernest Henley wrote—isn't some idealistic metaphor. It's a practical description of what you can become through conscious thought training.

Your transformation begins with the next page.

Allen would be proud.

Let's begin.

PART ONE

Days 1-7

"A man is literally what he thinks, his character being the complete sum of all his thoughts."
— **James Allen.**

Day 1: Your Thoughts Are Creating You

"As the plant springs from, and could not be without, the seed, so every act of a man springs from the hidden seeds of thought, and could not have appeared without them." — *James Allen.*

Marcus Thought He Was Stupid

At 34, he'd built a successful contracting business, employed twelve people, and had never missed a mortgage payment. But in his mind, he was still the kid who struggled in math class, the teenager whose teacher said he'd "never amount to much," the young man whose father shook his head whenever Marcus tried to explain an idea.

Marcus had believed for thirty years that his brain was fixed. That some people were smart, others weren't, and he fell into the second category. Every mistake reinforced this belief. Every moment of confusion proved it. Every time he had to ask someone to explain something twice, he heard that old teacher's voice: "You're just not college material, Marcus."

Then Marcus learned about neuroplasticity.

Allen's Timeless Insight

When James Allen wrote that thoughts are like seeds that grow into actions and character, he was describing something science wouldn't prove for another century. Allen understood intuitively that thoughts weren't just random mental events—they were the actual building blocks of personality, behavior, and life circumstances.

Allen saw what most people miss: you're not a passive victim of your thoughts. You're their active creator. And just as a gardener chooses which seeds to plant, you can choose which thoughts to cultivate.

"A man is literally what he thinks," Allen wrote, *"his character being the complete sum of all his thoughts."*

This wasn't metaphorical language. Allen meant literally. Your thoughts don't just influence your character; they create it, one neural pathway at a time.

The Science That Proves Allen Right

Modern neuroscience has vindicated Allen's insight in ways he never could have imagined. The discovery of neuroplasticity—the brain's ability to reorganize itself throughout your entire life—proves that you are literally sculpting your brain with every thought you think.

Here's what happens in your brain when you think:

Neural Activation: Every thought activates specific neural pathways. When you think "I'm not smart enough," particular neurons fire in a particular pattern.

Pathway Strengthening: Each time you repeat a thought, you strengthen the neural pathway associated with it. It's like walking through a forest—the first time requires pushing through undergrowth, but walk the same path daily, and soon you'll have a clear trail.

Myelination: With enough repetition, fatty tissue called myelin wraps around these neural pathways, making the signals faster and stronger. What once required conscious effort becomes automatic.

Default Networks: Eventually, frequently used thought patterns become your brain's default mode. The thoughts you practice most become the thoughts that arise most easily.

Dr. Sara Lazar at Harvard demonstrated this dramatically. Using MRI scans, she found that just eight weeks of meditation practice—focused thought training—literally thickened participants' prefrontal cortexes. Their brains physically changed in the areas responsible for attention, emotional regulation, and decision-making.

Marcus's brain had been practicing "I'm stupid" for three decades. No wonder it felt so true—he'd built neural superhighways to support that belief.

What This Means for You

That critical inner voice telling you that you "can't change" or you're "just not that kind of person"? It's not revealing the truth about your fundamental nature. It's revealing the truth about which thoughts you've been practicing.

You're not stuck with the brain you have. You're constantly creating the brain you'll have tomorrow through the thoughts you choose today.

The anxious person who practices calm thinking? Their brain builds stronger, calmer circuits.

The self-critical person who practices self-compassion? Their brain develops more robust self-soothing networks.

The scattered person who practices focused attention? Their brain creates better concentration pathways.

This isn't positive thinking or wishful manifestation. This is applied neuroscience based on Allen's fundamental insight: you become what you repeatedly think.

Marcus's Transformation

When Marcus learned that his brain could change, everything shifted. He realized that "I'm stupid" wasn't a fact about his intelligence; it was just a thought he'd practiced believing.

He started small. Instead of immediately jumping to "I don't understand this," he began practicing "I'm learning to understand this." Instead of "I'm not smart enough," he tried "I'm developing my intelligence."

The thoughts felt artificial at first. His brain kept defaulting to the old patterns. But Marcus persisted, treating it like physical training; you don't expect to bench press 200 pounds on your first day at the gym.

Within two months, Marcus was coming up with innovative solutions his competitors couldn't match. Within six months, he was teaching classes at the local community college. Within a year, his business had doubled.

"I'm the same person," Marcus told me recently. "But my brain works completely differently now. I actually feel smart for the first time in my life."

Today's Practice: The Thought Awareness Foundation

For the next 24 hours, you're going to begin noticing your thoughts without trying to change them. This is like Allen's idea of examining the seeds before you plant them.

The 5-Minute Thought Observation Exercise

When: Right after you wake up, before checking your phone

How long: 5 minutes (set a timer)

What to do:
- **Sit comfortably** anywhere, bed, chair, or floor
- **Close your eyes** and take three deep breaths

- **Simply notice your thoughts** as they arise: Don't judge them as good or bad | Don't try to change or stop them | Just observe them like clouds passing through the sky
- **When you notice you're lost in a thought** (and you will): Gently label it: "thinking" | Return to observing | Don't criticize yourself, noticing you were lost IS the practice
- **When the timer goes off**, take one deep breath and mentally note: "I am not my thoughts. I am the observer of my thoughts."

Throughout the day: Set three random phone alarms. When they go off, pause and ask: "What was I just thinking?" Don't judge, just notice.

Before bed: Write down three thought patterns you noticed today. Examples:
- "I kept thinking about everything that could go wrong."
- "I had the thought 'I'm behind on everything' multiple times."
- "I noticed judging other people's choices."

What to Expect

Your mind will feel chaotic. This is normal. You're not trying to create perfect, peaceful thoughts. You're building the skill of awareness.

You'll forget to do the practice. It's normal. When you remember, just start again without self-criticism.

You might feel overwhelmed by how many thoughts you have. The average person has 60,000-80,000 thoughts per day. You're not creating more thoughts by noticing them; you're becoming aware of what's already happening.

Some thoughts will surprise you. You might discover patterns you didn't know were there. This awareness is the first step toward conscious change.

Why This Practice Changes Everything

Allen wrote: *"Only by much searching and mining, are gold and diamonds obtained, and man can find every truth connected with his being, if he will dig deep into the mine of his soul."*

Thought observation is that mining process. You can't consciously direct thoughts you're not aware of having. You can't choose better mental seeds if you don't know what you're currently planting.

This practice builds what neuroscientists call "metacognition," awareness of your own thinking. It's the foundation of all mental mastery, and it's the skill that separates Allen's "wise master" from the "foolish master" who lets thoughts run wild.

The Bigger Picture

Today, you're taking the first step in a journey that transforms you from passenger to driver of your own mind. Allen understood that this shift, from unconscious to conscious thinking, is the difference between a life that happens to you and a life you actively create.

You're not trying to think perfectly. You're learning to think consciously. There's a profound difference.

Tomorrow, you'll discover why Allen compared the mind to a garden, and you'll learn the practical techniques for cultivating thoughts that serve your highest good.

Remember

Every thought you think is literally reshaping your brain. You've been doing this unconsciously your entire life. Now you're learning to do it on purpose.

As Allen wrote: *"Man is made or unmade by himself; in the armoury of thought he forges the weapons by which he destroys himself; he also fashions the tools with which he builds for himself heavenly mansions of joy and strength and peace."*

Today, you begin fashioning those tools.

Day 2: The Garden of Your Mind

"A man's mind may be likened to a garden, which may be intelligently cultivated or allowed to run wild; but whether cultivated or neglected, it must, and will, bring forth." — *James Allen.*

Sarah's Mind Was A Weed Factory.

Every morning, she'd wake up and immediately start worrying. About her presentation at work. About her teenage daughter's attitude. About whether she was saving enough for retirement. About her mother's health. About climate change. About whether she'd locked the front door.

By the time Sarah got to work, she'd already mentally rehearsed seventeen different catastrophes, none of which had actually happened. Her brain was so practiced at generating anxious thoughts that worry had become its default mode.

"I can't help it," Sarah would say. "I'm just a worrier. It's how I'm wired."

Sarah was half right. Worry had become how she was wired—but not because she was born that way. Because she'd been unconsciously training her brain to worry for so long that anxious thinking had become automatic.

When Sarah learned to see her mind as a garden that could be consciously cultivated, everything changed.

Allen's Garden Metaphor

James Allen's comparison of the mind to a garden is one of his most powerful insights. Just as a gardener chooses what to plant and tends their crops carefully, you can choose which thoughts to cultivate and which to weed out.

Allen observed: *"Just as a gardener cultivates his plot, keeping it free from weeds, and growing the flowers and fruits which he requires, so may a man tend the garden of his mind, weeding out all the wrong, useless, and impure thoughts, and cultivating toward perfection the flowers and fruits of right, useful, and pure thoughts."*

But here's what Allen understood that many people miss: if you don't consciously plant good seeds in your mental garden, weeds will grow automatically. Your mind won't stay neutral; it will fill with whatever thoughts grab your attention most frequently.

In Allen's time, those "weeds" might have been local gossip or personal worries. Today, your mental garden is under assault from 24/7 news cycles, social media algorithms designed to trigger strong emotions, and a culture that profits from your anxiety and dissatisfaction.

Conscious mental gardening isn't just useful, it's essential for mental health in the modern world.

The Neuroscience of Mental Gardening

Your brain has a fascinating feature called the Default Mode Network (DMN), essentially your mind's screensaver that runs when you're not actively focused on a specific task.

For most people, the DMN is like an untended garden, full of mental weeds:

- Worry about the future
- Regret about the past
- Self-criticism and judgment
- Rumination on problems
- Comparison with others

Neuroscientist Dr. Marcus Raichle discovered that people with depression and anxiety have hyperactive DMNs. Their brains literally can't stop generating negative thoughts when left to their own devices.

But brain imaging studies also show something hopeful: people who practice conscious thought cultivation—through meditation, mindfulness, or focused mental training—develop different DMN patterns. Instead of defaulting to worry and rumination, their minds naturally drift toward more peaceful, constructive thoughts.

Dr. Judson Brewer at Brown University found that experienced meditators show 60% less DMN activity during rest periods. Their mental gardens had been so well-tended that even the "weeds" that grew automatically were healthier.

You can literally reprogram your mind's default mode through conscious practice.

Sarah's Garden Transformation

When Sarah began seeing her mind as a garden she could tend, she started with one simple practice: she designated the first ten minutes after waking as "garden time."

Instead of immediately checking her phone and flooding her mind with news, emails, and other people's priorities, Sarah spent those ten minutes consciously planting positive thoughts for the day.

478

She'd think about three things she was grateful for, set one intention for how she wanted to show up, and visualize herself handling her day's challenges with calm confidence.

"At first, it felt forced," Sarah told me. "My brain kept wanting to jump to my worry list. But I treated it like actual gardening, you don't plant flowers once and expect them to flourish forever. You tend them daily."

Within two weeks, Sarah noticed she was naturally thinking more positive thoughts throughout the day. Within a month, her colleagues were commenting on how much calmer she seemed. Within three months, her teenage daughter said, "Mom, you're so much less stressed lately. What changed?"

What changed was that Sarah had learned to consciously cultivate her mental garden instead of letting it grow wild.

Today's Practice: The Mental Garden Tending

Building on yesterday's thought awareness, today you'll begin actively cultivating your mental garden. This is where Allen's philosophy becomes practical daily action.

The 10-Minute Morning Garden Practice

When: First thing after waking, before checking any devices

How long: 10 minutes

What to do:

Minutes 1-3: Weed Removal

- Notice any anxious, negative, or unhelpful thoughts from yesterday or overnight
- Don't fight them—simply acknowledge: "I notice the worry weed" or "I see the self-criticism weed."
- Gently set them aside like pulling weeds from the soil
- Take three deep breaths to clear your mental space

Minutes 4-6: Seed Planting

- Plant three specific positive thoughts for the day: One gratitude: "I'm grateful for..." (be specific) | One intention: "Today I choose to be..." (patient, focused, kind, etc.) | One confidence seed: "I have the ability to..." (handle challenges, learn new things, make a difference)
- Repeat each thought three times, feeling it in your body

Minutes 7-10: Garden Visualization

- Picture your mind as a beautiful, well-tended garden

- See the positive thoughts you just planted growing strong roots
- Visualize yourself throughout the day nurturing these thoughts
- Imagine how these mental "crops" will affect your mood, decisions, and interactions

The Weed Alert System

Throughout the day, when you notice negative thought patterns arising:

- **Pause and label**: "Weed alert—worry about the future."
- **Don't judge**: Weeds are natural; noticing them is good gardening
- **Consciously redirect**: "What helpful thought can I plant right now?"
- **Take one action**: Do something small that aligns with your planted intentions

Common Mental Weeds and Their Antidotes

Worry Weeds ("What if everything goes wrong?")

- **Antidote**: Present-moment awareness and action planning
- **Garden thought**: "I can handle whatever comes, one step at a time."

Comparison Weeds ("Everyone else has it figured out")

- **Antidote**: Focus on your own growth and unique path
- **Garden thought**: "My journey is exactly where it needs to be."

Scarcity Weeds ("There's not enough time/money/opportunity")

- **Antidote**: Abundance awareness and gratitude practice
- **Garden thought**: "I have enough, and I am enough."

Criticism Weeds ("I'm not good enough")

- **Antidote**: Self-compassion and a growth mindset
- **Garden thought**: "I'm learning and improving every day."

The Science Behind Garden Thinking

When you consciously practice positive, constructive thoughts, several things happen in your brain:

- **Neuroplasticity Activation**: You literally build new neural pathways associated with optimism, gratitude, and confidence.
- **Stress Hormone Reduction**: Positive thought patterns decrease cortisol and increase serotonin, creating a better mood and clearer thinking.
- **Attention Training**: You're training your Reticular Activating System to notice opportunities, resources, and positive aspects of your environment.
- **Emotional Regulation**: The prefrontal cortex—your brain's CEO—gets stronger at managing emotional reactions and making wise decisions.

What to Expect

Your mind will resist: Old thought patterns feel familiar and "true." New patterns feel forced and artificial at first. This is normal.

Weeds will keep growing: You won't eliminate negative thoughts entirely, nor should you try. The goal is conscious cultivation, not thought perfection.

Progress will be gradual: Like a real garden, mental cultivation requires consistent tending. Don't expect an overnight transformation.

Others will notice: As your inner garden becomes healthier, people around you will comment on your improved mood, patience, or calm presence.

Building on Yesterday

Yesterday, you learned to observe your thoughts. Today, you're learning to consciously influence them. You're moving from passive awareness to active cultivation—from being a victim of whatever thoughts arise to being a gardener who chooses what grows.

This is exactly what Allen meant when he wrote about discovering yourself as "the master-gardener of your soul, the director of your life."

Tomorrow's Preview

Tomorrow, you'll learn about one of the biggest obstacles to mental gardening: the autopilot patterns that have been running your mind unconsciously for years. You'll discover how to interrupt these automatic programs and install new ones that serve your growth.

Remember Allen's Promise

"By pursuing this process, a man sooner or later discovers that he is the master-gardener of his soul, the director of his life. He also reveals, within himself, the laws of thought, and understands, with ever-increasing accuracy, how the thought-forces and mind elements operate in the shaping of his character, circumstances, and destiny."

Today, you begin revealing those laws within yourself.

Your mental garden is ready for conscious cultivation. **Plant wisely.**

Day 3: Breaking Free from Mental Autopilot

"Man is made or unmade by himself; in the armoury of thought he forges the weapons by which he destroys himself; he also fashions the tools with which he builds for himself heavenly mansions of joy and strength and peace." — **James Allen.**

David was having the same argument with his wife again.

She'd made an innocent comment about his driving, and suddenly he was defensive, irritated, and pulling up every example from the past six months of times she'd criticized him. The rational part of his mind knew he was overreacting, but the words kept pouring out anyway.

Later, lying in bed after they'd both stormed off to separate rooms, David wondered: "Why do I keep doing this? I love my wife. I don't want to fight. But when she says certain things, it's like something else takes over."

That "something else" was David's mental autopilot, a collection of unconscious thought patterns that had been running his reactions for so long he didn't even know they existed.

David thought he was responding to his wife's comment. Actually, he was responding to a mental program installed decades earlier that interpreted any suggestion about his competence as an attack requiring immediate defense.

Until David learned to recognize and interrupt these autopilot patterns, they would continue running his life.

Allen's Understanding of Mental Programming

James Allen intuited something that modern psychology calls "automatic thoughts" and "cognitive schemas," mental programs that run below the level of conscious awareness but powerfully shape our responses to life.

Allen wrote: *"Thought in the mind hath made us, What we are / By thought was wrought and built."* He understood that most people's current thoughts, emotions, and behaviors weren't conscious choices, but the automatic result of mental patterns established in the past.

Allen saw that humans operate from what he called "long-cherished association" with certain types of thoughts. These associations become so habitual that people mistake them for their true nature rather than recognizing them as learned patterns that can be changed.

"A noble and Godlike character is not a thing of favour or chance," **Allen wrote,** *"but is the natural result of continued effort in right thinking, the effect of long-cherished association with Godlike thoughts."*

The reverse is also true: destructive patterns result from "long-cherished association" with destructive thoughts. The key insight is that all these associations—positive and negative—were learned, which means they can be unlearned and replaced.

The Science of Mental Autopilot

Your brain is an efficiency machine. Any pattern you repeat frequently enough gets automated so your conscious mind can focus on new challenges. This is why you can drive home while thinking about something else, or brush your teeth while planning your day.

This automation process works through several mechanisms:

- **Procedural Memory**: Your brain stores frequently used patterns in your basal ganglia, where they run automatically without conscious thought.
- **Neural Habits**: Repeated thought-emotion-behavior sequences create what neuroscientist Ann Graybiel calls "habit loops," cue, routine, reward cycles that run on autopilot.
- **Implicit Memory**: Emotional reactions and defensive responses often stem from implicit memories—past experiences stored below conscious awareness but triggered by similar situations.
- **Cognitive Schemas**: Your brain creates mental frameworks (schemas) that interpret new experiences through the lens of past patterns. These schemas run so quickly that they feel like immediate reality rather than interpretation.

Dr. Daniel Kahneman's research reveals that we have two thinking systems: System 1 (fast, automatic, unconscious) and System 2 (slow, deliberate, conscious). System 1 handles about 95% of your daily mental processing through automated patterns.

This is normally helpful—imagine having to consciously think through every step of getting dressed or making coffee. But when System 1 contains outdated or destructive patterns, you end up reacting to current situations based on old programming rather than present reality.

David's defensive reaction to his wife wasn't really about her comment—it was System 1 running an old program: "When competence is questioned, defend immediately."

Common Autopilot Patterns That Sabotage Growth

The Criticism Detector: Interprets neutral feedback as a personal attack

- **Trigger**: Any suggestion for improvement
- **Autopilot response**: Defensiveness, counter-attack, or withdrawal
- **Origin**: Often from early experiences with harsh criticism

The Perfectionism Program: Demands flawless performance to avoid shame

- **Trigger**: Making any mistake or facing uncertainty
- **Autopilot response**: Procrastination, over-preparation, or self-criticism
- **Origin**: Usually from conditional love or high-pressure environments

The Scarcity Scanner: Constantly searches for what's lacking or threatened

- **Trigger**: Any hint of competition or limitation
- **Autopilot response**: Hoarding, comparison, anxiety about the future
- **Origin**: Often from experiences of genuine lack or instability

The People-Pleasing Protocol: Prioritizes others' approval over authentic needs

- **Trigger**: Any possibility of disappointing someone
- **Autopilot response**: Over-giving, saying yes when you mean no, self-neglect
- **Origin**: Usually from early needs to maintain a connection for safety

David's Pattern Interruption Journey

When David learned about mental autopilot, he realized his marriage conflicts followed a predictable pattern:

- **Cue**: Wife makes a suggestion about his behavior
- **Automatic interpretation**: "She thinks I'm incompetent."
- **Emotional trigger**: Shame activates defensive anger
- **Routine**: Argue, bring up past grievances, prove his competence
- **Reward**: Temporary relief from shame (but damage to the relationship)

David began practicing what Allen might have called "watching the inner life" and what modern psychology calls "metacognitive awareness"—observing his own mental processes in real-time.

The next time his wife made a suggestion, David caught the autopilot pattern starting:

- He felt the familiar defensive surge
- Instead of immediately reacting, he paused and thought: "Autopilot pattern detected."

- He took three deep breaths and asked: "What if she's just trying to help?"
- He responded: "You might be right. Let me think about that."

The conversation that could have become a fight became a helpful discussion. David's wife was amazed. "You seem so much calmer lately," she said. "What changed?"

What changed was that David had learned to interrupt mental autopilot and choose his responses consciously.

Today's Practice: The Pattern Interrupt Technique

Today, you'll learn to catch autopilot patterns in action and consciously choose different responses. This is where Allen's philosophy becomes practical emotional intelligence.

The STOP Method for Autopilot Interruption

When you notice a strong emotional reaction or find yourself responding in familiar, unwanted ways:

S - STOP
- Physically pause whatever you're doing
- If possible, excuse yourself: "Give me just a moment."
- This creates space between the trigger and the response

T - TAKE A BREATH
- Three slow, deep breaths minimum
- Breathe in for 4 counts, hold for 4, exhale for 6
- This activates your parasympathetic nervous system

O - OBSERVE
- Ask: "What am I feeling right now?"
- Ask: "What story am I telling myself about what just happened?"
- Ask: "Is this a familiar pattern?"

P - PROCEED CONSCIOUSLY
- Ask: "How would my best self respond to this situation?"
- Ask: "What response would I be proud of tomorrow?"
- Choose one specific action aligned with these answers

The Daily Pattern Detection Exercise

Evening Reflection (5 minutes before bed):

1. **Identify one autopilot moment** from today: When did you react automatically? | What was the trigger? | How did you respond?
2. **Trace the pattern**: What thought arose immediately after the trigger? | What emotion followed? | What story did you tell yourself?

3. **Design a conscious alternative**: What conscious thought could you choose instead? | How would that change your emotional response? | What different action would that enable?
4. **Practice the new pattern**: Mentally rehearse the situation with your conscious response | Imagine how it would feel to respond differently | Set an intention to notice this pattern tomorrow

Advanced Pattern Work: The Origin Investigation

For patterns that feel particularly strong or persistent, try this deeper exercise:

Step 1: Identify when you first remember feeling this way

- How old were you?
- What was happening in your life?
- Who was involved?

Step 2: Understand the original function

- How did this pattern protect you then?
- What did it help you avoid or achieve?
- Why was it adaptive in that situation?

Step 3: Assess current relevance

- Is this pattern still serving you?
- Are you in the same circumstances as when it formed?
- What might be possible without this pattern?

Step 4: Thank and update

- Thank the pattern for its service
- Consciously choose to update it
- Install a new pattern that serves your current life

What to Expect from Pattern Work

Initial resistance: Autopilot patterns feel "true" and "natural." Conscious responses may feel forced or artificial at first.

Emotional intensity: When you interrupt old patterns, suppressed emotions may surface. This is normal and temporary.

Gradual change: New patterns take 21-66 days to feel automatic. Be patient with the process.

Relationship shifts: As you respond differently, other people may react with surprise or resistance to your changes.

Increased freedom: Each pattern you interrupt expands your range of conscious choice.

The Neuroscience of Pattern Change

When you consistently practice pattern interruption, several changes occur:

Strengthened prefrontal cortex: The brain region responsible for conscious choice gets stronger through practice.

Weakened automatic responses: Old neural pathways weaken when you stop using them.

Increased neural flexibility: Your brain develops more options for responding to triggers.

Improved emotional regulation: You become less reactive and more responsive to challenging situations.

Building on Previous Days

Day 1 taught you to observe thoughts.

Day 2 taught you to cultivate positive thinking.

Today, you're learning to interrupt destructive patterns and choose conscious responses.

You're developing what Allen called the capacity to be "the conscious and intelligent wielder of his mental powers."

Tomorrow's Preview

Tomorrow, you'll discover one of the most powerful applications of conscious thinking: programming your brain's attention system to notice opportunities, resources, and possibilities that align with your goals.

Remember Allen's Insight

"Man is always the master, even in his weaker and most abandoned state; but in his weakness and degradation, he is the foolish master who misgoverns his 'household.' When he begins to reflect upon his condition, and to search diligently for the Law upon which his being is established, he then becomes the wise master, directing his energies with intelligence, and fashioning his thoughts to fruitful issues."

Today, you begin the transition from foolish master to wise master—from unconscious reaction to conscious creation.

Your autopilot patterns served you once. Now you're learning to upgrade them for the life you want to create.

Day 4: Your Reticular Activating System

*"Men do not attract that which they want, but that which they are. Their whims, fancies, and ambitions are thwarted at every step, but their inmost thoughts and desires are fed with their own food, be it foul or clean." — **James Allen.***

Jennifer couldn't understand why some people seemed so lucky.

Her friend Maria landed job opportunities without even looking. Her colleague Tom always found great deals on everything from cars to vacation rentals. Her neighbor Susan seemed to meet helpful, interesting people wherever she went.

Meanwhile, Jennifer felt like she was swimming upstream. Opportunities passed her by. Problems seemed to find her. The world felt like a place of scarcity and struggle.

"Some people are just born lucky," Jennifer would say with resignation.

What Jennifer didn't understand was that she and her "lucky" friends were living in the same world, exposed to the same opportunities and possibilities. The difference wasn't luck—it was what their brains were programmed to notice.

Jennifer's Reticular Activating System was filtering reality for problems, threats, and evidence of struggle. Maria's was calibrated for opportunities, Tom's for bargains, and Susan's for connection.

When Jennifer learned to reprogram her mental filter, her "luck" changed dramatically.

Allen's Insight About Mental Attraction

James Allen observed something that wouldn't be scientifically explained until decades later: people don't attract what they consciously want, they attract what they unconsciously focus on most.

"The soul attracts that which it secretly harbours; that which it loves, and also that which it fears," Allen wrote. *"It reaches the height of its cherished aspirations; it falls to the level of its unchastened desires, and circumstances are the means by which the soul receives its own."*

Allen understood that your dominant thought patterns create a kind of magnetic field that draws matching experiences into your life, not through mystical forces, but through the practical mechanism of attention.

When your mind is consistently focused on problems, you notice more problems. When it's focused on solutions, you notice more solutions. When it's focused on scarcity, you see evidence of lack everywhere. When it's focused on abundance, you discover resources you previously overlooked.

Allen was describing what neuroscience now calls the Reticular Activating System—your brain's Google algorithm for reality.

The Science of Your Mental Filter

Reticular Activating System (RAS)

Your Reticular Activating System (RAS) is a network of neurons in your brainstem that acts as a gatekeeper between your subconscious and conscious mind. Every second, your senses pick up about 11 million bits of information. Your conscious mind can only process about 50.

Your RAS decides which 50 make the cut.

This filtering happens based on what your brain has been trained to consider important, relevant, or worthy of attention. The training occurs through:

- **Repetitive focus**: Whatever you think about most frequently
- **Emotional intensity**: Experiences that carry strong feelings
- **Personal relevance**: Information connected to your goals, fears, or identity
- **Recent priming**: What you've been exposed to lately

Dr. Daniel Simons' famous "invisible gorilla" experiment demonstrates this dramatically. Participants watching a video and counting basketball passes literally don't see a person in a gorilla suit walking through the scene. Their RAS was filtered for passes, so everything else became invisible.

This filtering happens constantly in your daily life: Pregnant women suddenly notice babies everywhere (they were always there) | When you're considering buying a blue Honda, blue Hondas appear on every street (they didn't multiply overnight) | People focused on financial problems notice every expense (but miss opportunities to save or earn) | Those focused on relationship issues spot every sign of discord (while overlooking gestures of love)

Your RAS isn't just passively filtering—it's actively searching for evidence to confirm whatever you've programmed it to find.

How Thought Patterns Program Your RAS

Every thought you repeat is essentially giving your RAS search instructions:

"I never have enough money." Program your RAS to notice:

- Every expense and bill
- Evidence of financial struggle
- Reasons you can't afford things
- Other people who seem better off

"I always find great opportunities." Program your RAS to notice:

- Potential openings and possibilities
- Resources and helpful people
- Creative solutions to challenges
- Evidence of abundance and growth

"People can't be trusted." Program your RAS to spot:

- Every disappointing interaction
- Signs of potential betrayal
- Reasons to be suspicious
- Evidence that confirms your cynicism

"I'm surrounded by good people." Program your RAS to see:

- Kindness and helpfulness in others
- Opportunities for connection
- Examples of human goodness
- Reasons to feel grateful and optimistic

The remarkable thing is that all of these programs can run in the same environment, with the same people, facing the same circumstances. Your RAS creates your experienced reality by determining what you notice.

Jennifer's RAS Reprogramming

When Jennifer learned about the RAS, she realized her brain had been programmed by years of focusing on what was wrong, missing, or threatening in her life.

She decided to experiment with reprogramming her mental filter. Instead of starting each day thinking about her problems, she began each morning with this simple practice:

Morning RAS Programming: "Today I'm looking for opportunities to grow, people who can help me, and evidence that good things are possible."

Within a week, Jennifer was amazed at what she began noticing:

- A conversation with a coffee shop customer led to a freelance project
- She spotted a flyer for a networking event that connected her with her next boss
- A casual comment from her neighbor revealed a potential solution to her biggest challenge

"It's like someone switched on lights I didn't know existed," Jennifer told me. "The opportunities were always there—I just wasn't programmed to see them."

Today's Practice: RAS Reprogramming Protocol

Today, you'll learn to consciously program your Reticular Activating System to search for evidence that supports your growth, goals, and highest potential.

The Morning RAS Setup Ritual

When: First thing in the morning, after your garden practice

How long: 5 minutes

What to do:

1. **Clear old programming** (1 minute): Notice what your mind has been automatically searching for | Common patterns: problems, threats, evidence of struggle | Gently say: "Thank you for trying to protect me, but I'm updating this program."

2. **Install new search parameters** (3 minutes): Choose three specific things you want your RAS to find today: "Today I'm looking for opportunities to _____" | "Today I'm noticing evidence that _____" | "Today I'm spotting examples of _____" Examples: "Opportunities to connect with interesting people" | "Evidence that I'm capable of learning new things" | "Examples of abundance and generosity in the world"

3. **Activate the search** (1 minute): Say: "My brain is now programmed to find these things"| Visualize your day with these new filters active | Feel excited about what you might discover

The Evening RAS Review

Before bed (5 minutes):

1. **Document your findings**: What did your newly programmed RAS help you notice? | What opportunities, evidence, or examples appeared? | How did this affect your mood and energy?

2. **Celebrate successful programming**: Acknowledge that you consciously directed your attention | Feel grateful for what your brain helped you discover | Recognize your power to filter reality

3. **Refine tomorrow's program**: What do you want to search for tomorrow? | How can you make the programming even more specific? | What would be most helpful to notice?

Advanced RAS Programming Techniques

The Specific Goal Filter: If you have a particular goal, program your RAS to find relevant opportunities:

- "I'm looking for ways to advance my career."
- "I'm noticing opportunities to improve my health."
- "I'm spotting chances to strengthen my relationships."

The Solution-Finder Program: For current challenges, program your RAS to find answers:

- "I'm looking for creative solutions to _____"
- "I'm noticing resources that could help with _____"
- "I'm spotting examples of people who've solved similar problems."

The Abundance Scanner: To counter scarcity thinking, program for abundance awareness:

- "I'm noticing all the ways I'm supported."
- "I'm looking for evidence of plenty in my life."
- "I'm spotting opportunities to give and receive."

The Growth Detector: To support personal development, a program for learning opportunities:

- "I'm looking for chances to develop new skills."
- "I'm noticing feedback that helps me improve."
- "I'm spotting examples of people who inspire my growth."

Common RAS Programming Mistakes

Being too vague: "I want good things to happen."

- Better: "I'm looking for specific opportunities to use my writing skills."

Programming for what you don't want: "I don't want to fail."

- Better: "I'm looking for evidence that I'm improving."

Expecting overnight results: RAS reprogramming takes consistent practice

- Better: Trust the process and maintain daily programming

Ignoring what you find: Your RAS will show you things, but you must consciously acknowledge them

- Better: Actively celebrate and document what you notice

The Science Behind RAS Reprogramming

When you consciously direct your attention through RAS programming:

- **Neural pathway strengthening**: You build stronger connections in brain regions associated with your chosen focus areas.
- **Confirmation bias redirection**: Instead of confirming limiting beliefs, you start confirming empowering ones.
- **Opportunity recognition**: You literally see possibilities that were always present but previously filtered out.
- **Mood enhancement**: Noticing positive evidence improves emotional state and energy levels.
- **Behavioral changes**: Seeing more opportunities leads to taking more beneficial actions.

Building on Your Week's Progress

You've now learned to:

- **Day 1**: Observe your thoughts consciously
- **Day 2**: Cultivate positive mental seeds
- **Day 3**: Interrupt destructive autopilot patterns
- **Day 4**: Program your brain's attention filter

You're developing what Allen called the ability to "command the hidden soil and seeds of being out of which circumstances grow."

Tomorrow's Preview

Tomorrow, you'll learn how to harness the power of purposeful thinking—directing your mental energy toward meaningful goals that inspire sustained motivation and clear action.

Remember Allen's Promise

"The world is your kaleidoscope, and the varying combinations of colours, which at every succeeding moment it presents to you, are the exquisitely adjusted pictures of your ever-moving thoughts."

Today, you learned to consciously adjust that kaleidoscope. Your RAS is now searching for evidence that supports your highest potential.

Pay attention to what it finds. You might be surprised by how "lucky" you become.

Day 5: The Power of Purposeful Thinking

"Until thought is linked with purpose, there is no intelligent accomplishment. With the majority, the bark of thought is allowed to 'drift' upon the ocean of life." — **James Allen.**

Michael had all the thinking tools but no direction.

He'd mastered meditation. He could interrupt negative patterns. He practiced gratitude daily. His friends envied his discipline and mental clarity. But Michael felt like he was spinning in place—busy but not building, active but not advancing.

"I'm really good at managing my thoughts," Michael told me, "but I don't know what to think about. I can focus my mind, but I don't know where to point it."

Michael had developed mental skills without a mental purpose. He was like a master archer with perfect technique but no target; all that power going nowhere.

When Michael learned to link his thinking to a meaningful purpose, everything changed. Instead of just managing his mind, he began directing it toward goals that energized him. His scattered mental energy became a focused force.

This is what Allen meant by "intelligent accomplishment," thought aligned with purpose, creating unstoppable momentum toward meaningful goals.

Allen's Insight About Purposeful Thinking

James Allen understood that thought without purpose is like steam without direction—lots of energy going nowhere useful. He observed that most people let their thoughts drift randomly, reacting to whatever captures their attention rather than consciously directing mental energy toward worthy aims.

"They who have no central purpose in their life," **Allen wrote,** *"fall an easy prey to petty worries, fears, troubles, and self-pityings, all of which are indications of weakness, which lead, just as surely as deliberately planned sins (though by a different route), to failure, unhappiness, and loss."*

Allen saw that purpose serves as an organizing principle for thought, a North Star that gives direction to mental energy. Without purpose, the mind becomes vulnerable to every distraction, worry, and negative influence.

This isn't about forcing every thought to be "productive" or eliminating all mental wandering. It's about having a meaningful direction that your thoughts can return to, especially when faced with challenges, decisions, or uncertainty.

The Neuroscience of Purpose-Driven Thinking

Modern research reveals why Allen's insight about purpose is so powerful. When your thinking is connected to meaningful goals, several remarkable things happen in your brain:

Enhanced Focus: Neuroscientist Dr. Adam Gazzaley's research shows that purpose-driven attention is significantly stronger than arbitrary focus. When you care about what you're thinking about, your brain allocates more resources to maintaining concentration.

Increased Motivation: Purpose activates the brain's reward systems differently than external motivators. Dr. Daniel Pink's research reveals that intrinsic motivation (purpose-driven) is more sustainable and satisfying than extrinsic motivation (reward-driven).

Improved Problem-Solving: Studies by Dr. Teresa Amabile show that people working on purpose-aligned goals demonstrate enhanced creativity and innovative thinking. Purpose literally makes you smarter.

Stress Resilience: Research by Dr. Kristin Neff reveals that people with a strong life purpose show better stress recovery and emotional regulation. Purpose provides perspective that reduces the impact of daily frustrations.

Neural Efficiency: Brain imaging studies show that purpose-driven individuals have more efficient neural networks—their brains work less hard to achieve better results because mental energy isn't scattered across competing priorities.

Dr. Patricia Boyle's longitudinal study of over 1,000 older adults found that those with high purpose scores were 2.4 times less likely to develop Alzheimer's disease. Purpose literally protects your brain from deterioration.

The Difference Between Goals and Purpose

Many people confuse goals with purpose, but they serve different functions in purposeful thinking:

Goals are destinations: Specific, measurable outcomes you want to achieve

- "Get promoted to director level."

- "Run a marathon"
- "Save $50,000"

Purpose is your compass: The deeper meaning that guides your direction

- "Develop human potential"
- "Create beauty in the world."
- "Reduce suffering"

How they work together:

- Purpose provides the "why" that sustains motivation
- Goals provide the "what" that directs action
- Purposeful thinking connects them: "I'm pursuing this goal because it serves this larger meaning."

Michael's Purpose Discovery Process

When Michael began exploring his deeper purpose, he used a process that Allen would have appreciated—careful observation of his own thoughts and energy patterns.

Michael noticed:

- He felt most energized when helping others solve complex problems
- He was naturally drawn to conversations about human potential
- He got excited about simplifying complicated systems
- His happiest memories involved teaching or mentoring

These observations pointed toward a purpose: "Help people unlock their capability by making complex things simple."

Once Michael connected his thinking to this purpose, everything shifted:

- His meditation became preparation for clearer thinking
- His problem-solving focused on how to help others more effectively
- His learning was directed toward skills that served his purpose
- Even routine tasks felt meaningful when connected to his larger mission

"It's like all my mental tools suddenly had a job to do," Michael said. "Instead of just maintaining my mind, I was building something meaningful with it."

Today's Practice: Purpose-Directed Thinking

Today, you'll learn to connect your daily thinking to deeper purpose, creating what Allen called "the royal road to self-control and true concentration of thought."

The Purpose Discovery Reflection

When: Morning, after your RAS programming

How long: 10 minutes

What to do:

1. **Energy Tracking** (3 minutes):
   - When do you feel most energized and alive?
   - What activities make you lose track of time?
   - What conversations excite you most?
   - When do you feel like you're using your best abilities?

2. **Values Identification** (3 minutes):
   - What principles matter most to you?
   - What injustices bother you most deeply?
   - What would you want to be remembered for?
   - If you could solve one problem in the world, what would it be?

3. **Natural Strengths** (2 minutes):
   - What do others frequently ask for your help with?
   - What seems easy for you but hard for others?
   - What compliments do you receive repeatedly?
   - What were you naturally drawn to as a child?

4. **Purpose Statement Draft** (2 minutes): Based on your reflections, complete this sentence: "My purpose is to _____ for/with _____ so that _____"

Examples:

- "My purpose is to simplify complex ideas for overwhelmed people so that they can make better decisions."
- "My purpose is to create beautiful spaces for busy families so that their homes become sanctuaries."
- "My purpose is to develop leadership skills in young professionals so that they can create positive change."

The Daily Purpose Connection Practice

Throughout the day, before major tasks or decisions, ask:

- "How does this connect to my purpose?"
- "How can I approach this in a way that serves my deeper mission?"
- "What would change if I did this task with purpose in mind?"

Before important conversations:

- "How can I show up in this interaction as someone living my purpose?"
- "What gift can I bring to this person that aligns with my mission?"

When facing challenges:

- "How is this difficulty helping me grow into my purpose?"
- "What is this situation teaching me that will help me serve others better?"

Advanced Purposeful Thinking Techniques

The Purpose Filter for Decisions: When facing choices, large or small, ask:

- "Which option better aligns with my purpose?"
- "How would someone fully living my purpose handle this?"
- "What choice will I be proud of when viewed through my purpose lens?"

The Purpose Reframe for Mundane Tasks: Transform routine activities by connecting them to purpose:

- Filing paperwork → "Organizing systems so I can serve others more effectively"
- Exercising → "Building energy to fulfill my purpose"
- Learning new skills → "Developing abilities that will help me serve better"

The Purpose Question for Problem-Solving: When stuck on challenges, ask:

- "How could solving this problem serve others with similar struggles?"
- "What would someone committed to my purpose do in this situation?"
- "How can this difficulty become a source of wisdom for future service?"

Common Challenges in Purposeful Thinking

"My purpose feels too big or overwhelming."

- Start with small expressions of purpose in daily life
- Remember: purpose is lived through accumulated moments, not single grand gestures

"I don't think I have a unique purpose."

- Everyone's combination of gifts, experiences, and perspectives is unique
- Focus on how you uniquely express universal values like love, growth, or service

"I feel guilty pursuing my purpose when I have responsibilities."

- True purpose often enhances rather than conflicts with responsibilities
- Living purposefully models authentic living for those you care about

"My purpose seems to keep evolving."

- Purpose can mature and deepen while maintaining core themes
- Evolution of purpose is growth, not inconsistency

The Science of Purpose-Driven Performance

Research consistently shows that purpose-directed thinking enhances performance:

Flow States: People are more likely to experience flow (optimal performance) when activities align with personal purpose.

Sustained Motivation: Purpose-driven goals show less motivational decay over time compared to purely external goals.

Enhanced Learning: Students learn faster and retain information longer when the material connects to personal purpose.

Improved Health: Purpose-driven individuals show better immune function, cardiovascular health, and longevity.

Greater Resilience: People with a strong purpose recover more quickly from setbacks and maintain optimism during challenges.

Building on Your Week

You've now developed:

- Thought awareness (Day 1)
- Mental cultivation (Day 2)
- Pattern interruption (Day 3)
- Attention programming (Day 4)
- Purpose-directed thinking (Day 5)

You're assembling what Allen called the tools to "build for himself heavenly mansions of joy and strength and peace."

Tomorrow's Preview

Tomorrow you'll learn how to install new thought habits that automatically support your growth, moving from occasional purposeful thinking to consistent mental patterns that serve your highest development.

Remember Allen's Vision

"Having conceived of his purpose, a man should mentally mark out a straight pathway to its achievement, looking neither to the right nor the left. Doubts and fears should be rigorously excluded; they are disintegrating elements, which break up the straight line of effort, rendering it crooked, ineffectual, useless."

Today, you conceived of your purpose and began marking out that straight pathway with your thoughts.

Tomorrow, you'll learn to walk it consistently.

Day 6: Thought Habits That Serve You

"A noble and Godlike character is not a thing of favour or chance, but is the natural result of continued effort in right thinking, the effect of long-cherished association with Godlike thoughts." — James Allen.

Lisa was exhausted from trying to think positively.

Every morning, she'd set intentions to be grateful and optimistic. By 10 AM, she was stressed about her workload. By noon, she was irritated with her coworkers. By evening, she was criticizing herself for "failing" at positive thinking again.

"I know what I should be thinking," Lisa said, "but I can't seem to make it stick. I'll have a good thought, then five minutes later, I'm back to my old patterns. It feels like I'm fighting my own brain."

Lisa was fighting her brain—specifically, she was trying to use willpower to overcome decades of established neural pathways. She was attempting to manually drive a car instead of simply changing the automatic transmission.

When Lisa learned to install new thought habits rather than forcing individual thoughts, everything became easier. Instead of constantly battling her mind, she programmed it to run better patterns automatically.

This is what Allen meant by "long-cherished association" with positive thoughts—making beneficial thinking so habitual that it becomes your natural way of processing life.

Allen's Understanding of Mental Habits

James Allen understood something that neuroscience would later prove: character is built through repeated thought patterns, not occasional positive thoughts or good intentions.

"As the physically weak man can make himself strong by careful and patient training," Allen wrote, "so the man of weak thoughts can make them strong by exercising himself in right thinking."

Allen saw that the mind operates like any other system—what you practice becomes automatic. Just as a musician develops muscle memory through repetition, you develop "mental memory" through consistent thought patterns.

"Thought and character are one," Allen observed. This isn't metaphorical; your habitual thoughts literally become your personality. The patterns you repeat most frequently become the mental "default settings" that shape how you automatically respond to life.

Allen understood that transformation doesn't come from occasional bursts of positive thinking but from what he called "continued effort in right thinking"—the patient installation of mental habits that align with your highest values and aspirations.

The Neuroscience of Thought Habits

Your brain operates on an efficiency principle: any pattern you repeat frequently enough gets automated to conserve mental energy. This happens through several mechanisms:

Myelin Development: When you repeat a thought pattern, fatty tissue called myelin wraps around the associated neural pathways, making signals faster and stronger. This is why practiced thoughts feel more "natural" and "true."

Synaptic Strengthening: Each repetition strengthens the connections between neurons involved in that thought pattern. As neuroscientist Donald Hebb discovered: "Neurons that fire together, wire together."

Automaticity Formation: After sufficient repetition (research suggests 66 days on average for complex habits), thought patterns transfer from conscious control to automatic processing. They run without willpower or effort.

Default Mode Programming: Your brain's Default Mode Network—its "screensaver"—gets programmed by your most frequent thought patterns. Whatever you practice thinking becomes what you think when you're not consciously directing your thoughts.

Neurochemical Conditioning: Repeated thought patterns create associated neurochemical responses. Habitually anxious thinking builds stronger stress response pathways. Habitually grateful thinking builds stronger joy response pathways.

Dr. Sarah Gottman's research on couples reveals this dramatically: partners who've practiced appreciative thinking about each other literally see more positive behaviors and fewer negative ones—their brains are wired to notice evidence that confirms their habitual thoughts.

The Difference Between Forced Thinking and Thought Habits

Forced Thinking:

- Requires constant willpower and effort
- Feels artificial and unsustainable
- Often creates internal resistance
- Works only when you remember to do it
- Exhausts mental energy

Thought Habits:

- Run automatically without effort
- Feel natural and authentic
- Create internal momentum
- Work even when you're not consciously monitoring
- Generate mental energy

The key difference: forced thinking fights your existing neural patterns, while thought habits gradually replace them.

Lisa's Habit Installation Process

Instead of trying to think positively all day, Lisa focused on installing one specific thought habit at a time. She chose to start with morning appreciation.

Week 1: Every morning, immediately upon waking, Lisa practiced the same thought pattern: "What am I grateful for right now?" She'd identify three specific things before getting out of bed.

Week 2: The pattern began feeling more natural. Lisa noticed her brain starting to automatically look for things to appreciate, even without conscious effort.

Week 3: The habit was so established that Lisa felt uncomfortable if she forgot to do it. Her brain had been rewired to expect this morning pattern.

Week 4 and beyond: Lisa added new thought habits one at a time:

- Before difficult conversations: "How can I be helpful here?"
- When facing challenges: "What is this situation teaching me?"
- Before sleep: "What did I do well today?"

Within three months, Lisa's colleagues were commenting on her improved mood and patience. Her stress levels had significantly decreased, and she felt more resilient when facing difficulties.

"The best part," Lisa told me, "is that I'm not trying to think positively anymore. I just naturally think more positively. My brain's been reprogrammed."

Today's Practice: Installing Your First Thought Habit

Today, you'll learn Allen's approach to developing a "long-cherished association" with beneficial thoughts through systematic habit installation.

The Thought Habit Selection Process

Step 1: Identify Your Current Mental Default (5 minutes) Notice what your mind automatically does in these situations:

- First thought upon waking
- Response to unexpected challenges
- Reaction to criticism or feedback
- Processing of mistakes or failures
- Mental state before sleep

Step 2: Choose One Pattern to Install (5 minutes). Select the situation where a new thought habit would be most beneficial. Start with just ONE:

Morning Moments:

- Instead of "What do I have to do today?" → "What opportunity does today offer?"
- Instead of checking phone first → "What am I grateful for right now?"

Challenge Responses:

- Instead of "Why is this happening to me?" → "What is this teaching me?"
- Instead of "This is too hard." → "I'm growing stronger by facing this."

Social Interactions:

- Instead of "What do they think of me?" → "How can I be genuinely helpful?"
- Instead of "They're judging me" → "Everyone is doing their best with what they know"

Evening Patterns:

- Instead of "What went wrong today?" → "What did I learn today?"
- Instead of worrying about tomorrow → "I trust my ability to handle whatever comes."

The 21-Day Installation Protocol

Week 1: Conscious Practice

- Set a specific trigger (alarm, visual cue, or situation)

- When the trigger occurs, consciously practice your new thought pattern
- Repeat the exact same thought sequence each time
- Track daily completion (simple checkmark system)

Week 2: Strengthening

- Continue daily practice
- Notice when the pattern starts arising naturally
- Celebrate each automatic occurrence
- Don't worry if you still forget sometimes

Week 3: Integration

- The habit should feel more natural now
- Focus on emotional connection—feel good about the new pattern
- Notice how this thought habit affects your mood and behavior
- Prepare to add a second habit if desired

Advanced Habit Installation Techniques

The Emotional Amplifier: Connect strong positive emotion to your new thought pattern:

- Feel genuine gratitude when practicing appreciation habits
- Experience real excitement when practicing opportunity-focused thinking
- Generate authentic compassion when practicing understanding-based thoughts

The Identity Link: Connect the habit to your desired identity:

- "I'm the kind of person who looks for the good in situations."
- "I'm someone who stays calm under pressure."
- "I'm a person who learns from every experience."

The Environmental Design: Create external supports for internal habits:

- Place visual reminders where you'll see them
- Use phone alarms with meaningful labels
- Ask trusted friends to gently remind you
- Change your environment to trigger new patterns

The Habit Stack: Attach new thought habits to existing routines:

- "After I brush my teeth, I'll practice my gratitude pattern."
- "Before I start my car, I'll set my intention for the drive."
- "When I sit down at my desk, I'll remind myself of my purpose."

Troubleshooting Common Installation Challenges

"I keep forgetting to practice the habit."

- Make the trigger more obvious (bigger reminders, phone alarms)
- Attach it to something you never forget (coffee, brushing teeth)

- Ask someone to gently remind you for the first week

"The new thought feels fake or forced."

- This is normal; all new habits feel artificial initially
- Focus on the intention behind the thought, not perfect execution
- Trust that authenticity develops through repetition

"I remember to do it, but then go back to old patterns immediately."

- One repetition of the new pattern + ten repetitions of the old pattern still creates progress
- Celebrate the new pattern without criticizing the old ones
- Consistency matters more than perfection

"I don't see any changes yet."

- Neural habit formation takes 21-66 days on average
- Benefits often accumulate below conscious awareness before becoming noticeable
- Trust the process—Allen's "continued effort" principle applies

The Compound Effect of Thought Habits

As you install beneficial thought habits, several things happen:

- **Reduced Mental Effort**: Beneficial thinking becomes automatic rather than forced
- **Improved Emotional State**: Better thought patterns create better feeling patterns
- **Enhanced Decision-Making**: Habitual wisdom thinking improves daily choices
- **Increased Resilience**: Automatic positive processing helps you bounce back faster
- **Stronger Relationships**: Beneficial thought habits improve how you interact with others

Building on Your Week's Foundation

You now have:

- Thought awareness (Day 1)
- Mental cultivation skills (Day 2)
- Pattern interruption ability (Day 3)
- Attention programming (Day 4)
- Purpose-directed thinking (Day 5)
- Thought habit installation (Day 6)

You're developing what Allen called "the conscious and intelligent wielder of mental powers."

Tomorrow's Preview

Tomorrow, you'll learn to integrate all these skills into what Allen called mastery of your "mental kingdom"—the ability to maintain beneficial thought patterns even during challenging circumstances.

Remember Allen's Promise

"The weakest soul, knowing its own weakness, and believing this truth that strength can only be developed by effort and practice, will, thus believing, at once begin to exert itself, and, adding effort to effort, patience to patience, and strength to strength, will never cease to develop, and will at last grow divinely strong."

Today, you began adding strength to strength through systematic thought habit development.

Trust the process. Your mental strength is growing with each repetition.

Day 7: Mastering Your Mental Kingdom

"Man is always the master, even in his weaker and most abandoned state; but in his weakness and degradation, he is the foolish master who misgoverns his 'household.' When he begins to reflect upon his condition, and to search diligently for the Law upon which his being is established, he then becomes the wise master, directing his energies with intelligence, and fashioning his thoughts to fruitful issues." **— James Allen.**

Today marks the completion of your first week—seven days of learning to reclaim conscious control over your mind. You've moved from being, in Allen's words, "the foolish master who misgoverns his household" toward becoming "the wise master, directing energies with intelligence."

But mastery isn't achieved through perfect conditions. Real mental mastery shows up when life gets difficult—when your teenager slams the door, when your boss criticizes your work, when unexpected expenses arrive, when your carefully laid plans fall apart.

This is when most people abandon their mental training and revert to old patterns. This is also when true masters prove their development.

Today, you'll learn to maintain your mental sovereignty regardless of external circumstances—to be, as Allen wrote, "the master of thought, the moulder of character, and the maker and shaper of condition, environment, and destiny."

Allen's Vision of Mental Mastery

James Allen understood that mental mastery isn't about eliminating life's challenges or achieving perfect emotional states. It's about maintaining conscious choice in your responses regardless of what happens around you.

"As a being of Power, Intelligence, and Love, and the lord of his own thoughts," Allen wrote, *"man holds the key to every situation, and contains within himself that transforming and regenerative agency by which he may make himself what he wills."*

Allen saw that the "key to every situation" isn't controlling external circumstances, it's maintaining control over your internal responses. External events will always be partially beyond your control. Your thoughts, reactions, and choices always remain within your power.

"Such is the conscious master," Allen explained, *"and man can only thus become by discovering within himself the laws of thought, which discovery is totally a matter of application, self-analysis, and experience."*

This week, you've been making that discovery through application, self-analysis, and experience. Now you'll learn to apply these laws even when circumstances test your resolve.

The Neuroscience of Stress-Tested Mastery

Your brain operates differently under stress than in calm conditions. When faced with threats (real or perceived), your amygdala can hijack your prefrontal cortex—the region responsible for conscious thought control.

This "amygdala hijack" explains why people who seem mentally disciplined in normal circumstances can become reactive, defensive, or destructive when stressed. Their thinking brain gets overwhelmed by their survival brain.

However, research by Dr. Sarah Maddux shows that people who consistently practice mental training develop what she calls "cognitive resilience"—the ability to maintain conscious choice even under pressure.

Brain scans reveal that experienced practitioners show:

- Stronger prefrontal cortex activation during stress
- Faster recovery from emotional disruption
- Better communication between the thinking and feeling brain regions
- More efficient stress response that activates and deactivates appropriately

Dr. Daniel Siegel's research demonstrates that this resilience comes from what he calls "mental integration," the developed ability to observe your mental state while experiencing it, maintaining conscious choice even during intense emotions.

This is exactly what Allen was describing when he wrote about becoming "the conscious master."

The Three Levels of Mental Challenge

Mental mastery develops through progressively handling more difficult circumstances:

Level 1: Calm Conditions

- Daily mental practices when life feels manageable
- Building basic skills of thought awareness and direction
- Establishing new neural pathways through repetition

Level 2: Moderate Stress
- Applying mental skills during everyday frustrations
- Work pressures, minor conflicts, routine setbacks
- Proving that your practices work in real-world conditions

Level 3: Intense Challenges
- Maintaining mental mastery during major difficulties
- Health crises, relationship conflicts, and financial pressure
- Demonstrating true sovereignty over your inner kingdom

Most people develop Level 1 skills but abandon them when facing Level 2 challenges. True masters learn to apply their training at all three levels.

Testing Your Mental Kingdom: Real-World Scenarios

Let's examine how the week's practices apply to common challenging situations:

Scenario 1: Workplace Criticism Your boss publicly criticizes a project you worked hard on.

   Old Pattern: Defensive anger, self-doubt, or rumination **Mastery Response**:
- **Thought Awareness** (Day 1): Notice defensive thoughts arising
- **Garden Tending** (Day 2): Choose growth-oriented thinking over victim mentality
- **Pattern Interrupt** (Day 3): STOP before reacting emotionally
- **RAS Programming** (Day 4): Look for learning opportunities in the feedback
- **Purpose Connection** (Day 5): How does handling this well serve your larger mission?
- **Thought Habit** (Day 6): Practice "This feedback helps me improve."

Scenario 2: Relationship Conflict. Your partner says something that triggers hurt and anger.

   Old Pattern: Attack back, withdraw, or replay grievances

   Mastery Response:
- **Thought Awareness**: Notice hurt feelings and angry thoughts
- **Garden Tending**: Choose understanding over blame
- **Pattern Interrupt**: Pause before speaking from emotion
- **RAS Programming**: Look for signs of your partner's positive intentions
- **Purpose Connection**: How does responding with love serve your relationships?
- **Thought Habit**: Practice "We're both doing our best with what we know."

Scenario 3: Financial Pressure Unexpected expenses strain your budget and trigger money fears.

   Old Pattern: Anxiety spiral, scarcity thinking, or avoidance

Mastery Response:

- **Thought Awareness**: Notice fear-based thoughts about security
- **Garden Tending**: Cultivate solution-focused rather than problem-focused thinking
- **Pattern Interrupt**: Stop catastrophic thinking before it spirals
- **RAS Programming**: Look for resources and opportunities you might have missed
- **Purpose Connection**: How can this challenge help you grow in wisdom?
- **Thought Habit**: Practice "I'm resourceful and capable of handling this."

Today's Practice: The Mental Mastery Integration

Today, you'll integrate all week's practices into a comprehensive system for maintaining mental sovereignty under pressure.

The Mastery Morning Preparation

When: First 15 minutes after waking

What to do:

1. **Mental Kingdom Assessment** (3 minutes):
   - How is your mental state today?
   - What challenges might test your mastery?
   - Which practices will be most important?
2. **Integrated Practice** (7 minutes):
   - **Thought Awareness**: 2 minutes of observing current mental state
   - **Garden Tending**: Plant three positive thoughts for the day
   - **RAS Programming**: Set your attention filters for growth opportunities
   - **Purpose Connection**: Connect today's activities to your larger mission
   - **Habit Activation**: Practice your chosen thought habit 3 times
3. **Mastery Intention** (5 minutes):
   - Visualize yourself maintaining mental mastery during today's challenges
   - See yourself applying your practices when tested
   - Feel the calm confidence of someone who owns their responses
   - Set intention: "I am the master of my thoughts and responses."

The Real-Time Mastery Protocol

When facing any challenging situation:

Step 1: Recognize the Test (10 seconds)

- Think: "This is an opportunity to practice mastery."
- Remind yourself: "I have tools for this."

Step 2: Apply Quick Integration (30 seconds)

- **Awareness**: What am I thinking and feeling right now?
- **Choice**: What response would I be proud of?
- **Purpose**: How does my best self handle this?

Step 3: Choose Conscious Response (Ongoing)

- Act from your training, not your emotions
- Use the situation to strengthen your mental muscles
- Celebrate choosing mastery over reaction

The Evening Mastery Review

Before bed (10 minutes):

1. **Review the day's tests** (5 minutes):
   - When was your mental mastery challenged?
   - How did you respond?
   - What practices served you best?
   - Where can you improve tomorrow?

2. **Celebrate growth** (3 minutes):
   - Acknowledge every moment you choose a conscious response
   - Appreciate your developing mental strength
   - Feel grateful for the opportunity to grow

3. **Set tomorrow's intention** (2 minutes):
   - What aspect of mastery will you focus on tomorrow?
   - How will you prepare for likely challenges?
   - What would increased mastery make possible?

Advanced Mastery Techniques

The Mental Aikido Method: Like martial arts aikido, use the energy of challenging situations for your growth:

- Criticism becomes information for improvement
- Conflict becomes an opportunity for understanding
- Setbacks become data for better strategies
- Pressure becomes training for resilience

The Observer Self: Develop the part of you that can watch your experiences without being overwhelmed:

- "I notice I'm feeling angry right now."
- "I see my mind creating worry stories."
- "I observe my impulse to react defensively."

- This observer self maintains choice even during intense emotions

The Mastery Question: In any challenging moment, ask: "What would someone who has mastered their mind do in this situation?" Let your highest vision of yourself guide your response.

Common Mastery Challenges and Solutions

"I forget to use my practices when I'm stressed."

- Practice more in calm moments to build stronger neural pathways
- Create environmental reminders for stressful situations
- Use physical cues (deep breath, hand on heart) to trigger mental training

"I use the tools but still feel overwhelmed sometimes."

- Mastery doesn't mean never feeling difficult emotions
- It means maintaining a conscious choice while feeling them
- Allow emotions while choosing wise responses

"I'm disappointed when I revert to old patterns."

- Every master faces setbacks—they're part of the growth process
- Focus on recovery speed rather than perfect consistency
- Each time you catch yourself and redirect, you're strengthening mastery

Your Week's Transformation

Look at how far you've traveled in seven days:

Day 1: You learned you're not a victim of your thoughts—you're their observer and director

Day 2: You discovered you can consciously cultivate positive mental states

Day 3: You developed the ability to interrupt destructive patterns and choose better responses

Day 4: You learned to program your brain's attention system for growth and opportunity

Day 5: You connected your thinking to a meaningful purpose and direction

Day 6: You began installing beneficial thought habits that run automatically

Day 7: You integrated these skills into a comprehensive mastery system

You've moved from unconscious thinking to conscious mental leadership. You've become, in Allen's words, "the wise master, directing energies with intelligence."

Preparing for Week Two

Next week, you'll build on this mental foundation to develop emotional mastery, learning to work with your feelings as skillfully as you now work with your thoughts.

But tonight, simply appreciate what you've accomplished. You've reclaimed sovereignty over your mental kingdom. You've proven that you can think consciously, even when circumstances invite unconsciousness.

Remember Allen's Ultimate Vision

"Man holds the key to every situation, and contains within himself that transforming and regenerative agency by which he may make himself what he wills."

This week, you found that key. You discovered the transforming and regenerative agency within yourself.

You are the master of your thoughts. You are the director of your mental energy. You are the conscious creator of your inner experience.

Tomorrow, you'll learn to become the master of your emotions as well.

Rest tonight in the knowledge that your mental kingdom is no longer running wild. You've become its wise and conscious ruler.

~End of Part One: Reclaim Your Mind~

Part One Summary: You've now learned the foundational skills of conscious thinking, from basic thought awareness through advanced mental mastery. These seven days have established your ability to observe, direct, and consciously choose your thoughts rather than being controlled by them. You've built the mental foundation that makes emotional mastery possible.

In Part Two, you'll discover how thoughts and emotions work together and how to develop the emotional intelligence that transforms reactive patterns into conscious responses.

PART TWO

Days 8-14

"The body is the servant of the mind. It obeys the operations of the mind, whether they be deliberately chosen or automatically expressed." **— James Allen.**

Day 8: Emotions Follow Thoughts

"At the bidding of unlawful thoughts the body sinks rapidly into disease and decay; at the command of glad and beautiful thoughts it becomes clothed with youthfulness and beauty." — James Allen.

Rachel was drowning in anxiety, and she couldn't understand why.

Her life looked good on paper—successful career, loving family, comfortable home. But every morning, she woke up with a knot in her stomach. Throughout the day, waves of worry would crash over her without warning. By evening, she was exhausted from fighting feelings that seemed to have no source.

"I have nothing to be anxious about," Rachel would tell herself. "Why can't I just stop feeling this way?"

Rachel was trying to fix her emotions directly, like adjusting the temperature on a thermostat while ignoring the furnace. She didn't realize that her anxious feelings weren't the problem—they were the symptom. The real source was a stream of unconscious worried thoughts that had been running in the background of her mind for months.

When Rachel learned that emotions follow thoughts—not the other way around—everything changed. Instead of fighting her feelings, she began examining the thoughts that were creating them.

What she discovered surprised her: her mind had been generating dozens of "what if" scenarios daily, each one triggering a small stress response. Her anxiety wasn't mysterious or random—it was the predictable result of anxious thinking.

Allen's Revolutionary Insight About The Mind-Body Connection

James Allen understood something that wouldn't be scientifically proven until decades later: emotions aren't random feelings that happen to you—they're the direct result of your thought patterns.

"Disease and health, like circumstances, are rooted in thought," **Allen wrote.** *"Sickly thoughts will express themselves through a sickly body. Thoughts of fear have been known to kill a man as speedily as a bullet, and they are continually killing thousands of people just as surely, though less rapidly."*

Allen saw that the body responds to the mind's directives with remarkable precision. When you think anxious thoughts, your body produces anxiety. When you think angry thoughts, your body generates anger. When you think peaceful thoughts, your body creates calm.

"Strong, pure, and happy thoughts build up the body in vigour and grace. The body is a delicate and plastic instrument, which responds readily to the thoughts by which it is impressed."

This wasn't metaphorical language for Allen; he meant it literally. Your thoughts are constantly sending chemical and electrical signals throughout your body, creating the physical sensations you experience as emotions.

The Modern Science of Thought-Emotion Connection

Contemporary neuroscience has validated Allen's insight with remarkable precision. We now understand exactly how thoughts create emotions through measurable biological processes:

The Neurochemical Cascade: When you think a thought, your brain immediately releases corresponding neurotransmitters and hormones:

- Worried thoughts trigger cortisol and adrenaline (stress response)
- Angry thoughts release norepinephrine (fight response)
- Sad thoughts affect serotonin and dopamine (mood regulation)
- Happy thoughts increase endorphins and oxytocin (pleasure response)

The Embodied Cognition Effect: Dr. Antonio Damasio's research shows that thoughts and emotions aren't separate systems—they're integrated. Your brain creates emotions by predicting what your body should feel based on your thoughts, then makes those predictions come true through hormonal and nervous system changes.

The Cognitive-Emotional Loop: Dr. Aaron Beck's research reveals that thoughts and emotions form feedback loops:

1. Thought triggers emotion
2. Emotion reinforces similar thoughts
3. More similar thoughts intensify emotion
4. Stronger emotions make those thoughts feel more "true."

The Interpretation Effect: Dr. Lisa Feldman Barrett's studies show that the same physical sensations can be interpreted as different emotions based on your thoughts. Increased heart rate can feel like excitement or anxiety, depending on your mental interpretation.

Dr. Candace Pert's groundbreaking research on "molecules of emotion" proved that emotional states are literally chemical states. Your thoughts direct the production of peptides and neurotransmitters that create the physical experience of feelings.

Rachel's anxiety made perfect sense once she understood this system. Her unconscious worried thoughts were continuously triggering her body's stress response, creating the physical sensation of anxiety—increased heart rate, muscle tension, and shallow breathing, which then made her think something must be wrong, creating more worried thoughts.

Common Thought-Emotion Patterns

Understanding how specific thought patterns create specific emotional states gives you tremendous power to influence how you feel:

Anxiety-Producing Thoughts:

- "What if something goes wrong?"
- "I can't handle this."
- "Something bad is about to happen."
- "I'm not prepared enough." Result: Body activates stress response—increased heart rate, muscle tension, shallow breathing

Depression-Inducing Thoughts:

- "Nothing ever works out for me."
- "I'm not good enough."
- "What's the point of trying?"
- "Nothing will change." Result: Body reduces energy production—low motivation, fatigue, heaviness

Anger-Generating Thoughts:

- "This isn't fair."
- "They're doing this on purpose."
- "I shouldn't have to deal with this."
- "They don't respect me." Result: Body prepares for conflict—increased blood pressure, muscle tension, heat

Joy-Creating Thoughts:

- "I'm grateful for this."
- "I'm learning and growing."
- "Good things are possible."
- "I appreciate this moment." **Result**: Body releases pleasure chemicals—relaxation, energy, warmth

Rachel's Thought-Emotion Discovery Process

When Rachel began tracking her thoughts-to-emotions patterns, she was amazed at what she discovered:

Morning anxiety came from immediately thinking about everything that could go wrong that day

Work stress intensified when she thought "I'm behind on everything" repeatedly

Evening worry spiked when she reviewed the day, focusing on what went wrong

Bedtime anxiety arose from thinking about tomorrow's potential problems

Rachel realized she'd been unconsciously training her body to feel anxious through her thought patterns. But this also meant she could train it to feel different emotions through different thoughts.

She began experimenting with intentional thought-emotion creation:
- When feeling anxious, she'd think: "I can handle whatever comes up."
- When feeling overwhelmed, she'd think: "I'll focus on one thing at a time."
- When feeling worried, she'd think: "Most of what I worry about never happens."

Within two weeks, Rachel's baseline anxiety had significantly decreased. "It's like I learned I had control over my emotional thermostat," she said. "I don't have to accept whatever emotions show up—I can consciously influence them through my thoughts."

Today's Practice: The Thought-Emotion Tracking System

Today, you'll develop conscious awareness of how your thoughts create your emotional experiences, giving you the power to influence both.

The Emotion Origins Investigation

Throughout the day, when you notice any strong emotion (positive or negative):

Step 1: Pause and Identify (30 seconds)
- What emotion am I feeling right now?
- Where do I feel it in my body?
- How intense is it on a scale of 1-10?

Step 2: Trace Back to Thought (1 minute)
- What was I thinking just before this emotion arose?
- What thoughts are present with this feeling?

- What story is my mind telling about the situation?

Step 3: Recognize the Connection (30 seconds)
- How might this thought have created this emotion?
- Does this make sense based on how the mind-body system works?
- Have I felt this way before when thinking similar thoughts?

Step 4: Document the Pattern (Write it down)
- Thought: "_____"
- Emotion: "_____"
- Body sensation: "_____"
- Pattern recognition: "_____"

The Conscious Emotion Creation Exercise

Evening practice (10 minutes):

Part 1: Emotion Generation (5 minutes) Practice consciously creating different emotional states through focused thinking:

1. **Generate Calm** (1 minute):
   - Think: "I am safe and peaceful right now."
   - Think: "I can breathe deeply and relax."
   - Notice how your body responds
2. **Generate Gratitude** (1 minute):
   - Think about someone you appreciate
   - Think: "I'm fortunate to have this in my life."
   - Feel the warmth in your chest
3. **Generate Confidence** (1 minute):
   - Think about a skill you've developed
   - Think: "I'm capable of learning and growing."
   - Notice the energy shift in your body
4. **Generate Compassion** (1 minute):
   - Think about someone struggling
   - Think: "Everyone is doing their best with what they know."
   - Feel the softness around your heart
5. **Generate Excitement** (1 minute):
   - Think about a positive future possibility
   - Think: "Good things are coming."
   - Notice the energy increase

Part 2: Pattern Analysis (5 minutes) Review your day's emotion-tracking:

- Which thought patterns created your most difficult emotions?
- Which thought patterns created your best emotions?
- What do you notice about the speed of the thought-emotion connection?
- How might you consciously use this knowledge tomorrow?

Advanced Thought-Emotion Techniques

The Emotion Prescription Method: When you want to feel a specific way, prescribe yourself the corresponding thoughts:

Want to feel more confident?
- "I've overcome challenges before."
- "I have valuable skills and abilities."
- "I can figure out whatever I need to learn."

Want to feel more peaceful?
- "This moment is exactly as it should be."
- "I don't need to control everything."
- "I can handle whatever arises with grace."

Want to feel more energized?
- "I'm excited about today's possibilities."
- "I have energy for what matters most."
- "Good things happen when I show up fully."

The Emotional Reframe Technique: Transform difficult emotions by changing the thoughts that create them:

Instead of: "This is terrible" (creates despair). *Try*: "This is challenging and I'm growing stronger" (creates resilience)

Instead of: "I can't handle this" (creates anxiety). *Try*: "I'm learning ..to handle this" (creates determination)

Instead of: "Nothing ever works out" (creates hopelessness). *Try*: "Some things work out, some don't, and that's normal" (creates acceptance)

Understanding Emotional Lag Time

Important: There's often a slight delay between changing thoughts and feeling emotional shifts. This happens because:

1. **Neurochemical clearing**: Stress hormones take time to metabolize
2. **Neural pathway switching**: Your brain needs moments to shift networks

521

3. **Body integration**: Physical sensations take time to change

Don't expect instant emotional transformation. Be patient as your body catches up to your new thought patterns.

The Difference Between Suppression and Direction

Emotional Suppression (doesn't work):

- Trying to force emotions away
- Telling yourself "don't feel this"
- Fighting or judging your feelings

Emotional Direction (does work):

- Acknowledging emotions while choosing helpful thoughts
- Understanding emotions as information while maintaining choice
- Gently guiding your mind toward more beneficial patterns

Building on Week One

Your first week's mental training now supports emotional mastery:

- **Thought awareness** helps you catch emotion-creating thoughts
- **Mental cultivation** lets you plant emotion-supporting thoughts
- **Pattern interruption** stops negative thought-emotion cycles
- **RAS programming** helps you notice emotion-supporting evidence
- **Purposeful thinking** creates meaningful, positive emotions
- **Thought habits** automatically generate beneficial feelings

What to Expect from Thought-Emotion Work

Increased awareness: You'll become much more conscious of the thought-emotion connection

Faster recognition: You'll catch unhelpful thought patterns before they create intense emotions

Greater choice: You'll realize you have more influence over your feelings than you thought

Improved emotional stability: Your emotional ups and downs will become less extreme

Enhanced well-being: You'll spend more time in positive emotional states

Tomorrow's Preview

Tomorrow, you'll learn to read your emotions like instruments on a dashboard—understanding what each feeling is trying to tell you and how to respond to that information wisely.

Remember Allen's Promise

"Change of diet will not help a man who will not change his thoughts. When a man makes his thoughts pure, he no longer desires impure food. Clean thoughts make clean habits."

Today, you discovered that changing your emotional diet starts with changing your thought diet. When you make your thoughts healthier, your emotions naturally become healthier too.

Your thoughts are the master, your emotions are the servant. Now you know how to give better instructions.

Day 9: Your Emotional Dashboard

*"If you would protect your body, guard your mind. If you would renew your body, beautify your mind. Thoughts of malice, envy, disappointment, despondency, rob the body of its health and grace." — **James Allen.***

Tom used to think emotions were inconvenient interruptions to rational thinking.

As an engineer, he prided himself on logic and objectivity. When feelings arose—frustration at work, sadness about his father's illness, anxiety about his teenage daughter's choices—Tom would push them down and try to "think his way through" problems.

"Emotions just cloud judgment," Tom would say. "I need to stay focused on facts and solutions."

But Tom's strategy was backfiring. By ignoring his emotional signals, he was missing crucial information about his relationships, health, and decision-making. His wife felt disconnected from him. His stress levels were rising. His work suffered because he couldn't read the interpersonal dynamics that drive most workplace problems.

When Tom learned to treat emotions like the sophisticated information system they are—rather than problems to be solved—his entire approach to life improved.

He discovered that emotions aren't obstacles to good thinking. They're essential data for wise living.

Allen's Understanding of Emotional Information

James Allen understood that emotions serve as messengers bringing valuable information about your inner state and external circumstances. The problem isn't having emotions—it's misunderstanding their purpose.

Allen wrote about the connection between emotional states and life outcomes: *"A sour face does not come by chance; it is made by sour thoughts. Wrinkles that mar are drawn by folly, passion, and pride."*

But Allen also recognized that emotions could serve wisdom: *"There is no physician like cheerful thought for dissipating the ills of the body; there is no comforter to compare with goodwill for dispersing the shadows of grief and sorrow."*

Allen saw that emotions weren't random feelings to be endured or suppressed, but responses to your thought patterns that could guide you toward better thinking and living. When you understand what your emotions are trying to tell you, you can use that information to make wiser choices.

The Science of Emotional Intelligence

Modern research reveals that emotions are sophisticated information-processing systems that evolved to help humans survive and thrive:

Emotional Data Processing: Dr. Antonio Damasio's research shows that emotions provide rapid assessments of situations faster than conscious thought. They signal whether something is safe or threatening, beneficial or harmful, aligned with your values or contradictory to them.

Decision-Making Enhancement: Studies by Dr. Daniel Kahneman reveal that people with emotional processing damage make poor decisions even when their logical reasoning is intact. Emotions provide crucial data that pure logic cannot.

Social Navigation: Dr. Paul Ekman's research demonstrates that emotions help you read social situations, understand others' intentions, and respond appropriately to complex interpersonal dynamics.

Body-Mind Communication: Dr. Candace Pert's work shows that emotions are how your body communicates with your mind about physical needs, energy levels, health status, and environmental responses.

Motivational Guidance: Research by Dr. Barbara Fredrickson reveals that emotions aren't just reactions—they're action signals that guide you toward beneficial behaviors and away from harmful ones.

Each emotion carries specific information:

Your Emotional Dashboard: What Each Feeling Tells You
Anger = Boundary Alert
- **Message**: "Something important to me is being violated or blocked."
- **Information**: Your values, needs, or goals are being compromised
- **Wise Response**: Identify what boundary needs protection and address it constructively

Fear = Safety Scanner

- **Message**: "Potential threat detected—prepare or get more information."
- **Information**: You may need to prepare, learn, or seek support
- **Wise Response**: Assess actual risk and take appropriate protective action

Sadness = Loss Processor

- **Message**: "Something valuable has been lost or changed."
- **Information**: You need time to grieve, adjust, or seek comfort
- **Wise Response**: Allow the processing time and seek appropriate support

Joy = Alignment Indicator

- **Message**: "This experience aligns with your values and wellbeing."
- **Information**: You're on a beneficial path worth continuing
- **Wise Response**: Savor the experience and note what created it

Anxiety = Preparation Signal

- **Message**: "Future uncertainty requires attention and planning."
- **Information**: You need more information, preparation, or support systems
- **Wise Response**: Break down the challenge and take concrete preparatory steps

Guilt = Values Calibrator

- **Message**: "Your actions don't align with your stated values."
- **Information**: You need to either change behavior or clarify values
- **Wise Response**: Make amends if needed and realign actions with values

Shame = Identity Alarm

- **Message**: "Core sense of self feels threatened or damaged."
- **Information**: You may need self-compassion or to challenge self-critical beliefs
- **Wise Response**: Separate actions from identity and practice self-compassion

Envy = Desire Revealer

- **Message**: "Something you want is possiblesomeone else has it"
- **Information**: Clarifies what you value and want to pursue
- **Wise Response**: Use the information to guide your own growth and choices

Tom's Emotional Dashboard Training

When Tom began treating emotions as information rather than interruptions, his decision-making improved dramatically:

At work: Instead of pushing through frustration, Tom recognized it as a signal that his boundaries were being crossed. He had productive conversations with colleagues about workload and expectations.

With family: Instead of dismissing anxiety about his daughter, Tom realized it was prompting him to have important conversations about safety and values. His worry contained wisdom about parenting.

About health: Instead of ignoring sadness about his father's illness, Tom recognized it as information about the importance of their relationship. He scheduled regular visits and meaningful conversations.

"It's like I upgraded from a car with no gauges to one with a full dashboard," Tom said. "I'm making much better decisions because I have better information about what's really happening."

Today's Practice: Reading Your Emotional Dashboard
Today, you'll learn to interpret your emotions as information rather than experiencing them as problems to solve.

The Emotional Check-In System

Set three alarms throughout your day (10 AM, 2 PM, 6 PM). When each alarm sounds:

Step 1: Emotion Identification (1 minute)
- What emotion(s) am I feeling right now?
- Where do I feel it in my body?
- What's the intensity level (1-10)?

Step 2: Information Extraction (2 minutes) Ask your emotion: "What are you trying to tell me?"
- **If anxious**: What am I uncertain about that needs attention?
- **If angry**: What boundary is being crossed that I need to protect?
- **If sad**: What loss am I processing that needs acknowledgment?
- **If excited**: What alignment am I experiencing that I should note?
- **If frustrated**: What obstacle is blocking something important to me?
- **If peaceful**: What conditions created this state that I should maintain?

Step 3: Wise Response Planning (1 minute)
- What action does this emotional information suggest?
- How can I honor this information while choosing my response consciously?
- What would be the wisest way to work with this feeling?

The Evening Emotional Dashboard Review

Before bed (10 minutes):

Part 1: Daily Emotional Weather Report (5 minutes) Review your day's emotional patterns:

- What were your primary emotions today?
- What information were they providing?
- Which emotions did you honor appropriately?
- Which emotions did you dismiss or fight against?

Part 2: Emotional Learning Integration (5 minutes) Ask yourself:

- What did my emotions teach me about my needs today?
- What did they reveal about my values and priorities?
- How did listening to emotional information improve, or could it have improved my decisions?
- What emotional patterns do I notice that might guide tomorrow's choices?

Advanced Emotional Dashboard Techniques

The Emotion Interview Process: When experiencing a strong emotion, have an internal conversation:

You: "Hello [emotion name]. I notice you're here. What do you need me to know?"

Emotion: [Listen for the answer that arises]

You: "What would help resolve this concern?"

Emotion: [Notice what response emerges]

You: "Thank you for this information. I'll consider how to respond wisely."

The Body Scan for Emotional Data: Your body often contains emotional information before your mind recognizes it:

1. **Head and neck**: Tension may indicate stress or mental overload
2. **Shoulders**: Carrying burdens or responsibilities
3. **Chest**: Heart emotions—love, grief, anxiety, excitement
4. **Stomach**: Gut feelings about situations or decisions
5. **Arms and hands**: Impulses toward action—reaching, pushing away, holding
6. **Legs and feet**: Readiness to move toward something or away from it

The Emotional Triangulation Method: When confused about what you're feeling, ask three questions:

- "What does my mind think about this situation?"
- "What does my body feel about this situation?"
- "What does my heart want in this situation?"

The intersection of these three perspectives often reveals the core emotional message.

Common Emotional Dashboard Reading Mistakes

Mistake 1: Judging emotions as "good" or "bad"

- All emotions carry useful information
- "Negative" emotions often contain the most important warnings
- "Positive" emotions help you know what to continue

Mistake 2: Trying to fix emotions immediately

- Emotions need to be heard before they can be resolved
- Rushing to solutions skips valuable information-gathering
- Some emotions (like grief) need time to complete their process

Mistake 3: Assuming emotions are facts about external reality

- Emotions are facts about your internal response to reality
- They reveal your needs, values, and interpretations
- They may or may not accurately reflect external circumstances

Mistake 4: Ignoring low-level emotional signals

- Subtle emotions often contain important early warnings
- Addressing small emotional signals prevents larger emotional crises
- Chronic low-level emotions (like mild resentment) reveal ongoing issues

Working With Difficult Emotional Information

Sometimes your emotional dashboard reveals uncomfortable truths:

If emotions reveal unmet needs:

- Acknowledge the need without immediately demanding it be met
- Consider healthy ways to address the need
- Communicate needs clearly to the relevant people

If emotions reveal value conflicts:

- Examine whether your actions align with your stated values
- Consider whether your values need updating or your actions need changing
- Seek guidance from trusted advisors if conflicted

If emotions reveal fears about the future:

- Distinguish between realistic concerns and anxiety-driven speculation
- Take practical steps to address legitimate concerns
- Develop comfort with uncertainty for things beyond your control

The Relationship Between Thoughts and Emotional Information

Yesterday, you learned that thoughts create emotions. Today, you're learning that emotions provide information that can guide thoughts:

Thought → Emotion Cycle:

- Your thoughts trigger emotional responses
- Emotions provide feedback about those thoughts
- This feedback can guide you toward better thinking

Example:

- Thought: "I'll never be successful."
- Emotion: Despair and hopelessness
- Information: This thought pattern isn't serving your well-being
- Better thought: "I'm learning skills that increase my chances of success."

Building Emotional Intelligence Through Dashboard Reading

Regular emotional dashboard reading develops:

Self-Awareness: Understanding your emotional patterns and triggers

Self-Management: Using emotional information to guide wise responses

Social Awareness: Better reading of others' emotional states

Relationship Management: More skillful navigation of interpersonal dynamics

Tomorrow's Preview

Tomorrow, you'll learn the crucial skill of creating space between emotional triggers and your responses—transforming automatic reactions into conscious choices.

Remember Allen's Insight

"As you cannot have a sweet and wholesome abode unless you admit the air and sunshine freely into your rooms, so a strong body and a bright, happy, or serene countenance can only result from the free admittance into the mind of thoughts of joy and goodwill and serenity."

Today, you learned to admit emotional information freely into your awareness, using it to create a stronger, brighter, more serene approach to living.

Your emotions aren't problems to solve; they're instruments providing essential data for wise living.

Listen to what they're telling you.

Day 10: From Reaction to Response

"The calm man, having learned how to govern himself, knows how to adapt himself to others; and they, in turn, reverence his spiritual strength, and feel that they can learn of him and rely upon him." — James Allen.

Sarah's morning had been perfect until her teenager rolled her eyes.

It was such a small gesture—barely a flicker of expression—but it hit Sarah like a lightning bolt. Instantly, she was furious. Before she could think, words were pouring out: lectures about respect, reminders of everything she'd sacrificed, threats about privileges being revoked.

Later, sitting in her car outside the office, Sarah felt terrible. "I don't know what happens to me," she thought. "One eye roll and I become this person I don't even recognize. I love my daughter, but when she does certain things, it's like something else takes over."

That "something else" was Sarah's automatic reaction system—millions of years of evolutionary wiring designed to respond to threats instantly, without conscious thought. In prehistoric times, this system saved lives. In modern family dynamics, it can often damage relationships.

Sarah's eye-roll reaction wasn't really about disrespect. It was about an old trigger that interpreted any sign of dismissal as a threat requiring immediate defensive action. Until Sarah learned to create space between trigger and response, she would continue reacting from ancient programming rather than present wisdom.

Allen's Vision of Conscious Response

James Allen understood that the difference between wise and unwise people isn't the absence of challenging emotions or difficult circumstances—it's the ability to choose responses rather than being controlled by automatic reactions.

"Calmness of mind is one of the beautiful jewels of wisdom. It is the result of long and patient effort in self-control," Allen wrote. *"Its presence is an indication of ripened experience, and of a more than ordinary knowledge of the laws and operations of thought."*

Allen saw that developing the ability to pause between stimulus and response was perhaps the most important skill a person could develop. In that pause lives your power to choose wisdom over reactivity, love over fear, growth over defense.

"The more tranquil a man becomes, the greater is his success, his influence, his power for good. Even the ordinary trader will find his business prosperity increase as he develops a greater self-control and equanimity."

Allen recognized that this skill didn't just improve personal wellbeing—it enhanced every area of life, from relationships to professional success.

The Neuroscience of Reaction vs. Response

Modern brain science reveals exactly what happens during the moments between trigger and action, and how you can gain conscious control over this process:

The Amygdala Hijack: Dr. Daniel Goleman's research shows that when your brain perceives a threat (real or imagined), your amygdala can "hijack" your entire nervous system in 1/20th of a second. This triggers:

- Stress hormone release (cortisol, adrenaline)
- Reduced blood flow to the prefrontal cortex (your thinking brain)
- Activated fight-or-flight responses
- Automatic defensive behaviors

The Prefrontal Cortex Recovery: Your thinking brain (prefrontal cortex) can regain control, but it takes time:

- 6 seconds for stress hormones to begin metabolizing
- 20 seconds for rational thinking to come back online
- 90 seconds for the full emotional chemical cycle to complete

The Neuroplasticity Factor: Dr. Sara Lazar's research demonstrates that regular practice of response choice strengthens neural pathways between your emotional brain and thinking brain, making conscious responses easier over time.

The Window of Tolerance: Dr. Dan Siegel's work reveals that everyone has a "window of tolerance"—the zone where you can experience emotions without being overwhelmed. Stress narrows this window; practice expands it.

The Anatomy of Triggers

Understanding what triggers automatic reactions helps you recognize them faster:

Personal History Triggers: Situations that remind your unconscious mind of past hurts, failures, or threats

- Criticism (reminds me of childhood shame)
- Dismissal (reminds me of feeling unimportant)

- Conflict (reminds me of family volatility)
- Uncertainty (reminds me of past lack of control)

Identity Triggers: Challenges to how you see yourself or want to be seen

- Competence questioned (for those who value being capable)
- Integrity challenged (for those who value being honest)
- Care criticized (for those who value being helpful)
- Control threatened (for those who value being organized)

Values Triggers: Situations that violate your deeply held principles

- Injustice (if you value fairness)
- Waste (if you value efficiency)
- Dishonesty (if you value truth)
- Disrespect (if you value dignity)

Stress Accumulation Triggers: When general stress levels are high, smaller irritations trigger bigger reactions than they normally would.

Sarah's Response Training Journey

When Sarah learned about the trigger-response gap, she realized her eye-roll reaction had nothing to do with her daughter's current behavior and everything to do with her own unhealed trigger around feeling dismissed.

Sarah began practicing response choice:

Step 1: Trigger Recognition. Sarah learned to recognize the physical sensation of being triggered: heat in her face, tension in her shoulders, the urge to speak immediately.

Step 2: The Pause Practice. When she felt triggered, Sarah practiced taking three deep breaths before speaking. "Just three breaths," she told herself. "I can handle three breaths."

Step 3: Response Choice. During those three breaths, Sarah would ask: "What response would I be proud of tomorrow?" This connected her to her values as a mother rather than her defensive programming.

Step 4: Conscious Action. Sarah would respond from her values: "I notice you seem frustrated. Do you want to talk about what's going on?"

The transformation was remarkable. Within two months, Sarah's relationship with her daughter had completely shifted. Her teenager later told her: "Mom, you're so much easier to talk to now. You don't immediately get upset about everything."

Today's Practice: The Response Choice Training System

Today, you'll learn to create conscious space between triggers and reactions, transforming automatic responses into chosen actions.

The STOP Technique for Trigger Moments

When you notice a strong emotional reaction arising:

S - STOP

- Physically pause whatever you're about to do or say
- If possible, excuse yourself: "Give me just a moment."
- This interrupts the automatic reaction sequence

T - TAKE THREE BREATHS

- Inhale slowly for 4 counts
- Hold for 4 counts
- Exhale slowly for 6 counts
- Repeat three times
- This activates your parasympathetic nervous system (calm response)

O - OBSERVE Ask yourself three questions:

- "What am I feeling in my body right now?"
- "What story is my mind telling about this situation?"
- "What old pattern might be getting triggered?"

P - PROCEED WITH PURPOSE Ask yourself:

- "What response would align with my values?"
- "How would my best self handle this?"
- "What would I want to model for someone watching?"
- "What response would I be proud of tomorrow?"

Then choose your action from this centered place.

The Daily Response Training Protocol

Morning Preparation (5 minutes):

1. **Identify likely triggers** for the day:
   - What situations might challenge your calm?
   - Which people or circumstances tend to trigger you?
   - What old patterns might get activated?

2. **Set response intentions**:
   - How do you want to show up in challenging moments?
   - What values do you want to guide your responses?

- What would a "successful" response choice look like today?
3. **Mental rehearsal**:
   - Visualize yourself using STOP in a challenging situation
   - See yourself choosing a response over a reaction
   - Feel the calm confidence of conscious choice

Evening Response Review (5 minutes):

1. **Assess the day's responses**:
   - When were you triggered today?
   - How did you respond?
   - Which responses made you proud?
   - Where could you have chosen differently?
2. **Extract learning**:
   - What patterns do you notice?
   - Which triggers are strongest for you?
   - What helps you remember to pause?
   - How is your response choice improving?
3. **Celebrate growth**:
   - Acknowledge every moment you choose a response over a reaction
   - Appreciate your developing emotional maturity
   - Feel grateful for the opportunity to grow

Advanced Response Choice Techniques

The 6-Second Rule: Stress hormones begin metabolizing after 6 seconds. If you can avoid reacting for 6 seconds, your rational brain starts coming back online. Practice counting slowly: "One Mississippi, two Mississippi..." through six.

The Reframe Response: During your pause, try reframing the trigger:
   - "This person is having a difficult day" (instead of "They're attacking me")
   - "This is an opportunity to practice patience" (instead of "This is unfair")
   - "They're doing their best with what they know" (instead of "They're being unreasonable")

The Future Self Check: Ask: "How will I feel about this response in one hour? Tomorrow? Next year?" This connects you to a longer-term perspective rather than immediate emotional impulse.

The Loving Observer Practice: Imagine watching this interaction from the perspective of someone who loves everyone involved. What response would that loving observer suggest?

The Values Compass: Before responding, quickly identify your core value in this situation:

- Kindness? Honesty? Growth? Fairness? Love?
- Let that value guide your response choice

Working With Intense Triggers

For very strong triggers that feel overwhelming:

The Physical Reset:

- Splash cold water on your face or wrists
- Take a brief walk, even just around the room
- Do 10 jumping jacks or push-ups
- This helps reset your nervous system

The Time-Out Strategy: "I need a few minutes to think about this. Can we continue this conversation in 10 minutes?" This isn't avoidance—it's responsible self-management.

The Journal Dump: Write out all your reactive thoughts before responding:

- "I'm feeling angry because..."
- "The story I'm telling myself is..."
- "What I want to say is..." This helps discharge emotional intensity before choosing your actual response.

Common Response Choice Challenges

"I forget to pause when I'm triggered."

- Practice STOP during calm moments to build the neural pathway
- Ask trusted people to gently remind you: "Take a breath."
- Use physical reminders (ring, bracelet) to cue conscious breathing

"Three breaths don't feel like enough."

- Take as much time as you need—three breaths is just the minimum
- Excuse yourself for longer breaks when needed
- Remember: responding late is better than reacting poorly

"I pause, but still react automatically."

- This is normal in early practice—the pause is still valuable
- Each pause strengthens your response choice muscles
- Focus on recovery speed: how quickly can you shift to conscious choice?

"Other people think I'm being weird or slow."

- Most people appreciate thoughtful responses over quick reactions
- Explain: "I want to give you a thoughtful response."
- Model conscious choice—others often adopt the practice

The Ripple Effects of Response Choice

When you consistently choose responses over reactions:

Personal Benefits:

- Reduced stress and anxiety
- Improved self-respect and confidence
- Better decision-making ability
- Increased emotional stability

Relationship Benefits:

- Deeper trust and connection
- Less conflict and drama
- Better modeling for children and colleagues
- More respect from others

Professional Benefits:

- Enhanced leadership presence
- Better team dynamics
- Improved conflict resolution
- Greater influence and respect

Building on Your Emotional Foundation

You've now learned:

- **Day 8**: How thoughts create emotions
- **Day 9**: How to read emotions as information
- **Day 10**: How to choose responses over reactions

You're developing what Allen called "self-control" and "equanimity"—the ability to remain centered and choose wisely regardless of circumstances.

Tomorrow's Preview

Tomorrow, you'll discover how the stories you tell yourself about situations create your emotional experiences, and how changing those stories transforms your entire relationship with challenging circumstances.

Remember Allen's Promise

"Tempest-tossed souls, wherever ye may be, under whatsoever conditions ye may live, know this: in the ocean of life the isles of Blessedness are smiling, and the sunny shore of your ideal awaits your coming. Keep your hand firmly upon the helm of thought."

Today, you learned to keep your hand firmly upon the helm of response. In the space between trigger and action, you found your power to choose wisdom over reactivity.

You are becoming the calm person Allen described—someone others can learn from and rely upon.

Day 11: The Stories You Tell Yourself

"Suffering is always the effect of wrong thought in some direction. It is an indication that the individual is out of harmony with himself, with the Law of his being." — James Allen.

Mark's marriage was falling apart, and he knew exactly why: his wife didn't appreciate him.

He had a detailed story to support this conclusion. She didn't thank him for working long hours to provide for the family. She didn't notice when he did the housework. She criticized his parenting while taking his financial support for granted. Clearly, she was selfish and ungrateful.

Mark's story was so compelling that his friends agreed with him. His family took his side. Even his therapist initially seemed to validate his perspective. The story felt completely true.

But Mark's story was destroying his marriage and his happiness.

When Mark learned that his suffering came not from his circumstances but from the story he was telling himself about those circumstances, everything changed. He discovered that the same factual events could be interpreted through entirely different narratives— narratives that created completely different emotional experiences.

Mark's wife wasn't the problem. Mark's story about his wife was the problem.

Allen's Insight About Mental Storytelling

James Allen understood that humans don't respond to events themselves; they respond to their interpretations of events. The stories you tell yourself about what happens create your emotional experience more than the actual occurrences.

"Circumstance does not make the man; it reveals him to himself," Allen wrote. *"No such conditions can exist as descending into vice and its attendant sufferings apart from vicious inclinations, or ascending into virtue and its pure happiness without the continued cultivation of virtuous aspirations."*

Allen saw that people create their own suffering not through their circumstances but through their mental responses to circumstances. Two people can face identical situations and have completely different experiences based entirely on how they interpret what's happening.

"Men do not attract that which they want, but that which they are," **Allen observed.**

This includes attracting experiences that match their dominant mental stories. If you consistently tell yourself stories of victimhood, you'll notice more evidence of victimization. If you tell stories of growth and possibility, you'll discover more evidence of opportunity.

Allen recognized that suffering wasn't caused by external events but by "wrong thought"— mental stories that create discord between your inner peace and outer experience.

The Science of Narrative Psychology

Modern research confirms Allen's insight that stories, not events, create emotional experiences:

Narrative Identity Theory: Dr. Dan McAdams' research shows that people literally construct their identities through the stories they tell about their experiences. These stories determine not just how you feel about your past, but how you approach your future.

Cognitive Reframing Studies: Research by Dr. Kevin Ochsner demonstrates that changing how you interpret an emotional situation changes your brain's response to it. The same event can trigger stress or growth, depending entirely on your narrative framework.

Post-Traumatic Growth Research: Dr. Richard Tedeschi's studies reveal that people who develop empowering stories about difficult experiences often emerge stronger, wiser, and more resilient than they were before the trauma. The facts don't change—the story does.

Meaning-Making Studies: Dr. Crystal Park's research shows that people who find meaning in difficult experiences recover faster and experience less ongoing distress than those who maintain victim narratives about the same events.

Therapeutic Storytelling: Narrative therapy research by Dr. Michael White demonstrates that helping people rewrite their personal stories is one of the most effective approaches to healing psychological distress.

Common Disempowering Story Patterns

Most suffering comes from a few predictable story templates:

The Victim Story: "Things happen TO me"

- "My boss is making my life miserable."
- "My family doesn't understand me."
- "Life is unfair to people like me."

- Creates: Helplessness, resentment, passivity

The Scarcity Story: "There's not enough"

- "I never have enough time/money/energy"
- "Good opportunities go to other people."
- "I always miss out."
- Creates: Anxiety, competition, hoarding mentality

The Inadequacy Story: "I'm not enough"

- "Everyone else is more capable than me."
- "I'm behind in life compared to others."
- "I don't have what it takes."
- Creates: Self-doubt, comparison, procrastination

The Catastrophe Story: "Everything is falling apart"

- "This situation is a disaster."
- "Things are getting worse and worse."
- "I can't handle much more."
- Creates: Overwhelm, panic, despair

The Betrayal Story: "People can't be trusted."

- "Everyone eventually lets you down."
- "People only care about themselves."
- "You can't rely on anyone."
- Creates: Isolation, cynicism, defensiveness

Mark's Story Transformation Process

When Mark learned about narrative psychology, he realized he'd been telling himself a very specific story about his marriage: "I'm the selfless provider and she's the ungrateful taker."

Mark decided to experiment with alternative stories using the same facts:

Alternative Story 1: "We're both stressed parents trying to balance work and family, and we've lost sight of how to appreciate each other."

Alternative Story 2: "I've been so focused on providing financially that I haven't been providing emotionally, and she's been trying to get my attention in ways I didn't understand."

Alternative Story 3: "We've fallen into negative patterns that don't reflect our love for each other, and we both want to reconnect but don't know how."

Each story created completely different emotions and suggested different actions. The victim's story created resentment and withdrawal. The collaborative stories created curiosity and hope.

Mark began testing the new stories through his behavior. Instead of working longer hours to "prove" his dedication, he came home earlier and asked his wife about her day. Instead of expecting gratitude for his financial contributions, he started expressing gratitude for her daily efforts with the children.

Within six months, Mark's marriage had transformed. "Same facts, completely different experience," Mark told me. "It turns out she did appreciate me—she just showed it differently than I expected. And I wasn't as generous as I thought I was. Changing my story changed everything."

Today's Practice: The Story Rewriting System

Today, you'll learn to identify the stories creating your suffering and experiment with narratives that create growth, connection, and possibility.

The Story Identification Process

Morning Story Audit (10 minutes):

1. **Identify current challenges** (3 minutes):
   - What situation is causing you stress or unhappiness?
   - What relationship feels difficult?
   - What aspect of your life feels stuck or problematic?

2. **Extract your current story** (4 minutes): Write out the story you're telling yourself about this situation:
   - "The reason this is happening is..."
   - "This situation means that..."
   - "The other people involved are..."
   - "My role in this is..."
   - "This will probably lead to..."

3. **Identify the story category** (3 minutes):
   - Is this a victim story? Scarcity story? Inadequacy story?
   - What emotions does this story create?
   - How does this story affect your behavior?
   - What actions does this story make possible or impossible?

The Alternative Narrative Exercise

Step 1: The Growth Story (5 minutes). Rewrite your situation as a growth story:

- "This situation is teaching me..."
- "I'm developing the skill of..."
- "This challenge is preparing me for..."
- "I'm becoming the kind of person who..."

Step 2: The Connection Story (5 minutes). Rewrite your situation as a story about connection:

- "The other people involved are also struggling with..."
- "We're all trying to..."
- "What we have in common is..."
- "This situation is an opportunity to..."

Step 3: The Empowerment Story (5 minutes) Rewrite your situation as a story about your agency:

- "What I can control in this situation is..."
- "The choices available to me include..."
- "I'm capable of..."
- "My next step could be..."

Step 4: Test Drive the New Stories (Throughout the day)

- Choose one alternative story to experiment with
- Notice how it affects your emotions and energy
- Act from this new story for one day
- Observe what becomes possible when you operate from a different narrative

Advanced Story Rewriting Techniques

The Future Self Story: Write about your current situation from the perspective of yourself five years from now:

- "Looking back, this difficult time was actually when I..."
- "I'm grateful this happened because it taught me..."
- "The person I became because of this experience is..."

The Wise Friend Story: Rewrite your situation as if advising a beloved friend:

- "If my best friend were facing this, I would tell them..."
- "The story I'd want them to believe about themselves is..."
- "The possibilities I'd want them to see are..."

The Hero's Journey Story: Frame your challenge as the classic hero's journey:

- "I've been called to the adventure of..."

543

- "The skills I need to develop are..."
- "My allies and resources include..."
- "The person I'll become through this quest is..."

The Contribution Story: Focus on how your experience serves others:

- "My struggle with this issue helps me understand others who..."
- "What I'm learning could help other people by..."
- "This situation is developing my ability to contribute..."

Recognizing Story-Based Suffering vs. Situation-Based Problems

Story-Based Suffering (changeable through narrative work):

- Emotional distress that continues even when thinking about the situation
- Feeling powerless or victimized by circumstances
- Ruminating about unfairness or others' behavior
- Suffering that seems disproportionate to actual events

Situation-Based Problems (require practical action):

- Concrete challenges that need specific solutions
- Health issues requiring medical attention
- Financial problems needing practical strategies
- Relationship conflicts requiring communication or boundaries

Often, situations have both practical and story elements. Handle both: take practical action while maintaining empowering narratives.

Working With Resistance to Story Change

"But my story is true!"

- Stories can be accurate and still unhelpful
- Multiple true stories can exist about the same events
- The question isn't "Is this true?" but "Is this useful?"
- Truth includes context, perspective, and interpretation

"I don't want to excuse bad behavior."

- Changing your story doesn't excuse others' harmful actions
- You can maintain boundaries while changing narratives
- Empowering stories often lead to more effective responses
- Victim stories rarely create positive change

"This feels like denial or positive thinking."

- Story rewriting acknowledges all aspects of situations
- It's about finding the most useful perspective, not denial
- Negative stories aren't more "realistic"—they're often distorted too

- Empowering stories often see situations more clearly than victim stories

The Relationship Between Stories and Reality

Your stories don't just interpret reality—they actively create it:

Behavioral Confirmation: Stories influence your actions, which create results that confirm the stories

Attention Direction: Stories determine what you notice and ignore

Expectation Fulfillment: Stories create expectations that influence others' responses

Emotional Reality: Stories generate emotions that become your lived experience

Building on Your Emotional Development

You now understand:

- **Day 8**: How thoughts create emotions
- **Day 9**: How emotions provide valuable information
- **Day 10**: How to choose responses over reactions
- **Day 11**: How stories create suffering or empowerment

You're developing sophisticated emotional intelligence—the ability to work with your entire emotional system consciously and skillfully.

Tomorrow's Preview

Tomorrow you'll learn emotional alchemy—the art of transforming difficult emotions into useful energy for growth, connection, and contribution.

Remember Allen's Truth

"The sole and supreme use of suffering is to purify, to burn out all that is useless and impure. Suffering ceases for him who is pure."

Today, you discovered that suffering often comes not from your circumstances but from the stories you tell about those circumstances. Change the story, transform the suffering.

You are not the victim of your life's plot. You are its author.

Write a better story.

Day 12: Emotional Alchemy

"Beautiful thoughts of all kinds crystallize into habits of grace and kindliness, which solidify into genial and sunny circumstances: pure thoughts crystallize into habits of temperance and self-control, which solidify into circumstances of repose and peace." — James Allen.

Lisa had been carrying anger for six months, and it was poisoning everything.

Her business partner had betrayed her trust, taking clients and proprietary information when he left to start a competing company. Lisa felt justified in her fury—what he'd done was genuinely wrong, unethical, and harmful to her livelihood.

But Lisa's anger was eating her alive. She couldn't sleep. She lost focus at work. Her friends were tired of hearing about the betrayal. She was suffering from chronic stress. The anger she'd hoped would fuel her fight for justice had become the very thing destroying her life.

"I have every right to be angry," Lisa would say. "What he did was terrible."

Lisa was absolutely right about having the right to be angry. She was absolutely wrong about letting that anger run her life unchecked.

When Lisa learned the art of emotional alchemy—transforming raw emotions into refined wisdom and energy—she discovered that anger could become a powerful force for positive change rather than destructive obsession.

Allen's Understanding of Emotional Transformation

James Allen understood that emotions themselves aren't the problem—it's what you do with them that creates either suffering or growth. Allen saw that all experiences, including difficult emotions, could be transmuted into wisdom and strength.

"Thoughts of courage, self-reliance, and decision crystallize into manly habits, which solidify into circumstances of success, plenty, and freedom," **Allen wrote**. He understood that even challenging experiences could be transformed into beneficial outcomes through conscious mental work.

Allen recognized that the same raw emotional energy that creates destruction when unconscious can create tremendous good when properly directed: *"He who has conquered weakness, and has put away all selfish thoughts, belongs neither to oppressor nor oppressed. He is free."*

Allen saw that emotional freedom didn't come from avoiding difficult feelings but from learning to work with them skillfully, transforming base emotional experiences into refined wisdom and purposeful action.

The Science of Emotional Transformation

Modern neuroscience reveals that emotions are fundamentally energy—electrochemical responses in your brain and body that can be directed toward different outcomes:

Emotional Energy Neutrality: Dr. Lisa Feldman Barrett's research shows that emotions are neither inherently positive nor negative—they're simply energy with different informational content. Anger and excitement use the same high-arousal energy system; sadness and peace both involve low-arousal states.

Neuroplasticity and Reframing: Studies by Dr. Kevin Ochsner demonstrate that you can literally rewire how your brain processes emotional experiences through conscious reframing techniques. The same emotional energy can create different neural patterns and behavioral outcomes.

Post-Traumatic Growth: Dr. Richard Tedeschi's research reveals that people who learn to transform difficult emotional experiences often develop greater resilience, wisdom, and life satisfaction than those who avoid or suppress challenging feelings.

Emotional Granularity: Research by Dr. James Gross shows that people who can distinguish between subtle emotional states have a greater ability to transform and utilize emotional energy effectively.

Flow State Research: Studies by Dr. Mihaly Csikszentmihalyi demonstrate that optimal performance occurs when emotional energy is fully engaged and directed toward meaningful activities.

The Alchemy Process: Transforming Emotional Lead into Gold

Anger → Boundaries and Justice

- Raw anger energy: Hot, aggressive, potentially destructive
- Alchemical transformation: Channel into clear boundary-setting and justice-seeking

- Refined outcome: Protected values, improved systems, empowered others

Sadness → Compassion and Connection

- Raw sadness energy: Heavy, withdrawing, potentially isolating
- Alchemical transformation: Channel into empathy for others' suffering
- Refined outcome: Deeper relationships, service to others, emotional wisdom

Fear → Preparation and Courage

- Raw fear energy: Anxious, paralyzing, potentially limiting
- Alchemical transformation: Channel into careful planning and brave action
- Refined outcome: Better preparation, calculated risks, expanded comfort zone

Guilt → Values Alignment and Amends

- Raw guilt energy: Self-attacking, ruminating, potentially paralyzing
- Alchemical transformation: Channel into value clarification and corrective action
- Refined outcome: Clearer integrity, repaired relationships, aligned behavior

Envy → Motivation and Appreciation

- Raw envy energy: Bitter, comparing, potentially resentful
- Alchemical transformation: Channel into personal goal-setting and gratitude
- Refined outcome: Inspired action, clearer desires, reduced comparison

Lisa's Anger Alchemy Journey

When Lisa learned about emotional alchemy, she realized her anger contained valuable energy that was being wasted on rumination and resentment. She decided to experiment with transforming that energy into something constructive.

Step 1: Honor the Anger. Instead of judging her anger as "bad," Lisa acknowledged it as appropriate information: "I'm angry because my trust was violated and my business was harmed. This anger shows me that I value integrity and fair dealing."

Step 2: Extract the Message. Lisa asked her anger: "What are you trying to protect or achieve?" The answer: "I want to protect other entrepreneurs from similar betrayals and create business relationships based on genuine integrity."

Step 3: Channel the Energy. Instead of using her anger energy to plot revenge or fuel resentment, Lisa channeled it into:

- Creating stronger contracts and partnerships in her new business
- Mentoring other entrepreneurs about red flags in business relationships
- Building a reputation for exceptional integrity in her industry

Step 4: Transform the Outcome. Within a year, Lisa's new business was more successful than her previous partnership had ever been. Her reputation for integrity attracted higher-quality clients and partners. She'd become a respected voice in her industry about ethical business practices.

"The anger didn't disappear," Lisa said, "but it stopped running my life. Instead, I put it to work creating the kind of business environment I want to see in the world."

Today's Practice: The Emotional Alchemy Laboratory

Today, you'll learn to transform raw emotional energy into refined wisdom, action, and contribution.

The Emotional Alchemy Process

Step 1: Identify Raw Emotional Material (5 minutes)

- What difficult emotion are you currently experiencing?
- What situation or person triggered this emotion?
- How intense is it on a scale of 1-10?
- Where do you feel it in your body?

Step 2: Honor the Emotion (5 minutes) Ask yourself:

- "What is this emotion trying to protect or achieve?"
- "What value or need does this emotion represent?"
- "If this emotion could talk, what would it say?"
- "How is this emotion actually trying to help me?"

Write down your answers without judgment. All emotions contain some form of wisdom or protective intention.

Step 3: Extract the Essential Message (5 minutes). Distill your emotion down to its core message:

- Anger often says, "A boundary has been crossed," or "Injustice needs addressing."
- Sadness often says: "Something important has been lost," or "I need comfort and connection."
- Fear often says, "Preparation is needed" or "Caution is required."
- Guilt often says, "My actions don't align with my values."
- Anxiety often says, "Uncertainty requires planning or acceptance."

Step 4: Design the Alchemical Transformation (10 minutes) Plan how to channel this emotional energy constructively:

For Anger:

- What boundary needs to be set or reinforced?
- What injustice could you work to address?

- How could you protect others from similar harm?
- What positive change could this energy fuel?

For Sadness:
- How could this experience help you connect with others who've suffered similarly?
- What compassion has this developed in you?
- How could you comfort others going through a similar loss?
- What appreciation for what remains can this cultivate?

For Fear:
- What preparation would actually address your concerns?
- What brave action could you take despite the fear?
- How could you help others face similar fears?
- What courage is this situation asking you to develop?

Step 5: Take Alchemical Action (Ongoing). Transform the emotion through specific actions:
- One immediate action you can take today
- One conversation you could have this week
- One longer-term project this energy could fuel
- One way to serve others through what you've learned

Advanced Emotional Alchemy Techniques

The Energy Redirection Method: When experiencing intense emotions:
1. **Feel the energy** in your body without acting on it
2. **Channel it into movement**: exercise, dancing, cleaning, creating
3. **Direct it toward goals**: use emotional energy to fuel meaningful work
4. **Transform it through service**: help others dealing with similar challenges

The Wisdom Extraction Process: Ask transformative questions:
- "What is this emotion teaching me about what I value?"
- "How is this making me stronger, wiser, or more compassionate?"
- "What would I want to tell someone else facing this same emotion?"
- "How could this experience serve something larger than my personal comfort?"

The Contribution Transformation: Turn personal emotional experiences into service opportunities:
- Use your struggle with anxiety to help others manage worry
- Transform your experience with loss into grief support for others
- Channel your anger about injustice into advocacy or volunteer work
- Convert your loneliness into reaching out to other isolated people

The Creative Alchemy Method: Express emotions through creative outlets:

- Write about your experience to help others
- Create art that captures your emotional journey
- Compose music that expresses your transformation
- Design solutions to problems that caused your difficulty

Common Alchemy Challenges and Solutions

"I don't want to 'use' my pain—I just want it to stop"

- Alchemy doesn't prolong suffering—it transforms it into meaning
- Meaning often reduces suffering more effectively than avoidance
- You can simultaneously seek healing and extract wisdom

"This feels like I'm excusing bad behavior or minimizing real problems."

- Alchemy doesn't excuse harmful actions—it transforms your response to them
- You can maintain boundaries while transforming emotional energy
- Justice and personal transformation can coexist

"I'm too overwhelmed to think about transformation."

- Start with basic emotional regulation (from previous days)
- Alchemy works best when you're not in crisis mode
- Sometimes the first alchemy is transforming overwhelm into clarity

"I don't see how my negative emotions could possibly help anyone."

- Your struggles often prepare you to help others with similar challenges
- The depth of your pain often equals the depth of wisdom you can offer
- Many of the world's greatest teachers and healers transformed personal suffering

The Compound Effect of Emotional Alchemy

Regular emotional alchemy practice creates:

Personal Benefits:

- Faster recovery from difficult emotions
- Increased sense of meaning and purpose
- Greater emotional resilience and wisdom
- Reduced victimization by circumstances

Relational Benefits:

- Deeper empathy and connection with others
- More helpful responses to others' struggles
- Modeling of healthy emotional processing
- Contribution to others' healing and growth

Societal Benefits:

- Transformation of personal pain into social good
- Reduction in cycles of emotional reactivity
- Creation of solutions to common human challenges
- Leadership through example in emotional maturity

Integration with Your Emotional Development

You now have a complete emotional mastery toolkit:

- **Day 8**: Understanding thought-emotion connections
- **Day 9**: Reading emotions as information
- **Day 10**: Choosing responses over reactions
- **Day 11**: Rewriting disempowering stories
- **Day 12**: Transforming emotions into wisdom and service

Tomorrow's Preview

Tomorrow you'll learn to build emotional resilience—the ability to maintain emotional stability and bounce back quickly from difficult experiences.

Remember Allen's Vision

"The circumstances which a man encounters with blessedness are the result of his own mental harmony. Blessedness, not material possessions, is the measure of right thought."

Today, you learned that blessedness comes not from avoiding difficult emotions but from transforming them into wisdom, service, and growth.

You are not a victim of your emotions. You are an alchemist who can transform any emotional experience into gold.

Day 13: Building Emotional Resilience

"The weakest soul, knowing its own weakness, and believing this truth that strength can only be developed by effort and practice, will, thus believing, at once begin to exert itself, and, adding effort to effort, patience to patience, and strength to strength, will never cease to develop, and will at last grow divinely strong." — James Allen.

David thought resilience was something you either had or you didn't.

When his company downsized and eliminated his position after fifteen years, David was devastated. While some of his colleagues seemed to bounce back quickly—updating resumes, networking, even expressing excitement about new opportunities—David felt paralyzed. He took the job loss personally, replayed every mistake he might have made, and couldn't imagine feeling optimistic about his future.

"Some people are just naturally resilient," David told his wife. "They don't take things as hard as I do. I'm just more sensitive."

David was partly right; people do have different baseline resilience levels. But what David didn't understand was that emotional resilience isn't a fixed trait you're born with. It's a skill set you can develop through practice, regardless of your starting point.

When David learned that resilience could be built like physical fitness, he began training his emotional strength systematically. Within six months, he'd not only found a better job but had developed a fundamentally different relationship with challenges and setbacks.

Allen's Understanding of Emotional Strength

James Allen recognized that emotional strength wasn't about avoiding difficulty but about developing the capacity to handle whatever life brings with grace and wisdom.

"The man who has conquered weakness and has put away all selfish thoughts belongs neither to oppressor nor oppressed. He is free," Allen wrote. He understood that true strength comes from internal development, not external circumstances.

Allen saw that resilience develops through what he called "continued effort" and "patient practice." Just as physical muscles grow stronger through repeated exercise, emotional muscles develop through consistently meeting challenges with wisdom rather than reactivity.

553

"Such is the conscious master, and man can only thus become by discovering within himself the laws of thought, which discovery is totally a matter of application, self-analysis, and experience," **Allen explained.** Resilience comes from learning to work with your mental and emotional systems consciously.

Allen understood that the strongest people aren't those who never face difficulties; they're those who've learned to transform difficulties into strength.

The Science of Emotional Resilience

Modern research reveals that resilience is indeed a trainable skill set involving specific mental, emotional, and behavioral capacities:

Neuroplasticity and Resilience: Dr. Richard Davidson's research shows that resilience training literally changes brain structure, strengthening areas responsible for emotional regulation while reducing reactivity in stress centers.

Cognitive Flexibility: Studies by Dr. Barbara Fredrickson demonstrate that resilient people develop broader repertoires of responses to challenges. Instead of defaulting to anxiety or despair, they can access curiosity, humor, gratitude, and problem-solving.

Stress Inoculation: Research by Dr. Salvatore Maddi reveals that controlled exposure to manageable stress builds resilience for handling larger challenges. Like a vaccine, small doses of difficulty build immunity to overwhelm.

Post-Traumatic Growth: Dr. Richard Tedeschi's studies show that people can develop greater strength, wisdom, and life satisfaction after difficult experiences—but only when they actively work with the challenge rather than avoiding it.

Social Connection: Dr. Robert Waldinger's Harvard Study of Adult Development proves that strong relationships are the most powerful predictor of resilience throughout life.

The Components of Emotional Resilience

Mental Flexibility: The ability to see multiple perspectives and generate various response options

- "This is one way to look at it, but there are others."
- "If Plan A doesn't work, I have Plans B, C, and D."
- "This setback might actually open new possibilities."

Emotional Regulation: The capacity to experience feelings without being overwhelmed by them

- "I can feel anxious and still take wise action."
- "This emotion is temporary and will pass."
- "I can surf this wave rather than being crushed by it."

Meaning-Making: The skill of finding purpose and growth in difficult experiences

- "What is this situation teaching me?"
- "How might this serve my development?"
- "What meaning can I create from this challenge?"

Social Connection: The ability to seek and provide support during difficult times

- "I don't have to handle this alone."
- "Others have faced similar challenges and survived."
- "I can both receive and offer support."

Self-Compassion: The practice of treating yourself with kindness during setbacks

- "Everyone struggles sometimes—I'm not alone in this."
- "I'm doing my best with what I know right now."
- "This difficulty doesn't define my worth or future."

David's Resilience Training Journey

When David began treating resilience as a skill to develop rather than a trait to possess, his entire approach to challenges changed:

Weeks 1-2: Building Awareness David began noticing his default patterns when facing difficulty:

- Catastrophic thinking ("This is the end of my career.")
- Self-blame ("I should have seen this coming.")
- Isolation ("No one understands what I'm going through.")
- Rumination (replaying the job loss repeatedly)

Weeks 3-4: Developing Mental Flexibility David practiced generating multiple perspectives on his situation:

- "This might be an opportunity to find better work."
- "Many successful people have been laid off."
- "I have skills and experience that companies need."
- "This could lead to career growth I wouldn't have pursued otherwise."

Weeks 5-8: Building Emotional Tolerance. David learned to experience difficult emotions without being overwhelmed:

- He practiced feeling disappointed without falling into despair

- He allowed himself to feel uncertain without creating anxiety stories
- He experienced grief about his lost identity without making it permanent

Weeks 9-12: Creating Meaning and Connection. David began seeing his experience as valuable for helping others:

- He joined a career transition support group
- He volunteered to mentor other professionals facing job loss
- He started viewing his experience as preparation for a more fulfilling career

Six months later, David had not only found a better position but had become someone others turned to for support during difficult transitions. "I'm actually grateful for the experience now," David said. "I learned I'm much stronger than I thought I was."

Today's Practice: The Resilience Building System

Today, you'll learn to develop emotional resilience through systematic training in each component.

The Daily Resilience Workout

Morning Resilience Preparation (10 minutes):

Mental Flexibility Training (3 minutes):

- Identify one current challenge in your life
- Generate three different ways to view this challenge: (1) The growth perspective: "This is developing my..." (2) The opportunity perspective: "This might lead to..." (3) The strength perspective: "I'm becoming someone who..."

Emotional Regulation Practice (3 minutes):

- Recall a recent stressful situation
- Practice the "observe and accept" approach: "I notice I'm feeling [emotion]" | "This feeling is temporary and will pass" | "I can feel this emotion and still choose wise action"

Meaning-Making Exercise (2 minutes):

- Ask about your current challenges: "What strength is this situation building in me?" | "What is this teaching me that could help others?" | "How might this serve my long-term development?"

Connection Intention (2 minutes):

- Identify one person you could reach out to today
- Plan one way you could offer support to someone else
- Remind yourself: "I don't have to handle challenges alone."

The Stress Inoculation Practice

Gradual Challenge Exposure: Build resilience by gradually exposing yourself to manageable stress:

Week 1: Take on one small challenge outside your comfort zone

- Have a difficult conversation you've been avoiding
- Try a new skill that feels slightly intimidating
- Express an opinion you usually keep to yourself

Week 2: Increase the challenge level slightly

- Volunteer for a project that stretches your abilities
- Address a conflict you've been postponing
- Take a social or professional risk

Week 3: Practice recovery and reflection

- Notice how you handled the previous weeks' challenges
- Identify what helped you stay resilient
- Plan how to apply these lessons to bigger challenges

Week 4: Integrate lessons and prepare for larger challenges

- Choose a meaningful goal that requires sustained effort
- Develop support systems for ongoing challenges
- Celebrate your increased resilience capacity

Advanced Resilience Techniques

The Resilience Bank Account: Build reserves for difficult times:

Deposits:

- Regular self-care practices
- Strong relationship maintenance
- Spiritual or philosophical grounding
- Physical health and energy
- Skill development and learning
- Meaningful work and contribution

Withdrawals:

- Major life stresses
- Health challenges
- Relationship conflicts
- Financial pressures
- Career transitions

- Loss and grief

Keep making more deposits than withdrawals to maintain resilience reserves.

The Anti-Fragility Principle: Move beyond resilience to anti-fragility—becoming stronger through stress:

- View challenges as strength training
- Extract lessons from every difficulty
- Use setbacks to refine goals and strategies
- Build systems that improve under pressure

The Support Network Architecture: Systematically build resilience through relationships:

- **Emotional Support**: People who listen and provide comfort
- **Practical Support**: People who offer concrete help
- **Informational Support**: People who provide advice and guidance
- **Social Support**: People who provide belonging and connection
- **Meaning Support**: People who share your values and purpose

Resilience During Crisis

When facing major challenges, use the RISE protocol:

R - Recognize what you're facing without minimizing or catastrophizing

I - Inventory your resources, strengths, and support systems

S - Strategize both immediate coping and longer-term recovery

E - Execute your plan while staying flexible and compassionate with yourself

Building Collective Resilience

Individual resilience is enhanced by community resilience:

- Share your challenges appropriately with trusted people
- Offer support to others facing difficulties
- Create or join groups focused on mutual support
- Model healthy resilience for family and colleagues
- Contribute to systems that support community wellbeing

Measuring Your Resilience Growth

Track resilience development through:

Recovery Speed: How quickly do you bounce back from setbacks?

Emotional Range: Can you access multiple emotions during challenges?

Perspective Taking: How many ways can you view difficult situations?

Meaning Making: How easily do you find purpose in difficulties?

Support Utilization: How effectively do you seek and provide help?

Growth Integration: What have you learned from recent challenges?

Common Resilience Building Challenges
"I don't want to become callous or insensitive."
- Resilience isn't about not feeling—it's about feeling without being overwhelmed
- Resilient people often have greater empathy because they're not consumed by their own reactivity

"Some challenges are too big for these techniques."
- Resilience building is gradual—start with smaller challenges
- Major trauma may require professional support along with resilience practices
- No technique works for everything, but all contribute to overall strength

"I feel like I'm just pretending to be strong."
- Resilience often feels artificial until it becomes natural
- "Fake it till you make it" is actually valid for building emotional strength
- Neurology follows behavior—acting resilient builds resilient neural pathways

Integration with Your Emotional Mastery
You've now developed:
- Understanding of thought-emotion connections
- Ability to read emotional information
- Skills for choosing responses over reactions
- Capacity to rewrite disempowering stories
- Tools for transforming emotions into wisdom
- Systems for building emotional resilience

Tomorrow's Preview

Tomorrow, you'll integrate all of your emotional mastery skills into what Allen called emotional freedom—the ability to remain centered and wise regardless of external circumstances.

Remember Allen's Promise

"Adding effort to effort, patience to patience, and strength to strength, will never cease to develop, and will at last grow divinely strong."

Today, you learned that emotional strength is built through practice, not granted through genetics. Every challenge you face consciously becomes training for greater resilience.

You are not at the mercy of life's difficulties. You are building the strength to meet them with grace.

Day 14: Emotional Freedom

Sarah stood in the airport, watching her vacation plans dissolve in real time.

Flight canceled. Hotel reservation in jeopardy. Her daughter's disappointed face. Her husband's frustrated sighs. A year of planning and saving for this family trip was seemingly wasted due to circumstances completely beyond her control.

Six months earlier, this situation would have sent Sarah into a spiral of stress, blame, and emotional overwhelm. She would have spent hours on the phone getting nowhere with airline representatives, snapped at her family, and turned the rest of the day into a drama of victimization and misery.

Instead, Sarah took three deep breaths and smiled.

"Well," she said to her family, "this is definitely not what we planned. But we're all together, we're healthy, and we have options. Let's see what adventure this detour might offer us."

What followed was one of their most memorable family experiences, an unplanned day exploring their own city like tourists, discovering places they'd never noticed despite living there for years.

This wasn't positive thinking or denial. This was emotional freedom, the ability to remain centered, creative, and connected regardless of external circumstances.

Allen's Vision of Emotional Mastery

James Allen understood that the ultimate goal of emotional development isn't the absence of challenging feelings or difficult circumstances; it's the presence of unshakeable inner peace that remains steady regardless of life's ups and downs.

"The calm man, having learned how to govern himself, knows how to adapt himself to others; and they, in turn, reverence his spiritual strength, and feel that they can learn of him and rely upon him," **Allen wrote.**

Allen saw that emotional freedom creates a kind of magnetic influence. People are naturally drawn to those who remain centered during storms, wise during chaos, and compassionate during conflict.

"The more tranquil a man becomes, the greater is his success, his influence, his power for good," Allen observed. This isn't about becoming emotionally flat or disconnected; it's about developing such deep emotional wisdom that you can feel deeply while responding wisely.

Allen's ultimate vision was of people who had become what he called "masters of themselves"—individuals who could maintain inner harmony regardless of outer circumstances, and through this mastery, contribute to the harmony of the world.

The Science of Emotional Freedom

Research reveals that emotional freedom—what psychologists call "emotional regulation mastery"—involves specific neurological and behavioral patterns:

Prefrontal Cortex Dominance: Brain imaging studies show that emotionally free individuals have stronger connections between their prefrontal cortex (thinking brain) and limbic system (emotional brain), allowing conscious choice to guide responses rather than automatic reactions.

Flexible Emotional Range: Dr. Barbara Fredrickson's research demonstrates that emotionally free people don't experience fewer emotions—they experience them more skillfully, accessing the full range of human feelings while maintaining perspective and choice.

Stress Resilience: Studies by Dr. Jon Kabat-Zinn show that people who develop emotional mastery have different physiological responses to stress—faster recovery, lower inflammation, and better immune function.

Social Impact: Research by Dr. Daniel Goleman reveals that emotionally free individuals create "emotional contagion" in positive directions—their calm presence actually helps regulate others' emotional states.

Cognitive Flexibility: Studies by Dr. Arne Dietrich demonstrate that emotional freedom correlates with enhanced creativity, problem-solving, and decision-making abilities.

The Characteristics of Emotional Freedom

Emotional Responsiveness Without Reactivity:

- Feeling emotions fully while maintaining perspective
- "I'm feeling angry about this injustice, and I choose to address it constructively."
- "I'm sad about this loss, and I can honor that sadness while staying open to life."

Presence Amidst Chaos:

- Remaining centered when others are overwhelmed
- "Everyone else is panicking, but I can think clearly."
- "This situation is chaotic, and I can be a calm presence within it."

Curiosity Instead of Judgment:

- Approaching emotional challenges with interest rather than resistance
- "This is an interesting response I'm having—what can I learn from it?"
- "I wonder what this situation is trying to teach me."

Compassion for All Emotional States:

- Treating yourself and others with kindness, regardless of emotional expressions
- "Everyone is doing their best with their current emotional capacity."
- "All emotions are valid information, even when they're uncomfortable."

Choice in Response Timing:

- Responding when you choose to, not when emotions demand it
- "I can feel this urgency and still take time to respond wisely."
- "This emotion is strong, and it doesn't have to control my timing."

Sarah's Journey to Emotional Freedom

Sarah's transformation didn't happen overnight. It was the result of integrating two weeks of emotional mastery training:

Foundation from Days 8-11:

- Understanding that thoughts create emotions gave Sarah the power to influence her feelings
- Reading emotions as information helped her extract wisdom from difficult feelings
- Learning to pause between trigger and response created space for conscious choice
- Rewriting stories about circumstances transformed her relationship with "problems"

Advanced Skills from Days 12-13:

- Emotional alchemy taught Sarah to transform difficult feelings into useful energy

- Resilience building gave her confidence that she could handle whatever arose

Integration into Freedom: At the airport, Sarah automatically applied all these skills:

- She recognized her initial frustration without being controlled by it
- She read the family's emotions and responded to their needs
- She paused before reacting and chose a response aligned with her values
- She reframed the story from "disaster" to "unexpected adventure"
- She transformed disappointment energy into creative problem-solving
- She drew on her resilience reserves to stay positive

"It wasn't that I didn't feel disappointed," Sarah explained later. "I felt it fully. But the feeling didn't own me. I could experience disappointment and choose adventure at the same time."

Today's Practice: The Emotional Freedom Integration System

Today, you'll integrate both weeks of emotional training into a comprehensive approach to emotional mastery.

The Freedom Morning Practice (15 minutes):

Emotional State Assessment (3 minutes):

- How am I feeling right now emotionally?
- What's my overall emotional energy level?
- Which emotions are present, even subtly?
- What do these emotions need or want to tell me?

Thought-Emotion Alignment (3 minutes):

- What thoughts have been creating my current emotional state?
- Are these thoughts serving my well-being and effectiveness?
- What thoughts would create the emotional state I want today?
- How can I plant those thoughts in my mental garden?

Response Preparation (3 minutes):

- What situations today might trigger automatic emotional reactions?
- What would wise responses look like for each situation?
- How do I want to show up emotionally for the people in my life?
- What emotional qualities do I want to embody today?

Story and Meaning Setting (3 minutes):

- What empowering story will I tell about today's challenges?

- How can I view any difficulties as opportunities for growth?
- What meaning and purpose can guide my emotional responses?
- How can my emotional state serve something larger than myself?

Freedom Intention (3 minutes):

- Today I choose to remain emotionally free by...
- When challenging emotions arise, I will...
- I commit to responding rather than reacting when...
- My emotional freedom will contribute to others by...

The Real-Time Freedom Protocol

When facing any emotionally challenging situation:

Step 1: Pause and Breathe (10 seconds)

- Three conscious breaths
- "I have emotional freedom and choice in this moment."

Step 2: Assess and Acknowledge (30 seconds)

- What emotion is arising?
- What information is it providing?
- What story am I telling about this situation?

Step 3: Choose and Respond (Ongoing)

- What response aligns with my values and wisdom?
- How can I transform this emotional energy constructively?
- What would emotional freedom look like right now?

The Evening Freedom Review (10 minutes):

Freedom Successes (3 minutes):

- When did I maintain emotional freedom today?
- What situations did I handle with emotional wisdom?
- How did my emotional freedom serve others?
- What am I proud of in my emotional responses?

Learning Opportunities (3 minutes):

- When was I less emotionally free than I wanted to be?
- What triggered automatic reactions?
- What would I do differently in the same situation?
- What additional skills would help me grow?

Freedom Evolution (2 minutes):

- How has my emotional freedom developed over these two weeks?
- What changes have others noticed in my emotional responses?

- What aspects of emotional mastery do I want to develop further?

Gratitude and Integration (2 minutes):

- What am I grateful for about this emotional development journey?
- How will I maintain and continue building my emotional freedom?
- What commitment will I make to ongoing emotional mastery?

Advanced Emotional Freedom Practices

The Emotional Weather System: Develop the ability to experience emotional "weather" without being controlled by it:

- "I notice it's stormy emotionally right now, and storms pass."
- "This is a cloudy emotional day, and I can still navigate clearly."
- "I'm experiencing emotional sunshine, and I'll appreciate it while it lasts."

The Emotional Aikido Master: Use challenging emotions and situations as opportunities to demonstrate mastery:

- When others are reactive, become more centered
- When situations are chaotic, they become more peaceful
- When pressures are high, become more graceful

The Emotional Service Practice: Use your emotional freedom to serve others:

- Be the calm presence in stressful situations
- Help others process difficult emotions without taking them on
- Model healthy emotional responses for family and colleagues
- Create emotionally safe spaces for others to grow

Maintaining Long-Term Emotional Freedom

Daily Practices:

- Continue morning emotional preparation
- Use real-time freedom protocols consistently
- End days with emotional review and integration

Weekly Practices:

- Deeper emotional pattern analysis
- Challenging situation rehearsal
- Emotional skill-building focus

Monthly Practices:

- Comprehensive emotional development review
- New emotional challenge goal setting
- Relationship impact assessment

Quarterly Practices:

- Major emotional pattern transformation work
- Life alignment with emotional wisdom assessment
- Service and contribution planning through emotional gifts

The Ripple Effects of Emotional Freedom

Personal Impact:

- Reduced stress and anxiety
- Increased life satisfaction and meaning
- Greater resilience and adaptability
- Enhanced creativity and problem-solving

Relational Impact:

- Deeper, more authentic connections
- Improved conflict resolution
- Greater trust and respect from others
- Positive influence on family and friend dynamics

Professional Impact:

- Enhanced leadership presence
- Better team collaboration
- Improved decision-making under pressure
- Increased influence and effectiveness

Societal Impact:

- Contribution to collective emotional intelligence
- Modeling of healthy emotional processing
- Reduction in reactive cycles and conflicts
- Creation of more harmonious communities

Your Emotional Mastery Achievement

Over these seven days, you've developed:

- **Day 8**: Understanding of thought-emotion connections
- **Day 9**: Ability to read emotions as valuable information
- **Day 10**: Skills for choosing responses over reactions
- **Day 11**: Capacity to rewrite disempowering emotional stories
- **Day 12**: Tools for transforming emotions into wisdom and service
- **Day 13**: Systems for building emotional resilience
- **Day 14**: Integration into comprehensive emotional freedom

You've moved from being controlled by emotions to working with them skillfully. You've transformed from emotional reactivity to emotional intelligence. You've evolved from emotional victimhood to emotional mastery.

Preparing for Week Three

Next week, you'll build on this emotional foundation to develop purposeful living—connecting your mental clarity and emotional wisdom to meaningful contribution and lasting fulfillment.

Remember Allen's Ultimate Vision

"Tempest-tossed souls, wherever ye may be, under whatsoever conditions ye may live, know this—in the ocean of life the isles of Blessedness are smiling, and the sunny shore of your ideal awaits your coming. Keep your hand firmly upon the helm of thought. In the bark of your soul reclines the commanding Master; He does but sleep: wake Him. Self-control is strength; Right Thought is mastery; Calmness is power."

Today, you awakened the commanding Master of your emotional life. You discovered that true power lies not in controlling external circumstances but in maintaining inner freedom regardless of what occurs.

You are no longer at the mercy of your emotions. You are their wise and compassionate master.

Tomorrow, you begin the journey toward living this mastery in service of meaningful purpose.

~End of Part Two: Master Your Emotions~

Part Two Summary: You've now developed comprehensive emotional intelligence, from understanding how thoughts create emotions through achieving emotional freedom. These seven days have equipped you with the ability to work with your entire emotional system consciously and skillfully. You can feel deeply while responding wisely, transform difficult emotions into useful energy, and maintain inner peace regardless of external circumstances.

In Part Three, you'll discover how to channel this mental clarity and emotional wisdom toward meaningful purpose, creating a life of authentic contribution and lasting fulfillment.

PART THREE

Live Your Purpose

Days 15-21

"He who cherishes a beautiful vision, a lofty ideal in his heart, will one day realize it. Columbus cherished a vision of another world, and he discovered it; Copernicus fostered the vision of a multiplicity of worlds and a wider universe, and he revealed it." **— James Allen.**

Day 15: Discovering Your North Star

*"The dreamers are the saviours of the world. As the visible world is sustained by the invisible, so men, through all their trials and sins and sordid vocations, are nourished by the beautiful visions of their solitary dreamers." — **James Allen.***

Michael felt like he was succeeding at everything that didn't matter.

At 38, he had the corner office, the impressive salary, and the respected title. His LinkedIn profile read like a catalog of achievements. His parents were proud. His peers were envious. By every external measure, Michael was winning.

But every Sunday night, Michael felt a familiar dread settling over him. Another week of work that felt meaningless. Another set of goals that excited no one, including himself. Another paycheck that bought comfort but not fulfillment.

"I should be grateful," Michael would tell himself. "I have everything I thought I wanted."

The problem wasn't that Michael lacked success, but that his success was disconnected from any deeper sense of purpose. He'd mastered the art of achievement without ever asking what was truly worth achieving. He'd become incredibly efficient at climbing a ladder without checking whether it was leaning against the right wall.

When Michael learned to align his considerable talents with genuine purpose, everything changed. His work became energizing instead of draining. His achievements felt meaningful instead of hollow. His success finally served something larger than his ego.

Allen's Understanding of Purpose and Vision

James Allen understood that all meaningful achievement begins with what he called "cherishing a beautiful vision" in your heart. He saw that purpose isn't something you find "out there" in the world, it's something you discover within yourself and then express through your actions.

"To desire is to obtain; to aspire is to achieve," **Allen wrote.** *"Shall man's basest desires receive the fullest measure of gratification, and his purest aspirations starve for lack of sustenance? Such is not the Law: such a condition of things can never obtain."*

Allen recognized that humans are naturally drawn toward meaning and contribution. When you align your daily actions with your deepest aspirations, you tap into a source of energy and persistence that no external motivation can match.

"Dream lofty dreams, and as you dream, so shall you become. Your Vision is the promise of what you shall one day be; your Ideal is the prophecy of what you shall at last unveil," **Allen wrote.** He understood that purpose begins as an internal vision that gradually manifests through sustained effort and aligned action.

Allen saw that people who live purposefully don't just achieve more, they achieve better. Their work carries an authenticity and power that comes from genuine alignment between inner values and outer expression.

The Science of Purpose and Wellbeing

Modern research has validated Allen's insights about purpose with remarkable consistency. Studies show that living purposefully isn't just spiritually fulfilling—it's biologically beneficial:

Longevity Research: Dr. Patricia Boyle's study of over 1,200 older adults found that those with high purpose scores lived significantly longer, even when controlling for other health factors. Purpose literally adds years to your life.

Stress Resilience: Research by Dr. Alia Crum shows that people with a strong life purpose demonstrate better stress recovery, lower inflammation markers, and improved immune function. Purpose acts as a biological buffer against life's challenges.

Brain Health: Studies by Dr. Rush University researchers reveal that purposeful living protects against cognitive decline and Alzheimer's disease. People with a strong purpose maintain sharper mental function as they age.

Sleep Quality: Research by Dr. Jason Ong demonstrates that individuals with a clear life purpose sleep better and are less likely to develop sleep disorders. Purpose provides the mental peace that allows deep rest.

Cardiovascular Health: Studies show that purposeful individuals have lower rates of heart disease and stroke. The alignment between values and actions creates cardiovascular harmony.

Neuroplasticity Enhancement: Dr. Adam Gazzaley's research reveals that purpose-driven activities stimulate brain plasticity more effectively than arbitrary tasks. Purpose literally helps your brain grow and adapt.

The Difference Between Goals and Purpose

Many people confuse goals with purpose, but they serve different functions in a meaningful life:

Goals are destinations:

- Specific, measurable outcomes
- "Get promoted to VP"
- "Run a marathon"
- "Save $100,000"
- "Write a book."

Purpose is your compass:

- The deeper "why" behind your goals
- "Develop human potential"
- "Create beauty and order."
- "Reduce suffering in the world."
- "Connect people with truth."

Integration Example:

- Goal: "Start a consulting business"
- Purpose: "Help overwhelmed leaders create sustainable success."
- Alignment: The business becomes a vehicle for expressing your purpose of reducing overwhelm and increasing sustainability

When goals align with purpose, you access sustainable motivation. When they don't, even achieved goals feel empty.

Michael's Purpose Discovery Journey

When Michael began exploring purpose, he used what Allen might have called "searching the mine of his soul" through careful self-observation:

Step 1: Energy Archaeology. Michael tracked his energy patterns for two weeks:

- When did he feel most alive and engaged?
- What activities made him lose track of time?
- When did work feel effortless despite being challenging?
- What conversations energized rather than drained him?

Step 2: Value Extraction. Michael identified what mattered most deeply to him:

- He cared about efficiency and effectiveness
- He was drawn to helping others reach their potential
- He valued systems that worked for everyone, not just the privileged
- He wanted his work to outlast his lifetime

Step 3: Pattern Recognition. Michael noticed recurring themes throughout his life:

- As a child, he organized neighborhood activities
- In college, he tutored struggling students
- His favorite work projects involved improving systems
- People sought his advice about career development

Step 4: Pain Point Analysis. Michael examined what problems in the world genuinely bothered him:

- Talented people stuck in roles that wasted their abilities
- Organizations that burn out good employees
- Systems that created unnecessary stress and inefficiency
- Leaders who achieved success at the cost of their humanity

Step 5: Purpose Synthesis. From this exploration, Michael's purpose emerged: "Help capable people and organizations achieve sustainable excellence without sacrificing their humanity."

Suddenly, Michael's career path became clear. Instead of climbing the corporate ladder for its own sake, he could use his position to transform how his company approached leadership development and employee wellbeing.

Today's Practice: The Purpose Discovery System

Today, you'll engage in the same systematic exploration that helped Michael discover his North Star.

The Four-Quadrant Purpose Exploration

Set aside 30 uninterrupted minutes for this exercise. Use pen and paper—handwriting accesses different neural pathways than typing.

Quadrant 1: Natural Energizers (8 minutes) Write continuously about:

- What activities make you feel most alive and engaged?
- When do you lose track of time in positive ways?
- What did you love doing as a child before others told you what was "practical"?
- What topics can you discuss for hours without getting bored?

- When do you feel like you're using your best abilities?

Quadrant 2: Deep Values (8 minutes) Write continuously about:

- What principles would you never compromise, regardless of consequences?
- What injustices or problems make you genuinely angry or sad?
- If you could solve one problem in the world, what would it be?
- What do you want to be remembered for after you're gone?
- When you read about people you admire, what are they usually doing?

Quadrant 3: Natural Gifts (7 minutes) Write continuously about:

- What do others frequently ask for your help with?
- What seems easy for you but difficult for others?
- What compliments do you receive repeatedly?
- What unique combination of skills and perspective do you bring?
- How are you different from most people in ways that could serve others?

Quadrant 4: Pain Points (7 minutes) Write continuously about:

- What suffering in the world do you feel called to address?
- What problems have you personally overcome that others struggle with?
- What inefficiencies or injustices do you notice that others overlook?
- What needs do you see in your community, workplace, or family?
- What would you want to fix if you had unlimited resources?

Purpose Statement Creation

After completing all four quadrants, look for patterns and connections. Create a purpose statement using this format:

"My purpose is to **[verb] [what]** for/with **[whom]** so that **[impact]**"

Examples:

- "My purpose is to simplify complex systems for overwhelmed leaders so that they can focus on what truly matters."
- "My purpose is to create beautiful, functional spaces for busy families so that their homes become places of peace."
- "My purpose is to teach practical life skills to young adults so that they can navigate independence with confidence."

Don't wordsmith endlessly. Version 1.0 is better than Version 0.0. Your purpose can evolve as you grow.

Advanced Purpose Clarification Techniques

The Deathbed Test: Imagine yourself at age 90, looking back on your life. What would you need to have done or become to feel deeply satisfied? What legacy would make you proud?

The Hidden Observer Exercise: Imagine an invisible, loving observer has been watching your entire life. What unique gifts would they say you're meant to share with the world? What contribution would they say only you can make?

The Time-Money Freedom Test: If you had unlimited time and money, how would you choose to spend your days? What problems would you work to solve? What beauty would you create? This reveals a purpose unclouded by practical constraints.

The Anger-to-Purpose Flip: What makes you angry about the current state of the world? Often, your deepest frustrations point toward your most important contributions. Anger at injustice suggests purpose in creating justice. Frustration with inefficiency suggests purpose in creating better systems.

Common Purpose Discovery Challenges

"I don't think I have a unique purpose."
- Everyone's combination of experiences, gifts, and perspectives is unique
- Purpose isn't about being special—it's about being useful
- Small purposes can have profound impacts on the people they touch

"My purpose feels too big or overwhelming."
- Purpose is lived through daily actions, not single grand gestures
- Start with how your purpose can express itself in your current circumstances
- Every meaningful purpose begins with small, consistent steps

"I have multiple interests—how do I choose one purpose?"
- Purpose can often integrate multiple interests under one umbrella
- Look for the common theme connecting your various passions
- Your purpose might be the unique way you combine different elements

"I feel guilty focusing on purpose when I have practical responsibilities."
- Purpose doesn't require abandoning responsibilities; it often enhances how you fulfill them
- Purposeful people are often more effective at meeting obligations
- Living purposefully models authentic engagement for those you care about

Purpose vs. Passion: An Important Distinction

Passion is about what you enjoy:

- "I'm passionate about photography."
- "I love working with numbers."
- "I'm excited by new technology."

Purpose is about how you serve:

- "I help people see beauty through photography."
- "I create financial clarity for confused business owners."
- "I use technology to solve real-world problems."

Passion can change; purpose typically endures. Passion is about you; purpose is about contribution. The most fulfilling lives often integrate passion in the service of purpose.

Building on Your Mental and Emotional Foundation

Your first two weeks of development now support purposeful living:

Mental Mastery provides:

- Clarity to recognize your authentic purpose
- Focus on pursuing it consistently
- Mental flexibility to adapt your approach
- Thought patterns that support meaningful work

Emotional Intelligence provides:

- Awareness of what truly energizes you
- Ability to work through fears about following one's purpose
- Resilience to persist when the purpose gets challenging
- Emotional freedom to choose meaning over comfort

Tomorrow's Preview

Tomorrow you'll learn how to align your daily thoughts and actions with your discovered purpose, creating what Allen called "the centralizing point" that gives direction and power to all your efforts.

Remember Allen's Promise

"Cherish your visions; cherish your ideals; cherish the music that stirs in your heart, the beauty that forms in your mind, the loveliness that drapes your purest thoughts, for out of them will grow all delightful conditions, all heavenly environment; of these, if you but remain true to them, your world will at last be built."

Today, you began cherishing the vision of your authentic purpose. You started the process of building a world aligned with your deepest values and highest aspirations.

Your North Star is becoming visible. Tomorrow, you'll learn to navigate by its light.

Day 16: Aligning Thoughts with Purpose

*"Until thought is linked with purpose, there is no intelligent accomplishment. With the majority, the bark of thought is allowed to 'drift' upon the ocean of life. Aimlessness is a vice, and such drifting must not continue for him who would steer clear of catastrophe and destruction." — **James Allen.***

Jennifer had discovered her purpose, but she couldn't figure out how to live it.

After yesterday's exploration, Jennifer felt clear about her calling: "Help working parents create harmony between career success and family connection." It resonated deeply, explained her life patterns, and excited her about future possibilities.

But Monday morning arrived with the same old reality. Demanding boss. Endless emails. Kids need rides to activities. Household tasks multiply faster than she can complete them. By Tuesday afternoon, Jennifer's beautiful purpose felt like just another item on an impossible to-do list.

"I know what I'm supposed to be doing," Jennifer said, "but I can't figure out how to actually do it. My purpose feels inspiring in theory, but impossible in practice."

Jennifer was experiencing the gap between purpose discovery and purpose alignment, the difference between knowing your North Star and actually navigating by it.

When Jennifer learned how to consistently align her thoughts with her purpose, her entire relationship with daily life transformed. Instead of feeling pulled in multiple directions, she began experiencing what Allen called "intelligent accomplishment," focused energy that created meaningful progress toward what truly mattered.

Allen's Insight About Thought-Purpose Integration

James Allen understood that purpose without aligned thinking remains merely a pleasant idea, while aligned thinking without purpose becomes scattered effort. The power comes from their integration.

"A man should conceive of a legitimate purpose in his heart and set out to accomplish it. He should make this purpose the centralizing point of his thoughts," **Allen wrote.** *"It may take the form of a spiritual ideal, or it may be a worldly object, according to his nature at the time being; but whichever it is, he should steadily focus his thought-forces upon the object, which he has set before him."*

Allen saw that most people's thoughts drift aimlessly because they lack a central organizing principle. Purpose provides that principle, a North Star that gives direction to mental energy.

"He should make this purpose his supreme duty, and should devote himself to its attainment, not allowing his thoughts to wander away into ephemeral fancies, longings, and imaginings," Allen continued. This doesn't mean rigid thinking, but rather a consistent return to purposeful focus.

Allen understood that when thoughts and purpose align, you access what he called "concentrated thought," mental energy that creates results far beyond scattered effort.

The Neuroscience of Purpose-Aligned Thinking

Modern research reveals why Allen's approach to thought-purpose alignment is so powerful:

Enhanced Focus Networks: Dr. Adam Gazzaley's research shows that purpose-driven attention activates stronger focus networks in the brain. When you think about meaningful goals, your prefrontal cortex allocates more resources to sustained concentration.

Reduced Cognitive Load: Studies by Dr. Kathleen Vohs demonstrate that having clear priorities reduces the mental effort required for decision-making. Purpose-aligned thinking eliminates hundreds of micro-decisions about what deserves your attention.

Improved Memory Consolidation: Research by Dr. Lynn Nadel reveals that information related to personal goals receives preferential treatment in memory formation. You literally remember purpose-related information better than random facts.

Motivational Persistence: Dr. Edward Deci's research on intrinsic motivation shows that purpose-driven thinking activates different reward pathways than external motivation. Purpose-aligned thoughts sustain energy longer and recover from setbacks faster.

Default Mode Network Optimization: Studies by Dr. Marcus Raichle show that people with strong life purpose have different default mode network patterns. Instead of defaulting to worry or rumination, their minds naturally drift toward purpose-related planning and problem-solving.

The Three Levels of Thought-Purpose Alignment

Level 1: Daily Thought Direction. Consciously directing your thinking toward purpose-related topics throughout the day:

- "How can my current work project serve my purpose?"
- "What would someone living my purpose do in this situation?"
- "How can I approach this conversation with my purpose in mind?"

Level 2: Problem-Solving Through Purpose Lens. Using purpose as a filter for decisions and challenges:

- "Which option better aligns with my purpose?"
- "How can this obstacle become preparation for better purpose expression?"
- "What would I do if my purpose were my primary priority?"

Level 3: Identity Integration. Thinking of yourself as someone who embodies your purpose:

- "I am someone who helps working parents find harmony."
- "I naturally look for ways to express my purpose."
- "My purpose is my compass for all major decisions."

Jennifer's Alignment Journey

When Jennifer learned systematic thought-purpose alignment, her experience of daily life completely shifted:

Week 1: Morning Purpose Priming. Jennifer began each day by spending five minutes thinking about her purpose:

- How could she help working parents today?
- What opportunities might arise to express her purpose?
- How could she approach her own work-family balance as research for helping others?

Week 2: Purposeful Problem-Solving. When facing challenges, Jennifer filtered them through her purpose:

- Meeting conflict with her boss → "How can I model the kind of professional boundary-setting I'd want working parents to learn?"
- Kids fighting over screen time → "How can I handle this in a way that demonstrates effective family communication?"
- Overwhelming work deadline → "How can I manage this stress in a way that preserves family connection?"

Week 3: Identity Shift. Jennifer began thinking of herself as someone already living her purpose:

- Instead of "I want to help working parents," she thought, "I am someone who helps working parents."
- Instead of "Someday I'll do meaningful work," she thought, "My current work is preparation for my purpose."
- Instead of "I don't have time for my purpose," she thought, "Everything I do can express my purpose."

Week 4: Natural Integration. Purpose-aligned thinking became automatic:

- Jennifer naturally noticed opportunities to help other working parents
- Her conversations shifted toward topics related to work-life harmony
- She began documenting insights about family-career balance
- Colleagues started asking her for advice about managing work and family

"It wasn't that my external circumstances changed dramatically," Jennifer said. "It was that I started seeing everything through the lens of my purpose. Suddenly, my regular life became preparation for the work I really want to do."

Today's Practice: The Thought-Purpose Alignment System

Today, you'll learn to make purpose the "centralizing point" of your thoughts, as Allen recommended.

The Morning Purpose Priming Protocol (10 minutes)

Purpose Connection (3 minutes):

- Read your purpose statement from yesterday
- Feel the energy and meaning it contains
- Ask: "How can I express this purpose today?"
- Set intention: "Today, my thoughts will return to this purpose."

Opportunity Scanning (3 minutes):

- Review your day's schedule through purpose lens
- Which activities could serve your purpose?
- What conversations could advance your purpose?
- Where might unexpected purpose opportunities arise?
- How can mundane tasks connect to meaningful aims?

Challenge Reframing (2 minutes):

- What difficulties might you face today?
- How could each challenge serve your purpose development?
- What would someone fully living their purpose do with these challenges?
- How can obstacles become preparation for better service?

Identity Affirmation (2 minutes):

- "I am someone who [your purpose]"
- "I naturally look for ways to express my purpose."
- "My purpose guides my thoughts and decisions."
- "Everything I do can serve my larger mission."

The Purpose of Thought Redirection Practice

Throughout the day, when you notice your thoughts drifting, use this sequence:

Step 1: Gentle Redirect (10 seconds)

- "I notice my thoughts wandering."
- "Let me return to my purpose."

Step 2: Purpose Question (30 seconds) Ask one of these questions:

- "How does my current situation relate to my purpose?"
- "What would someone living my purpose think about this?"
- "How can I approach this with my purpose in mind?"
- "What opportunity might this situation offer for purpose expression?"

Step 3: Aligned Action (Ongoing)

- Take one small action aligned with the purposeful thought
- It could be as simple as listening more carefully
- Or as significant as offering help to someone
- The key is connecting thought to purpose-aligned action

Advanced Purpose-Thinking Techniques

The Purpose Problem-Solving Method: When facing any decision or challenge:

- **State the situation clearly**: "I need to decide whether to take this job offer."
- **Apply purpose lens**: "How does each option serve my purpose of helping working parents?"
- **Consider purpose development**: "Which choice will better prepare me to serve my purpose?"
- **Assess alignment**: "Which option feels most aligned with who I'm becoming?"
- **Choose and commit**: Make the decision that best serves purpose fulfillment

The Daily Purpose Integration Review: Each evening, ask:

- When did I think about my purpose today?
- How did purpose-aligned thinking affect my decisions?
- What opportunities did I notice when thinking purposefully?
- How can I integrate purpose thinking more naturally tomorrow?

The Purpose Story Technique: Reframe daily experiences as chapters in your purpose story:

- "Today's difficult customer interaction was training in the patience I'll need for my purpose."
- "Managing family chaos today taught me skills for helping other working parents."
- "Solving this work problem developed abilities I'll use in my purposeful work."

Overcoming Common Alignment Challenges

"My purpose feels disconnected from my current responsibilities."

- Look for ways your current role develops purpose-relevant skills
- Find aspects of current work that align with purpose values
- Use current situations as research for future purpose expression
- View present responsibilities as preparation for purposeful service

"I keep forgetting to think about purpose."

- Set phone reminders throughout the day
- Write your purpose on cards and place them where you'll see them
- Ask trusted friends to occasionally ask about your purpose
- Create environmental cues that prompt purpose thinking

"Purpose thinking feels forced or artificial."

- Start with small doses—even 30 seconds of purpose thinking helps
- Focus on curiosity rather than forcing specific outcomes
- Remember that all new mental habits feel artificial initially
- Trust that alignment becomes natural with consistent practice

"I don't see how mundane tasks connect to my purpose."

- Every skill can serve larger purposes (organization, communication, patience)
- Current work often develops capacities needed for purposeful work
- Daily interactions are practice for purposeful relationships
- Managing current life well demonstrates readiness for purpose expansion

The Power of Purpose-Aligned Questions

Transform your mental habits by consistently asking purpose-centered questions:

Throughout the day:
- "How can this serve my purpose?"
- "What would my purpose have me do here?"
- "How is this preparing me for better purpose expression?"

During challenges:
- "How can this difficulty develop my purpose-related abilities?"
- "What is this teaching me that will help me serve others?"
- "How would someone committed to my purpose handle this?"

In relationships:
- "How can I bring my purpose qualities to this interaction?"
- "What does this person need that relates to my purpose?"
- "How can I practice purpose-related skills in this relationship?"

Before decisions:
- "Which option better serves my purpose?"
- "How do these choices align with my deepest values?"
- "What would I choose if purpose were my primary criterion?"

Building Purpose Momentum

Week 1: Focus on morning purpose priming and basic thought redirection

Week 2: Add purpose, problem-solving, and evening integration reviews

Week 3: Experiment with identity thinking and purpose story framing

Week 4: Develop natural, automatic purpose-aligned thinking patterns

Monthly: Review and refine your purpose statement based on lived experience

Quarterly: Assess how well your major life areas align with your purpose

The Compound Effect of Aligned Thinking

When you consistently align thoughts with purpose:

Increased Clarity: Decisions become easier because you have a clear decision-making criterion

Enhanced Energy: Purpose-aligned thinking generates sustainable motivation

Improved Focus: Mental energy stops scattering across random concerns

Greater Opportunities: You notice chances to express purpose that others miss

Authentic Confidence: Acting from purpose creates genuine self-assurance

Natural Service: You automatically look for ways to contribute meaningfully

Building on Your Development

Your growing capacities now support purposeful thinking:

- **Mental mastery** provides the ability to direct thoughts consciously
- **Emotional intelligence** helps you notice when thinking feels aligned vs. scattered
- **Purpose clarity** gives direction to your mental and emotional energies

Tomorrow's Preview

Tomorrow you'll learn to overcome the inevitable obstacles that arise when you begin aligning your life with authentic purpose—and how to transform these challenges into strength for more effective service.

Remember Allen's Vision

"Those who are not prepared for the apprehension of a great purpose should fix the thoughts upon the faultless performance of their duty, no matter how insignificant their task may appear. Only in this way can the thoughts be gathered and focused, and resolution and energy be developed."

Today, you learned to gather and focus your thoughts around your authentic purpose. You began developing the mental discipline that transforms purpose from inspiration into reality.

Your thoughts are no longer drifting aimlessly. They're aligned with your North Star, creating the intelligent accomplishment Allen envisioned.

Day 17: Overcoming Purpose Obstacles

"Doubts and fears should be rigorously excluded; they are disintegrating elements, which break up the straight line of effort, rendering it crooked, ineffectual, useless. Thoughts of doubt and fear never accomplished anything, and never can." **— James Allen.**

Three months after discovering his purpose, "helping small business owners create sustainable success without burnout," Marcus felt more stuck than ever.

The initial excitement had worn off. Reality had set in. Every time Marcus tried to move toward his purpose, obstacles appeared: He didn't have the "right" credentials. He couldn't afford to leave his steady job. His family thought he was being impractical. He had no network in the consulting world. He was probably too old to start over.

By month three, Marcus had convinced himself that his purpose was just a nice idea that didn't fit his real life. He was facing what everyone encounters when they begin aligning with authentic purpose: the inevitable gap between inspiration and implementation.

"Maybe some people are meant to live their purpose, and others are meant to be practical," Marcus told himself. He was ready to abandon his calling before he'd even begun pursuing it.

Marcus was experiencing what Allen understood as the natural resistance that emerges when you attempt to align your outer life with your inner truth. This resistance isn't a sign that you're on the wrong path; it's often proof that you're on the right one.

Allen's Understanding of Purpose Obstacles

James Allen recognized that the path toward purpose is never smooth or straightforward. He understood that obstacles aren't impediments to purpose; they're part of the development process that prepares you to serve effectively.

"He who has conquered doubt and fear has conquered failure. His every thought is allied with power, and all difficulties are bravely met and wisely overcome," **Allen wrote**. He saw that the obstacles themselves often contain the very qualities needed for purpose fulfillment.

Allen understood that doubt and fear are natural responses to growth: *"The will to do springs from the knowledge that we can do. Doubt and fear are the great enemies of knowledge, and he who encourages them, who does not slay them, thwarts himself at every step."*

"Thought allied fearlessly to purpose becomes creative force," Allen observed. The key isn't avoiding obstacles but learning to work with them as preparation for greater service.

Allen saw that every purpose worth pursuing will be tested by circumstances that seem to prove it's impossible. These tests aren't meant to stop you—they're meant to strengthen you.

The Science of Obstacle Psychology

Research reveals why obstacles to purpose feel so intense and how to work with them effectively:

Cognitive Dissonance: Dr. Leon Festinger's research shows that when your current situation conflicts with your values (pursuing purpose), your brain creates discomfort designed to restore consistency. This discomfort often manifests as self-doubt or rationalization.

Fear of Identity Change: Studies by Dr. Carol Dweck demonstrate that pursuing purpose often requires identity shifts, which trigger psychological resistance. Your brain prefers familiar discomfort to unfamiliar growth.

Impostor Syndrome: Research by Dr. Pauline Clance reveals that 70% of people experience impostor syndrome when pursuing meaningful goals. Feeling "not qualified" is normal, not disqualifying.

Status Quo Bias: Dr. William Samuelson's research shows that humans have a strong preference for keeping things as they are, even when change would be beneficial. This bias makes purpose pursuit feel unreasonably difficult.

Social Pressure: Studies by Dr. Shelly Taylor demonstrate that changing your path often triggers resistance from others who feel threatened by your growth or left behind by your choices.

The Five Universal Purpose Obstacles

Obstacle 1: The Credibility Question. *"Who am I to do this? I don't have the right experience/education/background."*

- **The Truth**: Purpose doesn't require permission or perfect credentials. Your unique combination of experiences, including your struggles, often provides exactly the perspective needed for your particular contribution.
- **Allen's Response**: *"A man may rise to high success in the world, and even to lofty altitudes in the spiritual realm, and again descend into weakness and wretchedness by allowing arrogant, selfish, and corrupt thoughts to take possession of him."* Character and commitment matter more than credentials.

Obstacle 2: The Practicality Trap. *"This is nice in theory, but I have bills to pay and responsibilities to others."*

- **The Truth**: Purpose and practicality aren't opposites. Most purposes can be developed gradually while maintaining current responsibilities. Purpose often enhances rather than threatens practical success.
- **Allen's Response**: *"He who would accomplish little must sacrifice little; he who would achieve much must sacrifice much; he who would attain highly must sacrifice greatly."* The sacrifice often involves comfort and familiarity, not necessities.

Obstacle 3: The Timing Objection. *"I'm too young/old/busy/unprepared. This isn't the right time."*

- **The Truth**: There's never a perfect time for meaningful change. The best time is always now, starting with small steps that fit your current circumstances.
- **Allen's Response**: *"The greatest achievement was at first and for a time a dream. The oak sleeps in the acorn; the bird waits in the egg."* Purpose begins with small seeds planted in imperfect soil.

Obstacle 4: The Support Shortage. *"Nobody understands what I'm trying to do. I don't have a network or mentors."*

- **The Truth**: Purpose pursuit often requires building new communities and relationships. The people you need often appear when you begin taking action, not before.
- **Allen's Response**: *"When he begins to reflect upon his condition, and to search diligently for the Law upon which his being is established, he then becomes the wise master."* Self-reliance builds the strength needed for eventual collaboration.

Obstacle 5: The Comparison Catastrophe. *"Others are already doing this better than I ever could. What's the point?"*

- **The Truth**: Your purpose isn't about being the best—it's about offering your unique contribution. The world needs multiple expressions of similar purposes serving different people in different ways.
- **Allen's Response**: *"Your circumstances may be uncongenial, but they shall not long remain so if you but perceive an Ideal and strive to reach it."* Focus on your ideal, not others' achievements.

Marcus's Obstacle Transformation Process

When Marcus learned to view obstacles as development opportunities rather than roadblocks, his entire approach changed:

Step 1: Obstacle Inventory. Marcus identified his specific barriers:

- Lack of business consulting credentials
- Fear of leaving financial security
- Family skepticism about career change
- No network in his target industry
- Self-doubt about age (he was 47)

Step 2: Obstacle Reframing. Marcus transformed each obstacle into an asset:

- Lack of credentials → Real-world experience that business owners could relate to
- Financial concerns → Motivation to create value quickly and efficiently
- Family skepticism → Opportunity to demonstrate purposeful decision-making
- No network → Chance to build authentic relationships based on service
- Age concerns → Wisdom and stability that younger consultants lacked

Step 3: Gradual Implementation. Instead of requiring dramatic change, Marcus began expressing his purpose within his current circumstances:

- Started informal coaching conversations with struggling business owners
- Developed expertise by solving problems in his current company
- Built credibility through documented results
- Created content sharing lessons learned
- Developed systems that could eventually become his methodology

Step 4: Evidence Collection. Marcus documented every piece of evidence that his purpose was viable:

- Positive feedback from colleagues he'd helped
- Successful projects that applied his problem-solving approach
- Growing expertise in sustainable business practices
- Building confidence in his unique perspective

Within a year, Marcus had transitioned to part-time consulting while maintaining financial security. Within two years, he was fully supporting his family through purpose-aligned work.

"The obstacles didn't disappear," Marcus said. "But they stopped being reasons to quit and became reasons to get creative."

Today's Practice: The Obstacle Transformation System

Today, you'll learn to transform purpose obstacles from roadblocks into stepping stones.

The Obstacle Inventory and Reframe Process (20 minutes)

Step 1: Complete Obstacle Identification (8 minutes) Write down every obstacle you perceive to living your purpose. Be exhaustive:

Internal Obstacles:

- Self-doubt and impostor syndrome
- Fear of failure or judgment
- Lack of confidence in specific areas
- Perfectionism or procrastination
- Identity conflicts

External Obstacles:

- Financial constraints
- Time limitations
- Lack of credentials or experience
- Family or social pressure
- Market competition

Practical Obstacles:

- Geographic limitations
- Technology or skill gaps
- Resource shortages
- Regulatory or institutional barriers
- Timing challenges

Step 2: Obstacle-to-Asset Transformation (12 minutes) For each obstacle, complete this sentence: "This apparent obstacle is actually preparing me for my purpose by..."

Examples:

- "My lack of formal training is actually preparing me by forcing me to learn through real experience, which makes my eventual teaching more practical and relatable."
- "My financial constraints are actually preparing me by teaching me to be resourceful and helping me understand the challenges my future clients face."
- "My age is actually preparing me by giving me the wisdom and perspective that younger people in this field lack."

Advanced Obstacle-Working Techniques

The Obstacle Investigation Method: For each major obstacle, ask:

- "What is this obstacle trying to protect me from?"
- "What would I need to develop to handle this challenge?"
- "How might overcoming this obstacle serve my eventual purpose?"
- "What would someone committed to my purpose do with this situation?"

The Future Self Consultation: Imagine yourself five years from now, successfully living your purpose:

- "What would my future self say about this current obstacle?"
- "How did my future self overcome this challenge?"
- "What advice would they give me about working with this difficulty?"
- "What would they want me to know about this apparent problem?"

The Obstacle Gratitude Practice: For your biggest current obstacle, write:

- "I'm grateful for this obstacle because it's teaching me..."
- "This challenge is developing my capacity for..."
- "Overcoming this will prepare me to help others with..."
- "This difficulty is making me the kind of person who..."

The Physics of Purpose Obstacles

Understanding why obstacles appear helps you work with them more skillfully:

- **Obstacles Test Commitment**: Like a river flowing toward the ocean, purpose encounters resistance that tests whether you're genuinely committed or just casually interested.
- **Obstacles Develop Capability**: Just as muscles grow through resistance training, your purpose-related abilities develop through overcoming challenges.

- **Obstacles Clarify Direction**: Like a prism that separates white light into distinct colors, obstacles help clarify which aspects of your purpose are most important to you.
- **Obstacles Attract Resources**: Taking action despite obstacles often brings the support, information, and opportunities you need to continue.
- **Obstacles Create Credibility**: Having overcome challenges makes you more qualified to help others facing similar difficulties.

Working with Specific Obstacle Types

For Fear-Based Obstacles:

- "What's the worst that could realistically happen?"
- "How could I handle that worst-case scenario?"
- "What's the cost of not pursuing my purpose?"
- "What small step would move me forward despite the fear?"

For Resource-Based Obstacles:

- "How can I express my purpose with current resources?"
- "What creative alternatives exist to traditional approaches?"
- "Who might benefit from my purpose enough to support its development?"
- "How can I start small and build gradually?"

For Social Pressure Obstacles:

- "Who truly has my best interests at heart?"
- "How can I honor others' concerns while staying true to my purpose?"
- "What evidence can I gather to demonstrate purpose viability?"
- "How can I find community among others pursuing similar purposes?"

The Obstacle Integration Protocol

Daily Obstacle Work (5 minutes each morning):

1. **Identify today's likely obstacles**: What resistance might you face?
2. **Reframe as development**: How could each obstacle serve your growth?
3. **Plan creative responses**: What would someone committed to your purpose do?
4. **Set learning intention**: What do you want to learn from today's challenges?

Weekly Obstacle Review (15 minutes):

1. **Assess obstacle work**: How did you handle this week's challenges?
2. **Extract lessons**: What did obstacles teach you about yourself or your purpose?
3. **Adjust strategies**: How can you work more effectively with resistance?
4. **Celebrate progress**: What growth resulted from working with difficulties?

Building Anti-Fragile Purpose

Move beyond overcoming obstacles to using them as fuel for a stronger purpose expression:

- **Document lessons learned** from each challenge to help others
- **Develop systems** that work even when conditions aren't ideal
- **Build resilience** that makes you more capable of serving others
- **Create value** from the unique perspective your obstacles provide

Tomorrow's Preview

Tomorrow, you'll learn how to build momentum toward your purpose through small, consistent actions that compound into significant progress over time.

Remember Allen's Truth

"Thought allied fearlessly to purpose becomes creative force: he who knows this is ready to become something higher and stronger than a mere bundle of wavering thoughts and fluctuating sensations; he who does this has become the conscious and intelligent wielder of his mental powers."

Today, you learned to ally your thoughts fearlessly with your purpose, transforming obstacles from enemies into allies. You're becoming the conscious and intelligent wielder of both your mental powers and life circumstances.

Obstacles are not the end of your purpose journey. They're preparation for its fulfillment.

Day 18: Small Steps, Big Purpose

"All that a man achieves and all that he fails to achieve is the direct result of his own thoughts. In a justly ordered universe, where loss of equipoise would mean total destruction, individual responsibility must be absolute." — James Allen.

Diana had discovered her purpose, "helping introverts build authentic confidence," and overcome her major obstacles through reframing and creative problem-solving. But she still felt overwhelmed by the gap between where she was and where she wanted to be.

"I know what I want to do," Diana said, "but it feels so big. How do I go from being a shy accountant to helping thousands of introverts? How do I build a platform, create programs, find clients, and establish credibility? When I think about everything I need to do, I feel paralyzed."

Diana was experiencing what many people face when they clarify their purpose: the intimidation of transformation. She was looking at the mountain peak instead of the trail, the finished book instead of the first page, the established business instead of the first conversation.

When Diana learned the power of purpose-aligned micro-actions—small steps that seem insignificant but compound into extraordinary results—her journey became not only manageable but enjoyable.

Within six months, Diana had helped over 50 introverts, created a popular blog series, and developed a waiting list for her confidence-building program. She achieved this transformation not through dramatic gestures but through consistent, small actions aligned with her purpose.

Allen's Understanding of Small, Consistent Effort

James Allen understood that all meaningful achievement comes through accumulated small efforts rather than single large actions. He saw that consistent daily practice creates more transformation than sporadic, intense effort.

"In all human affairs, there are efforts, and there are results, and the strength of the effort is the measure of the result," Allen wrote. He recognized that the quality and consistency of effort matter more than the intensity of individual actions.

Allen observed that most people fail not because their goals are too ambitious, but because they try to accomplish everything immediately: *"Not having commenced to manfully control his thoughts, he is not in a position to control affairs and to adopt serious responsibilities."*

"As the physically weak man can make himself strong by careful and patient training, so the man of weak thoughts can make them strong by exercising himself in right thinking," **Allen** explained. He understood that strength, whether physical, mental, or purposeful,develops gradually through consistent practice.

Allen saw that small, daily actions aligned with purpose create what he called "concentrated effort"—focused energy that accumulates into remarkable achievement over time.

The Science of Small Steps and Compound Growth

Modern research validates Allen's insight about the power of incremental progress:

The Compound Effect: Research by mathematician Edward Lorenz demonstrates that small changes in initial conditions can lead to dramatically different outcomes over time. In human development, daily 1% improvements compound into 37x growth over a year.

Neuroplasticity and Micro-Practice: Dr. Alvaro Pascual-Leone's studies show that brief, regular practice creates stronger neural pathways than intensive, sporadic practice. The brain responds better to consistent small inputs than irregular large ones.

Behavioral Momentum: Research by Dr. Stephen Rollnick reveals that completing small actions builds psychological momentum that makes larger actions feel more achievable. Success breeds success through neurochemical reinforcement.

Identity Shifts Through Micro-Actions: Dr. James Clear's research shows that small, consistent actions gradually shift identity. Each purpose-aligned action becomes a vote for the person you're becoming.

Stress Reduction: Studies by Dr. Kelly McGonigal demonstrate that breaking large goals into small steps reduces the stress response that often sabotages goal achievement. Small steps feel safe to your nervous system.

The Architecture of Purpose-Aligned Small Steps

Micro-Actions (1-5 minutes):

- Write one paragraph about your purpose topic
- Have one conversation related to your purpose
- Read one article in your purpose field
- Take one small action to help someone in your purpose area

Mini-Habits (5-15 minutes daily):

- Daily purpose journaling
- Regular skill-building practice
- Consistent content creation
- Ongoing relationship building

Milestone Projects (Weekly/monthly):

- Complete one small project related to your purpose
- Attend one networking event or learning opportunity
- Create one piece of valuable content
- Help one person in a significant way

Diana's Small Steps Strategy

Diana transformed her overwhelming purpose into a series of manageable daily actions:

Weeks 1-2: Foundation Building

- **Daily micro-action**: Write one paragraph about introvert challenges
- **Weekly project**: Research three successful introvert coaches
- **Purpose practice**: Have one meaningful conversation daily
- **Skill building**: Read 15 minutes about confidence psychology

Weeks 3-4: Audience Connection

- **Daily micro-action**: Comment helpfully on one introvert-related post
- **Weekly project**: Start a weekly blog about introvert experiences
- **Purpose practice**: Share one vulnerability or insight with a friend
- **Skill building**: Practice one confidence technique daily

Weeks 5-8: Value Creation

- **Daily micro-action**: Answer one question from introverts online
- **Weekly project**: Create one resource for fellow introverts
- **Purpose practice**: Help one person with a confidence challenge
- **Skill building**: Study one coaching conversation technique weekly

Weeks 9-12: Service Expansion

- **Daily micro-action**: Reach out to one person who might benefit from support
- **Weekly project**: Offer a free mini-coaching session to one person
- **Purpose practice**: Share lessons learned publicly
- **Skill building**: Develop one group activity or exercise

By month three, Diana's small steps had created remarkable momentum:

- 50+ people read her blog regularly
- 15 people she'd helped through mini-sessions
- Growing reputation as someone who understands introvert challenges
- Clear evidence that her purpose was viable and valuable

"I never felt overwhelmed because I was only focusing on today's small step," Diana said. "But when I looked back after three months, I couldn't believe how much had accumulated."

Today's Practice: The Small Steps Purpose System

Today, you'll design a daily practice of purpose-aligned micro-actions that build unstoppable momentum toward meaningful contribution.

The Purpose Micro-Action Design Process (25 minutes)

Step 1: Purpose Breakdown (8 minutes) Break your purpose into component skills and activities:

Knowledge Areas: What do you need to learn?

- Industry insights, skills, methodologies
- Understanding the people you want to serve
- Best practices from others doing similar work

Relationship Building: Who do you need to connect with?

- People who share your purpose
- Potential mentors or collaborators
- People you want to serve
- Communities relevant to your purpose

Value Creation: How can you start serving now?

- Content that helps your target audience
- Direct help to individuals
- Resources or tools that solve problems
- Examples or inspiration for others

Skill Development: What abilities need strengthening?

- Communication and teaching skills
- Technical or professional competencies
- Personal development areas
- Purpose-specific methodologies

Step 2: Daily Micro-Action Selection (10 minutes) Choose ONE micro-action from each category that you can do daily:

Learning Micro-Action (5-10 minutes daily): Examples:

- Read one article about your purpose topic
- Watch one educational video in your field
- Listen to 10 minutes of a relevant podcast
- Study one technique or methodology

Connection Micro-Action (5-10 minutes daily): Examples:

- Comment meaningfully on one relevant post
- Send one message to someone in your purpose field
- Join one conversation about your purpose topic
- Express appreciation to someone doing purpose-related work

Service Micro-Action (5-10 minutes daily): Examples:

- Answer one question related to your purpose
- Share one helpful insight or resource
- Offer encouragement to someone struggling in your purpose area
- Create one small piece of valuable content

Development Micro-Action (5-10 minutes daily): Examples:

- Practice one skill related to your purpose
- Journal about one purpose-related insight
- Work on one small improvement project
- Reflect on one lesson learned

Step 3: Implementation Planning (7 minutes) Design your daily practice:

- **Time Selection**: When will you do each micro-action?
- **Sequence Design**: What order works best for your schedule?
- **Accountability Method**: How will you track completion?
- **Environmental Setup**: What do you need to make this easy?
- **Flexibility Plan**: How will you adapt when life gets busy?

Advanced Small Steps Strategies

The 2-Minute Rule: Make your micro-actions so small they take less than 2 minutes to complete. This eliminates resistance and builds consistency. You can always do more, but you're only committed to the minimum.

The Chain Method: Use a calendar to mark each day you complete your micro-actions. Focus on not breaking the chain rather than on dramatic results. Consistency becomes its own motivation.

The Compound Documentation: Keep a simple log of your micro-actions and their results:

- What you did
- Who did it help, or how did it serve your purpose
- What you learned
- What became possible as a result

Review weekly to see the accumulating impact.

The Seasonal Focus: Every 90 days, emphasize one category while maintaining the others:

- Spring: Learning and skill development
- Summer: Relationship building and networking
- Fall: Service and value creation
- Winter: Reflection and strategic planning

Working with Small Steps Resistance

"These actions feel too small to matter."

- Remember that all massive achievements began with small steps
- Trust the compound effect—small improvements accumulate exponentially
- Focus on consistency rather than individual impact
- Document results to see the accumulating progress

"I want to do more, but don't have time."

- Start smaller—even 1 minute daily creates momentum
- Use transition times (commute, waiting, breaks)
- Replace less purposeful activities with micro-actions
- Remember that consistency beats intensity

"I don't see results fast enough."
- Most compound growth is invisible initially
- Focus on process metrics (actions taken) rather than outcome metrics (results achieved)
- Celebrate small wins and progress markers
- Trust that sustained effort creates inevitable results

"It's hard to stay motivated for small actions."
- Connect each micro-action to your larger purpose and vision
- Track the people you're helping, even in small ways
- Find accountability partners doing similar work
- Remember that motivation follows action, not the reverse

The Psychology of Small Steps Success

Small steps work because they:
- **Reduce Overwhelm**: Breaking large purposes into small actions makes them feel manageable rather than impossible
- **Build Confidence**: Completing daily actions creates evidence that you can make progress toward your purpose
- **Create Identity Shifts**: Each purpose-aligned action reinforces your identity as someone who lives their purpose
- **Generate Momentum**: Success in small areas builds energy for larger challenges
- **Develop Skills**: Daily practice builds competency gradually and sustainably
- **Attract Opportunities**: Consistent action often brings unexpected resources and connections

Scaling Your Small Steps

As your capacity grows, evolve your practice:
- **Month 1**: Establish consistent micro-actions
- **Month 2**: Add weekly projects that serve your purpose
- **Month 3**: Introduce monthly challenges that stretch your skills
- **Month 4**: Begin quarterly goals that integrate all your development

Always maintain the daily micro-actions as your foundation, even as you add larger projects.

Building Community Around Small Steps

Find Purpose Partners: Connect with others taking small steps toward similar purposes

Share Progress: Document your journey to inspire and encourage others

Offer Support: Help others design and maintain their own small steps practice

Create Accountability: Form groups focused on consistent purpose-aligned action

Tomorrow's Preview
Tomorrow you'll learn to embody your highest self consistently—living from the identity of someone who has already achieved their purpose rather than someone still striving toward it.

Remember Allen's Promise

"Achievement, of whatever kind, is the crown of effort, the diadem of thought. By the aid of self-control, resolution, purity, righteousness, and well-directed thought, a man ascends."

Today, you learned to create the well-directed thought and consistent effort that leads to purpose achievement. You discovered that the crown of effort isn't won in single heroic moments but through accumulated daily choices aligned with your deepest values.

Your purpose doesn't require giant leaps. It requires small steps taken with great consistency.

Start where you are. Use what you have. Do what you can. Trust the compound effect.

Day 19: Living as Your Highest Self

*"You will become as small as your controlling desire; as great as your dominant aspiration. Your Vision is the promise of what you shall one day be; your Ideal is the prophecy of what you shall at last unveil." — **James Allen.***

Rachel had been working toward her purpose for months—"helping busy mothers create peaceful, organized homes"—but she noticed something troubling: she only felt purposeful when actively working on purpose-related activities.

When organizing her own home, she felt scattered and overwhelmed. When dealing with her children's chaos, she lost patience quickly. When facing her own domestic challenges, she forgot all the wisdom she shared with others.

"I feel like a fraud," Rachel confided. "I help other mothers create peace in their homes, but my own life is still chaotic half the time. How can I teach what I haven't fully mastered myself?"

Rachel was experiencing the gap between purpose work and purpose identity—the difference between doing purposeful activities and being a purposeful person. She was practicing her purpose as something external to herself rather than expressing it as something integral to who she was.

When Rachel learned to live from the identity of her highest self—the person she was becoming through her purpose—everything shifted. Instead of having good days and bad days, she had more and less polished expressions of the same centered identity.

Allen's Vision of Identity-Based Living

James Allen understood that true transformation comes not from changing what you do but from changing who you are. He saw that the most powerful people live from their ideals rather than toward them.

*"Dream lofty dreams, and as you dream, so shall you become," **Allen wrote.** "Your Vision is the promise of what you shall one day be; your Ideal is the prophecy of what you shall at last unveil."*

Allen recognized that most people live from their current circumstances while occasionally reaching toward their aspirations. But truly purposeful people live from their aspirations while occasionally being pulled back by circumstances.

"He who cherishes a beautiful vision, a lofty ideal in his heart, will one day realize it," Allen observed. The key word "cherishes"—holding your ideal so close that it becomes your natural way of being.

Allen saw that when you live from your highest self consistently, external circumstances gradually align with internal reality. The world responds to who you are, not who you're trying to become.

The Science of Identity-Based Change

Modern psychology reveals why living from your highest self is more effective than striving toward it:

- **Identity-Behavior Consistency**: Research by Dr. Leon Festinger shows that people naturally act in ways that align with their identity. When you see yourself as a peaceful person, peaceful actions feel natural rather than forced.
- **Self-Schema Theory**: Studies by Dr. Hazel Markus demonstrate that your self-concept acts as a cognitive framework that filters perceptions and guides decisions. Operating from your highest self identity creates consistency across all life areas.
- **Embodied Cognition**: Research by Dr. Amy Cuddy reveals that physical posture and behavior influence internal states. When you act like your highest self, you begin feeling like your highest self.
- **Neural Pathway Reinforcement**: Dr. Joe Dispenza's research shows that repeatedly embodying a new identity strengthens associated neural networks, making that identity increasingly natural and automatic.
- **Social Identity Confirmation**: Studies by Dr. William Swann reveal that others tend to treat you according to the identity you consistently express, creating a positive feedback loop that reinforces your highest self.

The Architecture of Highest Self Living

Level 1: Embodied Presence. Carrying yourself physically as your highest self:

- Posture that reflects your purpose (confident, open, grounded)
- Energy that matches your ideals (calm, focused, compassionate)
- Movement that expresses your values (intentional, graceful, purposeful)

Level 2: Emotional Consistency. Responding emotionally as your highest self:

- Patience when facing delays or difficulties
- Compassion when others are struggling
- Enthusiasm for opportunities to serve

- Equanimity during challenging circumstances

Level 3: Mental Habits. Thinking patterns that reflect your highest self:

- Curiosity instead of judgment
- Solution-focused instead of problem-focused
- Growth-mindset instead of fixed-mindset
- Service orientation instead of self-focus

Level 4: Behavioral Integration. Acting from your highest self in all situations:

- Professional interactions guided by purpose and values
- Personal relationships expressing your ideals
- Daily routines reflecting your principles
- Crisis responses demonstrating your growth

Rachel's Highest Self Integration Journey

When Rachel began living from her identity as someone who embodied peace and organization, her entire experience shifted:

Weeks 1-2: Identity Clarification. Rachel defined her highest self clearly:

- "I am someone who creates calm in chaos."
- "I naturally find simple solutions to complex problems."
- "I embody the peace I want to see in my home."
- "I respond to stress with wisdom and grace."

Weeks 3-4: Physical Embodiment. Rachel began carrying herself as this peaceful, organized person:

- Slower, more intentional movements
- Deeper breathing during stressful moments
- Organized personal space that reflected inner calm
- Physical presence that naturally calmed others

Weeks 5-8: Emotional Consistency. Rachel practiced responding emotionally as her highest self:

- When children were chaotic, she remained centered
- When unexpected challenges arose, she found creative solutions
- When feeling overwhelmed, she remembered her peaceful identity
- When helping others, she drew from authentic, embodied experience

Weeks 9-12: Lifestyle Integration. Rachel's entire life began reflecting her highest self identity:

- Her home naturally became more organized
- Family interactions became more harmonious

- Work with clients felt more authentic
- Daily routines supported rather than conflicted with her purpose

"The amazing thing," Rachel said, "is that I stopped feeling like a fraud. I wasn't teaching what I hoped to become, I was sharing what I was actively practicing and embodying. My clients could sense the authenticity."

Today's Practice: The Highest Self Embodiment System

Today, you'll learn to live consistently from the identity of your most purposeful, developed self.

The Highest Self Definition Process (20 minutes)

Step 1: Vision Clarification (8 minutes). Imagine yourself five years from now, fully living your purpose. Describe this person:

How do they carry themselves physically?

- Posture, energy, presence
- How they move through space
- Their natural demeanor and bearing

How do they respond emotionally?

- Their typical emotional state
- How they handle stress and challenges
- Their way of relating to others
- Their response to setbacks and successes

How do they think about situations?

- Their default mental frameworks
- How they process problems and opportunities
- Their attitude toward learning and growth
- Their perspective on service and contribution

How do they behave in various contexts?

- Professional interactions
- Personal relationships
- Daily routines and habits
- Crisis responses and decision-making

Step 2: Identity Statement Creation (7 minutes). Write 5-10 "I am" statements that capture your highest self:

Examples:

- "I am someone who brings calm to chaotic situations."
- "I am naturally curious about people's experiences and perspectives."
- "I am a person who sees possibilities where others see problems."
- "I am someone who creates beauty and order wherever I go."
- "I am a natural teacher who helps others discover their strengths."

Step 3: Daily Embodiment Planning (5 minutes). For each "I am" statement, identify:

- **One physical way** to embody this quality today
- **One emotional expression** of this identity
- **One mental habit** that reflects this aspect
- **One behavioral choice** that demonstrates this quality

The Highest Self Morning Practice (10 minutes)

Identity Activation (3 minutes):

- Stand in a posture that reflects your highest self
- Breathe in a way that embodies your purpose
- Feel the energy of your most developed identity
- Say your "I am" statements with conviction

Day Preview (4 minutes):

- Review your day's schedule as your highest self
- Identify where this identity will be most important
- Visualize yourself embodying these qualities consistently
- Set the intention to live from this identity, not toward it

Energy Anchoring (3 minutes):

- Choose one physical gesture that connects you to your highest self
- Practice this gesture while feeling your purposeful identity
- Use this anchor throughout the day to return to your highest self
- Commit to embodying this identity in challenging moments

Advanced Highest Self Practices

The Identity Check-In Method: Set random alarms throughout the day. When they sound, ask:

- "Am I being my highest self right now?"
- "How would my highest self handle this current situation?"
- "What adjustment would bring me back into alignment?"
- "How can I express my best qualities in this moment?"

The Highest Self Problem-Solving: When facing any challenge, ask:

- "How would my highest self interpret this situation?"
- "What would my most developed identity do here?"
- "What opportunity does this challenge offer for embodying my ideals?"
- "How can I use this difficulty to practice my highest qualities?"

The Integration Review Process: Each evening, reflect:

- "When did I most fully embody my highest self today?"
- "Where did I fall back into old identity patterns?"
- "What helped me stay connected to my purposeful identity?"
- "How can I embody my highest self more consistently tomorrow?"

Working with Identity Resistance

"This feels fake or like I'm pretending."

- All identity development initially feels artificial
- You're not pretending—you're practicing your emerging identity
- Authenticity comes through embodiment, not the reverse
- Your highest self is already within you; you're just expressing it more consistently

"I can't maintain this when life gets stressful."

- Start with low-stakes situations to build the neural pathways
- Use stress as a practice opportunity for identity strengthening
- Remember that your highest self includes grace for imperfection
- Focus on recovery speed rather than never falling back

"Others notice I'm different and seem suspicious."

- Authentic growth often triggers others' discomfort with change
- Stay consistent with your identity regardless of others' reactions
- Some people will be inspired by your transformation
- Your embodied growth gives others permission for their own development

"I don't feel worthy of this identity yet."

- Worthiness develops through practice, not prerequisites
- Your highest self includes compassion for your current limitations
- Growth identity is about direction, not perfection
- You become worthy by consistently choosing to embody worthiness

The Ripple Effects of Highest Self Living

Personal Impact:

- Increased self-respect and confidence

- Greater consistency between values and actions
- Reduced internal conflict and self-criticism
- Enhanced ability to handle challenges gracefully

Relational Impact:

- Others feel more comfortable and inspired around you
- Deeper, more authentic connections
- Natural leadership through example
- Positive influence on family and colleague development

Professional Impact:

- Work becomes an expression of identity rather than a separate role
- Enhanced credibility and trustworthiness
- Natural authority in your purpose area
- Attraction of opportunities aligned with your highest self

Societal Impact:

- Modeling of conscious living for others
- Contribution to collective elevation
- Creation of environments that support others' growth
- Living proof that transformation is possible

Integrating All Three Weeks

Your highest self embodies everything you've learned:

- **Mental Mastery**: Your highest self thinks consciously, purposefully, and skillfully
- **Emotional Intelligence**: Your highest self feels deeply while responding wisely
- **Purpose Alignment**: Your highest self naturally serves your deepest calling

Living as your highest self integrates all these capacities into one consistent identity.

Preparing for Life Mastery

Tomorrow you'll learn to maintain your highest self-identity during life's inevitable storms—demonstrating that your transformation is real, durable, and unshakeable.

Remember Allen's Truth

"And you, too, youthful reader, will realize the Vision (not the idle wish) of your heart, be it base or beautiful, or a mixture of both, for you will always gravitate toward that which you, secretly, most love."

Today, you learned to love and embody your highest self so consistently that gravitating toward it becomes natural and automatic.

You are not becoming someone new. You are unveiling who you truly are.

Live from that truth.

Day 20: Mastering Life's Storms

*"Tempest-tossed souls, wherever ye may be, under whatsoever conditions ye may live, know this—in the ocean of life the isles of Blessedness are smiling, and the sunny shore of your ideal awaits your coming. Keep your hand firmly upon the helm of thought." — **James Allen.***

At 2:47 AM on a Tuesday, everything in Susan's world fell apart.

The phone call from the hospital. Her teenage son's car accident. The three-hour surgery. The financial implications of extended medical care. The work project that couldn't wait. The other children who needed stability amidst chaos.

Six months earlier, this crisis would have shattered Susan completely. She would have been consumed by anxiety, blame, and overwhelming fear. Her carefully constructed life would have collapsed into reactive crisis management.

But Susan had spent those six months developing what Allen called "mastery of thought." She'd learned to direct her mind consciously, work with emotions skillfully, and live from her highest self consistently.

When the storm hit, Susan discovered something remarkable: her transformation wasn't just for fair weather. The mental clarity, emotional intelligence, and purposeful identity she'd developed had created what Allen called "unshakeable foundation"—inner stability that could weather any external chaos.

This is the ultimate test of any personal development: not how you feel during easy times, but how you respond when life unleashes its full force.

Allen's Understanding of Storm Mastery

James Allen understood that the true measure of personal development is how you handle life's inevitable difficulties. He saw that challenges don't create character; they reveal it.

*"Calmness of mind is one of the beautiful jewels of wisdom. It is the result of long and patient effort in self-control. Its presence is an indication of ripened experience, and of a more than ordinary knowledge of the laws and operations of thought," **Allen wrote.***

Allen recognized that storms serve a purpose in human development: *"The strong, calm man is always loved and revered. He is like a shade-giving tree in a thirsty land, or a sheltering rock in a storm."*

"In the bark of your soul reclines the commanding Master; He does but sleep: wake Him," Allen declared. He understood that within every person lies the capacity for unshakeable peace, but this capacity must be developed through practice and proven through testing.

Allen saw that people who develop true mastery don't avoid storms—they learn to sail through them with wisdom, grace, and purpose intact.

The Science of Stress Resilience and Post-Traumatic Growth

Modern research reveals how conscious development creates genuine resilience during major life challenges:

- **Stress Inoculation**: Dr. Salvatore Maddi's research shows that people who've practiced stress management in small situations develop greater capacity for handling major crises. Training with daily challenges builds resilience for extraordinary difficulties.
- **Cognitive Flexibility Under Pressure**: Studies by Dr. Barbara Fredrickson demonstrate that people with broader emotional ranges and thinking patterns maintain more options during crises. They can access curiosity, gratitude, and humor even in difficult circumstances.
- **Meaning-Making During Adversity**: Research by Dr. Crystal Park reveals that people who can find meaning in difficult experiences recover faster and often emerge stronger than before the crisis. Purpose provides resilience during purposelessness.
- **Social Connection During Crisis**: Dr. Sheldon Cohen's studies show that people with strong relationship skills maintain better support networks during difficulties. Emotional intelligence becomes social resilience during storms.
- **Neuroplasticity and Trauma Recovery**: Research by Dr. Rick Hanson demonstrates that brains trained in mindful awareness recover more quickly from traumatic experiences and are less likely to develop PTSD.

The Anatomy of Life Storms

Personal Health Crises: Illness, injury, mental health challenges

Relationship Upheavals: Divorce, betrayal, family conflicts, loss of loved ones

Financial Catastrophes: Job loss, business failure, economic downturns

Professional Setbacks: Career derailment, public failure, workplace conflict

Existential Challenges: Loss of faith, identity crisis, meaning collapse

Each type of storm tests different aspects of your development:

- Health crises test your relationship with mortality and control
- Relationship storms test your capacity for love and forgiveness
- Financial challenges test your security and self-worth concepts
- Professional setbacks test your identity and resilience
- Existential crises test your meaning-making and purpose connection

Susan's Storm Navigation Process

When the hospital call came, Susan automatically applied the three weeks of training she'd developed:

Mental Mastery in Crisis:

- She noticed her mind's impulse to catastrophize and gently redirected it
- She focused on what she could control (being present, making decisions) rather than what she couldn't (the accident itself)
- She used purposeful thinking: "How can I be the mother my son needs right now?"

Emotional Intelligence in Emergency:

- She felt her fear fully without being paralyzed by it
- She read her other children's emotions and provided stability
- She chose responses that served the situation rather than reacting from overwhelm
- She practiced self-compassion when moments of breakdown occurred

Purpose Alignment in Chaos:

- She remained connected to her identity as a loving, capable mother
- She used the crisis as an opportunity to model resilience for her children
- She drew strength from her larger purpose: "Supporting families through difficult transitions."

The Results:

- Susan remained functional and present throughout the crisis

- Her son recovered more quickly, partly due to the calm environment she maintained
- Her other children learned that difficulties could be handled with grace
- The experience strengthened rather than weakened her family relationships
- Susan discovered reserves of strength she didn't know she possessed

"I kept waiting for the breakdown," Susan said later, "but it never came. Not because I wasn't affected—I was deeply scared and sad. But the fear and sadness moved through me without taking over. I could feel everything and still think clearly and act wisely."

Today's Practice: The Storm Mastery Preparation System

Today, you'll learn to prepare for and navigate life's inevitable storms using all the skills you've developed over the past three weeks.

The Storm Readiness Assessment (15 minutes)

Mental Preparedness Evaluation (5 minutes):

- How quickly can you redirect catastrophic thinking during stress?
- Can you focus on controllable factors when facing uncertainty?
- Do you maintain purposeful thinking when circumstances are chaotic?
- How effectively do you use your mental tools under pressure?

Emotional Resilience Check (5 minutes):

- Can you feel difficult emotions without being overwhelmed by them?
- Do you maintain emotional intelligence when others are reactive?
- How quickly do you recover from emotional intensity?
- Can you provide emotional stability for others during crises?

Purpose Anchor Assessment (5 minutes):

- Does your purpose provide strength during difficult times?
- Can you access your highest self identity when challenged?
- Do you maintain service orientation even when personally struggling?
- How does your purpose help you find meaning in difficulties?

The Storm Navigation Protocol

When facing any significant life challenge, use this systematic approach:

Phase 1: Immediate Stabilization (First 24-48 hours)

1. **Breathing Reset**: Use extended exhales to activate the parasympathetic nervous system

2. **Present Moment Anchoring**: Focus on immediate needs rather than future projections
3. **Support Activation**: Reach out to your strongest relationships immediately
4. **Basic Needs Attention**: Ensure sleep, nutrition, and hydration despite crisis

Phase 2: Conscious Response Design (Days 2-7)

1. **Situation Assessment**: What exactly has happened vs. what stories am I adding?
2. **Control Identification**: What can I influence vs. what must I accept?
3. **Resource Inventory**: What strengths, skills, and support do I have available?
4. **Response Planning**: What actions align with my values and highest self?

Phase 3: Meaning Integration (Weeks 2-4)

1. **Learning Extraction**: What is this experience teaching me?
2. **Growth Recognition**: How am I becoming stronger through this challenge?
3. **Service Connection**: How might this experience help me serve others better?
4. **Purpose Alignment**: How does navigating this well serve my larger mission?

Phase 4: Post-Storm Integration (Ongoing)

1. **Wisdom Documentation**: What did I learn about myself and life?
2. **Relationship Strengthening**: How can I use this experience to deepen connections?
3. **Resilience Building**: What additional skills do I want to develop?
4. **Gratitude Practice**: What am I grateful for about this experience?

Advanced Storm Mastery Techniques

The Eye of the Hurricane Method: Find the calm center within external chaos:

- Remember that you are not the storm—you are experiencing the storm
- Access the part of you that can observe the situation with clarity
- Breathe into the space between you and your circumstances
- Act from this centered place rather than from reactive overwhelm

The Purposeful Storm Response: Use difficulties to strengthen rather than abandon your purpose:

- "How can I serve my purpose even in this difficult situation?"
- "What would someone committed to my mission do here?"
- "How can this challenge develop the capabilities I need for my purpose?"
- "How might this experience prepare me to help others facing similar storms?"

The Storm as Teacher Practice: Approach each difficulty as a demanding but wise teacher.

- "What is this situation trying to teach me?"

- "What strength is this developing in me?"
- "How is this experience expanding my capacity for service?"
- "What would I want someone to learn if they faced this same challenge?"

Common Storm Navigation Challenges

"I feel like I should be handling this better."

- Perfect storm navigation is impossible—focus on conscious response, not flawless response
- Use self-compassion as actively as you use other tools
- Remember that growth includes temporary setbacks and learning curves
- Measure success by intention and effort, not by perfect execution

"I can't find any meaning or purpose in this suffering."

- Some storms are too fresh for immediate meaning-making
- Focus first on navigating well, then look for lessons later
- Meaning often emerges gradually through reflection and time
- Sometimes, the meaning is simply developing greater compassion for others who suffer

"My support system seems to disappear when I need it most."

- Crisis often reveals who your true allies are—this information is valuable
- Some people feel overwhelmed by others' storms and withdraw to protect themselves
- Focus on the support that is available rather than what's missing
- Use this as motivation to be the kind of person who stays present during others' storms

"I feel like I'm losing all my progress and development."

- Storms often temporarily disrupt practiced skills—this is normal
- Your development is deeper than you realize and will resurface
- Crisis is the test that proves and strengthens your growth
- Each storm you navigate consciously increases your permanent resilience

Building Storm-Proof Foundation

Daily Resilience Practices:

- Regular stress inoculation through small challenges
- Consistent application of mental and emotional tools
- Ongoing connection to purpose and highest self identity
- Maintenance of strong relationships and support systems

Crisis Preparation Planning:

- Identify likely storm types for your life circumstances
- Develop response strategies for each potential challenge
- Create emergency action plans for maintaining your development during a crisis
- Build reserves of mental, emotional, and practical resources

Post-Storm Growth Integration:

- Document lessons learned from each difficulty navigated
- Share your storm wisdom to help others facing similar challenges
- Use storm experiences to refine and strengthen your development practices
- Celebrate your growing capacity to handle life's full range

The Unexpected Gifts of Storms

When navigated consciously, life storms often provide:

- **Clarity About Priorities**: Crisis strips away non-essentials and reveals what truly matters
- **Strength Discovery**: You often find capabilities you didn't know you possessed
- **Relationship Deepening**: Shared difficulties often strengthen authentic connections
- **Compassion Development**: Personal struggle increases empathy for others' pain
- **Meaning Enhancement**: Overcoming challenges often increases appreciation for life
- **Service Preparation**: Your storm navigation wisdom becomes a gift for others facing similar challenges

Tomorrow's Preview

Tomorrow, in your final day, you'll integrate everything you've learned into a sustainable way of being, establishing practices and perspectives that will continue your growth long after this 21-day journey ends.

Remember Allen's Promise

"Self-control is strength; Right Thought is mastery; Calmness is power. Say unto your heart, 'Peace, be still!'"

Today, you learned that true mastery isn't about avoiding life's storms—it's about maintaining your peace, purpose, and power while navigating through them.

You have become the sheltering rock in the storm, not just for yourself, but for all those whose lives you touch.

When the next storm comes—and it will—you'll be ready.

Day 21: Your New Way of Being

"Self-control is strength; Right Thought is mastery; Calmness is power. Say unto your heart, 'Peace, be still!'" — **James Allen**

Today marks not an ending, but a graduation.

Twenty-one days ago, you began a journey from unconscious living to conscious creation. You started as someone whose thoughts, emotions, and actions were largely automatic, shaped by circumstances, genetics, and conditioning you didn't choose.

You're completing this journey as someone fundamentally different: a conscious creator who can direct thoughts purposefully, work with emotions skillfully, and live from authentic purpose regardless of external circumstances.

This transformation isn't theoretical; it's practical, measurable, and permanent. You've literally rewired your brain, developed emotional mastery, and connected with your deeper calling. You've become what Allen called "the wise master, directing energies with intelligence."

But this isn't the end of your development. It's the beginning of what's possible when someone learns to think, feel, and live consciously. Today, you'll establish the practices and perspectives that will sustain and expand your growth for years to come.

Allen's Vision of Mastery

James Allen understood that true mastery isn't a destination but a way of being—a consistent commitment to conscious living that creates continuous growth and contribution.

"Such is the conscious master, and man can only thus become by discovering within himself the laws of thought, which discovery is totally a matter of application, self-analysis, and experience," Allen wrote. You've spent three weeks in exactly this discovery process.

Allen saw that mastery expresses itself through what he called "ripened experience"—the wisdom that comes from applying principles consistently until they become natural ways of being.

"The calm man, having learned how to govern himself, knows how to adapt himself to others; and they, in turn, reverence his spiritual strength, and feel that they can learn of him

618

and rely upon him," Allen observed. This is what you're becoming: someone others naturally turn to for wisdom, stability, and inspiration.

"The more tranquil a man becomes, the greater is his success, his influence, his power for good," Allen promised. Your growing mastery serves not just your own fulfillment but the elevation of everyone whose life you touch.

Your Transformation: A 21-Day Review

Week One: Mental Mastery

- **Day 1**: You discovered your brain's neuroplasticity and began conscious thought observation
- **Day 2**: You learned to cultivate your mental garden, choosing thoughts that serve your growth
- **Day 3**: You developed pattern interruption skills, breaking automatic mental habits
- **Day 4**: You programmed your Reticular Activating System to notice opportunities and possibilities
- **Day 5**: You connected thinking to purpose, giving direction to your mental energy
- **Day 6**: You installed beneficial thought habits that run automatically
- **Day 7**: You integrated all mental skills into comprehensive thought mastery

Week Two: Emotional Intelligence

- **Day 8**: You understood how thoughts create emotions and began influencing your feeling states
- **Day 9**: You learned to read emotions as valuable information rather than problems to solve
- **Day 10**: You developed the ability to choose responses over reactions, creating space for wisdom
- **Day 11**: You discovered how stories create suffering and learned to rewrite disempowering narratives
- **Day 12**: You mastered emotional alchemy, transforming difficult feelings into useful energy
- **Day 13**: You built emotional resilience, developing the capacity to bounce back from setbacks
- **Day 14**: You achieved emotional freedom, maintaining inner peace regardless of external circumstances

Week Three: Purposeful Living

- **Day 15**: You discovered your authentic purpose through systematic self-exploration

- **Day 16**: You learned to align daily thoughts and actions with your deeper calling
- **Day 17**: You transformed purpose obstacles from roadblocks into stepping stones
- **Day 18**: You developed small-steps strategies that build unstoppable momentum toward meaningful goals
- **Day 19**: You began living from your highest self identity rather than striving toward it
- **Day 20**: You learned to maintain mastery even during life's inevitable storms
- **Day 21**: You're integrating everything into a sustainable way of conscious living

Your New Operating System

You've upgraded from unconscious living to conscious creation. Your new operating system includes:

Mental Architecture:

- Conscious thought direction instead of mental drift
- Purpose-aligned thinking instead of random worry
- Growth mindset instead of fixed limitations
- Solution focus instead of problem obsession

Emotional Intelligence:

- Emotional awareness instead of reactive overwhelm
- Feeling wisdom instead of emotional avoidance
- Response choice instead of an automatic reaction
- Emotional alchemy instead of suffering prolongation

Purpose Integration:

- Authentic calling instead of external expectations
- Daily meaning instead of weekend fulfillment
- Service orientation instead of pure self-focus
- Highest self embodiment instead of future self aspiration

Today's Practice: The Mastery Integration System

Today, you'll establish the practices that will sustain and expand your consciousness for years to come.

The Daily Mastery Trinity (15 minutes each morning)

Mind Mastery Check-In (5 minutes):

- What thoughts are present as I begin this day?
- How can I direct my thinking purposefully today?
- What mental habits will I practice?
- Where might I need conscious thought redirection?

Emotional Intelligence Preparation (5 minutes):

- What emotions am I experiencing right now?
- What information are these feelings providing?
- How do I want to respond emotionally to today's challenges?
- What would emotional mastery look like in my anticipated situations?

Purpose Alignment Intention (5 minutes):

- How can I express my purpose today?
- What opportunities might arise for meaningful service?
- How can I embody my highest self in today's activities?
- What would purpose-driven living look like in my current circumstances?

The Evening Mastery Review (10 minutes each night)

Growth Celebration (3 minutes):

- What evidence of mastery did I demonstrate today?
- Where did I successfully apply the skills I've learned?
- How did my conscious living serve others?
- What am I proud of in today's choices and responses?

Learning Integration (4 minutes):

- Where did I fall back into old patterns?
- What triggered unconscious reactions?
- What would I do differently in the same situations?
- How can I strengthen my mastery for tomorrow?

Evolution Planning (3 minutes):

- What aspect of mastery do I want to develop further?
- What new challenges might help me grow?
- How can I deepen my practice and service?
- What would the next level of consciousness look like for me?

The Mastery Maintenance System

Daily Practice (15 minutes morning + 10 minutes evening):

- Never negotiate with the daily practice—it's your foundation
- Adapt the length if necessary, but never skip entirely
- View this as essential maintenance, like brushing teeth
- Use the practice to prevent problems rather than just solve them

Weekly Review (30 minutes each Sunday):

- Assess the week's mastery development
- Identify patterns and areas for growth

- Plan the following week's focus areas
- Celebrate progress and learn from setbacks

Monthly Evolution (2 hours, first Saturday of each month):

- Deep review of mastery development across all three areas
- Reading from sources that support continued growth
- Goal setting for the coming month's development
- Connection with others on similar growth journeys

Quarterly Integration (Half-day retreat every three months):

- Comprehensive assessment of life alignment with mastery principles
- Major goal setting and life direction evaluation
- Planning new challenges that will promote continued growth
- Service expansion planning—how can your mastery serve others better?

Advanced Mastery Practices

The Teaching Practice: Begin sharing what you've learned with others:

- Informal mentoring of friends, family, and colleagues
- Documenting your journey to inspire others
- Creating content that helps others develop consciousness
- Modeling mastery in all your relationships and interactions

The Challenge Seeking Practice: Actively pursue experiences that will develop your mastery:

- Take on responsibilities that require your highest self
- Engage in conversations that challenge your perspective
- Volunteer for opportunities that stretch your capabilities
- Place yourself in situations where mastery is essential

The Service Integration Practice: Make a conscious contribution central to your life:

- Look for ways your unique combination of skills can serve others
- Use your mastery development as preparation for greater service
- Connect with communities and causes aligned with your purpose
- View your continued growth as service to the collective consciousness

Common Post-Training Challenges

"I'm worried about losing momentum without daily guidance."

- Your internal guidance system is now stronger than external direction
- Trust your developed intuition and wisdom
- Use the maintenance systems to stay connected to growth

- Remember that mastery is a practice, not a perfect state

"I feel pressure to maintain this level of consciousness constantly."

- Mastery includes self-compassion for human imperfection
- Focus on recovery speed rather than never falling back
- Use setbacks as opportunities to practice your skills
- Progress is measured over months and years, not days

"People around me seem resistant to my changes."

- Others' resistance often reflects their own fear of change
- Model mastery without preaching or forcing it on others
- Some relationships may evolve or end as you grow
- Find community with others committed to conscious living

"I don't know what goals to pursue now."

- Your purpose provides direction for meaningful goal-setting
- Focus on service and contribution rather than just personal achievement
- Trust that opportunities for growth and service will emerge naturally
- Use your mastery to help others discover their own purpose and potential

The Ripple Effects of Your Mastery

Your transformation creates expanding circles of influence:

- **Personal Impact**: You experience greater peace, fulfillment, and authentic power
- **Family Impact**: Your conscious living models a possibility for loved ones
- **Professional Impact**: Your mastery enhances leadership and contribution
- **Community Impact**: Your presence elevates the consciousness of your environment
- **Global Impact**: Every person who develops mastery raises collective consciousness

Your Continuing Education

Mastery is a lifelong curriculum. Continue growing through:

Reading: Study works by those who've walked the path of conscious development

Practice: Maintain daily disciplines that strengthen your capacities

Teaching: Share your learning to deepen your own understanding

Service: Use your gifts in the service of others' growth and well-being

Challenge: Continuously stretch yourself in ways that promote evolution

A Personal Message

As you complete this 21-day journey, I want you to know something important: you've accomplished something remarkable. In a world where most people live unconsciously, reacting to circumstances and following cultural programming, you've chosen to wake up.

You've developed the capacity to think consciously, feel skillfully, and live purposefully. You've become someone who creates rather than just consumes, serves rather than just takes, and contributes rather than just criticizes.

This doesn't make you better than others; it makes you more useful to others. Your mastery is a gift you offer to the world simply by being who you've become.

The path of conscious living isn't always easy, but it's always worthwhile. There will be days when you forget your training, moments when you react unconsciously, times when purpose feels distant. This is all part of the journey.

What matters is that you've learned to return to consciousness, to choose response over reaction, to live from purpose rather than just impulse. You've developed what Allen called "the master key" to creating the life you want.

Your Graduation Commitment

As you complete this program, consider making this commitment to yourself and to the world:

- *"I commit to living consciously, thinking purposefully, and serving authentically.*
- *I will continue developing my capacity for wisdom, compassion, and contribution.*
- *I will use my gifts in the service of others' growth and well-being.*
- *I will model the possibility of conscious living through my daily choices and responses.*
- *I am no longer someone who happens to live; I am someone who creates life consciously and purposefully."*

Remember Allen's Ultimate Promise

"In the ocean of life, the isles of Blessedness are smiling, and the sunny shore of your ideal awaits your coming. Keep your hand firmly upon the helm of thought. In the bark of your soul reclines the commanding Master; He does but sleep: wake Him."

Today, you have awakened the commanding Master of your life. You've learned to keep your hand firmly upon the helm of thought. The sunny shore of your ideal is no longer a distant dream, it's the reality you're creating through conscious living.

You are no longer who you were 21 days ago. You are the conscious creator of your thoughts, the wise master of your emotions, and the authentic expression of your highest purpose.

Live from this truth. The world needs what you've become.

Welcome to your new way of being.

~End of Part Three: Live Your Purpose~

Complete Book Summary: Over 21 days, you've transformed from unconscious reaction to conscious creation through three integrated phases: Mental Mastery (Days 1-7), which taught you to direct thoughts purposefully rather than being controlled by them. Emotional Intelligence (Days 8-14) developed your ability to work with feelings skillfully and choose responses over reactions. Purposeful Living (Days 15-21) connected your mental clarity and emotional wisdom to authentic service and contribution. You've become what James Allen envisioned, the conscious and intelligent wielder of your mental powers, living from your highest self in service of your deepest purpose.

Your journey continues beyond these 21 days, but you now have the foundation, tools, and practices to create the life Allen described: one of conscious thought, wise emotion, and purposeful action. You are the master of your fate, the captain of your soul, the conscious creator of your destiny.

Conclusion

"You are today where your thoughts have brought you; you will be tomorrow where your thoughts take you." — *James Allen.*

The Master of Your Fate

Twenty-one days ago, you opened this book carrying the weight of unconscious thinking, reactive emotions, and unclear purpose. You may have felt like a passenger in your own life, buffeted by circumstances and controlled by automatic patterns you didn't choose and couldn't seem to change.

Today, you close it as the conscious architect of your inner world.

This transformation didn't happen by accident. It occurred because you chose to engage with one of the most profound truths ever articulated: that you have the power to shape your life from the inside out through the deliberate cultivation of your thoughts.

James Allen knew this truth over a century ago. You've now lived it for three weeks.

Allen's Final Wisdom

In the concluding words of "As A Man Thinketh," Allen offered a final instruction that encompasses everything you've learned: *"Say unto your heart, 'Peace, be still!'"*

These six words contain the essence of mastery. They represent the ultimate goal of all your practice: the ability to bring calm to any storm, peace to any chaos, stillness to any turbulence—not by controlling external circumstances, but by accessing the unshakeable center within yourself.

Allen understood that this phrase isn't just beautiful poetry—it's a practical instruction. When your mind churns with worry, you can say "Peace, be still!" When your emotions rage with reactivity, you can say "Peace, be still!" When your life feels overwhelming with complexity, you can say, "Peace, be still!"

This isn't about suppressing your humanity or becoming emotionally flat. It's about accessing the wise, calm, centered part of yourself that can meet any situation with grace and intelligence. It's about becoming what Allen called "the master"—not of others, not of circumstances, but of yourself.

Allen saw this mastery as the highest human achievement: *"Self-control is strength; Right Thought is mastery; Calmness is power."* You've spent 21 days developing each of these

626

qualities. You've learned that self-control comes through conscious choice rather than willpower. You've discovered that the right thought is simply thinking in ways that serve your wellbeing and growth. You've experienced that calmness isn't the absence of challenge but the presence of wisdom.

The person who can say "Peace, be still!" to their own heart and mean it—who can access calm in the midst of any storm—possesses a power that no external circumstance can touch. This is what Allen meant by becoming "master of your fate."

You are becoming that person.

Your Transformation

What You've Accomplished in 21 Days

The changes you've experienced aren't minor adjustments—they represent a fundamental shift in how you relate to your own mind, emotions, and life purpose.

In Week One, you reclaimed your mind from unconscious autopilot. You discovered that thoughts aren't things that happen to you—they're choices you make. You learned to:

- Notice automatic thought patterns that previously ran undetected
- Interrupt mental loops that didn't serve your well-being
- Consciously plant thoughts that support your goals and values
- Program your attention to notice opportunities and resources
- Link your thinking with meaningful purpose
- Build empowering mental habits through repetition

In Week Two, you mastered your emotional life. You transformed from being controlled by feelings to working with them skillfully. You developed the ability to:

- Understand how thoughts create emotional experiences
- Read emotions as valuable information rather than problems to solve
- Choose responses instead of reacting automatically
- Rewrite disempowering stories that create unnecessary suffering
- Transform difficult emotions into wisdom and useful energy
- Build resilience that allows you to bounce back from any setback
- Maintain inner freedom regardless of external circumstances

In Week Three, you connected your mental clarity and emotional wisdom to meaningful purpose. You learned to:

- Discover your unique contribution through aligned thinking

- Direct your mental energy toward goals that matter
- Overcome obstacles through conscious thought redirection
- Build purposeful habits that compound over time
- Embody your highest self through identity-based living
- Apply all your tools during difficult challenges
- Integrate everything into a sustainable way of being

These aren't just techniques you've learned, they're capacities you've developed. You haven't simply read about Allen's principles; you've embodied them through daily practice until they've become part of how you naturally think and respond.

How Allen's Wisdom Lives in Your Daily Life

Allen's insights are no longer philosophical concepts you admire from a distance. They've become practical tools you use throughout each day:

When you wake up, you don't just hope for a good day; you consciously set the mental and emotional tone that creates one. You've learned that your first thoughts program your entire day's experience.

When challenges arise, you don't automatically fall into stress or victimhood; you pause, breathe, and choose responses that align with your values and wisdom. You've discovered that you have far more choice in difficult moments than you ever realized.

When emotions surge, you don't suppress them or let them control you—you read them as information and transform their energy into constructive action. You've developed the emotional intelligence that Allen called "calmness of mind."

When pursuing goals, you don't rely on motivation alone; you link your thoughts with purpose and build systems that make progress inevitable. You've learned what Allen meant by "intelligent accomplishment."

When relating to others, you don't react from old patterns, you respond from the centered, wise part of yourself that can see beyond immediate triggers. You've become someone others can rely upon, just as Allen described.

Allen's wisdom isn't something you occasionally apply when you remember, it's become your natural way of processing life. You've internalized his insights so deeply that they operate automatically, like a new operating system for your consciousness.

The Compound Effect Ahead

The transformation you've experienced in 21 days is just the beginning. Allen understood that conscious thinking creates compound growth—small daily improvements that build exponentially over time.

In the next month, the neural pathways you've been building will become stronger and more automatic. The conscious effort required to choose your thoughts and responses will decrease as these new patterns become your natural default.

In the next three months, people in your life will comment on how much you've changed. Your increased calm, wisdom, and emotional stability will be evident to others, often before you fully recognize it yourself.

In the next year, you'll look back and hardly recognize the person who started this journey. The compound effect of daily conscious thinking will have created changes in your relationships, career, health, and overall life satisfaction that seemed impossible when you began.

In the next five years, you'll have become a completely different person—not through dramatic personality changes, but through the consistent application of Allen's principles. You'll have developed what he called "divine strength" through "continued effort in right thinking."

This compound effect works because each day of conscious thinking builds upon all previous days. Every moment you choose response over reaction strengthens your capacity for future choices. Every time you transform a difficult emotion into wisdom, you develop greater skill for handling future challenges. Every day you align your thoughts with purpose, you increase your power to create meaningful results.

Allen wrote: *"The weakest soul, knowing its own weakness, and believing this truth that strength can only be developed by effort and practice, will, thus believing, at once begin to exert itself, and, adding effort to effort, patience to patience, and strength to strength, will never cease to develop, and will at last grow divinely strong."*

You've begun this development. The compound effect ahead will make you "divinely strong."

The Continuing Journey

Advanced Practices

Your 21-day foundation now supports advanced applications of Allen's principles:

- **Thought Leadership**: Use your mental mastery to influence positive change in your family, workplace, and community. Your calm presence in stressful situations will naturally make you someone others look to for guidance.

- **Creative Expression**: Channel your emotional intelligence into artistic, entrepreneurial, or innovative endeavors. When your thoughts are clear and emotions are balanced, creativity flows naturally.

- **Service Integration**: Apply your purpose clarity to serve causes larger than yourself. Allen believed that personal mastery naturally leads to contribution to others' well-being.

- **Relationship Mastery**: Use your response-choice skills to transform difficult relationships. Your ability to remain centered while others are reactive can heal family dynamics, improve partnerships, and enhance professional collaboration.

- **Crisis Leadership**: Your emotional resilience will be most valuable during difficult times—both your own and others'. You'll find yourself naturally becoming a stabilizing force during community, family, or workplace challenges.

- **Mentorship and Teaching**: As your own transformation becomes evident, others will seek your guidance. You'll discover that sharing Allen's principles deepens your own understanding and accelerates your growth.

Community and Support

Allen's path of conscious thinking isn't meant to be walked alone. Your continued growth will be enhanced by connecting with others who share this commitment:

- **Find Your Tribe**: Seek out individuals, groups, or communities focused on personal growth, conscious living, and purposeful contribution. Whether online or in person, surrounding yourself with people who value inner development will support your continued evolution.

- **Create Study Groups**: Organize regular meetings with friends, family, or colleagues to discuss Allen's principles and share experiences applying them. Teaching others reinforces your own learning and creates accountability for continued practice.

- **Professional Development**: Consider working with coaches, therapists, or mentors who understand and support conscious thinking approaches. Professional guidance can help you navigate deeper patterns and more complex applications.

- **Service Communities**: Join or create groups focused on serving others through the principles you've learned. Volunteering, mentoring, or contributing to causes you care about multiplies the impact of your personal development.

Remember that your growth doesn't exist in isolation—it ripples out to affect everyone in your life. As you continue developing Allen's mastery, you become a positive influence on your family, workplace, and community.

Your Role in Sharing These Principles

Allen wrote his insights not to keep them to himself but to share them with anyone ready to apply them. You now have the same opportunity and responsibility.

Model the Principles: Your most powerful teaching tool is your own transformation. As others notice your increased calm, wisdom, and effectiveness, they'll naturally become curious about how you've changed.

Share Your Story: When appropriate, tell others about your journey with Allen's principles. Your authentic experience will be more compelling than any theoretical explanation.

Recommend Resources: Introduce others to "As A Man Thinketh" and practical approaches to applying its wisdom. Sometimes, the gift of the right book at the right time can change someone's entire life trajectory.

Create Opportunities: Organize workshops, discussion groups, or informal gatherings focused on conscious thinking and emotional mastery. You don't need to be an expert— you just need to be someone willing to explore these ideas with others.

Live the Example: In your daily interactions, demonstrate what it looks like to choose responses over reactions, to remain calm during chaos, and to pursue meaningful goals with persistent thought and action.

Allen's influence has continued for over a century because people like you have taken his principles seriously, applied them consistently, and shared them generously. You now have the opportunity to extend that influence into your own sphere of relationships and community.

Final Integration

The progression you've followed over these 21 days reveals a fundamental truth about human development: mastery builds from the inside out.

- **Thought Mastery** (Week One) had to come first because thoughts are the foundation of everything else. Until you can consciously direct your mental energy, you remain at the mercy of random mental conditioning and unconscious patterns. Allen knew that "the mind is the master-weaver" of all experience.

- **Emotional Mastery** (Week Two) became possible once you understood how thoughts create emotions. You couldn't have developed emotional intelligence without first learning to work with your thoughts consciously. Emotions are too powerful to control directly—they must be influenced through the thoughts that generate them.

- **Purposeful Living** (Week Three) emerged naturally from the combination of mental clarity and emotional wisdom. When your thoughts are conscious and your emotions are balanced, your true values and meaningful goals become clear. Purpose isn't something you find through external searching—it's something you uncover through inner development.

This progression reflects Allen's insight that lasting change must start with thought. External techniques, willpower approaches, and environmental modifications can only create temporary improvements. But when you change how you think, everything else changes naturally and permanently.

Your New Toolkit for Life

You now possess a comprehensive system for conscious living that will serve you for the rest of your life:

- **For Mental Challenges**: You have tools for noticing, interrupting, and redirecting unhelpful thought patterns while cultivating thoughts that serve your growth and goals.

- **For Emotional Difficulties**: You can read emotions as information, choose responses over reactions, transform difficult feelings into useful energy, and maintain emotional freedom regardless of circumstances.

- **For Life Direction**: You know how to discover your purpose through aligned thinking, overcome obstacles through conscious choice, and build habits that create meaningful progress.

- **For Relationship Issues**: You can remain centered during conflict, respond wisely to others' reactivity, and use your emotional mastery to improve all your connections.

- **For Professional Challenges**: You possess the calm presence, clear thinking, and purposeful action that naturally create leadership opportunities and career advancement.

- **For Crisis Management**: You have the resilience, perspective, and practical tools to handle any difficulty with grace and wisdom.

This isn't a collection of separate techniques—it's an integrated approach to living that touches every aspect of your experience. Allen's principles provide a complete framework for human flourishing.

The Master You've Become

Twenty-one days ago, you began this journey hoping to improve your life. You've accomplished something far more significant: you've become a different person.

You've transformed from someone controlled by unconscious patterns to someone who chooses conscious responses. You've evolved from emotional reactivity to emotional intelligence. You've grown from unclear direction to purposeful living.

Most importantly, you've discovered what Allen knew: that the power to create your life from the inside out was always within you. You didn't gain new abilities through this journey—you uncovered capacities that were always present but previously undeveloped.

Allen wrote: *"Tempest-tossed souls, wherever ye may be, under whatsoever conditions ye may live, know this—in the ocean of life the isles of Blessedness are smiling, and the sunny shore of your ideal awaits your coming. Keep your hand firmly upon the helm of thought. In the bark of your soul reclines the commanding Master; He does but sleep: wake Him."*

You have awakened the commanding Master within yourself. You've learned to keep your hand firmly upon the helm of thought. You've discovered that the Isles of Blessedness aren't distant destinations—they're available in any moment when you access the wisdom and peace that live within you.

You are no longer the victim of your circumstances, the prisoner of your emotions, or the slave of your past conditioning. You are the conscious creator of your character, the wise manager of your emotional life, and the purposeful director of your future.

You have become what Allen called "master of your fate."

This mastery isn't a destination you've reached—it's a way of traveling through life. Every day offers new opportunities to apply your wisdom, deepen your understanding, and extend your influence in positive directions.

Allen concluded his masterpiece with words that now apply directly to you: *"Self-control is strength; Right Thought is mastery; Calmness is power. Say unto your heart, 'Peace, be still!'"*

You possess this strength. You've developed this mastery. You have access to this power.

The journey continues, but you no longer walk it as a seeker hoping for transformation. You walk it as someone who has transformed, continuing to grow in wisdom, contributing to others' growth, and demonstrating daily what it means to live as the conscious master of your inner world.

Allen would be proud of who you've become. Even more importantly, you can be proud of who you've become.

The future you dream of isn't somewhere ahead of you; it's emerging from within you, one conscious thought at a time.

"You are today where your thoughts have brought you; you will be tomorrow where your thoughts take you." — **James Allen.**

Your tomorrow begins now.

Appendices for Thoughts That Matter

Appendix A: Quick Reference Guide

Part One: Reclaim Your Mind (Days 1-7)

Day 1: The Thought Awareness Exercise

- Practice: 5 minutes of simply noticing thoughts without judgment
- Track patterns in a simple journal
- Goal: Develop consciousness of automatic thought patterns

Day 2: The 5-Minute Mental Garden Tending

- Weed out one negative thought pattern
- Plant one positive thought seed
- Goal: Begin conscious cultivation of mental environment

Day 3: The Pattern Interrupt Technique

- Catch one automatic thought during the day
- Replace with conscious choice
- Goal: Break free from mental autopilot

Day 4: The Attention Programming Exercise

- Set one specific intention for what you want to notice
- Observe how reality responds throughout the day
- Goal: Program your Reticular Activating System

Day 5: The Purpose-Thought Alignment

- Choose one important goal
- Direct thoughts toward it for 10 minutes
- Goal: Link thought with purpose for intelligent accomplishment

Day 6: The New Thought Habit Installation

- Choose one empowering thought
- Practice it 10 times throughout the day
- Goal: Build helpful mental habits through repetition

Day 7: The Mental Mastery Review

- Assess your week of practice
- Choose your strongest tool for ongoing use
- Goal: Integrate mental sovereignty skills

Part Two: Master Your Emotions (Days 8-14)

Day 8: The Thought-Emotion Tracking System

- Track thought → emotion sequences throughout the day
- Practice shifting one feeling through thought change
- Goal: Understand how thoughts create emotions

Day 9: The Emotional Dashboard Reading

- Check in with emotions 3 times daily (10 AM, 2 PM, 6 PM)
- Ask each emotion: "What are you trying to tell me?"
- Goal: Read emotions as information rather than problems

Day 10: The STOP Technique

- S-Stop, T-Take three breaths, O-Observe thoughts, P-Proceed with purpose
- Use during three triggering moments throughout the day
- Goal: Create space between stimulus and response

Day 11: The Story Reframe Exercise

- Identify one painful story you tell yourself
- Create three alternative empowering versions
- Goal: Transform suffering through narrative change

Day 12: The Emotional Alchemy Process

- Transform one difficult emotion into constructive energy
- Channel emotional energy toward meaningful action
- Goal: Convert emotional lead into wisdom gold

Day 13: The Daily Resilience Workout

- Morning resilience preparation (10 minutes)
- Gradual challenge exposure throughout the day
- Goal: Build emotional strength through systematic training

Day 14: The Emotional Freedom Integration

- Morning emotional state assessment and intention setting
- Real-time freedom protocol during challenges
- Evening review of emotional mastery moments
- Goal: Maintain centered wisdom regardless of circumstances

Part Three: Live Your Purpose (Days 15-21)

Day 15: The Purpose Discovery Exercise

- Identify patterns in what energizes you
- Connect energy patterns to potential service
- Goal: Discover your north star through aligned thinking

Day 16: The Purpose Alignment Practice

- Choose one way to serve your purpose today
- Notice how purpose-aligned action affects thinking
- Goal: Direct thoughts toward meaningful goals

Day 17: The Obstacle Transformation Exercise

- Identify your biggest purpose obstacle
- Create a thought-based solution strategy
- Goal: Overcome purpose barriers through conscious thinking

Day 18: The Daily Purpose Practice

- Take one small action aligned with your purpose
- Notice effects on thoughts and energy
- Goal: Build purposeful habits through micro-commitments

Day 19: The Highest Self Exercise

- Act from your best self for one focused hour
- Notice required thought patterns for excellence
- Goal: Embody identity-based purposeful living

Day 20: The Storm Mastery Test

- Apply all tools to one current challenge
- Demonstrate integrated growth under pressure
- Goal: Prove mastery during difficult circumstances

Day 21: The Integration Ceremony

- Celebrate a 21-day transformation
- Commit to continued conscious growth
- Goal: Honor achievement and establish an ongoing practice

Emergency Techniques for Difficult Moments

When Overwhelmed by Negative Thoughts:

1. **The 3-3-3 Technique**: Name 3 things you see, 3 sounds you hear, 3 things you can touch
2. **The Thought Labeling**: Simply say "thinking" when you notice rumination
3. **The Mental Reset**: Ask "Is this thought helpful right now?" If no, choose a better one

When Emotions Feel Uncontrollable:

1. **The 6-Second Rule**: Count slowly to 6 while breathing—stress hormones begin metabolizing
2. **The Physical Reset**: Splash cold water on face/wrists or do 10 jumping jacks
3. **The RAIN Technique**: Recognize, Allow, Investigate, Non-attachment to the emotion

When Losing Sense of Purpose:
1. **The Values Compass**: Ask "What do I care about most right now?"
2. **The Service Question**: "How can I help someone else in the next hour?"
3. **The Gratitude Pivot**: Name 3 things you appreciate about your current circumstances

When Feeling Reactive:
- **The Pause and Breathe**: 3 conscious breaths before any response
- **The Future Self Check**: "How will I feel about this response tomorrow?"
- **The Loving Observer**: "What would someone who loves everyone involved suggest?"

When Doubting the Process:
- **The Evidence Review**: List 3 ways you've already grown from these practices
- **The Patience Reminder**: "Lasting change takes time—I'm building neural pathways."
- **The Allen Connection**: Read one original quote from "As A Man Thinketh."

Appendix B: Allen's Original Wisdom

The Power of Thought

Allen's Original: "A man is literally what he thinks, his character being the complete sum of all his thoughts."

Modern Translation: Your personality, habits, and life outcomes are the direct result of your dominant thought patterns. You're not stuck with who you are—you can reshape yourself by changing how you think.

Allen's Original: "As the plant springs from, and could not be without, the seed, so every act of a man springs from the hidden seeds of thought."

Modern Translation: Every behavior, decision, and action in your life originates from a thought. If you want to change your actions, start by changing your thoughts.

Allen's Original: "Mind is the master-weaver, both of the inner garment of character and the outer garment of circumstance."

Modern Translation: Your thoughts create both your internal personality and your external life conditions. Change your thinking, and you change both who you are and what happens to you.

Mental Cultivation

Allen's Original: "A man's mind may be likened to a garden, which may be intelligently cultivated or allowed to run wild."

Modern Translation: Your mind requires conscious cultivation like a garden. Without deliberate care, it will grow whatever random thoughts take root—usually weeds of worry, doubt, and negativity.

Allen's Original: "Just as a gardener cultivates his plot, keeping it free from weeds, and growing the flowers and fruits which he requires, so may a man tend the garden of his mind."

Modern Translation: You can systematically remove unhelpful thought patterns and deliberately plant thoughts that create the character and life you want.

Circumstances and Choice

Allen's Original: "Circumstance does not make the man; it reveals him to himself."

Modern Translation: External situations don't determine who you are—they show you who you've become through your thought patterns. Your response to circumstances reveals your character.

Allen's Original: "Men do not attract that which they want, but that which they are."

Modern Translation: You don't attract what you consciously desire—you attract what matches your dominant internal state. Your outer world reflects your inner world.

Allen's Original: "Every man is where he is by the law of his being; the thoughts which he has built into his character have brought him there."

Modern Translation: Your current life situation is the natural result of your past thinking patterns. You're exactly where your thoughts have led you.

Emotions and The Body

Allen's Original: "The body is the servant of the mind. It obeys the operations of the mind, whether they be deliberately chosen or automatically expressed."

Modern Translation: Your physical body responds to your mental commands, whether you're conscious of those commands or not. Your thoughts directly influence your health and energy.

Allen's Original: "Strong, pure, and happy thoughts build up the body in vigour and grace."

Modern Translation: Positive, clear thinking creates physical vitality and attractiveness. Your mental diet determines your physical condition.

Allen's Original: "Disease and health, like circumstances, are rooted in thought."

Modern Translation: Your mental patterns significantly influence your physical health. While not all illness is mentally caused, mental health strongly affects physical well-being.

Purpose and Achievement

Allen's Original: "Until thought is linked with purpose, there is no intelligent accomplishment."

Modern Translation: Random positive thinking doesn't create results. You must connect your thoughts to specific, meaningful goals to achieve anything worthwhile.

Allen's Original: "He who cherishes a beautiful vision, a lofty ideal in his heart, will one day realize it."

Modern Translation: When you consistently hold inspiring goals in your mind and align your thoughts with them, you create the conditions for their achievement.

Allen's Original: "You will become as small as your controlling desire; as great as your dominant aspiration."

Modern Translation: Your life will expand or contract to match the size of your primary mental focus. Think small thoughts, live a small life. Think great thoughts, create a great life.

Self-Mastery and Freedom

Allen's Original: "Self-control is strength; Right Thought is mastery; Calmness is power."

Modern Translation: True strength comes from controlling your responses, mastery comes from directing your thoughts, and real power comes from maintaining inner peace.

Allen's Original: "Calmness of mind is one of the beautiful jewels of wisdom. It is the result of long and patient effort in self-control."

Modern Translation: Inner peace isn't a personality trait you're born with—it's a skill you develop through consistent practice of conscious thinking.

Allen's Original: "The calm man, having learned how to govern himself, knows how to adapt himself to others."

Modern Translation: When you master your internal responses, you become more effective in all your relationships and external interactions.

Appendix C: The Science Behind the Practices

Neuroplasticity: The Brain's Ability to Change

Key Research: Dr. Sara Lazar, Harvard Medical School (2005) *Finding*: Just 8 weeks of meditation practice measurably thickens the prefrontal cortex—the brain region responsible for focus, decision-making, and emotional regulation. *Application*: Allen's "thought cultivation" practices literally reshape your brain structure.

Key Research: Dr. Norman Doidge, "The Brain That Changes Itself" (2007) *Finding*: The brain remains plastic throughout life, capable of forming new neural pathways at any age. *Application*: You're never too old to change thought patterns and develop Allen's "mental mastery."

Reticular Activating System: Attention and Perception

Key Research: Dr. Arne Dietrich, American University of Beirut (2004) *Finding*: The brain's filtering system (RAS) determines what information reaches conscious awareness based on current mental focus. *Application*: Allen's insight that "men attract what they are" is neurologically accurate—your thoughts program what you notice.

Key Research: Dr. Daniel Simons, University of Illinois (1999) *Finding*: The "selective attention" studies show people miss obvious stimuli when focused elsewhere. *Application*: Changing your dominant thoughts literally changes what opportunities and resources you perceive.

Cognitive-Behavioral Science: Thoughts Create Emotions

Key Research: Dr. Aaron Beck, University of Pennsylvania (1976) *Finding*: Thoughts directly influence emotional responses through predictable cognitive-behavioral patterns. *Application*: Allen's teaching that thoughts create character and circumstances is scientifically validated.

Key Research: Dr. Kevin Ochsner, Columbia University (2008) *Finding*: Cognitive reframing—changing how you think about situations—measurably changes brain activity in emotional processing centers. *Application*: Allen's story-rewriting and perspective-shifting practices work at the neurological level.

Stress Response and Emotional Regulation

Key Research: Dr. Daniel Goleman, "Emotional Intelligence" (1995) *Finding*: The 6-second rule—stress hormones begin metabolizing after 6 seconds, allowing rational thought to return. *Application*: Allen's emphasis on "pause and choose" responses is neurologically optimal.

Key Research: Dr. Jon Kabat-Zinn, University of Massachusetts (1982) *Finding*: Mindfulness practices reduce activity in the amygdala (fear center) while strengthening prefrontal cortex connections. *Application*: Allen's "calmness" and "self-control" practices create measurable brain changes.

Post-Traumatic Growth and Resilience
Key Research: Dr. Richard Tedeschi, University of North Carolina (1996) *Finding*: People who actively work with difficult experiences often emerge stronger than before the trauma. *Application*: Allen's teaching about transforming suffering into strength is psychologically documented.

Key Research: Dr. Barbara Fredrickson, University of North Carolina (2001) *Finding*: Positive emotions broaden cognitive capacity and build psychological resources. *Application*: Allen's "beautiful thoughts" practices create measurable cognitive enhancement.

Meaning-Making and Purpose
Key Research: Dr. Viktor Frankl, "Man's Search for Meaning" (1946) *Finding*: People who find meaning in suffering experience better psychological outcomes. *Application*: Allen's emphasis on linking thought with purpose is psychologically essential.

Key Research: Dr. Kristin Neff, University of Texas (2003) *Finding*: Self-compassion practices reduce depression and anxiety while increasing motivation. *Application*: Allen's gentle approach to mental cultivation is scientifically superior to self-criticism.

Habit Formation and Behavioral Change
Key Research: Dr. Charles Duhigg, "The Power of Habit" (2012) *Finding*: Habits form through consistent repetition of cue-routine-reward loops, typically taking 66 days. *Application*: Allen's daily practices create lasting change through neurological habit formation.

Key Research: Dr. BJ Fogg, Stanford University (2009) *Finding*: Small, consistent behaviors are more effective for lasting change than large, sporadic efforts. *Application*: Allen's simple daily practices are optimally designed for sustainable transformation.

How Thoughts Physically Change the Brain
When you practice Allen's thought-cultivation techniques, specific neurological changes occur:

- **Synaptic Strengthening**: Repeated thought patterns strengthen neural connections through increased myelin production

- **Gray Matter Changes**: Focused attention practices increase gray matter density in regions associated with learning and memory
- **Default Mode Network Modification**: Conscious thinking practices reduce activity in the brain's "autopilot" system
- **Neurotransmitter Optimization**: Positive thought practices increase serotonin, dopamine, and GABA production

The Stress-Thought-Health Connection

Research shows Allen's mind-body insights are measurably accurate:

- **Cortisol Reduction**: Conscious thinking practices lower chronic stress hormones
- **Immune Enhancement**: Positive mental states improve immune system function
- **Inflammatory Response**: Negative thought patterns increase harmful inflammation
- **Cardiovascular Health**: Mental stress directly affects heart health through measurable pathways

Appendix D: Troubleshooting Common Challenges

"What If I Miss A Day?"

The Reality: Missing days are normal and expected. Perfectionism often sabotages progress more than occasional lapses.

The Solution:

- Start immediately where you left off—don't restart from Day 1
- Use the "minimum effective dose": If you missed the full practice, do just 2 minutes
- Focus on consistency over perfection: 80% completion is better than 0% because you quit after missing one day
- Build buffer days: Expect to miss 2-3 days and plan accordingly

Mindset Reframe: Allen wrote about "patient effort"—this includes patience with your own human imperfection. Missing days provides opportunities to practice self-compassion, which is itself valuable growth.

Practical Strategies:

- Set phone reminders for your practice time
- Find an accountability partner doing the same program
- Keep the book/practices visible in your environment
- Prepare "emergency mini-practices" for busy days (1-2 minutes maximum)

"What If It Doesn't Seem To Work?"

Common Reasons Practices Feel Ineffective:

1. **Expecting immediate dramatic results**: Neuroplasticity requires 21+ days for measurable change
2. **Practicing mechanically without engagement**: Going through motions without genuine intention
3. **Focusing on what's not changing**: Attention bias toward problems rather than progress
4. **Practicing during crisis**: Starting when overwhelmed rather than building a foundation first

Troubleshooting Steps:

Week 1: If no noticeable changes

- **Check your expectation timeline**: Are you expecting month-long changes in days?
- **Verify genuine practice**: Are you actually doing the exercises or just reading about them?
- **Document subtle shifts**: Keep a daily journal of small changes you might be missing

Week 2: If you are still feeling stuck

- **Assess life context**: Are major stressors overwhelming your practice capacity?
- **Modify intensity**: Start with smaller, easier versions of practices
- **Seek support**: Discuss your experience with friends, mentors, or counselors

Week 3: If practices still feel ineffective

- **Consider professional help**: Sometimes, underlying issues (depression, trauma, anxiety) need additional support
- **Try different practices**: Some techniques resonate better with different personalities
- **Focus on process over outcome**: Sometimes the benefit is in the effort itself, not dramatic results

Signs of Subtle Progress (that people often miss):

- Catching negative thoughts faster than before
- Feeling slightly less reactive to usual triggers
- Others are commenting that you seem different
- Better sleep or energy levels
- Increased interest in personal growth topics

Allen's Perspective: He wrote about "long and patient effort"—the work itself is valuable, regardless of immediate visible results. Trust the process.

"How Do I Maintain This Long-Term?"

The Challenge: Initial motivation fades, life gets busy, and old patterns feel easier than new ones.

Long-Term Sustainability Strategies:

Monthly Maintenance:

- **Practice rotation**: Use different daily practices to prevent boredom
- **Difficulty progression**: Gradually increase the challenge as skills develop
- **Community connection**: Join or create groups focused on conscious thinking
- **Regular review**: Monthly assessment of growth and practice effectiveness

Quarterly Renewal:

- **Reread Allen's original**: Return to "As A Man Thinketh" for inspiration
- **Major pattern work**: Address deeper issues that surface through practice
- **Goal alignment**: Ensure practices support your evolving life direction
- **Celebration rituals**: Acknowledge growth and renewed commitment

Annual Integration:

- **Life design review**: How have practices influenced major life decisions?
- **Teaching others**: Share what you've learned to deepen your own understanding
- **Advanced training**: Explore related practices (meditation, therapy, coaching)
- **Legacy planning**: How can your growth serve others and future generations?

Creating Your Personal System:

Daily Non-Negotiables (choose 1-2):

- 5-minute morning thought cultivation
- Evening reflection on growth moments
- Trigger-response practice during challenging moments

Weekly Practices (choose 1):

- Deeper emotional processing session
- Planning session for applying insights
- Connection with an accountability partner or group

Monthly Reviews:

- What patterns am I noticing in my thinking and emotions?
- Which practices are most helpful and why?
- How has my growth served my relationships and work?
- What do I want to focus on developing next?

Dealing With Motivation Cycles:

- **High motivation periods**: Build strong habits and systems

- **Low motivation periods**: Rely on minimal effective practices
- **Crisis periods**: Return to basic techniques (breathing, pausing, reframing)
- **Growth periods**: Experiment with advanced applications

The Integration Principle: Eventually, these practices become so natural they're no longer separate "practices"—they become how you naturally think and respond. Allen's goal wasn't a lifelong effort but rather developing wisdom that operates automatically.

Allen's Promise: He wrote that this work leads to becoming "master of yourself." Masters don't need to constantly practice basic skills—they've integrated them into natural competence. Trust that consistent practice leads to integrated wisdom.

Final Support Structure: Create a personal mission statement based on Allen's principles that you can return to during difficult periods. Example: "I am committed to conscious thinking, emotional wisdom, and purposeful living, knowing that my inner development serves not only my own growth but the well-being of everyone in my life."

Remember: These appendices are designed to support your ongoing journey with Allen's timeless wisdom. Return to them whenever you need quick reference, deeper understanding, or renewed motivation. The path of conscious thinking is not a destination but a way of traveling through life with greater wisdom, peace, and purpose.

Bibliography

Primary Source

Allen, James. *As A Man Thinketh*. 1903. Reprint, New York: Dover Publications, 1999.

Neuroscience and Brain Research

Davidson, Richard J., et al. "Alterations in Brain and Immune Function Produced by Mindfulness Meditation." *Psychosomatic Medicine* 65, no. 4 (2003): 564-570.

Dietrich, Arne. "Neurocognitive Mechanisms Underlying the Experience of Flow." *Consciousness and Cognition* 13, no. 4 (2004): 746-761.

Doidge, Norman. *The Brain That Changes Itself: Stories of Personal Triumph from the Frontiers of Brain Science*. New York: Penguin Books, 2007.

Lazar, Sara W., et al. "Meditation Experience Is Associated with Increased Cortical Thickness." *NeuroReport* 16, no. 17 (2005): 1893-1897.

Ochsner, Kevin N., et al. "Rethinking Feelings: An fMRI Study of the Cognitive Regulation of Emotion." *Journal of Cognitive Neuroscience* 14, no. 8 (2002): 1215-1229.

Siegel, Daniel J. *The Developing Mind: How Relationships and the Brain Interact to Shape Who We Are*. 2nd ed. New York: Guilford Press, 2012.

Simons, Daniel J., and Christopher F. Chabris. "Gorillas in Our Midst: Sustained Inattentional Blindness for Dynamic Events." *Perception* 28, no. 9 (1999): 1059-1074.

Emotional Intelligence and Regulation

Barrett, Lisa Feldman. *How Emotions Are Made: The Secret Life of the Brain*. Boston: Houghton Mifflin Harcourt, 2017.

Beck, Aaron T. *Cognitive Therapy and the Emotional Disorders*. New York: International Universities Press, 1976.

Damasio, Antonio. *Descartes' Error: Emotion, Reason, and the Human Brain*. New York: Putnam, 1994.

Ekman, Paul. *Emotions Revealed: Recognizing Faces and Feelings to Improve Communication and Emotional Life*. New York: Times Books, 2003.

Goleman, Daniel. *Emotional Intelligence: Why It Matters More Than IQ*. New York: Bantam Books, 1995.

Gross, James J. "Emotion Regulation: Affective, Cognitive, and Social Consequences." *Psychophysiology* 39, no. 3 (2002): 281-291.

Neff, Kristin D. "Self-Compassion: An Alternative Conceptualization of a Healthy Attitude Toward Oneself." *Self and Identity* 2, no. 2 (2003): 85-101.

Pert, Candace B. *Molecules of Emotion: The Science Behind Mind-Body Medicine*. New York: Scribner, 1997.

Positive Psychology and Resilience

Fredrickson, Barbara L. "The Role of Positive Emotions in Positive Psychology: The Broaden-and-Build Theory of Positive Emotions." *American Psychologist* 56, no. 3 (2001): 218-226.

Kabat-Zinn, Jon. "An Outpatient Program in Behavioral Medicine for Chronic Pain Patients Based on the Practice of Mindfulness Meditation." *General Hospital Psychiatry* 4, no. 1 (1982): 33-47.

Maddi, Salvatore R. "The Story of Hardiness: Twenty Years of Theorizing, Research, and Practice." *Consulting Psychology Journal* 54, no. 3 (2002): 173-185.

Tedeschi, Richard G., and Lawrence G. Calhoun. "Posttraumatic Growth: Conceptual Foundations and Empirical Evidence." *Psychological Inquiry* 15, no. 1 (2004): 1-18.

Waldinger, Robert J., and Marc S. Schulz. "What's Love Got to Do with It? Social Functioning, Perceived Health, and Daily Happiness in Married Octogenarians." *Psychology and Aging* 25, no. 2 (2010): 422-431.

Cognitive Psychology and Decision-Making

Csikszentmihalyi, Mihaly. *Flow: The Psychology of Optimal Experience*. New York: Harper & Row, 1990.

Kahneman, Daniel. *Thinking, Fast and Slow*. New York: Farrar, Straus and Giroux, 2011.

Narrative Psychology and Meaning-Making

Frankl, Viktor E. *Man's Search for Meaning*. Boston: Beacon Press, 1946.

McAdams, Dan P. "The Psychology of Life Stories." *Review of General Psychology* 5, no. 2 (2001): 100-122.

Park, Crystal L. "Making Sense of the Meaning Literature: An Integrative Review of Meaning Making and Its Effects on Adjustment to Stressful Life Events." *Psychological Bulletin* 136, no. 2 (2010): 257-301.

White, Michael, and David Epston. *Narrative Means to Therapeutic Ends*. New York: Norton, 1990.

Habit Formation and Behavioral Change

Duhigg, Charles. *The Power of Habit: Why We Do What We Do in Life and Business*. New York: Random House, 2012.

Fogg, BJ. "A Behavior Model for Persuasive Design." *Proceedings of the 4th International Conference on Persuasive Technology*. ACM, 2009.

Lally, Phillippa, et al. "How Are Habits Formed: Modelling Habit Formation in the Real World." *European Journal of Social Psychology* 40, no. 6 (2010): 998-1009.

Classical References

Henley, William Ernest. "Invictus." 1875.

Lao Tzu. *Tao Te Ching*. Translated by Stephen Mitchell. New York: Harper & Row, 1988.

Contemporary Applications

Clear, James. *Atomic Habits: An Easy & Proven Way to Build Good Habits & Break Bad Ones*. New York: Avery, 2018.

Covey, Stephen R. *The 7 Habits of Highly Effective People*. New York: Free Press, 1989.

Dweck, Carol S. *Mindset: The New Psychology of Success*. New York: Random House, 2006.

Note: This bibliography represents the foundational research and sources that inform the practical applications presented in *Thoughts That Matter*. While James Allen's original insights were based on philosophical observation rather than scientific study, modern neuroscience and psychology have validated many of his core principles through rigorous empirical research. The citations provided offer readers opportunities for deeper exploration of the scientific foundations underlying Allen's timeless wisdom.

Your Journey Continues

As you reach the end of this book, remember: the true value lies not just in what you've learned, but in what you choose to do next. Growth is not a single event; it's a lifelong journey, built on small, consistent steps and fueled by your willingness to keep moving forward, even when progress feels slow.

The principles and practices you've explored here are meant to be lived, revisited, and refined. Some days will be easier than others. There will be setbacks, doubts, and moments when old habits resurface. This is all part of the process. What matters most is your commitment to begin again, each day, with compassion and courage.

You are now part of a larger community of readers and learners who, like you, have decided to focus on the things that truly matter. The *About Things That Matter* series is your ongoing companion, offering new tools, fresh perspectives, and encouragement for every stage of your journey.

As you close this book, ask yourself:
- What is one small action you can take today to move closer to the life you envision?
- Who can you invite to join you on this path, offering support and accountability?
- How will you celebrate your progress, no matter how incremental?

Thank you for letting us be part of your story. The best is yet to come. Keep investing in yourself. Keep daring to create change that matters. Keep learning, keep growing, and keep moving forward, one meaningful step at a time.

The next chapter of your story is yours to write, one intentional step at a time.

Stay curious. Stay compassionate. Stay committed to the things that matter.

Share your journey: Tell a friend or accountability partner what you've learned and what you plan to do next.

Choose the next book that fits your current needs, or read the whole series for the most powerful results. Visit http://aboutthingsthatmatter.com

Please take 2 minutes to give us your feedback https://bit.ly/3ZZjERJ

Your Gift

As a way of saying thanks for your purchase, I'm offering you the first book in the series **About Things That Matter** as a gift.

This book is exclusive to my readers. You will not find this book anywhere else.

You're invited to pause, reflect, and reconsider what truly defines a meaningful life. In a world conditioned to chase money, status, and material achievements, this book challenges the conventional yardsticks of success. Through incisive insight and refreshing authenticity, it guides readers to shift their focus from external validation to the internal foundations that cultivate real fulfillment, purpose, and enduring happiness. It's a call to eliminate distractions, clarify values, and build a life anchored in what matters most.

Visit this link to download your free copy of About Things That Matter or type this address into your browser https://BookHip.com/HLAJBFP

Visit the series page https://mybook.to/Aboutthingsthatmatter

About JC Ryan

JC Ryan is a bestselling author renowned for his intricate espionage, archaeological thrillers, and conspiracy mysteries. With over 30 acclaimed novels, including the popular Rex Dalton K9 Thrillers, Rossler Foundation Mysteries, and Carter Devereux Mystery Thrillers, Ryan has captivated readers around the globe.

Drawing from his diverse professional background—as a military officer, lawyer, and IT manager—Ryan creates compelling narratives that skillfully blend historical accuracy with thrilling adventure. He is celebrated as a master storyteller, known for crafting riveting plots, meticulous historical details, and engaging, multidimensional characters. Ryan's meticulous research lends authenticity and depth to each story, immersing readers in richly constructed worlds filled with intrigue, suspense, and adventure.

Fans of David Baldacci, Lee Child's Jack Reacher, Tom Clancy's Jack Ryan, Nelson DeMille's John Corey, Vince Flynn's Mitch Rapp, Mark Greaney's Gray Man, Gregg Hurwitz's Orphan X, Robert Ludlum's Jason Bourne, Daniel Silva's Gabriel Allon, Brad Taylor's Pike Logan, Brad Thor's Scot Harvath, James Rollins' Sigma Force, Steve Berry's Cotton Malone, and Dan Brown's Robert Langdon will find JC Ryan's novels equally compelling and unforgettable.

When not writing, Ryan enjoys spending time with his college sweetheart, whom he married in 1978. They are proud parents of two daughters, have two sons-in-law, and are grandparents to two grandchildren.

Also by JC Ryan

Rex Dalton K9 Thrillers

Here's what readers are saying about the series:

"A great read, started and couldn't stop until the end!!!"

"Just gets better and better. Can't wait to read the next in the series."

"Rex and Digger return. The continuing story of Rex Dalton and Digger is a suspenseful and intriguing work."

"What's A Dog To Do? 5 stars. I love reading about Rex Dalton's exploits, but my favorite character has to be Digger, his military-trained super-intelligent dog."

"JC Ryan scores again. I was not a fan of the first Rex Dalton book, but I plunged ahead with the second, hoping JC Ryan would not disappoint. I loved it. Now here I am after reading the third book in this series. I had a hard time putting it down and found myself wondering about it when I was not reading. Rex has added several new ports of call to this adventure. He sure gets into more trouble than any person I know who just wants to become a sightseer. With the help of Digger (his new comrade-in-arms), we are once again trying to correct the wrongs inflicted on the weak."

Visit The Rex Dalton Series Page http://viewbook.at/RexDaltonSeries

The Rossler Foundation Mysteries

http://myBook.to/RosslerFoundation

Here's what readers are saying about the series:

"A brilliant series by a master of the techno thrillers turning old much debated mysteries into overwhelming modern engrossing sagas of adventure, heroism and a sense of awe for the many mysteries still unexplained in our universe. Enjoy!"

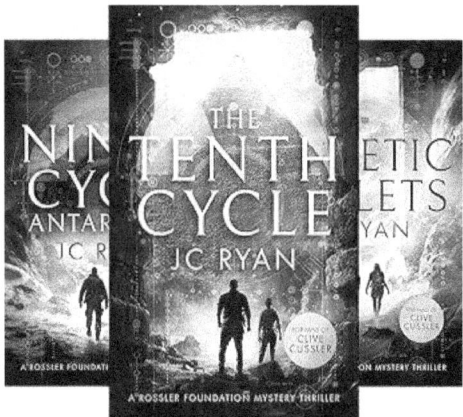

"I LOVED this series! It's readily apparent that the author drew from a large body of knowledge in writing this series. It's just believable enough to think it could happen someday, and in fact, aligns quite well with some of the current relationships that exist between present-day countries and the USA."

The Carter Devereux Mystery Thrillers

myBook.to/CarterDevereux

Here's what readers are saying about the series:

"Omg, this series is awesome. Full of adventure, action, romance, and suspense. If you start reading, you are hooked. Carter and all characters are awesome, you will fall in love with all of them they become like family. I love the way J C weaves the human and animals together in the story. Try it you will love it."

"The best! What a joy to read these four books about Carter and Mackenzie Devereux and their adventures. A very good read. I will look for more of JC Ryan's books."

"Suspenseful! Fabulous just fabulous! I enjoyed reading these books immensely. I highly recommend these books. Bravo to the author! You won't regret it."

"What a wonderful and intriguing book. Kept me glued to what was going to happen next. Not a normal read for me. But a very enjoyable series that I would recommend to everyone who likes adventure and thrills."

Satire and Humor

In a world where words are outlawed, news is tranquilized, and history is bubble-wrapped, The Snark Files dares to ask the questions everyone else is too comfortable to touch. Each file is a darkly comic record of society's most absurd attempts to outlaw reality, rebrand common sense, and algorithm-proof the obvious.

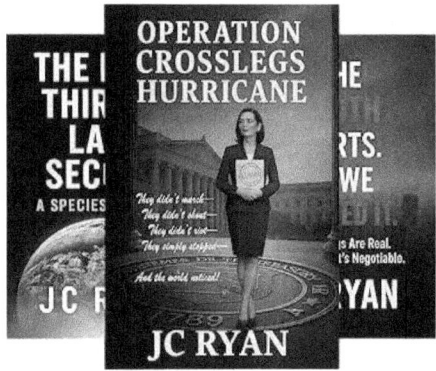

From professors fired for quoting Aristotle, to news anchors forced to deliver "comfort reports," to bureaucrats panicking over a lost Manual of Common Sense, the series exposes the hilarious fragility of a culture addicted to feelings, euphemisms, and spin.

Wry, biting, and disturbingly plausible, The Snark Files read like classified documents accidentally left on the copier—records of a civilization so desperate to protect itself from offense that it banned the very tools of truth.

Think Orwell with a laugh track. Swift with Wi-Fi. Douglas Adams at a government hearing.

If you've ever wondered how far nonsense can go before it collapses under its own contradictions, this is your front-row seat.